THE

MAYORS

THE

MAYORS

The Chicago Political Tradition

Third Edition

Edited by Paul M. Green and Melvin G. Holli

SOUTHERN ILLINOIS UNIVERSITY PRESS
Carbondale

Grateful acknowledgment is extended to Lyceum Books, Inc., for permission to reprint Monroe Anderson, "The Sawyer Saga: A Journalist, Who Just Happened to Be
the Mayor's Press Secretary, Speaks," from Paul M. Green and Melvin G. Holli,
eds., *Restoration, 1989: Chicago Elects a New Daley* (Chicago: Lyceum Books, 1991).

Library of Congress Cataloging-in-Publication Data

The Mayors : the Chicago political tradition / edited by Paul M. Green and Melvin
G. Holli.—3rd ed.
   p. cm.
  Includes bibliographical references and index.
  1. Mayors—Illinois—Chicago—Biography. 2. Chicago (Ill.)—Politics and
government. I. Green, Paul Michael. II. Holli, Melvin G.
F548.25.M39 2005
977.3'11'0099—dc22   2004017077
ISBN 0-8093-2612-4 (pbk. : alk. paper)

Printed on recycled paper. ♻

For Sharon and Betsy,

*our professors, Richard Wade, Arthur Mann,
Sidney Fine, and John Higham,*

*and our good friend and colleague,
Steve Neal—a man we will miss*

CONTENTS

PLATES

PREFACE TO THE THIRD EDITION

In the eighteen years since *The Mayors* was first published, Chicago politics has become more genteel, more docile, and more predictable. This dampening of the city's once red-hot political coals is due to domination by one man: Mayor Richard M. Daley (RMD).

No previous mayor (including his legendary father, Richard J. Daley) has so clearly, so decisively, and so thoroughly bundled up the diverse aspects of city life as the current mayor. In short, Chicago is not Rich Daley's *kind* of town—it is his town. Critics label him a dictator and a boss, while his allies describe him as a workaholic whose political and managerial shrewdness is constantly being underestimated.

Given RMD's rise to historically important power within Chicago's mayoral tradition, the new material in this third edition centers mainly on his mayoral performance. From many different viewpoints, authors analyze how and why this individual, who lost his first attempt at the mayoralty in 1983, has risen to such dominance. And given the fact that in Chicago, the concept of "term limits" is an oxymoron, all new contributors to this edition agree that Richard M. Daley's mayoral run is far from over.

PREFACE TO THE FIRST EDITION

This book was conceived as an effort to provide a political road map for the past century, charting where Chicago has been with its principal executive office, the mayoralty and its leading occupants, and where it may be going in the future. We have omitted some of the lesser mayors who served in the period after the Great Fire of 1871 (Heath, Roche, Cregier, Washburne, Swift, Hopkins, and Carter Harrison I, whose substance and style can be seen in Carter II) but covered all of the movers and shakers who have occupied city hall. Much of the city's dynamic and turbulent political history is surprisingly poorly known even to Chicagoans, who pride themselves as experts on the byzantine labyrinth that honeycombs and undergirds Chicago politics. Most of the "historic" knowledge of politics seldom extends farther back than the Richard J. Daley era or stretches beyond the memory span of those who think, write, and talk about politics in the Windy City. We hope this distillation of Chicago's mayoral history will help to fill at least a part of that hiatus and enable Chicagoans to see their present in a historical perspective.

Many debts were incurred in the process of putting together such a book. First we wish to thank the contributors, who wrote freshly commissioned pieces which appear here for the first time (with the exception of the Richard J. Daley selection, a revision of an earlier work). We would also like to thank the Illinois Humanities Council and the Chicago Historical Society, who funded and hosted the first draft of this book which was presented on 2 December 1985 at an all-day conference. Thanks also go to former mayor Jane Byrne, to Mayor Harold Washington and members of his staff, and to a crew of lively political commentators and writers who squeeze out more interpretation per column inch or fifteen-minute broadcast than any in the nation: Basil Talbott (Chicago *Sun-Times*), Sharon Alter (William Rainey Harper College), Milton Rosenberg (WGN Radio–Extension 720 and the University of Chicago), and Robert Starks (Northeastern Illinois University). We would also like to acknowledge the aid of a sharp-minded group of critics who helped significantly in shaping some of the ideas in this book: Louis Masotti (Northwestern University), Paul McGrath (Northwestern University), and Phil Krone (political consultant).

THE

MAYORS

I.

JOSEPH MEDILL: CHICAGO'S FIRST MODERN MAYOR

David L. Protess

Joseph Medill is not often remembered for his term as Chicago's first chief executive after the Great Fire of 1871, despite the historical importance of his regime. Medill's years as mayor were largely overshadowed by his other occupations. For most of the second half of the nineteenth century, Medill ran the Chicago *Tribune*. During those years, he played a seminal role in the development of the national Republican party and was instrumental in the making of the Lincoln presidency. Between 1871 and 1873 Medill also attempted to run Chicago. He proved to be less successful as the city's twenty-first mayor than as a newspaper publisher and political kingmaker. Nonetheless, his term as mayor was vital to the establishment of Chicago's unique political tradition.

In many respects, Medill was a contemporary urban mayor. His administration was preceded by more than three decades of mayors who were ceremonial figureheads, single-mindedly dedicated to promoting economic expansion during their two year, parttime terms. Medill, on the other hand, was able to expand considerably the authority of the mayor's office. Medill's increased power was accompanied by increased burdens for handling a variety of major conflicts and crises, many of which have persisted to the present time.

The legacy of the Medill mayoralty is in its precedent-setting efforts to manage complex urban problems. His administration was pressured to spend and to save, to be more efficient and more democratic, to distribute spoils and to establish a meritocracy. At the same time, it endeavored to mediate among interest groups with markedly different visions for the city.

While seeking to cope with these conflicting pressures, Medill presided over the city's first "reform" administration.[1] He also rebuilt the city with fireproof buildings, established its public library system, and used his self-generated mayoral charter to revamp the police and fire departments. More important than his ideological stamp and tangible accomplishments, however, was Medill's unprecedented willingness to *attempt* to govern the city. In the course of this effort, Medill went beyond the "transition mayor" status conventionally assigned to him[2] and became the first mayor of the city's modern political era.

Joseph Medill's Chicago

The City after the Fire

In 1871, Chicago was the fastest growing city in the country. As the result of a massive influx of immigrants in the previous decade, Chicago surpassed Saint Louis in population to become the fourth largest American city. According to the 1870 census, half of the city was foreign-born, with one of every six Chicagoans being a native of Germany. Chicago's changing demographic picture made for rivalries that would affect profoundly the political landscape of the city for more than a century.

These conflicts were temporarily put aside when fire devastated the city in October of 1871. In three days, four-fifths of Chicago burned. Thirteen thousand two hundred dwellings were destroyed, leaving 350,000 people homeless. The city was in a state of financial ruin.

Chicago's elected representatives were ill-equipped to handle the crisis. Mayor Rosewall Mason's formal authority was virtually nonexistent, while the forty members of the city council were too disorganized and preoccupied with the plight of their own businesses to be able to assume a leadership role. City Hall was one of many official buildings that burned to the ground, forcing the city's decision-makers to meet in temporary headquarters. The city treasury was quickly bankrupt by the effort to provide relief to the homeless and clean up the ruins.

With less than one month remaining before the November election for city officeholders, a coalition of business and civic leaders led by Carter Harrison decided to slate Joseph Medill for mayor on a bipartisan "Citizens Fire-Proof" ticket. The choice of Medill was not surprising. His life had been devoted to public causes. Trained as an attorney, he had gradually abandoned the practice of law to become a newspaper editor and publisher in Cleveland in the early 1850s. Medill's newspaper generally supported Whig party candidates and principles. However, he became increasingly disillusioned with the Whigs after their defeat in the national election of 1852. In 1854, Medill spearheaded the move to create a probusiness, antislavery political organization that he named the Republican party.

In the 1850s, Medill moved to Chicago and became editor and part-owner of the Chicago *Tribune*. He used the voice of the *Tribune* and his personal lobbying ability to convince the new Republican party to nominate Abraham Lincoln for President. Medill campaigned vigorously for Lincoln and became the first Republican president's close advisor and confidant. Locally, he was a delegate to the Illinois Constitutional Convention in 1869. In 1871, he served as a member of the first U.S. Civil Service Commission. In each position, he exhibited strong, tough-minded leadership traits; he made decisions with ideological fervor but was not incapable of compromise.

Despite his commitment to public affairs and dedication to Chicago, Medill proved to be a reluctant mayoral candidate. The supposedly fireproof Tribune Tower was virtually destroyed by the blaze, and Medill devoted almost all of his energy to the continued publication of his newspaper. Further, Medill resisted the overtures of Harrison and the others because he believed that "the powers of the mayor were so restricted that he did not amount to much more than a figurehead."[3]

Consequently, Medill initially declined the nomination for mayor. Undeterred, the leaders of the coalition applied constant pressure on Medill to head their ticket. After several days, he finally agreed to accept the nomination on the condition that the Illinois legislature would enact a new city charter that would greatly expand the powers of the mayor's office. Typical of his autocratic style, Medill's acceptance speech threatened that "if it [the legislature] rejected the bill then I would feel at liberty to resign the office and slip down and out; but if the amended charter bill became a law I would serve to the best of my ability."[4]

Medill's opponent in the election was Charles C. P. Holden, the alderman of the Tenth Ward and president of the city council during the Mason administration. Holden was nominated by a poorly organized local Democratic party whose main support was in the city's predominately immigrant wards. Following a two week campaign, Medill overwhelmingly defeated Holden by a vote of 16,125 to 5,988. The Fire-Proof candidates for city treasurer and city collector were also victorious. Significantly, however, seven aldermanic candidates supported by the Democratic party were elected, providing an incipient core of opposition to Medill's programs by one-third of the city council.[5]

The Medill Regime

As mayor, Joseph Medill inherited a crisis that was unprecedented in Chicago's history. His term of office was affected profoundly by the emergency conditions of 1871 and 1872. Nonetheless, Medill's mayoral programs helped to mold the city's postfire environment as much as they were circumscribed by the conditions of the times.

Medill's policies emerged from his efforts to manage a variety of paradoxical tendencies in the life of Chicago after the fire. The roles Medill played in handling five such dilemmas were particularly significant for shaping the character of his administration. First, in performing a "ministerial" role,

3

Medill sought to expand the authority of his office to cope with severe urban problems, while being mindful of the prerogatives of the city council and numerous other governmental units. Secondly, as a "developer" he was responsible for rebuilding the city, while conserving its scarce resources. Thirdly, in the role of "kingmaker" Medill was faced with the dilemma of advancing the careers of partisan loyalists or establishing procedures for nonpolitical merit appointment. Fourthly, as a power "broker" he had to mediate between patrician and immigrant groups who were fighting for control of the city. Fifthly, Medill as "imagemaker" had to manage the press and other public forums to develop a persona that appealed to different and often incompatible urban interests. Most significantly, Medill's willingness to assume these roles created leadership themes that have persisted through the mayoral regimes of the twentieth century.

The Ministerial Role. The first issue that Medill attended to after the election was his ability to govern. Since the duties of city officials were defined entirely by state law, Medill devised a strategy to convince the Illinois legislature to modify the existing city charter to increase mayoral authority. Even before he assumed the office of mayor on 4 December 1871 Medill appointed the well-respected Judge Murray F. Tuley to draft a "Mayor's Bill" for submission to the Springfield lawmakers in their next session.

Medill and Tuley used several arguments in lobbying for the new law: it was needed to allow for efficient executive response to the emergency conditions in the city; it was to be a temporary measure, not to extend beyond Medill's two year term of office; and it would not preempt the existing authority of the city council. After considerable arm twisting, the state of Illinois enacted the Mayor's Bill on 9 March 1872.[6] Medill was relieved of having to act on his campaign promise to resign in the absence of its passage, and he immediately rewarded Judge Tuley's efforts by making him the city's corporation counsel.

The new charter established the modern day authority of the mayor's office. The mayor was provided with the following new responsibilities:

—To appoint all nonelected city officials, with the advice and consent of the city council;
—To remove all nonelected city officials, while only having to inform the city council of the reasons for the removal;
—To serve as the presiding officer of the city council;
—To appoint the standing committees of the city council and to serve as *ex officio* member of those committees;
—To veto any ordinance, including all or part of an appropriations ordinance, with a two-thirds vote of the city council necessary to override the veto;
—To exercise special police powers, including the authority to license, regulate, and maintain order in the city.

In Medill's inaugural address, the new mayor made it clear that he would not hesitate to use the powers of his office to make Chicago work. In this first speech to the city council, he attacked aldermanic budgeting practices, the pervasive presence of spoils and corruption, and the inability of city government to prevent and cope with the conflagration. He promised "a complete overhauling of all expenditures in all departments of the city," warning that "the services of hundreds of persons now on the pay-rolls can be dispensed with. . . ." "Good government" was Medill's answer to Chicago's problems, and he outlined an array of programs that he believed would achieve it.[7] In doing so, Medill asserted a strong leadership position from the outset of his regime, and directly challenged those aldermen who might resist his efforts to change the direction of city government.

Despite the adversarial tone set by his inaugural address, Medill's first year in office met with a minimum of formal legislative resistance. The city's atmosphere of crisis and the broadness of his electoral coalition allowed him to implement many of his programs. Further, Medill chose to gradually and cautiously use his expanded authority during 1872, always recognizing the Council's legislative prerogatives and generally working toward the establishment of a stronger executive in city government.

While he vetoed an historically unprecedented eleven council ordinances in his first year in office, most dealt narrowly with specific "wasteful" financial practices. None of the vetoes was overriden. He also was successful in obtaining council approval of his appointments and removals, in part because the magnitude of the former fell far short of his inaugural threats.

His expanded ministerial responsibilities included the appointment of members to the newly constituted Chicago Board of Education and of commissioners of the city's first public library. His selections were unanimously approved by the council. When the new city charter went into effect on July 1, Medill sidestepped the potential aldermanic resentment of his takeover as their presiding officer by allowing the council to choose a series of acting chairmen. He good-naturedly told the council that a hearing impairment would prevent him from serving effectively in that capacity.

In performing a ministerial role in the first part of his administration, Medill was often preoccupied with intergovernmental issues. In addition to his effort to obtain the Mayor's Bill from the state, he lobbied furiously for financial aid to Chicago. Illinois law prohibited the direct appropriation of funds to the city. However, Medill convinced the legislature to pass a special act to reimburse Chicago for $2.9 million it had expended on the state-owned Illinois and Michigan canal.[8]

Medill also pressured the national government for assistance. While grants-in-aid did not yet fall within the domain of the federal government, Medill used his numerous contacts in Washington as he had in Springfield to obtain other means of support. In Medill's third month in office, he wrote to Vice-

President Schuyler Colfax urging the passage of a tariff rebate bill that would increase the supply of inexpensive materials needed to rebuild the city.[9] The legislation ultimately passed despite the strong opposition of organized lumber interests. Medill also coordinated the city's national relief effort, convincing President Grant to send a one thousand dollar contribution and collecting more than five million dollars in gifts and loans from individuals and cities from around the world.

At the end of his first year in office, Medill had managed to stabilize the city's fiscal affairs. He negotiated a budget with the city council that put the city "in better condition than before the Fire." [10] In his annual message to the council, Medill thanked the aldermen for their cooperation and expressed special appreciation to Tenth Ward Alderman Lester Bond, who was Chairman of the Finance Committee. He reviewed the traumatic events of the previous year and "look[ed] back to that dark and dismal time with a shudder." [11] In fact, the troubles of his regime were really only about to begin.

The second year of Medill's administration proved to be filled with turbulence as the mayor attempted to expand upon his ministerial duties. At the first meeting of the city council, Medill announced that for the first time he would exercise his power under the Mayor's Bill to select the chairmen and members of the council committees. Most of those chosen to top posts of important committees were Medill loyalists; aldermen from the immigrant wards received lesser consideration.

In the first three months of 1873, Medill vetoed five council ordinances. The vetoes included an important appropriations bill and an effort by the council to purchase a school lot that Medill believed was under the sole control of his board of education. In addition, Corporation Counsel Tuley was instructed to provide legal opinions to the council on why they did not have the authority to hire additional police officers or prevent the mayor's removal of police board members.

As the year progressed, council votes became increasingly divided. While the growing opposition was not sufficient to override the mayor's legislative initiatives, several of his personal choices were rejected for the first time. Moreover, Medill's move to shake up the police department met with effective aldermanic resistance.

By mid-1873, the mayor and council were at loggerheads over the city's licensure and appropriations powers. In a major dispute that will be discussed in detail later in this article, the council challenged the mayor's authority to revoke saloon licenses. The council also rejected Medill's proposals to cut budgetary spending. The mayor responded by using his line item appropriations veto repeatedly, and the council in turn made their first successful efforts to override most of the vetoes.

Medill had never experienced such direct challenges to his authority. He began to suffer from a variety of ailments that were related to the burgeoning conflicts over city government.[12] In August, Medill decided to take an extended European vacation. In accordance with the city charter, he informed the council that he would "be absent from the city for an unspecified length of time," requiring the aldermen to "appoint an 'Acting Mayor' to serve during my contemplated absence."[13] In a close vote taken on the same day of Medill's announcement, the council elected Lester Bond (Tenth Ward) to be the city's first acting mayor. Medill did not return to the city until 1874, and Bond completed the remainder of his term of office.

How may this dramatic turn of events be explained? First, Medill's initial successes were due in part to the traditional honeymoon period afforded most elected chief executives. The emergency circumstances under which he took office undoubtedly contributed to the postponement of opposition to his regime. This opposition increasingly crystallized as the crisis eased, allowing the underlying social conflicts in the Chicago of the 1870s to surface.

Moreover, the nature and timing of the controversies coincided with a major shift in Medill's performance of his ministerial role. In the first year of his regime, Medill was able to maintain a sense of equilibrium between the mayor's office and other governmental agencies. In the second half of his term in office, however, Medill's policies infringed upon the prerogatives of the council, the Police Board, and even the Illinois legislature. In the name of efficiency, Medill engaged in actions that were perceived to be antidemocratic.

In sum, Medill's ministerial efforts ultimately failed when he attempted to autocratically govern Chicago as if it were the Chicago *Tribune*, and he was its editor. In this light, the city council's vehement opposition to a move by the state legislature to reenact the Mayor's Bill can be understood. By a vote of 34 to 2, the Council resolved in 1874: "that we are unalterably opposed to the enactment of any law which shall continue in operation for one second beyond its lease of life that pestiferous relic of the Medillian era, the 'Mayor's Bill.'"[14] Medill's personal inability to maintain his broad but obviously fragile electoral coalition proved fatal to his administration and eviscerated the ministerial responsibilities of Chicago mayors for years to come.

The Developer Role. Despite the brevity of Medill's term of office, his administration was able to affect profoundly the physical landscape of the city. As in the performance of his ministerial role, Medill faced significant conflicts in his efforts to rebuild Chicago after the fire. Following the precedent of three decades of mayoral leadership, Medill was pressured to support a policy of unregulated development. At the same time, his electoral promises as a "Citizens Fire-Proof" candidate and his conservative fiscal views led him to consider adopting a more cautious strategy.

In his first inaugural address, Medill responded to Democratic party leaders and special interest groups who wanted to provide relief to the homeless by immediately constructing pine buildings with paper and tar roofs. He argued that: "If we rebuild the city with this dangerous material, we have a moral certainty, at no distant day, of a recurrence of the catastrophe. . . . The outside walls of every building hereafter erected within the limits of Chicago, should be composed of materials as incombustible as brick, stone, iron, concrete or slate." [15] He recommended the immediate appointment of a special committee of the city council to draft a new building code for the city that complied with this mandate.

On 12 February 1872, the council by a vote of 26 to 6 passed an ordinance that prohibited the construction of wooden frame buildings inside the city limits. Within this regulatory limitation, Medill presided over a period of construction that was unparalleled in the city's history. During the first year after the fire, over $45 million was expended on the erection of ten thousand new buildings. By the end of Medill's mayoral term, historians commented that "a stranger visiting the city would not have imagined, from anything he could see, that any disastrous event had ever occurred." [16]

While most of the construction was for private dwellings, Medill was also concerned with public development projects. In August 1872, Medill proposed the construction of a new City Hall and County Building to be built on the site which it currently occupies. In addition, the new Chamber of Commerce building was completed and dedicated by Medill on the first anniversary of the fire. Finally, Medill's administration proposed and implemented the use of the present-day decimal system for numbering city streets (with State and Madison at the vortex.)

Nonetheless, public opposition to Medill's development initiatives quickly surfaced in various forms. As the city council debated the new fire code, a large demonstration of citizens calling for immediate construction of frame housing disrupted the meeting and resulted in its adjournment. Later, Medill was forced to use his veto power for the second time when the council voted to allow the completion of frame buildings that were already in the process of construction. Medill's veto message expressed sympathy for the builders and the homeless they sought to help, but refused to tolerate any exception to his fire regulations. When the Council later attempted to circumvent Medill's policy by passing an ordinance that permitted the limited construction of frame buildings, Medill used his veto power once again. Such disputes increased in frequency over the course of his term, although the basic provisions of the code were never successfully challenged.

A second dispute related to Medill's performance of his developer role centered on the use of the city's fiscal resources. Medill stated repeatedly that he was unwilling to rebuild the city at the expense of sound financial practices. In his first year in office, Medill moved the city from the verge of bankruptcy to a nearly balanced budget. This process did not occur without political costs.

The mayor and aldermen frequently locked horns on the expenditure of public money for neighborhood improvement projects. In February 1872, Medill vetoed an ordinance for the curbing and paving of a long stretch of city streets because it would place "an additional burden . . . upon the now over-burdened city treasury."[17] The single largest number of Medill's vetoes were explained by his interest in fiscal rationing. When he item-vetoed a porkbarrel appropriations ordinance in July 1873, the council had had enough; the aldermen rebelled with their first veto overrides.

Medill also proved to be as parsimonious in his social welfare policies as he was in his bricks-and-mortar programs. In April 1872, the mayor asked the Chicago Relief and Aid Society to return to their traditional practice of caring only for the sick, aged, and infirm. Further issues of stoves, furniture, bedding, and clothing to victims of the fire were ceased. Later in the month, hundreds of widows protested the change in policy to the mayor, but it took a city council ordinance to alter the system of providing relief.[18]

In sum, Medill's administration produced an amalgam of development programs. His regime broke with tradition by attempting to balance the conflicting pressures to spend and to save. Where trade-offs were necessary, it is clear that regulated development and fiscal conservatism were more desirable to Medill than uncontrolled economic expansion. In this respect, Medill's role as developer was more akin to a Chicago mayor of the 1980s than a nineteenth century chief executive.

Kingmaker Role. One of Medill's most difficult tasks as mayor was to select employees for public service. His role as kingmaker proved to be laden with conflicts and paradoxical choices. On the one hand, Medill was committed to the principle of merit appointment. The antispoils movement was sweeping the nation, and Medill's *Tribune* was one of its leading voices. Medill himself served as one of the first federal civil service commissioners. On the other hand, Medill as mayor had to face certain pragmatic realities. The use of partisan political criteria in government hiring was endemic to the city by the 1870s. Significant numbers of aldermen of both political parties benefitted by the use of the spoils system. As mayor, Medill was in the tempting position of being able to expand upon his own sphere of influence by exercising the new appointment powers of the Mayor's Bill.

Personally, Medill was no stranger to partisan political intrigue. He had played the role of kingmaker frequently on the national political scene. Medill was both a Lincoln partisan and benefactor. And he was part of an unsuccessful effort to have the Republican party nominate Horace Greeley instead of Ulysses S. Grant for president in 1872.

In performing his kingmaker role as mayor, Medill's ambivalence was often apparent. As a reformer, he took steps that virtually removed spoils from the Chicago Fire Department.[19] He made similar efforts with the Chicago Police Department. Medill's first formal communication to the council after his inaugural address provided for the election of police constables. He also fired the incumbent police superintendent and replaced him with a "good government"-oriented chief from outside of the city.[20] Medill's initial appointments to the new library and school boards were considered to be blue ribbon candidates whom the council approved without resistance.

As a pragmatic politician, Medill also proved to be sensitive to local political realities. He proposed no formal ordinance or program to eliminate the spoils system from the city. In fact, he generally tolerated the practice by the city's aldermen. Medill never made good on his inaugural threat that he would "dispense with" hundreds of city employees whom he believed were payroll-padders.[21]

Medill could be politically heavy-handed in his own right. He repeatedly juggled members of the police board when they differed with his policies, replacing them with political loyalists. In the second year of his term, the council rejected several of the mayor's nominees to boards and commissions on the grounds that they were more loyal to Medill than capable of holding public office.

On balance, Medill went further than any previous mayor to implement the goals of civil service reformers, while not neglecting partisan considerations in hiring public employees. Several years after his regime, he perhaps best summarized his philosophy of personnel selection by stating: "Change the heads [of departments], but let the subordinates alone, if they are expert and faithful, is the Golden Mean that should be adopted in the Civil Service and let their performance depend upon their honesty and capability."[22] In articulating and performing his role as kingmaker, Medill had once again adopted the complexities of modern day mayoral administrators.

The Broker Role

Perhaps the most challenging of Medill's mayoral roles was to mediate between the competing patrician and immigrant social classes. It also proved to be his most problematic effort. While Medill often was able to manage the demands of many specialized interest groups, he ultimately was unable to achieve peace between the city's most powerful warring factions. The struggle between Anglo-Saxon and ethnic groups was an important undercurrent in Medill's dispute with the city council, and significantly contributed to the untimely end of his regime.

To some extent Medill was a victim of urban demographic trends. As mentioned previously, his mayoral term occurred at a time when Chicago was divided almost equally between patricians and immigrants. Clearly, however, the latter were increasing at an exponential rate and becoming highly organized politically. Differences in customs between the social classes and among immigrants themselves accelerated the mounting tension.

Nonetheless, Medill managed in general to keep the conflict off of the city's governmental agenda during his first year in office. He accomplished this in a variety of ways. First, Medill used the atmosphere of crisis after the fire to pull together the traditional adversaries. He coordinated the relief effort with the assistance of all leading factions and made certain that each part of the city was receiving necessary assistance.

Second, he used his appointment power to ensure a fair representation in city government of immigrants and patricians alike. In July 1872, he selected library commissioners and members of the board of education from among leaders of the various groups, although some Irish spokesmen complained that they had been unfairly excluded.[23] He also allowed the city council, itself an ethnically heterogeneous body, to continue to sponsor city jobholders from their neighborhoods.

Third, Medill attempted to accommodate the different views and social customs of the city's residents. In this effort, the temperance issue became the most difficult and significant problem for him to manage. On the one hand, the patricians strongly supported measures to close taverns early on weekdays and to enforce the existing Sunday closing laws. On the other hand, most immigrant groups supported limited regulation of saloons. The latter included many Germans, a mainstay of Medill's Republican constituency.

For awhile, Medill successfully mediated between these factions by offering compromises and making promises to both. To appease the patricians, he fired the highly tolerant Police Superintenent W. W. Kennedy and replaced him with Elmer Washburne, a law-and-order former warden of the Joliet penitentiary. The police were ordered to crack down on public drunkenness and crime in the vicinity of saloons. Medill, a teetotaler himself, also spoke publicly of his "hatred for drunkenness."[24] At the same time, he was unwilling to support proposals to limit further the hours that taverns were open and instructed the police not to enforce the Sunday closing law. In September 1872, when petitioned by his police board to support tavern-closing initiatives, he expressed sympathy for their position but called the measures "impractical" and "discriminative." He claimed that there were not enough Chicago policemen to enforce any such law in an evenhanded manner.[25]

In sum, Medill played his role as broker effectively during the first year of his administration. However, as his term of office progressed, the demands of each side became more organized and strident, with the temperance issue becoming the focal point of their dispute. By the fall of 1872, Medill's tightrope had become almost impossible to walk.

In October, German saloonkeepers organized a mass meeting to oppose the growing demands for new restrictions on the sale of alcoholic beverages. They passed a resolution, which was submitted to the city council, calling all such efforts unconstitutional and threatened to "support only those candidates for public office [who] are known to favor our views."[26] The same month, Police Superintendent Washburne submitted a draft ordinance to the council requiring taverns to close at eleven p.m. instead of midnight. When the council tabled the ordinance, the stage was set for a battle to control the police department.

On the first anniversary of Medill's assumption of the duties of mayor, the police board suspended Superintendent Washburne for "negligence of duty, incompetency and disobedience of the orders of the Board." [27] The underlying issues in the dispute were Washburne's increase in the length of police shifts and his protemperance initiatives. Medill could no longer avoid taking action. He responded to the removal of his police chief by firing two members of the police board and replacing them with Medill and Washburne loyalists. When antitemperance aldermen challenged the mayor's authority to shake up the board without providing adequate reasons for his actions, Medill retaliated by using the Mayor's Bill to deny them key council committee posts. In March 1873, the newly constituted police board and the reinstated superintendent again proposed the passage of an eleven p.m. tavern closing ordinance. This time, the mayor lent his support to the ordinance, which was finally passed by a heavily divided council in April. On April 23, the superintendent on behalf of the mayor finally issued an order to the police to enforce the Sunday closing law.

At this juncture, there was no turning back for Medill. In May, various immigrant groups formed a People's party coalition opposed to the Medill regime. In early June, the Mayor took two actions that sealed the fate of his administration. First, following a police crackdown on taverns he revoked the licenses of ten saloonkeepers for failing to obey the Sunday closing law. When the council passed a resolution challenging his authority to take this action, Medill vetoed the measure. Second, the mayor vetoed a council ordinance that would have restored the closing times of taverns to midnight. While the aldermen from the immigrant wards did not have sufficient votes to override the vetoes, they had made it clear that the remainder of Medill's regime would be filled with acrimony and strong legislative resistance.

By August, Medill was physically and emotionally unable to complete his term and announced his decision to leave the city. Politically, he was no longer able to play the vital role of brokering disputes. The changing conditions of city life had made political decision making a "zero sum game," replacing the politics of mediation and compromise. When ultimately forced to choose, Medill had supported the patrician cause that was consistent with his background and ideological perspective. Having done so, he was personally incapable of backing down or taking steps to defuse the controversy.

While Medill recovered in Europe, Chicagoans in the next municipal election voted overwhelmingly for every candidate on the People's party ticket. Harvey D. Colvin was elected as the city's new mayor. Defeated were candidates of the Law and Order party, an offshoot of the Citizens Fire-Proof coalition. Shortly thereafter, Elmer Washburne resigned as police superintendent and the city council asserted its control over police department affairs. The city was moving into a new era of immigrant-dominated machine politics.

The Image-maker Role. In performing his various roles as mayor, Medill appreciated the importance of projecting a positive image to his constituency. He was, by training, both a journalist and a politician and was sensitive to how the public viewed his performance during his tumultuous regime. Consequently, he made a concerted effort as mayor to manage the flow of information about city affairs.

While in office, Medill remained active in the management of the *Tribune* and made certain that the coverage of his administration was favorable. Concerned about expanding his sphere of press influence as well as about the appearance of a conflict of interest, one of Medill's first actions in office was to approve the designation of the Chicago *Evening Post* as the city's official newspaper and the Chicago *Staats-Zeitung* as its foreign language newspaper of record. At various points, he arranged for stories to be published that were supportive of his candidacy for congress and even for president. Medill was also fond of providing lengthy public explanations for his actions as mayor. His inaugural address was one of the most detailed in the city's history, and he made a similar speech to the council at the end of his first year of office that enumerated his accomplishments. Almost all of the actions he took on ordinances were accompanied by mayoral messages, with his explanations for vetoes being especially detailed. These actions were reported verbatim by the three above named newspapers.

Nonetheless, Medill did not escape problems in the performance of his image-making role. As social and political conflicts began to flourish in the city in 1873, managing the press's portrayal of his regime became more difficult. Medill's city treasurer was accussed by the *Staats-Zeitung* of improperly investing city funds for personal gain. The German newspaper seized upon the alleged scandal as a means of discrediting Medill's temperance policies and later even suggested that he left office "to escape moral responsibility and public censure." [28] While these charges later proved to be unfounded, they lingered and became an important issue in the November municipal election.

Further, an enduring paradox existed between Medill as a public figure and as a private person. While Medill publicly projected the persona of a political man intent on exerting influence in all areas of public life, he was privately a very sedate and dour individual who felt uncomfortable in the presence of most people. As one historian put it: "Medill valued his time too highly to waste a second chatting with a friend. One result was that he had no close friends at all." [29] He dressed out of fashion and disdained smoking, drinking, and other social customs of the times. He seemed to be most at ease when barking orders from his editor's chair at the *Tribune*. (He had an "obsession with power," [30] another historian concluded.)

Medill's public policies sometimes reflected his personal contradictions. He was quick to advocate war, yet lost his brother in the Civil War and complained to Lincoln that too many Chicagoans were being drafted to fight. [31] He was a leading abolitionist, yet was openly racist and stated publicly that "In future wars . . . we will not be so careful about spilling the blood of niggers."[32] As indicated earlier, his actions on patronage and temperance were often contradicted by both his public and private behavior.

In conclusion, Medill's performance of his role as image-maker was as complex as his other roles. His concern with the press's coverage of his regime distinguished him from all of his predecessors.[33] His mixture of successes and failures in managing the press is consistent with the experience of contemporary urban mayors. In these ways, Medill's term of office may be described as a watershed in the city's political history. The mayor's strong but highly enigmatic personality blended with the complicated circumstances of the times to create a multifaceted regime that contributed immeasurably to the richness of Chicago's political tradition.

The Medill Legacy

When Joseph Medill returned to Chicago in 1874, he scarcely recognized the city he had left the previous year. Some of the limitations he had imposed on the city's physical development had been lifted by the Colvin administration, and thousands of new structures of every kind had been erected. Governmentally, the balance of power had shifted from the mayor to the city council, with the aldermen from the immigrant wards wielding considerable influence. Politically, the spoils system flourished once again, even in the police department where Medill's reform efforts had been quickly undone. Chicago had become an open city in which saloons and vice flourished.

Had the Medill administration proved to be a failure? In the short run, at least, it is fair to conclude that Medill had fallen far short of his mayoral objectives. His decision to leave office before the end of his term was a tacit acknowledgment of his inability to govern the city at even the most minimally acceptable level. In the long run, however, the Medill mayoralty had a profound and lasting impact on the city. It marked the first time that a Chicago mayor had asserted a broad claim of executive authority. While the move in 1874 to reenact the Mayor's Bill was resoundingly defeated, the formal and informal powers of the office were gradually restored by the Illinois legislature and the practices of Medill's twentieth-century successors. The modern authority of the mayor's office is clearly derived from the regime of Joseph Medill.

More importantly, Medill's *use* of mayoral authority established policy-making precedents that have become a routine part of the contemporary urban agenda. Medill was the catalyst for moving the pendulum of economic growth towards a more stable position, for introducing merit appointment practices to city government, and for attempting to manage the city's social problems. Regardless of the short-term outcome of these initiatives, they raised issues that have preoccupied each of Chicago's mayors over the past century.

Medill's influence on the movement of the urban pendulum persisted well beyond his mayoral regime. In 1874, he purchased a controlling interest in the Chicago *Tribune* with a loan from businessman Marshall Field. As the newspaper's editor-in-chief for most of the remainder of the nineteenth century, Medill remained involved in local public affairs. His *Tribune* became the leading midwestern Republican journal, crusading for municipal reform and against the manifestations of machine politics and the trade union movement. The former mayor's interest in economic development led him to return briefly to public office in 1893 as a member of Chicago's World's Fair planning committee. Two years later, he witnessed the achievement of a longstanding goal when the Illinois legislature passed the state's first civil service law.

On 17 March 1899, Medill died in San Antonio, Texas, at the age of seventy-five. Before his death, Medill assured that his political perspective and family tradition would persist well into the twentieth century by turning over control of the *Tribune* to his son-in-law, Robert W. Paterson. He also spent time during his last years grooming his third grandson, Robert R. McCormick, for an eventual leadership position in the newspaper.[34] Outspoken to the end, Medill wrote a short editorial on the day before he died that McCormick took to the San Antonio telegraph office. It appeared in the *Tribune* the following morning, in the same issue that announced the news of his death.

At the first city council meeting after Medill's death, Chicago's aldermen passed the following memorial tribute to his mayoral leadership:

> As Mayor . . . he rendered conspicuous service to this municipality in its highest office. . . . The Mayor's Bill, embodying the reforms which he suggested, enabled him to give the city a systematic, efficient and successful administration. . . . Among the good things accomplished by the administration of Mayor Medill was the complete divorcement of the Fire Department from politics and a similar temporary divorcement of the Police Department therefrom and the establishment of the Chicago Public Library.[35]

To be sure, the city council that expressed these sentiments was a very different one from the legislature presided over by Joseph Medill, but one that was a direct outgrowth of the political tradition that he established.

2.

CARTER H. HARRISON II: THE POLITICS OF BALANCE

Edward R. Kantowicz

For a man who served five terms as mayor of Chicago, a man whose father before him had also served five terms, one who lived on well into his nineties, and who wrote not one but two autobiographies, Carter H. Harrison II is remarkably little known or remembered in Chicago. No monuments or memorials commemorate him. (Harrison Street is named for President William Henry Harrison, a distant relative, and Harrison High School for Carter H. Harrison I.) No scholar has written his life. When I viewed his grave on a historical tour of Graceland Cemetery, the guide simply identified him as, "the mayor who closed down the whorehouses." As we shall see, whorehouses did play a large role in his career, but he deserves to be remembered for more than that.[1]

Harrison's lack of recognition is partly due to the general historical amnesia of our time. In addition, Richard J. Daley so dominated recent Chicago politics, both in fact and in myth, that any politician predating Daley has fallen into the background. Above all, though, Carter Harrison's relative obscurity is due to his style of leadership. Neither a flamboyant politico nor a crusading zealot, Harrison combined some of the qualities of both boss and reformer, thus blurring his image and making him hard to define. In short, Harrison practiced the politics of balance; he was a harmonizer and a unifier.

The politics of balance may sound boring, the stuff of safe-and-sane conservatism; but nothing could be further from the truth. In fact, maintaining a political balance in a rapidly growing, factionalized city is a highly dynamic, even daring act. The English writer G. K. Chesterton, in discussing what he called the "romance of orthodoxy," described the Catholic Church as "a huge and ragged and romantic rock, which, though it sways on its pedestal at a

16

touch, yet, because its exaggerated excrescences exactly balance each other, is enthroned there for a thousand years."[2] The politics of balance is like that, with city hall rocking violently from one seemingly impossible point of equipoise to another. No one performed this balancing act, this juggling extravaganza, better than the Carter Harrisons, father and son.

The Age of Harrison

Chicago politics, for thirty-five years before the outbreak of World War I, may be termed the Age of Harrison.[3] The Harrisons won ten of the seventeen mayoral elections held during that period, each of them serving five terms. Yet, though a Harrison reigned as mayor more often than not, he did not control the politics and politicians of Chicago. No organization like the Tammany machine in New York, or the Daley machine later in Chicago, dominated the scene; Chicago politics was a bipartisan jungle of rival bosses and factions. The Harrisons owed their success to personal skill and charisma, not to the support of a disciplined machine. They were able to accommodate, with amazing dexterity and flexibility, the explosive growth and bewildering diversity of Chicago at the turn of the century.

Chicago's growth was astounding. When Carter Harrison I was first elected mayor in 1879, the city held nearly a half million inhabitants; but it was in many ways an overgrown village. The city's physical limits stretched from Fullerton Avenue on the north to 39th Street on the south, and west from the lakefront to Crawford (now Pulaski) Avenue; but much of the land within those boundaries still lay vacant.[4] Carter II grew up during the 1860s and '70s in a semirural atmosphere at Ashland Avenue and Jackson Boulevard, "with cows, horses, goats, chickens, [and] turkeys" in the backyard. Young Harrison remembered skating on the frozen prairies west of his home in wintertime; he and his boyhood chums could "sweep over the smooth unmarked ice to Riverside, a good ten miles distant." The elder Harrison avowed that in 1879 "there were not ten miles of paved street in the whole city over which a light vehicle could move rapidly without injury to wheel or axle."[5]

By 1915 when the younger Harrison left office, Chicago extended out nearly to its present borders and housed over 2,400,000 people. The *City Manual* published during Harrison's last mayoral year reported 1,800 miles of paved streets, 914 miles of streetcar tracks, 155 miles of elevated railway tracks, and 313,667 buildings which, the *Manual* remarked, "upon being placed side by side . . . would make one continuous line of homes extending from New York to San Francisco."[6]

Just as striking as this rapid growth was the city's startling diversity. Immigrants from every country in Europe poured into the city looking for work in its steel mills, foundries, slaughterhouses, tanneries, and rail yards. A full 77 percent of Chicago's population in 1900 were immigrants or the children of immigrants. The Germans and the Irish formed the two largest ethnic groups, but the Poles were increasing in numbers rapidly, eventually making Chicago the largest Polish city outside of Warsaw. Scandinavians, Bohemians, Lithuanians, Italians, Russian Jews, and many others added to the mix. Each of these groups clustered in highly segregated enclaves, centered around their churches or synagogues, their shops, and their ethnic fraternals.[7]

The city was fragmented along class and geographic lines as well. As street-cars and rapid transit lines stretched to the horizon, the largely native-born, Anglo-Saxon middle class moved out to the periphery, leaving the inner wards to the immigrant working-class. The customs, habits, values, and lifestyles of the Protestant middle class differed sharply from those of Catholic and Jewish immigrants. Under the influence of repeated evangelical revivals, Chicago Protestants campaigned against liquor and vice and strove to keep Sunday sacred and quiet. Catholics and Jews saw nothing immoral in beer, wine, or spirits and believed in celebrating the Lord's Day in more lively fashion.[8]

Turn-of-the-century Chicago, then, was a divided, segregated city comprising gold coast and slum, semisuburban retreat and teeming immigrant ghetto, slaughterhouses and counting houses, red lights and blue noses. In 1914, Chicago counted 1,077 churches and over 7,000 saloons.[9]

Carter Henry Harrison I was an old-fashioned city booster who wedded his fortunes to the growth of this brash, boisterous boomtown. He unblushingly called the city "his bride." The elder Harrison had been born on a Kentucky plantation on 15 February 1825. His family traced its Southern lineage back to the colonial Virginia of John Smith and Pocahontas. A Protestant but no Puritan, Harrison imbibed liberal attitudes and acquired a wide-ranging knowledge of people and languages on two extensive journeys through Europe and the Near East as a young man. Finding plantation life too slow, he took his young wife north in 1855 in search of fortune and frolic. After visiting St. Louis and Galena, the couple settled in Chicago, sold their Kentucky property, and invested the proceeds in Chicago real estate. "A buyer rather than a seller of real estate," Harrison invested for the long term; thereafter, the city's growth also meant the growth of his fortune.[10]

Drawn into political life after the great fire of 1871, Harrison served a term as county commissioner, then two terms in congress. His congressional service was distinguished mainly by a flamboyant, spread-eagle style of oratory. Returning to the city to run for mayor in 1879, he was elected to four consecutive two-year terms. He retired in 1887 and went on a sixteen month world tour. His attempt at a mayoral comeback in 1891 fell short, but in 1893 he won a final term, just in time to host the World's Fair. Admirably suited by his broad-minded attitudes and wide travels to greet visitors from all over the world, Harrison made a perfect World's Fair mayor.

Harrison cut a dramatic figure throughout his mayoral years. Readily identifiable by the black felt slouch hat he wore constantly, he crisscrossed the city's dusty streets on his white mare, often at a full gallop. He held court for the public in City Hall daily and applied himself in a businesslike fashion to the financial and administrative details of his office, restoring the city's credit by a policy of retrenchment during his first term. The city's first fulltime professional politician, he built a personal following of loyal retainers, particularly among the saloonkeeper-politicians. Holding decidedly broadminded views on gambling, liquor, and prostitution, Harrison never attempted to enforce Sunday closing ordinances or any other blue laws that the city council might pass. A rip-roaring stump speaker, able to discourse off-the-cuff for hours and utter a convincing phrase or two in nearly every European language, Harrison appealed forcefully to immigrant voters. Throughout his mayoral years, he combined the support of the business classes with the working masses, though the press, the Protestant pulpit, and the evangelical middle class usually opposed him.

During his final term, however, his optimistic Chicago boosterism united the city behind him. On Saturday, 28 October 1893, in the waning days of the fair, he greeted the mayors of cities from all over the United States with a final soaring speech:

> Genius is but audacity, and the audacity of the wild and woolly west, and of Chicago has chosen a star and has looked upward to it and known nothing that it cannot accomplish. This is a city that was a morass when I came into the world 68½ years ago. . . . What is it now? The second city of America. . . . I intend to live for more than a half century[!] and, at the end of that half century London will be trembling lest Chicago shall surpass her.[11]

That evening, at his home on Ashland Avenue, Harrison was shot to death by a disappointed office-seeker, Patrick Eugene Prendergast. One of the city's ethnic newspapers summed up perfectly the administrations of this optimistic city booster: "His career was a series of dramatic incidents enveloped in a haze of festivities."[12]

What we might call today the "Chicago-fest mentality" served Carter Harrison I admirably, but it would not suffice for his son, who faced even greater challenges and more complicated times.

Carter Henry Harrison II was born on 23 April 1860 in a house at the corner of Clark and Harrison Streets, on the first parcel of land his father bought in Chicago.[13] When only six months old his family moved to the semirural surroundings of the west side prairies, an area lightly settled by a number of Kentuckians, all engaged in land speculation. Harrison's mother never loved the city as much as his father did, so in 1873 she took young Carter and his sister and brother for an extended stay in Germany. Carter studied three years in a German *gymnasium,* returning in 1876 after his mother's death. The public school authorities in Chicago did not know how to evaluate his unorthodox educational background and temporarily refused him admittance to high school. So he enrolled at the Catholic prep school run by the Jesuit Fathers, then called St. Ignatius College, and took the equivalent of his high school and undergraduate schooling there. From 1881 to 1883 he attended his father's *alma mater,* Yale, and received a law degree.

The young Harrison of Chicago, newly emerged from Yale, resembled in many ways the young Theodore Roosevelt of New York, his close contemporary in age. Like Roosevelt, who wrote in his autobiography, "My father was the best man I ever knew," Carter Harrison idolized his wealthy, handsome father. Both young men traveled extensively in Europe, learned their French and German firsthand, and attended the best schools (Roosevelt attended Harvard). Neither really needed to work for a living, and therefore each spent a good deal of time "finding himself." Teddy headed West in the 1880s to punch cows and write history, whereas Harrison spent that decade knocking about Chicago, writing poetry, and practicing journalism under the pseudonym Cecil H. Harcourt. His poetry was of the "ode to spring" variety—"Winter's furious power is past, Sing the merry measure!"[14] Both Roosevelt and Harrison abandoned the gentlemen's callings of their birth and background for the hurlyburly of politics. Roosevelt put the matter strikingly:

> The big business men and lawyers told me that politics was low . . . that I would find them run by saloon-keepers, horsecar conductors, and the like, and not by men with whom I would come in contact outside. . . . I answered that if this were so it merely meant that the people I knew did not belong to the governing class, and that the other people did—and that I intended to be one of the governing class.[15]

Harrison's plunge into low politics came easier, for he had already met saloonkeepers and horsecar conductors in his father's house.

There were, of course, many differences between Roosevelt and Harrison. The future president was a Republican and the mayor's son a southern Democrat. Harrison lacked TR's boundless energy, his bellicose temperament, and his "ninety-pound-weakling-body-builder" mentality. In fact, Carter Harrison enjoyed a far more stable, balanced personality. Yet both men were well-bred, somewhat effete patricians, who plunged into the rough and tumble of politics in a turbulent era and gave as good as they got. Had Harrison not been caught between five political chieftains at the 1904 Democratic Convention, he might have opposed Teddy Roosevelt as Democratic presidential candidate that year, rather than the forgettable Alton B. Parker.[16]

Despite the failure of his long-nourished presidential ambitions, Carter Harrison II's background suited him perfectly for a career in Chicago politics. A Protestant by birth, educated in Germany, at Irish-Catholic St. Ignatius, and at Waspy Yale, he was nearly a balanced ticket all by himself. His wife, Edith Ogden Harrison, was a Louisiana belle of cultured, aristocratic habits who acquitted herself well in the parlors of the Potter Palmers and Marshall Fields.

She was also a Catholic and raised their two children as Catholics. Harrison felt equally at home in a poker game with party hacks or at a reception on the Gold Coast or in the Art Institute. He lacked his father's platform oratory and flamboyant style, but he was a good-looking, athletic man with a trim mustache, a handsome face, and a strong personal presence. "He was admired by men and adored by women." Like his father, he cultivated a businesslike administrative image, championed the rights of workingmen to enjoy a glass of beer on Sunday, and tossed off appeals to every immigrant nationality in the city. But when he entered politics in 1897, he also developed reform credentials which attracted some of the Anglo-Saxon middle class. Balancing and juggling Chicago's rival political factions, reaching out to diverse constituencies throughout the expanding city, Harrison served four consecutive two-year terms as mayor from 1897 to 1905 and a final four-year term from 1911 to 1915.

A Reform Boss

Carter Harrison was, in his fashion, a progressive reformer. This news would have startled some of his contemporaries, and it does not represent the consensus opinion of present-day historians. The uncertainty about his reform credentials is largely due to the wide variety of reformers and the amorphousness of turn-of-the-century progressivism. Many different kinds of reformers pursued many separate reform causes in a broad, diffuse movement of civic betterment. Harrison championed some of these reforms but not others. Furthermore, he allied his brand of reform with a motley crew of ward bosses and immigrant politicos, further blurring his image. Relying on machine-like methods to win elections but pursuing many reform goals, Harrison might best be labeled a "reform boss." [17]

The progressive movement on the urban scene encompassed three broad categories: moral reform, political reform, and what could be termed socioeconomic reform but which I prefer to call civic reform. Moral reform represented the evangelical Protestant impulse at its purest, attacking the immoderate use of liquor and attempting to repress gambling, prostitution, and all other forms of vice and crime. Political reformers fought the evils of bossism, graft, and patronage, and proposed to run city governments in a more businesslike, efficient fashion through a civil service system and a nonpartisan city council. Civic reformers attempted to use the power of government to make urban life more humane and comfortable, extending city services rapidly to keep up with urban growth. Ideally, they believed that city governments should own and operate all essential utilities ("sewer socialism" it was called), but if that was impossible, they insisted that private contractors not exploit the city but provide honest, efficient service and pay a just compensation for any profits or privileges they secured. [18]

In Chicago, each of these reform causes exploded on the scene in a sensational manner. The assassination of Carter Harrison I in 1893 by a disappointed office-seeker galvanized local civil service reformers. Just as the murder of President James Garfield under similar circumstances had led to passage of a national civil service law, so too Harrison's death prompted the Illinois legislature to prescribe the merit system for most city and state employees.[19]

Moral reform found its champion in William T. Stead, a crusading English journalist who published a sensational book, *If Christ Came to Chicago*, in 1894. Stead's expose left no doubt that the Lord would be displeased at the open vice and crime of Chicago's First Ward. "The Levee" was an unofficial title for several centers of gambling and prostitution in and around the Loop which the elder Carter Harrison had left unmolested. Stead found that the Nineteenth precinct of the First Ward, covering Dearborn Street, Custom House Place (today Federal Street), and Clark Street between Polk and Harrison, contained thirty-seven brothels, forty-six saloons, and eleven pawnshops. Two First Ward bosses, a Laurel and Hardy-like pair named "Bathhouse" John Coughlin and Michael "Hinky Dink" Kenna, presided over these dens of iniquity. Stead's revelations led to a series of mass meetings in Chicago and the founding of the Civic Federation to attack the evils of vice and crime.[20]

Economic or civic reform received its impetus from a series of sensational grafting scandals during the administration of Mayor John Hopkins, elected to fill out Carter Harrison I's unexpired term. Businessmen spread large amounts of money ("boodle" it was called) around the city council to buy lucrative street railway and utility franchises. In 1895, for instance, the council passed the Ogden gas ordinance, creating a new gas company whose major stockholders included Mayor Hopkins and his political ally, Roger Sullivan. The clear intent of this ordinance was to "sandbag" legitimate companies into buying out Ogden Gas's franchise rights. Repeated boodle ordinances prompted a movement to drive out the grafters, to insist on adequate compensation for franchise privileges, and to secure municipal ownership and operation of public utilities.[21]

These sensational events, occurring between the death of Carter Harrison I and the election of his son in 1897, defined the reform issues in Chicago for a generation—the prohibition of liquor and the repression of vice and prostitution; political honesty, the merit system, and nonpartisanship; and municipal ownership of utilities or, at least, adequate compensation paid by private business for the grant of public privileges. Carter Harrison II did not favor moral reform; he waffled a good deal on political reform, often trying to play both sides of the street; but he stood steadfast on issues of civic reform, blocking many audacious franchise grabs and introducing numerous small civic improvements.

During his first four terms, Harrison refused to join the aroused forces of moral reform. Like his father before him, he held a live-and-let-live attitude towards drinking, gambling, and the "social evil." Harrison knew that the European immigrants opposed the prohibition of liquor and that many respectable men who signed on as moral reformers at Stead's mass meetings privately patronized the Levee. He considered gambling and prostitution necessary evils which never could be suppressed. So he championed "personal liberty," the right to drink beer or liquor without undue restrictions, and pursued a policy of "segregated vice," restricting the brothels and gaming houses to a few small areas where they would be out of sight of respectable people but under police surveillance. When the downtown business district encroached too closely on the Old Levee that Stead had inspected, Mayor Harrison pressured the underworld elements to move. In 1903, they set up a new Levee between 18th and 22nd Streets along State and Dearborn, where it remained for a decade. Harrison's policy of segregated vice served him well politically. It placated middle-class sentiment for a time by keeping open vice out of respectable neighborhoods, it pleased those who indulged themselves in the fleshpots, and it earned the political loyalty of First Ward bosses Kenna and Coughlin. Until the very end of his career, the First Ward bosses furnished Harrison's most dependable political support, marching thousands of flophouse residents to the polls at every election to vote for the mayor and the candidates he supported.[22]

Despite his father's shocking murder by a spoilsman, Harrison never adopted a consistent position on civil service. He recognized the value of the merit system for municipal administration but did not wish to apply it until he had cleared out holdover Republican officeholders. So in his first term of office, his corporation counsel found numerous loopholes in the law, and Harrison took the opportunity to reward loyal Democrats. Later in his tenure, he spoke more favorably of the merit system, even going so far as to publicly apologize to two Republican civil service commissioners he had removed. On other political reform issues, he proved more straightforward. The Civic Federation had spun off another reform organization in 1896, the Municipal Voters' League (MVL), which worked for the election of honest aldermen on a nonpartisan basis. An honest politician himself, Mayor Harrison encouraged the MVL and worked hard to form an honest, unbought majority in the city council. In 1902, he caucused with the president of the MVL and representatives of both political parties to appoint city council committees on a nonpartisan basis. Harrison also championed other political reforms, such as home rule for municipalities, direct primaries, and referendum votes on public policy questions. Ever the juggler, he tried to satisfy political reformers whenever he could but still reserve the power to reward his friends.[23]

Harrison's progressivism stood out most clearly on the complex of social and economic issues I have termed civic reform. The mayor highlighted the essential point of civic reform in his 1905 annual message: "From the very beginning I determined that during my service as mayor no private use of public property should be allowed without requiring just and adequate compensation to the community for the privilege." If anyone wanted a favor from the city, whether it was permission to hang an awning over the sidewalk or to rip up the streets to lay streetcar tracks, the individual or corporation should not have to bribe aldermen but rather should pay a just and equitable fee into the city treasury. In pursuit of this principle, Harrison vetoed numerous utility franchises bought with boodle. Only one of his vetoes was ever overridden, the notorious Commonwealth Electric ordinance of 1897, which created a dummy company that promptly sold out to the Edison Company. But in 1900, when Messrs. Hopkins and Sullivan tried to duplicate this success with an ordinance permitting Ogden Gas to sell its franchise to other companies, Harrison made his veto stick. The Sullivan crowd had to wait until 1906, when Harrison was out of office, to cash in Ogden Gas.[24]

Besides this negative type of civil reform (stopping boodlers), Harrison introduced small, unspectacular, but useful improvements in the city's environment. One of the most important was railroad track elevation. As the nation's transportation hub, Chicago was crisscrossed by railroad tracks, all of which crossed the city's streets at grade level and exacted a frightful toll on human life due to frequent collisions. In 1892, before Harrison took office, the city began pressing railroad companies to elevate their tracks on embankments and eliminate grade crossings, but only a few miles of track were elevated in the next five years. At Harrison's urging in 1897, the city council appointed a special committee on track elevation, with a fulltime engineering expert, John O'Neill, to expedite the work. In Harrison's first six years, 286 grade crossings were eliminated and fifty-five miles of mainline track were elevated. In accord with the politics of balance, track elevation served several purposes. It not only ended the carnage in the neighborhoods through which railroads ran, it provided an estimated 115,000 jobs, all at no cost to the city.[25]

Harrison often needed someone else to pay for his civic improvements, for the state and county governments—usually controlled by Republicans—kept Chicago's finances on a short leash. Harrison's comptroller found that the city's area had increased 420 percent between 1888 and 1900 and its population 110 percent but that its tax revenue had increased only 35 percent. Harrison employed numerous stratagems to stretch these slender resources. In 1900, he declared that the outmoded center pier bridges in the Chicago River were obstacles to the free flow of water which the Sanitary District was legally mandated to maintain, so the Sanitary District should pay to replace them with modern bascule bridges. In 1899, he appointed a Small Parks Commission to open playgrounds in crowded immigrant slums. Lacking firm legal authority or adequate funding, the commission appealed to private philanthropists to donate vacant lots for parks. To provide wintertime play opportunities, Mayor Harrison, recalling his childhood skating on the open Chicago prairie, offered a free permit and free city water to any landowner who would flood his property for a skating rink. Sixty such rinks opened in the winter of 1900.[26]

Harrison squeezed out a tiny appropriation to open a Municipal Reference

Library and establish a Bureau of Statistics. Progressive reformers believed in gathering and broadcasting comparative urban statistics as a means of improving city government and building up a civic spirit. Harrison's Bureau of Statistics published an annual *City Manual* which combined encyclopedic statistics with stories of Chicago's growth and progress. The *City Manual* provided a more sophisticated, updated variety of urban boosterism than the elder Harrison's rip-roaring speeches. Harrison's successor gutted the Bureau of Statistics and cancelled the *City Manual*, but the Municipal Reference Library survived.[27]

The Traction Wars

Above all else, Carter Harrison II earned his reputation as a reformer by his firm and successful stand in Chicago's traction controversies. ("Traction" was the standard phrase used to describe electric streetcar companies. The name derives from the traction method of powering cable cars. Though cable cars were swiftly replaced by overhead electric trolleys in the 1890s, the name stuck.) The traction issue was a long and complex wrangle which kept Chicago politics in turmoil for decades. The first street railway franchises, permitting private companies to use the public streets and carry passengers at a profit, were granted by the Chicago City Council in 1858 for a period of twenty-five years. Then in 1865 a corrupt state legislature passed the infamous ninety-nine year act over the governor's veto, extending the corporate rights of streetcar companies to a total length of ninety-nine years. Widespread doubt about the constitutional validity of this act, however, kept a cloud of uncertainty hanging over the companies' traction rights. In 1883, when the original franchises expired, Harrison I worked out a compromise which simply extended the companies' rights for another twenty years but deferred settlement of the ninety-nine-year question. This bequeathed the whole problem to the next generation, led, as it turned out, by his son.[27]

In the meantime, however, streetcar lines and elevated roads had expanded to all corners of the city; and a new actor appeared on the scene in the person of traction magnate Charles Tyson Yerkes. The very prototype of a robber baron, the model for Theodore Dreiser's novel *The Titan*, Yerkes came to Chicago from Philadelphia in 1881 and began buying up streetcar lines in 1886. He planned to unify all the lines in the city into one grand system and enrich himself enormously in the process. He succeeded admirably in the second aim, amassing a fortune estimated at $29 million in 1896, but numerous obstacles slowed his unification schemes.[28]

By 1896, Yerkes controlled the streetcar lines of the west and north sides and he decided to settle the extent of their privileges with one grand ordinance of the state legislature. Senator John Humphrey, an obscure legislator from rural parts of Cook County and evidently a Yerkes stooge, introduced a series of bills early in 1897 extending Yerkes's franchises for fifty years and granting minimal compensation to the city. Yerkes's efforts to ram the Humphrey bills through the legislature with a liberal application of boodle blew up in his face due to the reform ferment which had been brewing in the mid-90s.

The thirty-six-year-old Carter Harrison, newly elected primarily on the strength of his father's name, jumped into the Humphrey Bill controversy and made the traction issue peculiarly his own. He raced to Springfield in the company of reform aldermen and helped lobby enough votes to defeat the Humphrey Bill. Yerkes then changed tactics and had another rural stooge, Representative Charles Allen of Vermilion County, introduce a bill which authorized city councils to grant fifty-year franchises. The Allen Bill passed, so the struggle shifted to the Chicago City Council.

Yerkes let the situation cool awhile, going off to Europe for eighteen months, but on 5 December 1898 he had a fifty-year franchise extension introduced in council. Mayor Harrison called on the citizenry to surround City Hall at the next council meeting and publicly vowed, "If Yerkes can pass an ordinance over my veto I'll eat my old brown fedora." At the December 19 council meeting, Harrison killed the fifty-year franchise without a veto. Employing a parliamentary stratagem, he buried the ordinance in a friendly committee, winning the roll call by a single vote. Harrison's live-and-let-live policy on the vice issue had already paid dividends, for "Bathhouse" John and "Hinky Dink" Kenna, the Lords of the Levee, voted with Harrison against Yerkes. They decided to avoid Yerkes's big boodle and stick to their protected vice rackets. Harrison helped win a major civic victory by abandoning moral reform.[29]

It may be objected that Harrison exercised no real leadership during the Yerkes fight but merely followed the wave of public opinion in opportunistic fashion. There's no doubt he hoped to capitalize politically on the issue, but had his motivation been totally cynical, he wouldn't have taken so strong and visible a stand. He not only opposed the fifty-year franchise extension, he vowed to fight any franchise extension, no matter how favorable the terms appeared, until the legislature repealed the Allen Law. His stubbornness paid off; it was repealed in 1899.[30]

Yerkes left the city permanently after his Allen Law defeat, but the traction issue did not go away. The major streetcar franchises all would expire in 1903 and the companies were sure to assert their ninety-nine-year rights under the old 1865 law. Most reform organizations favored a swift and early settlement with the several streetcar companies while Yerkes's memory was fresh in the public mind and the companies were on the defensive. Had Harrison been a mere opportunist, he would have followed this line of least resistance. Instead, he dug in his heels and delayed a final settlement of the traction controversy.

For the rest of his first four terms, Harrison pursued a firm and consistent traction policy, but it was a complex policy not easy to communicate to the public. He expressed it most clearly in a special message to the city council on

6 January 1902. He highlighted five essential conditions which the public interest demanded in any traction settlement: a definite and marked improvement in the speed, comfort, and safety of streetcar service; adequate compensation to the public for franchise rights; an unequivocal legal waiver of any supposed ninety-nine-year rights; provision for the city to purchase and operate the streetcar lines at some future date; and the referral of any final settlement to a referendum for popular approval. Harrison did not believe the city had enough money or expertise to buy out the traction companies immediately and proceed to a municipally owned and operated transportation system; but he wanted to be sure the city possessed the legal authority to do so at a future date. Therefore, he stalled any franchise extension until the state legislature granted Chicago this authority. He pointed out shrewdly, "It is easier to stop than to pass legislation. Give the companies what they want and they will successfully block Chicago's attempt to get what the citizens want." Finally, in 1903, the legislature passed the Mueller Law, authorizing any city in the state to own and operate street railways.[31]

Harrison was now ready to settle the traction question; but the companies asserted their ninety-nine-year rights, as expected, and litigation dragged on until 1907 when the Illinois Supreme Court finally overruled the ninety-nine-year franchise act. In the meantime, public dissatisfaction built up against Harrison's delaying policy, a widespread movement for immediate municipal ownership sprang up, and Harrison decided to retire in 1905. Judge Edward F. Dunne, another reform Democrat, was elected on a platform of immediate municipal ownership. Dunne, however, failed to leap through all the financial and legal hoops of municipal ownership, and the city council finally negotiated franchise extension ordinances with the existing streetcar companies in 1907.[32]

The "Settlement Ordinances" of 1907 vindicated Carter Harrison's traction policy. They embodied his politics of balance by striking a compromise, with something for everyone. The streetcar companies agreed to rehabilitate and upgrade their rickety cars under the direction of a Board of Supervising Engineers, thus providing tangible benefits to the riding public. Municipal ownership advocates were placated with a clear option for the city to purchase the lines at any time. The companies were guaranteed a 5 percent return on capital, but all profits over and above that amount were split 55 percent to the city and 45 percent to the companies. Finally, in accord with Harrison's longstanding policy, the ordinances required popular approval, which was granted at a referendum in April 1907. The long traction controversy was finally settled, largely on the terms Harrison had held out for. The settlement, of course, was far from perfect. It did not deal with the elevated lines or with the possibility of digging a subway, and eventually it was outmoded by the rapid rise in automobile use and the resulting drop in transit ridership. Yet the traction settlement did provide improved transit service and adequate compensation to the city for at least ten years after its passage.[33]

Harrison's firm stand against Yerkes in the traction war and his honest, if sometimes inconsistent, cooperation with political reformers of the Municipal Voters' League earned the mayor some often grudging but significant backing from business and middle-class reform groups. In the midst of the Allen Law uproar, a Chicago newspaper summed up his reform appeal: "We may thank our stars for the presence in the mayor's office of an honest man with a club." [34] In addition, his cosmopolitan background and liberal views on personal liberty earned him consistent immigrant support. The Poles of Chicago, for instance, gave 73 percent of their votes to Harrison in his first four elections. [35] Finally, Harrison's unholy alliance with "Hinky Dink" and "Bathhouse" delivered a dependable, controlled vote of flophouse denizens which often made the difference in close elections. The Harrison coalition, then, embraced the immigrant nationalities, the Skid Row wards, and many thousand middle-class independents and Republicans. The only groups in the city that he spurned were the big boodlers—Yerkes, Roger Sullivan, and the Ogden Gas crowd—and the moral reformers. Eventually, these two groups brought him down.

Harrison Loses His Balance

Harrison's balance had begun to totter toward the end of his first four terms. His complex traction policy frustrated the more ardent reformers, and a vocal movement for immediate municipal ownership swept Judge Dunne into office. Harrison had a valid personal reason for withdrawal—he needed to move his son to California for his health—but he probably could not have won reelection had he stayed in town. He returned briefly in 1907 but could not secure the party nomination. Then in 1911 the city scheduled its first direct mayoral primary, and Harrison won an extremely narrow victory over exmayor Dunne and Roger Sullivan protégé, Andrew Graham. The faithful First Ward bosses produced Harrison's 2,000 vote margin in the primary.

The progressive movement in Chicago rose to a crescendo in the mayoral election of 1911. Much had happened while Harrison was away. Daniel Burnham had issued his bold Chicago Plan of civic betterment in 1909, with its striking vistas of broad boulevards, green parks, and sparkling lakefront facilities. A University of Chicago professor, Charles E. Merriam, serving his first term as a reform alderman, had headed a 1909 inquiry into municipal finances which unearthed multiple scandals. In 1910, a growing agitation against the segregated vice district led Republican Mayor Fred Busse to appoint a vice commission, chaired by Episcopalian Dean Charles T. Sumner, to investigate conditions in the Levee. Then at the end of 1910, alderman-professor Merriam had announced his candidacy for mayor and had swept to a surprising victory in the Republican primary.

Harrison's campaign against Merriam in the 1911 mayoral election was a model of successful progressive politics in a diverse, divided, polyglot city. [36]

He got on the reform bandwagon right away, adopting Burnham's visions as his own, but he carefully avoided the dynamite threatening to go off in the vice commission and thus cemented his normal First Ward alliances. To keep the immigrant vote, he branded Merriam as a prohibitionist, fronting for blue-nosed, silk-stocking bigots in Hyde Park. Above all, he learned from his own experience and kept his reform appeals simple and concrete—"We plan to wage this fight on the theory that public utility corporations should be our servants instead of our masters. I believe the gas company can sell its product at not more than 70 cents for 1000 cubic feet." Seventy-cent gas gave Harrison a specific, easily understood issue he could sell in every ward of the city, to immigrant and Wasp alike. Whenever possible, he portrayed himself as an experienced, pragmatic reformer and Merriam as a bookish, impractical professor. Harrison won a narrow victory; but it proved to be his "last hurrah" as his carefully balanced coalition fell apart during his final term.

Just after the election the vice commission dynamite exploded. The lords and ladies of the Levee had overplayed their hands by too openly flaunting their illegal activities. Bathhouse John's outrageous First Ward Balls and the elegant debauchery of the Everleigh Club brothel had earned Chicago a nationwide reputation for sin and decadence. Dean Sumner's vice commission produced a hard-hitting expose of the "social evil" in all its aspects, counting over 1,000 brothels, 1,800 pimps and madames, and at least 4,000 prostitutes in the Levee, raking in an annual revenue of $60,000,000. The commission called for an end to protected vice and a policy of total repression. Mayor Harrison stalled for time, hoping to retain his First Ward allies by letting the public clamor cool down. In October 1912, he took the highly visible and symbolic action of closing the Everleigh Club but proceeded no further. Then the following year, a lame-duck Republican states attorney, John E. Wayman, forced his hand by sending his own agents to close down the remaining brothels in the Levee. Belatedly, Harrison sent in city police to join the crackdown. Once launched on the new policy of repression, Harrison went all the way. He fired his police chief, reorganized the department, and sent the police crashing into the Levee for a final series of raids in 1914. Hinky Dink and Bathhouse, who had long furnished Harrison his staunchest support, abandoned the Mayor and joined Roger Sullivan's wing of the party.[37] Harrison and Sullivan were archenemies. Notorious for his boodle ordinances in the city council, Roger Sullivan was a businessman-politician who had become a rich man selling the Ogden Gas franchise to Peoples Gas in 1906 for six million dollars. Yet Sullivan was also a shrewd and skillful politician who quietly forged many bosses and factions together into the nucleus of a Democratic machine. Only the personal popularity of Harrison and Sullivan's own noxious reputation prevented him from dominating the Democratic party in Chicago.

By the second decade of the century, however, so much had happened in Chicago that Sullivan's gas ring reputation had begun to fade, and he had nearly convinced the voters that he was a statesman. Sullivan wanted badly to end his career in the U.S. Senate, and he devoted all his energies to obtaining the senate nomination in 1914. Had Harrison retained his usual sure-footed balance, he might have made a deal with Sullivan, and the machine leader's forces would easily have compensated for the loss of the First Ward bosses. Washington was far away and it might not have cost Harrison too much to support Sullivan's senate bid. But Harrison's hatred for Sullivan had become a vendetta; his opposition to civic boodlers was absolute. So he desperately, and unsuccessfully, tried to block Sullivan's nomination. It came as small comfort that Sullivan lost the general election to a Republican.[38]

By the end of his four-year mayoral term, Carter Harrison was physically worn down, frustrated, and politically isolated. His uncharacteristic foray into moral reform had alienated his First Ward allies but had earned him no new adherents, for the crusading ministers didn't vote in Democratic primaries and didn't trust Harrison anyway. Roger Sullivan had gathered together anyone dissatisfied with Harrison and was ready to unseat the mayor in 1915 with a loyal lieutenant, Robert A. Sweitzer. Sweitzer, a Catholic of mixed Irish and German parentage, even cut into Harrison's immigrant support and handily defeated the mayor in the 1915 primary. Harrison exited bitterly. Years later, he wrote, "I had the sentiment but Sweitzer had the sediment."[39] Roger Sullivan and his allies were better at winning nominations than elections; Sweitzer went down to defeat in the 1915 mayoral election at the hands of Republican William Hale "Big Bill" Thompson.

A Civic Patriot

The multiple administrations of Carter Harrison II are surrounded by paradoxes and might-have-beens. Harrison was a realist, willing to take the world as it was and tolerate many sordid realities. He never entertained illusions about his unsavory political allies. Harrison once asked Hinky Dink about his flamboyant partner, "Tell me, Mike, do you think John is crazy or just full of dope?" Kenna replied, "To tell you th' God's truth, Mr. Mayor, they ain't found a name for it yet."[40] Nor did the five-time mayor repent his tolerant views on vice. Late in life, he often remarked, "Is Chicago . . . more moral or a better place to live in today than was the Chicago of 1893? Under pressure in 1914 I closed the red light district. . . . My action did not end the evil, it merely scattered it . . . and brought it close to the homes."[41] His two autobiographies present a somewhat world-weary, I've-seen-everything-in-my-day self-image.

Yet he had an idealistic side as well. He loved Chicago—glorying in the title of "Chicago's first native-born mayor"—and enjoyed city life—sharing the dream of fellow-progressives Frederic Howe and Tom Johnson for a kind of civic renaissance. Harrison's 1902 traction message expressed his progressive civic vision:

I admit today with many others that municipal operation [of the transit lines] under present conditions would not today be desirable. But he who fails to see it will be desirable even before the time limit of the franchise extension . . . expires is not keeping abreast with the times. The improvement in the personnel of your own Honorable Body [the city council, reformed by the MVL] so marked in the past few years, shows the tendency of the times. . . . Why should we on the threshhold of the new century bind ourselves with the same shackles with which our fathers bound themselves. . . .[42]

To read Carter Harrison's mayoral messages and the pages of the *City Manual* he inspired is to imbibe the optimism of a new century, of a generation that believed the city was "the hope of democracy."[43]

Had all five of his terms been of four-year duration, relieving him of the continual reelection burden; had he more consistently opposed the spoils system and improved the quality of civic administration more than he did; had the automobile not wrecked his dream of comfortable, efficient public transit; had the Levee denizens not flaunted their activities quite so extravagantly and brought about his downfall, perhaps the civic renaissance might have come about. Instead, Chicago wound up with Big Bill Thompson, Al Capone, the refurbished Roger Sullivan Democratic machine, and an international reputation for crime and corruption.

The most frequent criticism of Carter Harrison, both in his own time and by later historians, was his failure to lead the city vigorously enough. Historians use such phrases as "lackadaisical," "easygoing," "slipshod" in describing him.[44] During his final term, the public became impatient for more visible signs of action in implementing the Burnham plan, just as earlier they had chafed at his policy of delay on the traction issue. The mayor defended himself against these charges in his final message to the city:

Captious criticism has been directed at the supposed failure of this administration to do things. There are two ways of doing things. Things may be done slowly but right. Things may be done in a hurry . . . and a generation be caused to suffer because of what has been done. If a great work is to be done right, more time will be required for the planning than in actual construction.[45]

Chicago suffered no lack of leaders early in this century. Indeed, the city was bursting with energy. Daniel Burnham, Jane Addams, Walter Fisher of the MVL, and many others were all "making no little plans" for Chicago. What the city government required was a balancer, a harmonizer, a unifier, someone to focus all this energy and keep it from exploding. Carter Harrison succeeded in this task until his fifth and final term.

A more valid criticism concerns Harrison's failure to perpetuate or institutionalize his civic vision. Political control and civic policy can be perpetuated in only two ways, by building a political machine or by entrenching a profes-

31

sional civil service bureaucracy. Harrison did neither, so his politics of balance proved impermanent. He had no real successor. His legacy, therefore, was a memory of civic patriotism and city unity.

The *City Manual* for 1913 captured the spirit of Harrison's tenure in office:

> It was local patriotism, civic pride, that moved Saint Paul on a forever memorable occasion to exclaim, "I am a citizen of no mean city. . . ." Should every intelligent inhabitant of Chicago adopt these his noble words as his own, the resulting increase of pride in the city would be prodigiously great.[46]

And Harrison himself provided his best epitaph: "I have always been a little in advance of public opinion in Chicago. It is true I have not been so far ahead the people could not see me."[47]

3.

EDWARD F. DUNNE: THE LIMITS OF MUNICIPAL REFORM

John D. Buenker

For two tumultuous years between April 1905 and April 1907, Chicago was widely regarded as "the most radical city in America," one presided over by a "socialist" mayor who loaded his administration with "long-haired friends and short-haired women." The chief executive who evoked such furor was a fifty-two-year-old, former Cook County circuit court judge with no previous executive experience, a devout Catholic and devoted family man whose announced intention was to be remembered as the father of thirteen children and municipal ownership of the transit system. Although Edward F. Dunne's crusade for "immediate municipal ownership" failed for a complex of reasons, many of his own making, it did help force a resolution of the issue that had dominated Chicago politics for over a decade, leaving the city with a greatly improved transit system.[1]

In a broader view, the Dunne administration tried, with some success, to make government responsive to the concerns of several hitherto under-represented constituencies, such as organized labor, consumer groups, social workers, teachers, and intellectuals, and to promote the welfare of the middle and working classes in the areas of utility regulation, tax equity, education, and environmental protection. By the same token, Dunne forged a political coalition that, for a time at least, combined elements of the "old politics"—parochial, partisan, nonideological, and ethnocultural—with those of the "new"—issue-oriented, nonpartisan, candidate-centered, and reliant upon mass communications. Most importantly, his failure to achieve municipal ownership and to gain reelection clearly delineated the limits of reform politics in a city that was so fragmented, on the one hand, and so dominated by the business ethic, on the other.

Charges of radicalism or socialism notwithstanding, Dunne was squarely in the mainstream of municipal reform, usually dubbed "social reform" or "urban liberalism," that stressed sharing political power with the lower social orders, support for organized labor, toleration of ethnocultural differences and human weakness, and the expansion of urban services at costs affordable to all city dwellers. Although not as nationally renowned as Tom Johnson of Cleveland, Hazen Pingree of Detroit, Samuel "Golden Rule" Jones or Brand Whitlock of Toledo, or Mark Fagan of Jersey City, Dunne corresponded regularly with these luminaries, shared speech platforms with them, and contributed articles to the same "progressive" journals. He was a prominent member of several prestigious, municipal reform organizations and was a frequent speaker in major cities, especially on the topic of municipal ownership of utilities. From 1913 to 1917, he earned national recognition for his advocacy of numerous progressive measures as governor of Illinois, the only Chicago mayor to achieve that office.

The sources of Dunne's urban liberalism are complex but relatively easy to identify. His Irish-American identity, continuously reinforced by his leadership role in Irish causes and organizations, gave Dunne a lifelong empathy with the disadvantaged and the oppressed. Equally important was his belief in "Catholic social liberalism," a world view founded on a corporatist conception of society that stressed the interdependence of social classes, the responsibility of the more fortunate for the less, moderation in the acquisition and use of all earthly goods, a fair price, a just wage, and prohibition against usury. His Irish Catholic identity not only informed Dunne's judicial decisions and political utterances but also constituted an emotional and rhetorical link to the ethnocultural groups who were his staunchest supporters. In a vital sense, Dunne was Chicago's first "co-ethnic" mayor, the first to be "of" one of the city's substantial minorities and to serve as a conduit between his compatriots and mainstream institutions.

Dunne's ethnocultural orientation was reinforced and broadened by his legal education and by his fourteen years as a Chicago attorney and thirteen years on the circuit court bench. As a jurist he enjoyed a national reputation as a "people's judge," a defender of the underdog, and a foe of those who misused wealth and power. His outlook was further developed through his continuous association with almost every progressive cause of the day with a virtual "who's who" of Chicago social critics, independent radicals, activist intellectuals, settlement house workers, and labor leaders. Finally, it was given political structure by his leadership role in the most liberal wing of the Democratic party, that committed to William Jennings Bryan and Illinois Governor John Peter Altgeld.[2]

The rise and fall of Dunne as mayor was inextricably intertwined with the fortunes of municipal ownership (MO) of the transit system, a struggle that contemporary political scientist John Fairlie observed rivaled "in duration and intensity the Trojan War."[3] Dunne's blending of advanced Catholic social thought and populist Democracy convinced him that "the people were the ultimate repository of wisdom and goodness and that the public weal has to be constantly guarded against the machinations of predatory private interests." The granting of long-term franchises to "traction buccaneers," he charged, was to give them control over "the streets which belong to the people of Chicago." Summing up the case against privatism, Dunne accused the transit company owners of "corruption of public officials, the stealing of private property, favoritism in the selection of employees, strikes, inefficient service, exhorbitant charges, and insolence toward and defiance of the public."[4]

Dunne's conviction that municipal ownership (MO) could eliminate these evils was based upon a comparison of Chicago with MO cities that he derived from his 1900 tour of Europe and from data contained in expert studies. Dunne cited reams of statistics in support of the contention that European cities with MO provided superior service at significantly lower rates and with little of the corruption or labor strife that characterized the granting of franchises to privately owned utilities. Although his data seemed overwhelmingly persuasive to many, critics replied that they were misleading because European cities were generally more spatially compact, had long traditions of public responsibility, and enjoyed a measure of home rule denied to American cities. Nonetheless, Dunne indicted the Chicago system for its high costs, dirty cars, congestion, and lack of seating room for the average straphanger.[5]

Dunne also contended that "the wages paid by publicly owned companies are always higher than those paid by private companies," thus minimizing labor strife and strikes. Because he believed that a goodly portion of the fare went to pay inordinately high profits on watered stock, Dunne argued that it would actually be possible to raise wages while lowering fares. With no franchises to grant in exchange for graft, he insisted, the major source of municipal corruption would be virtually eliminated. To the charge that MO would create a bonanza of patronage jobs, he replied that while the privately owned gas and transit utilities were manned largely by political appointees, the municipally owned water utility was run almost entirely by civil service appointees. Although Dunne's MO speeches and writings used the transit system as a point of departure, the evidence and examples were usually selected from the entire range of public utilities, making it clear that he favored universal municipalization.[6]

As public frustration with the traction stalemate increased, Dunne gained in popularity and stature by advocating what seemed to many to be a workable plan to achieve immediate municipal ownership. Brushing aside technicalities and complexities, he boldly asserted that the Mueller Law "empowers the city which desires to own and operate public utilities to condemn the property and franchises of existing companies and, under the eminent domain act, hail them to court and compel them to surrender their property at fair cash value to the people." Dunne insisted that the city should immediately cease all negotiations with the companies and grant them only short-term three month extensions upon their current franchises. Once the voters approved application of the

Mueller Law to Chicago, he continued, the city should fix a fair market value for the companies' property and franchises and raise the necessary purchase price operating revenue, and funds for rehabilitation through the issuance of street car certificates.[7]

Publicly, at least, Dunne made no concession to the argument that the certificates might well be invalidated by the courts on the grounds that the legislature had no authority to exempt them from the constitutional limitation on the city's indebtedness. To those who contended that investors would not purchase certificates of such questionable validity, he replied that previous investors had purchased badly inflated transit company stock primarily because of the value added by the possession of twenty year franchises. Would not investors place at least equal value on franchises possessed by the city in perpetuity, he asked, especially if the municipality pledged itself to retain the five cent fare until the certificates were paid off at interest? In addition, they could earn five percent interest as opposed to the three percent paid by banks on savings deposits. Within ten years, Dunne concluded streetcar certificates would be paid in full, and the people would own the system.[8]

Dunne's emergence coincided with a sharp decline in the political fortunes of Carter Harrison. Harrison's renomination chances were severely imperiled by organized labor's endorsement of immediate municipal ownership (IMO) to which Harrison was cool and by the bitter factional fights that marred the Democratics county, state, and national conventions in 1904. The combination of Harrison's challenge to Hearst's presidential candidacy in 1904 and his seeming vacillation on MO cost the mayor the publisher's support. Withdrawing as a candidate for reelection, Harrison persuaded the council to submit the tentative ordinances, which Dunne condemned vehemently, to a referendum at the upcoming mayoral elections.[9]

Dunne, who proclaimed his mayoral candidacy in January 1905, was an outspoken leader for immediate municipal ownership. In 1903, he moved his large family back into the city from River Forest. On 26 June 1904, at a picnic of Democratic faithful, Dunne blasted Harrison for betraying the party's pledge to MO. In December, Dunne denied rumors that he planned to run as an independent, stating that he was a lifelong Democrat. About the same time, former Judge William Prentice of the Chicago Federation of Labor threatened to run as an independent MO candidate unless Dunne secured the Democratic nomination. In an open letter to the people of Chicago on 15 January, Murray Tuley, a distinguished jurist and Dunne mentor, styled MO as a struggle for control of the city's streets between Wall Street and the people and averred that the only hope of victory was for the Democrats to nominate a mayoral candidate "who would inspire confidence throughout the city in his determination and ability to carry out the municipal ownership policy for which he would stand." Tuley opined that any possible Republican candidate would be too committed to privatism to fill the bill and that an independent candidate would have little hope of success.[10]

Just eight days later, Dunne announced that Tuley's letter had led to delegations from thirty-three of the city's thirty-five wards urging him to run for mayor and that he was willing to accept the nomination as a public duty. Explaining that he would not resign his judicial seat until he began campaigning, Dunne pledged that he would accept no corporate contributions, even if "it may be that the campaign will have to be conducted from the street corners." Although the Harrison-controlled, Democratic Central Committee refused to endorse anyone, Dunne had the enthusiastic backing of Bryan-Altgeld and Hearst Democrats and organized labor and at least encountered no overt opposition from the Sullivan-Hopkins faction or from such powerful ward bosses as Mike Kenna, John Coughlin, Johnny Powers, John Brennan, Stanley Kunz, and Ed Cullerton. Most bosses were motivated either by a desire to punish Harrison for his cooperation with a good government crusader or by a recognition that Dunne was a likely "winner." Their attitude was probably best summarized in a statement that a *Chronicle* reporter attributed to City Sealer James Quinn in late February 1905: "I care nothing for municipal ownership. I'm for Judge Dunne. I have a good job in city hall and I'd be a fool to oppose him. Another reason I'm for him, I'm for an open town, I want to see North Clark Street like it was in the old days." In his acceptance speech, the candidate insisted that he agreed to run "chiefly . . . for putting into actual operation the principle of municipal ownership and operation of the streetcars of Chicago." [11]

In an apparent effort to blunt the appeal of Dunne and IMO, the Republicans nominated John M. Harlan, the maverick who had run on an MO platform in 1897. Since then Harlan had moderated his position significantly, first supporting the tentative ordinances and then hedging on MO saying "when the city shall be legally and financially able successfully to adopt it." Although some reformers campaigned for Harlan, many of his 1897 supporters switched openly to Dunne, including Clarence Darrow, Louis Post, Jane Addams, and Donald Richberg. The Non Partisan Harlan Club, organized by Harold Ickes, Raymond Robbins, Graham Taylor, and William Kent, supported Harlan because of his demands for a new city charter and in protest against Dunne's alliance with the Democratic ward bosses. Significantly, Harlan's major support came from sources that had previously opposed him—the business and financial community, the regular Republican organization, and the GOP press—or from such good government groups as the Municipal Voters League (MVL) and the Civic Federation that opposed IMO. [12]

Despite his inexperience in the rough and tumble of electoral politics, Dunne's campaign was an ingenious blending of traditional ethnocultural, partisan, pragmatic, ward-based politics with ideological appeals to independent voters through the press and political action committees. In a speech to Democratic ward leaders on 10 March, Dunne praised them as the officers of "the Democratic army of Chicago, 175,000 strong" and as practical men who knew their duties far better than he did. Because their party was committed to municipal ownership, however, Dunne insisted, it had been elevated to a higher plane, one where there could be no Dunne, Hopkins, Harrison, Sullivan, or Hearst men, "but only municipal ownership Democratics." At the same time, he emphasized the need to reach the fifty thousand independent voters "that will side with the party that is in the right" and who held the balance of power. He admonished party leaders to "go out and get the stragglers . . . and get their votes."[13]

To mobilize the party faithful, Dunne held Democratic rallies in every ward and made partisan and ethnocultural appeals. Even though several ward bosses were running for reelection, Dunne generally refrained from endorsing or opposing them unless they took a forthright position on IMO. In the Nineteenth Ward, where John Powers was a vocal critic of the policy, Dunne supported independent Democrat Simon O'Donnell, who was committed to IMO, but refrained from attacking Powers himself. In the end, the Nineteenth was Dunne's best ward, giving him better than a 3,900 vote plurality, while Powers edged out O'Donnell by just over 400 votes. In the First Ward, where Hinky Dink Kenna urged his supporters to vote for the judge because he was going to give the streetcars to the people, Dunne responded with an effusive endorsement of one of the most notorious Gray Wolves. The First Ward voters gave Dunne more total votes than did any other and a plurality of 3,800. Since Kenna's plurality was more than 5,600, it is clear that Dunne benefited from being the organization candidate. Dunne's elaborate praise of Hinky Dink prompted the Republican press and the good government organizations to argue that IMO was a spoilsmen's plot. To placate the Harrison faction, Dunne agreed to replace his candidate for city treasurer, John Traeger, with Fred Blocki. Where expedient, he also traded low-level patronage for support of IMO.[14]

But Dunne also proved himself to be an adept practitioner of ideological, independent politics. His closest advisors were Bryan-Altgeld Democrats, labor leaders, social reformers, intellectuals, or leaders of the Municipal Ownership League (MOL) or of the Municipal Ownership and Referendum League (MORL), and it was from that pool that he later made most of his high-level appointments. His decision to make the campaign on the single issue of IMO (Immediate Municipal Ownership) was designed primarily to appeal to voters who would have been largely immune to or incensed by ethnocultural or partisan appeals. Similarly, Dunne's refusal to resign his judicial position reinforced his image of independence and his stature as a highly educated, successful professional. To supplement the organizational and mobilization efforts of the ward organizations and to reach progressive Republicans and independents, Dunne supporters relied upon a series of volunteer political action clubs designed to demonstrate the support of various segments of society for IMO. City-wide, his candidacy was pushed by the MOL, MORL, and the newly formed MO Campaign Committee. Most of the volunteer political action clubs were organized by occupation, sex, ethnic group, geography, or some combination thereof, and illustrate Dunne's attempt to weave together elements of the old and the new politics.[15]

The success of that strategy was borne out on 4 April 1905 when Dunne defeated Harlan by a vote of 163,189 to 138,671. His vote total was almost 7,000 more than Harrison's best effort in 1901, and over 17,000 better than the latter's 1903 showing. Dunne carried twenty-two wards, all but one of which were on the Near North Side or in the core city bounded by North Avenue on the north, 55th Street on the south, South 46th Avenue or Kedzie on the west, and the lakefront north of 12th Street on the east. The latter was the traditional Democratic bastion, included the bailiwicks of the major ward bosses, contained the city's major industrial and commercial areas, and was inhabited primarily by working and lower middle-class Irish, Germans, or southern and eastern Europeans. The Near North Side was more of a swing area, containing some of the city's wealthiest and poorest residents and a mixture of normally Republican and Democratic ethnic groups. In the seventeen core Democratic wards, Dunne's political affiliation and/or ethnocultural ties were more important than his stand on IMO, as he outpolled the latter by totals ranging from 150 to over 3,500. In the most boss-dominated wards, Dunne's margin over IMO averaged better than two to one and he ran significantly behind the Democratic aldermanic candidate in about half those districts. In the Eighteen and Nineteenth, however, Dunne significantly outpolled Brennan and Powers as well as IMO, indicating that Dunne the partisan ethnic reformer was a formidable candidate. Apart from the First and Nineteenth wards, his strongest showing came in the city's largest Irish-Catholic community, where Dunne polled about two-thirds of the mayoral vote and ran about 1,300 votes ahead of IMO. In the Near North Side wards, Dunne received about the same vote totals as had Harrison in 1903, ran between 500 to 1,000 votes ahead of IMO, and won largely due to a drop-off in the usual Republican vote. In the far southeast Eighth ward, Dunne ran 250 votes ahead of Harrison's 1903 pace and outpolled IMO by just under 500.[16]

By contrast, Dunne's role as the transit companies' severest critic benefited him significantly in most of the thirteen largely peripheral, normally Republican wards carried by Harlan. Except for the Second, Third, and Fifteenth, these were virtually suburban wards inhabited primarily by upwardly mobile Yankees or second- and third-generation Americans of British, Scandinavian, German, or Irish descent. Their higher socioeconomic status reinforced the normal Republic proclivities of the Protestant residents and undermined the Democratic loyalties of many of the Irish and German Catholics. The Second and Third wards contained the city's largest concentration of blacks, who joined Yankee, Scandinavian, and German Protestant voters in keeping the districts solidly Republican. The Fifteenth was predominantly Jewish and Scandinavian and located in the zone of emergence where the inner city flowed into the periphery, making it a natural swing ward. Eleven of these thirteen wards were the only ones in the city where IMO received more votes than did Dunne. By contrast, the inner city, staunchly Republican Second and Third wards were the only ones where Dunne outpolled IMO and lost. In every Harlan ward save the Fifteenth, Dunne improved upon Harrison's 1903 total by margins ranging from 200 to 1,200 votes.[17]

Although it was clear that Chicago voters preferred Democrat Dunne to Republican Harlan for mayor in 1905, it was much less certain what they wanted him to do about the transit problem. The three propositions on the advisory ballot were worded in such a way that IMO supporters could only vote against some alternative course of action. On the question of whether the council should pass the tentative ordinances, they voted in the negative by 150,785 to 64,391. They were even more emphatic in rejecting the granting of any franchise to the Chicago City Railway Company and in instructing the council not to grant any franchise to any railway company. Since Dunne had made his entire campaign on IMO and since the correlation between his vote total and that of IMO was upwards of 90 percent, it was reasonable for the victorious candidate to claim an overwhelming mandate.

Although Dunne had tried all in his power to make the election a referendum on IMO and had engineered what seemed to be a smashing victory, there was still ample room for opponents to deny that he had received a clear mandate. But the vote against the tentative ordinances was nearly 30,000 more than that by which the voters approved IMO and 2,500 less than that by which they favored adoption of the Mueller Law in 1904, indicating that many may have viewed IMO primarily as a threat. Adding to the confusion was the fact that in such banner GOP wards as the Third, Sixth, and Seventh, the voters rejected the tentative ordinances by margins ranging from 1,700 to 4,200 and then overwhelmingly reelected aldermen who were members of the city council's Committee on Local Transportation (CLT) and staunch advocates of regulation. Finally, the support of such Gray Wolves as Kenna for IMO was highly tenuous at best, while several other Democratic aldermen who were indifferent to or hostile toward the prospect had been reelected.[18]

Dunne as Mayor

While the calibre of his appointments to top level administrative positions was perhaps the highest of any city administration in history, Dunne left them largely to their own devices and provided little coordination or communication. Because these were men and women of exceptional intelligence and expertise but little previous governmental experience, they frequently clashed with bureaucrats, politicians, and the mayor himself. As Jane Addams astutely observed, Dunne believed that if "citizens representing social ideas and reform principles were appointed to office, public welfare must be established." To his credit, Dunne later admitted that he "made some serious mistakes in taking the advice of some of those who had my confidence" and that he "left political matters to a large extent to be taken care of by men I trusted, but who were not adept in politics."[19]

Even though he had promised "immediate" municipal ownership and had momentum on his side, Dunne delayed for nearly three months before submitting his MO proposal to the CLT. While part of this delay was due to a teamsters strike that occupied much of his time and energy, a great deal of it was consumed by travel and speech—making statements on the benefits of MO. Dunne further alienated the CLT by ignoring much of its expertise and relying instead on outside advisers supplied by Hearst, Johnson, and other MO advocates. This tendency even led him to send for a traction expert from Glasgow, Scotland, who turned out to be both the wrong man and an unfriendly witness, to Dunne's embarrassment.[20]

Finally, Dunne fluctuated greatly in his plans to achieve MO and in his relations with his various traction advisers. His first message to the CLT contained two proposals, a city plan that called for Chicago to construct and operate its own system and a contract plan that contemplated the creation of a private corporation headed by five prominent citizens to build, acquire, and operate a system. When the council refused to adopt either plan, the mayor, with the help of several of the Gray Wolves, secured authorization to conduct a referendum on the policy of using Mueller certificates to purchase the existing lines. When the voters gave him that authority but failed to bestow upon the city the right to operate the system, Clarence Darrow resigned as City Corporation Counsel and was replaced by Walter Fisher. Dunne then proposed to CLT chairman Charles Werno that the city enter into an agreement to purchase the system and to build new lines out of a sinking fund created by sharing in all company profits above 5 percent. When Fisher negotiated such an agreement, Dunne found it so filled with "jokers" that he vetoed the so-called settlement ordinances, fired Fisher, and based his reelection campaign on rejection of the ordinances and a continued battle for MO. This apparent vacillation, along with his other shortcomings, convinced some ardent MO advocates that Dunne bungled their golden opportunity and allowed his opponents to portray him as a quixotic dreamer.[21]

But even had he done everything right, it is highly unlikely that Dunne or any other Chicago mayor could have achieved IMO. Neither as mayor nor as party leader did he have sufficient clout to overcome significant opposition. Constrained by a two year term and with limited patronage, he had little leverage with which to compel recalcitrant aldermen. He had no real recourse other than popular appeal if the council refused to act favorably upon his recommendations, while aldermen could override his veto with a two-thirds vote. Nor could Dunne derive much clout from his status in the Democratic party, where he was at most the leader of only one faction. He never gained control of either the city or county central committees and failed to forge any solid alliance with the Harrison or Sullivan-Hopkins factions. Real power lay with the ward bosses, who functioned autonomously, and Dunne commanded the consistent loyalty of only about one-third of the Democratic aldermen.[22]

Dunne's IMO efforts were further damaged by the intrusion of other issues that distracted his time and energy, alienated some supporters, and gave additional ammunition to his opponent. The first of these was a paralyzing teamsters strike that gripped the city for the first hundred days of his administration. A firm supporter of organized labor and a beneficiary of its political support, Dunne refused to call in the militia or take any other steps to break the strike. He spent long hours mediating between the union and the Employers Association, but was unable to effect a settlement. In the end, the union capitulated, costing Dunne some labor support, while his handling of the matter gave credence to conservative charges that he was both a prolabor radical and an incompetent chief executive.[23]

The opponents of IMO were also able to make a great deal of political capital out of Dunne's efforts to reform the school board. While judge, Dunne had ruled in favor of a Chicago Teachers Federation (CTF) suit forcing the State Board of Equalization to collect the full amount of taxes from the city's corporations in order to raise teacher's salaries. The CTF gave him strong backing in 1905. As mayor, Dunne appointed such reformers as Addams, Post, Robins, and Dr. Cornelia DeBey, a physician prominent in social work, to the school board, along with labor leaders and educators. Although they often disagreed among themselves, the Dunne appointees generally supported such radical causes as the creation of teachers councils to evaluate performance, restrictions on the powers of the superintendent, teacher unionization, higher salaries, and attacks on the "textbook trust." Most radical of all was their unsuccessful effort to break the long-term leases of school property at low rentals that several corporations, especially such newspapers as the *Tribune,* had cajoled out of a cooperative board in 1895. Not surprisingly, these efforts earned Dunne the violent condemnation of most Chicago newspapers, with the *Tribune* denouncing his appointees as "freaks, cranks, monomaniacs, and boodlers."[24]

Even more damaging were Dunne's efforts to cope with the highly explosive liquor issue. His Irish Catholicism mandated a preference for personal temperance over legislated prohibition and he understood the role that the saloon played in the social and political life of ethnic, working-class neighborhoods. He was also aware that no Democratic politician could afford to risk the political consequences of making concessions to antisaloon sentiment. But the reformer in him also recognized the abuses that occurred in the city's more disreputable saloons and the political and police corruption that attended their operation. Accordingly, he trod a middle course between moral reform and toleration that ended by alienating elements in both the dry and wet camps. Specifically, he proposed to enforce the Sunday closing ordinance and to raise the license fee from $500 to $1000, especially for those saloons deemed to be disreputable. The revenue engendered by the latter policy was also designed to finance the hiring of a substantial number of new policemen to improve the general quality of law enforcement. At one point, he pursued a policy of revoking the licenses of 104 disreputable saloons and restoring them if they cleaned up their act, but the state legislature prohibited the restoration of revoked licenses. His police even went so far as to close one of the Kenna's saloons for a time.[25]

None of this was enough for the Sunday Closing League and other anti-saloon groups who forced a grand jury investigation of the administration and the police. It was far too much, however, for the Liquor Dealers Association, the saloon keepers, ward bosses, and many of their patrons who vowed revenge in 1907. Anton Cermak, the rising Czech-American politician, formed the United Societies for Local Self-Government, a multiethnic organization that claimed over two hundred thousand members pledged to "personal liberty" and heavily financed by the liquor industry. Cermak worked for the defeat of his fellow Democrat, Dunne, in 1907 because Republican candidate Fred Busse advocated a wide-open city. The *Tribune* reported that an irate worker condemned Dunne at a union meeting because "he has closed the saloons and dance halls and everything. He has sacrificed everything for municipal ownership." There can be little doubt that the liquor question cost him votes in both the dry and wet camps, especially among the latter. It mattered little to many Chicagoans who owned the trolley cars if you couldn't ride them to and from your favorite saloon.[26]

More significantly, Dunne failed to achieve IMO because his philosophy presented a direct challenge to the values and interests of the city's power brokers. Each of these, from slightly different perspectives, were too firmly committed to privatism to acquiesce in an innovation that struck at the very heart of that system. Although the ward bosses publicly supported MO when it was to their advantage, they were too canny not to realize that it would mean an end to the practice of exchanging franchises for money, jobs, and other economic and political considerations. While some astute business leaders acknowledged that the system was corrupt and inefficient and adversely effected the city's economic climate, nearly all of them felt that the answer lay in better-managed, or at most regulated, private enterprise. The mainstream newspapers generally reflected this viewpoint since their publishers were a part of the business community. Ironically, the moderate reformers who populated the MVL, CLT, and Civic Federation opposed MO on the grounds that it created a patronage bonanza and increased political corruption, while the ward bosses opposed it in the belief that it would destroy the bonanza that they already had. Throughout the entire transit crisis, the moderates remained consistent in their preference for regulated private enterprise and in their strategy of using MO as a lever to achieve consolidation, regulation, and a share of the profits for the city.[27]

Finally, Dunne failed to achieve IMO because it is highly unlikely that a majority of Chicago voters ever unequivocally supported the notion, despite the apparent evidence of the various referenda. About 20 percent of the city's eligible voters failed to vote at all, and about one-third of those who did ignored the referendum questions, meaning that close to one-half of them never expressed any opinion. In all the referenda from 1902 to 1906, the pro-MO vote fluctuated between a low of 110,225 on the 1906 question of issuing Mueller certificates to a high of 152,135 on the 1905 question of denying a franchise to any railway company. Conversely, opposition to these propositions steadily grew from a low of 27,998 in 1902 to a high of 110,323 who voted against municipal operation of the transit lines in 1906. Apparently, the more "real" that MO became, the more reservations it raised among the voters.

When the issue was fairly clearly joined in 1907 between regulated private ownership and continued agitation toward MO, the total vote reached nearly 300,000 (compared to about 170,000 in 1902) and those who voted chose the settlement ordinances 165,846 to 132,720. It seems reasonable to accept the judgment of contemporary political scientist Arthur Bentley who argued that middle class voters supported MO when regulation seemed impossible and regulation when MO seemed stymied, while working class people followed the lead of their union officials and politicians. The election returns seemingly corroborated the findings of a *Tribune* poll whose respondents overwhelmingly believed that settlement meant improved service while rejection promised only delay and further agitation. There seems little reason to doubt that tens of thousands of Chicagoans concurred with one of the poll's respondents that as long as the service was improved significantly, it was all the same who got the nickel.[28]

The three-sided struggle over MO among the Dunne administration, the city council, and the transit companies raged on during most of the mayor's two-year term. As the 1907 mayoral election approached, Dunne again demonstrated that he was better at electoral politics than he was at the administrative or legislative variety. He skillfully quashed a Harrison challenge to his renomination by courting the Sullivan-Hopkins forces and a few ward bosses. On 21 February, Dunne won the primary of the Democratic convention for mayor 624 to 259 over Harrison, carrying the peripheral wards and those controlled by Powers, Sullivan, and former Harrison Lieutenant Robert Burke. Ominously, though, Harrison won the First Ward of Kenna and Coughlin, Loeffler's westside domain, and the predominantly German Near North Side, always a Harrison stronghold. Many wards bosses were incensed by Dunne's reformist policies and his public stance in favor of civil service. Perhaps more importantly, he now seemed a likely loser.[29]

The Dunne-dictated platform committed the party to defeat of the settlement ordinances and lauded the administration's accomplishments. Campaign strategy, however, consisted of stressing MO in those wards where it seemed to benefit Dunne in 1905 and emphasizing party loyalty and the mayor's personal qualities in traditionally Democratic bailiwicks. The mayor himself gave so many speeches that he eventually lost his voice, but he seemed to gain more applause when pleading his own reelection cause rather than urging defeat of the settlement ordinances. The Hearst papers were the only mainstream dailies to support his reelection and to urge rejection of the settlement ordinances, but even that was a mixed blessing. The candidate who pledged to save the city from sinister Wall Street bankers in 1905 now had to defend himself against charges that he was the tool of a radical and malevolent New York publisher. The Republican dailies kept up a steady barrage of denunciations of Dunne, while their cartoonists portrayed the mayor as a wildeyed radical riding an MO hobby horse.[30]

In an effort to placate those regulars alienated by Harlan's 1905 candidacy, the Republicans nominated Fred Busse, a German-American coal and ice dealer and professional politician. For his part, Busse endorsed settlement but concentrated his limited oratory on the need for a "greater Chicago" and businesslike government, a stance facilitated by his minor injury in a train accident early in the campaign. At that time the Republican papers portrayed the contest as an uneven one between a healthy Dunne and an injured Busse, much to the mayor's disadvantage.[31]

Much of the campaign against Dunne and for the settlement ordinances was conducted by two political action committees, the Chicago Non-Partisan Traction Settlement Association and the Straphanger League. The former was a front for the Real Estate Board and the Commercial Association, sponsors of the Chicago Plan, and it sent slick prosettlement brochures to every registered voter. The traction and liquor interests spent heavily in the campaign, with estimates ranging as high as $600,000. The Chicago City Railway Company alone spent $350,000 in promoting settlement. A sizeable portion of the money was spent in Democratic wards whose bosses had declared in favor of settlement and a wide-open town.[32]

The election of 2 April 1907 marked the end of both Dunne's mayoral career and MO. Busse outpolled Dunne 164,702 to 151,779, while the settlement ordinances were adopted 167,367 to 134,281, meaning that the Republican candidate trailed settlement by about 2,500 votes, while Dunne ran almost 17,500 ahead of the position he advocated.[33] The correlation between Dunne's showing and opposition to the settlement ordinances was about 90 percent. The prosettlement vote carried twenty-four wards and swept the entire lakeshore, everything south of 55th Street, and everything north of Van Buren, except for the Near North Twenty-fourth, the riverfront Sixteenth, 55th street on the South, and those dominated by the Irish-American community. Dunne carried ten of the eleven opposition wards. In each of them he ran ahead of antisettlement opinion. Even more than was the case in 1905, Dunne's personality, ethnoreligious identity, and/or partisan affiliation earned him the votes of many who were indifferent or hostile to MO.[34]

But Dunne's defeat should not obscure his contributions to Chicago and its political tradition. Although the 1907 election and referendum was primarily a realization of the moderate reformers' policy and probably reflected the viewpoint of the majority of Chicagoans, it is hard to see how that end could have been accomplished without the pressure generated by Dunne's IMO crusade. Emboldened by Grosscup's partial upholding of the eternal monopoly laws in 1904, the transit companies were reluctant to accept even the tentative ordinances, let alone the 1907 settlement. In collaboration with the Gray Wolves, Dunne's IMO advocates prevented further negotiations with the companies in 1906 and forced a referendum that resulted in the authorization of purchase by Mueller certificates and the prohibition of further franchise extentions. Almost simultaneously, the administration's legal counsels persuaded the Supreme Court to overrule Grosscup and invalidate most of the companies' claims under the ninety-nine-year laws. It was only at that point that the companies were willing to entertain serious consideration of regulation and consolidation.

Dunne's Werno letter outlined many of the terms later included in the settlement ordinances, and his later opposition was largely responsible for forcing the intense public debate that dominated the early months of 1907. Finally, his opposition to settlement clearly joined the issue and motivated unprecedented participation in the April 1907 referendum. None of this is to suggest that the adoption of the settlement ordinances was the outcome of any conscious design on Dunne's part. He was absolutely committed to MO and was even more convinced that any delay was a betrayal of the goal. Dunne's role in achieving regulation and consolidation was clearly unintended but nevertheless highly significant.[35]

Nor were Dunne's achievements by any means limited to his part in forcing the traction settlement. The central focus of his administration was on regulating of the rates and service of public utilities, with an eye toward eventual municipal ownership. It was clear from his speeches and writings that Dunne saw municipalization as the ultimate solution for all utilities; he backed a provision granting such authorization proposed by the charter commission. Typically, Dunne demanded more regulation than the city council was willing to endorse. In late April 1905, the new mayor led the Committee of Fifty, composed of moderate reformers and radical Democrats, to Springfield to lobby for the passage of a law permitting the city to regulate gas and utility rates. When the legislature passed the gas rate legislation, Dunne immediately asked the city council to reduce the price from the prevailing $1.00 per cubic foot to 75¢. His position was strengthened when the voters approved a public policy referendum permitting the city to sell surplus electricity and to fix rates for the supply of gas and electricity by private distributors. After the gas companies claimed that they could go no lower than 90¢, the administration filed suit to open their books. When the city council passed an 85¢ ordinance, Dunne vetoed it on the grounds that the rate was unfair and excessive, only to have the council override.[36]

Dunne also fought with the council and won an estimated 25 percent reduction in electrical rates as well as scaled-down telephone rates. Charging that

$175 a year for unlimited telephone service was exorbitant, the Dunne administration convinced the Illinois Supreme Court to mandate a $125 rate. Dunne used such tactics as opposing franchise extensions and threatening to invite rival companies to force even lower rates and greater efficiency in service. Because the city owned and operated the water utility, it was considerably easier to effect rate reduction for most consumers. This was accomplished by raising the rate for larger corporations from 4¢ per 1,000 gallons to 7¢ and correspondingly lowering the household rate from 10¢ to 7¢.[37]

The Dunne administration's legal department, headed by corporation counsels J. Hamilton Lewis, Clarence Darrow, and Glenn E. Plumb, focused on corporate privileges, and won its most famous victory when the Supreme Court's rejected the "eternal monopoly" laws. Dunne's legal department also bore down on tax evasion by wealthy corporations and persuaded the state Board of Review to examine the valuations and assessments of several estates and corporations, resulting in the recovery of nearly $2 million in revenue. The city health department vigorously pursued enforcement of health and environmental codes, nearly doubling the number of prosecutions during the first year. Spurred by the publication of *The Jungle* and the resultant passage of the federal Meat Inspection Act, the department confiscated ten million pounds of decayed and diseased meats and cooperated fully with U.S. inspectors in enforcing higher standards. However, the administration's efforts at curtailing the smoke from factories was considerably less effective.[38]

Other city departments also concerned themselves with consumer protection and business regulation. The city sealers' office waged a highly publicized campaign to eliminate dishonest weights and measures that cost customers millions of dollars per year. Building department head Peter Bartzen, a young and enthusiastic Dunne appointee, ruffled important feathers with his aggressive inspection and code enforcement policies. His department revoked numerous building permits and shut down several businesses for code violations. Bartzen's most famous exploit was the closing of Marshall Field's department store during two business hours for fire escape violations.[39]

Equally controversial were the activities of the public works department, headed by Joseph Medill Patterson, scion of *The Tribune* family who had deserted his rock-ribbed Republican upbringing to work for Dunne. He insisted upon open and honest bidding on all public works projects and sought to enforce civil service regulations in what was perhaps Chicago's biggest patronage machine. He compounded the latter by bringing assistant street commissioner and Sixth Ward committeeman Frank Solon up before the Civil Service Commission on charges of demanding campaign contributions of city hall employees. Solon's dismissal was one of the major incidents that contributed to the ward bosses' dissatisfaction with administration patronage practices. Following another of Dunne's favorite notions, Patterson vigorously pursued the collection of rents from corporations utilizing public streets, sidewalks, and tunnels. After ten months in office, Patterson resigned, praising Dunne's crusade for municipal ownership, excoriating waste, delay, and graft in government and business, and announcing his conversion to socialism.[40]

With the exception of MO itself, the Dunne administration's greatest challenge to the status quo came over the school board. Nowhere was the design to make government more representative of new constituencies more evident. In defending his appointments from the almost hysterical attacks of his critics, Dunne contended that "labor and middle class people are better able to determine what is good for their children than the merchants club." Not surprisingly, his controversial appointments were vigorously endorsed by Margaret Haley, president of the CTF, who deemed it "the most remarkable Board of Education I have ever known in Chicago or any other city," one that "so clearly saw so far ahead that it took hold of the large problems of the school." And, she added, "never did we have a board so opposed by the newspaper." Much of the latter's ire was attributable to the Dunne appointees' efforts to make them pay more for their long-term leases of school property, an action largely responsible for the *Tribune*'s charge that the mayor had packed the board with freaks, cranks, and boodlers. Dunne promptly called for a grand jury investigation and filed a one hundred thousand dollar civil suit against the paper. The grand jury returned no indictments but commended Dunne as an "honest public official," while the *Tribune* published a qualified retraction. Although the Dunne appointees achieved only minor successes, such as increase in teacher salaries, they aimed at decentralization and democratization of the school system and a drastic curtailment of the superintendent's powers.[41]

Dunne and the Chicago Political Tradition

The Dunne administration mounted the most serious challenge to the existing order ever managed in Chicago. It organized and operated municipal affairs for two years with officials recruited largely from the ranks of "outsiders." Although failing to achieve municipal ownership of the transit system, it applied much of the pressure that forced the companies to accept consolidation and regulation. It forced significant rate reductions from nearly all of the city's utility companies and induced many of them to pay rentals for use of public throughfares. It championed the right of teachers and parents to play a major role in the determination of educational policy. It brought the power of the state down upon some of the city's wealthiest corporations and estates, forcing them to pay delinquent taxes. By collecting rentals, delinquent taxes, and fines and by raising saloon license fees, it produced the largest surplus in the city's history. Taken as a whole, the Dunne administration's effort merited its leader's description of "militant civism."[42]

Yet it is still Dunne's failure to achieve MO and reelection that provides us with a distinct sense of the limits of political reform in Chicago. The successful reformer must not only be an effective practitioner of electoral politics, but also proficient at administrative and legislative politics. Dunne was not and clearly failed either to forge a coordinated administrative machine or to lobby his program through the city council where his approach was too confrontational.

Even if Dunne had been an effective administrator and legislative leader, however, he would still have been defeated by the fragmented nature of Chicago's life and by the realities of power. The strong council-weak mayor system severely inhibited any positive action by the latter and the virtual autonomy of individual aldermen and municipal departments exacerbated the problem. This fragmentation was also reflected in the factionalism of the party structure that severely undermined party discipline.

Dunne's frontal assault on privatism attacked the business and financial community's belief in its right to manage its own affairs, to make as much money as possible, and to use public property for private gain, values generally shared by the majority of Chicagoans. It was also an assault on the practice of exchanging franchises and contracts for jobs, money, and other favors that was the politicians' life blood. Dunne had tried to innovate faster and to push policy further than his predecessors but had run his administration aground when he reached the limits of municipal reform.

4.

FRED A. BUSSE:
A SILENT MAYOR IN TURBULENT
TIMES

Maureen A. Flanagan

Mayor Fred A. Busse's political personality may be suggested by the fact that during the entire mayoral campaign in 1907 he gave no speeches, made no campaign appearances. This was due partially to circumstance. At the start of the campaign, while returning to Chicago from Washington, Busse was seriously injured in a train wreck. Although he was then confined to bed under doctor's orders, one gets the impression from reading the newspapers that the accident was a rather fortuitous event: had he really wanted to, or if the Republican party had wanted him to, he might have risen from his bed of pain and gone speechmaking a few times. However, as one observer of the campaign cogently remarked of the accident, "this relieved him from the necessity of a speechmaking campaign, which would not have been at all to his liking. He rarely talks in public."[1] Busse's public reticence in the long run was to prove a handicap, especially given the bombastic style of Chicago politics at the time, but in early 1907 he was precisely what the Chicago Republicans were looking for. He was a solid Republican with no hint of scandal; a party man who promised to be amenable to promoting the party line; and a German with the potential to attract some ethnic voters away from the Democrats.

Fred Busse was born in Chicago in 1866 to German immigrant parents. His father was a small businessman engaged in hardware, and the son took a similar business path. After working in his father's hardware business for a time, Fred moved into the coal business, ultimately becoming president first of the Busse-Reynolds Coal Company and then of the Busse Coal Company. He joined the Republican party and entered the political arena in 1891 at age twenty-five. Over the next two decades, he carved for himself a solid, if not spectacular, political career. He was elected to his first public office in 1891, that of town clerk of North Chicago. After serving as a court bailiff and deputy sheriff for a time, Busse broadened his political aspirations and went into state politics. First, he held two terms in the Illinois House of Representatives in 1894 and 1896 and then followed with his election in 1898 as state senator from the Twenty-first District. After serving his four-year term as senator, he was elected state treasurer in 1902. Four years later, President Roosevelt appointed Busse postmaster of Chicago, a position he occupied until his election as mayor of Chicago in April 1907.

During his tenure in these public offices, Fred Busse did little to draw attention to himself as anything other than a competent officeholder, a man who made himself available to his constituents, and one who had made few enemies. Although he was the political boss of the North Side faction of the Republican party in the city, he was relatively unsullied by political graft and corruption, being neither a flamoyant political boss nor a practitioner of the more flagrantly corrupt aspects of the machine politics of the day. And his personal life, if dull, was above reproach. Until he married in 1908 at the age of forty-two, he lived at home with his parents. Newspaper accounts during the campaign are full of references to his mother fending off reporters and well-wishers who would invade her son's convalescent room. Moreover, while he was by no means the darling of the liberal reform element of the Republican party, he was an uncontroversial figure to whom few men would object openly, a factor that enabled the party to display a unity of purpose that otherwise would have been impossible behind other potential candidates.

And in 1907 the Republicans wanted to present a united party to the voters. In that year, the party thought it stood a good chance of regaining the mayor's office—a seat it had not controlled in well over a decade. The incumbent mayor, Edward Dunne, had alienated many Chicago voters either by being too wishy-washy or, from the opposite perspective, too radical on some important municipal issues. Moreover, the factions of the Democratic party were not in line firmly behind Dunne, and this interparty feuding gave the Republicans hope that their rivals would not be able to make a strong showing at the polls. This mayoral contest was especially important to the Republicans first of all because the winner would serve the first four-year term in that office. But they also wanted to have their man in office because the next four years promised to be critical ones for determining the shape of Chicago's future development.

Chicago, in 1907, was in the throes of the reforming spirit of the Progressive Era,[2] and the perception in the city was that whoever occupied the mayoral seat, and by extension his party, would exert tremendous influence over the outcome of these reforms. A new municipal charter that could centralize the powers and configuration of Chicago's government would be put to a referendum of Chicago voters; the proponents of municipal ownership of public utilities were promising an all-out campaign to achieve their goal of transferring utilities, especially the municipal transit systems, from the hands of private entrepreneurs to the city; the financing and direction of the public school system was in open dispute among the city's residents, particularly in regard to the composition, powers, and selection of the board of education; and the question of liquor regulation had become a hot issue not only within the city, but in the relations between the city and the state.

As a personality Busse pales in significance when set against contemporaries Carter Harrison and William Hale Thompson, both strong, flamboyant individuals who between them spent twenty-five years in the mayor's office from 1897 to 1931. Nor can Busse be easily described as machine or reform; he is one of those Progressive Era figures who falls between the cracks in the definitions, both an ethnic machine-oriented politician, and a businessman comfortably backed by the most reform-minded, antimachine businessmen of the Republican party. But, because the issues at stake in the first decade of the twentieth century were never satisfactorily resolved, they continue to be controversial problems today: the school system, mass transit, the structurally noncentralized municipal government.

So with its nonloquacious candidate safely confined to bed, the Republican party assumed complete control of the mayoral campaign and turned it into one of the more scurilous Chicago mayoral races, not an easy task for a city that has seemed to specialize in dirty politics. By all accounts of the 1907 mayoral race, the single, most rancorous issue, and one that caused much anguish for the Dunne forces, was that of traction reform. Under Chicago's existing system, the municipal government granted franchises to private companies to build and run transit lines in the city. By the turn of the century, Chicagoans clearly agreed among themselves that the franchise system, as it then functioned, was hopelessly corrupt and unable to provide sufficient or affordable public transportation. But Chicagoans did not agree on how to remedy the situation. They split into two distinct camps. There were those people who wanted to accomplish reform by tightening municipal regulation of franchises: issuing them for twenty years instead of the prevailing fifty year grants, setting more rigorous regulations on construction and provision of services, and making the traction companies pay more compensation to the city in return for their right to use municipal property. Opposing these proponents of regulation were those residents who believed that the franchising of public utilities itself was the problem and thus believed that regulation would never sufficiently guarantee adequate and affordable public services. These people, instead, advocated direct municipal ownership and operation as the only viable solution.

The issue of regulation versus municipal ownership had intruded heavily into the two previous mayoral contests of 1903 and 1905.[3] First Carter Harrison and then Edward Dunne had supported the idea of immediate municipal ownership, but once elected neither man carried out his campaign pledge. Now in 1907 the traction issue was again a focal point of the mayoral campaign, particularly because the existing franchises had expired and some decision had to be made about how to continue furnishing public transit. Dunne helped insure his defeat by turning several flip-flops on the issue. Although he had promised municipal ownership in 1905, soon after taking office he had appointed Walter Fisher as his official traction advisor. Fisher was committed to moderate franchise reform, and he and Dunne agreed to the course of renegotiating the existing franchises to receive better terms for the city than they had managed in previous franchise agreements. However, no sooner had Fisher accomplished this and presented new traction agreements to the city council for approval, than Dunne repudiated Fisher and the agreements. Labeling them neither sufficiently protective of the rights of the people who had to depend on public transit nor remunerative enough to the city, he vetoed the agreements after they had passed the city council and renewed his earlier call for immediate municipal ownership.

In the ensuing uproar over Dunne's about-face, the Republican party saw its opportunity to move back into city hall and they determined to get as much political mileage as possible out of the issue. Party leaders believed that the people had grown so tired of unfulfilled promises and political wrangling on this issue while at the same time watching public transit services continue to deteriorate in the city, that they could be swayed to vote for the man who promised to settle the problem once and for all by signing the pending traction agreements which Walter Fisher had negotiated. To this end they hoped that by agreeing unanimously upon Fred Busse as their candidate and by tying together Busse's election with the ratification of the agreements, their man would win the election.

The fight over traction reform was more than a disagreement over the proper means to reform, for it contained within it fundamentally different views of city life and good municipal government. It was this aspect of the issue, and of other municipal issues also as we will see, that made them so controversial and helped turn the 1907 mayoral campaign into a mudslinging affair. To many Republicans, the traction problem was a business matter to be settled by businessmen sitting down together and hammering out the best deal for all concerned— that is, for all the businessmen concerned. Speaking at a Busse campaign rally, state Attorney General William H. Stead ridiculed any other means to reform as absurd. "The one thing needed in the present crisis," he said, "is plain, everyday common sense and business judgment." Underlying this stance on traction reform was the ideological position that the business of the city was to accommodate business and that traction service should have as its main objective the enhancement of business. The campaign arguments of party leaders and their citizen supporters on this issue, therefore, stressed that business needs should always take precedence over any other municipal needs or desires since business made the city. Hence, as a proponent of moderate reform, Republican Alderman Milton Foreman dismissed opposing arguments that the renegotiated franchises did not bring in sufficient revenue to the municipal government by saying "what do we care whether the city makes $1 or $1 million out of the deal? The thing we are vitally interested in is keeping a straight spine by getting a seat." Or, as one Chicago banker put it most succinctly, "the building up of a new street car system is absolutely indispensable to the business life of the city. It would pay the people of Chicago to spend almost any amount of money and upon almost any terms to create an adequate transportation system for themselves in the shortest possible time."[4] For the Chicago business community, the compensation to the city negotiated in traction franchises was far less important than getting new franchises that promised to provide the kind of transit system that it desired, running over the routes that it declared the most desireable.

Many supporters of Mayor Dunne, on the other hand, could not agree with these arguments. For them, municipal ownership was not just a way of operating a mass transit system; it was also an ideological view opposed to the perspective of those persons favoring franchises. Municipal ownership contained the possibility of the people themselves, rather than just businessmen, having a say in the crucial decisions to be made about the transit system: where and when, for instance, traction lines would be built and how much the fares would be. As one of Dunne's backers put it, "If the voter is for private corporate control of the streets and street railways . . . he should vote for the election of Mr. Busse for mayor."[5] Many voters in the city were sympathetic to this argument, fearing that, in fact, the Republicans were in league with the companies currently holding traction franchises with the purpose of getting the best deal for the businessmen involved rather than for the people of the city.[6] These suspicions could only have been furthered when one of the franchise holders, the City Railway Company, announced pay raises for its employees if the traction agreements were ratified, "the way for which was paved by James Pease of the Republican county central committee and other friends of Mr. Busse."[7] Nor could they have been much comforted by Busse's record on traction. As a state representative, he had voted to extend the ninety-nine years the traction franchises of the notorious Charles Yerkes who had steadfastly refused to increase the number of streetcars on his routes in Chicago, saying it was "the straphangers who pay the dividends." Busse only reversed his stand two years later when the outraged public threatened to unseat at the next elections anyone who voted for franchise extensions again. Busse's supporters preferred not to bring up his original vote, or at best to attribute it to his newness in office.[8]

In this campaign, as was their wont with the numerous other current municipal issues bedeviling Chicago, the Republicans refused to acknowledge any legitimate opposition to their position. The Chicago *Tribune,* the strongest supporter of the Republican cause among the city's dailies, day after day during the campaign viciously ridiculed Dunne and anyone supporting him. Headlines such as "Hysteria Rules Demo[crat]-M[unicipal] O[wnership] Camp," "Chicago Suffers by Dunne Fiasco," "Dunne 'Loses' Use of Voice, But Abuses Opponents," were matched against ones saying "Busse a Fighter: Credit to City" and "Busse Managers Stick to Issue; Better Traction and Clean City Urged, While the Dunne Followers Sling Mud." The political cartoons did much the same: the "mild-mannered" Busse was depicted reading in his sick bed while Dunne supporters, all dressed in black with masks over their faces, sneak up to throw buckets of mud on him.[9] Every speech made by Dunne, every statement issued by him or his campaign, was mercilessly ridiculed; to read the *Tribune* accounts of his campaign, hardly a person ever showed up for his campaign appearances. All the while, Busse was safely tucked away in his bed, never having to face the public, a delightful situation for the Republican campaign committee that as much as possible answered any Democratic challenges to its candidate by referring indignantly to the poor man laid up in bed just wishing that he could respond in person, but alas it could not be.

Other daily newspapers at times gave more measured coverage to the campaign, but the *Tribune* coverage helps expose the underlying political tensions within the city in 1907 that were in fact central to determining the outcome of the elections and subsequent reform proposals. A tone of political hysteria emerges from its pages, conveying the sense that at least some Republicans held Busse's election essential to reverse a trend in Chicago toward radical municipal government. In a poll conducted among real-estate men during the campaign, one respondent urged Busse's election because it would "settle for many years the question as to whether the long haired men and short haired women are going to rule and ruin this town." The same sentiment was echoed by Thomas D. Knight, who, when presiding over a meeting of the Republican businessmen's Hamilton Club, declared the club to be against the "long haired management of city affairs." In cartoons, Dunne and his "cronies" were seen hanging out the City Hall windows, all wild-eyed and long-haired.[10] Partially this hysteria was a legacy from Haymarket and the confrontations with the radical labor movement of the 1870s and 1880s. It also reflected the fears of more conservative Republicans that Dunne's reelection might guarantee municipal ownership and other municipal reforms that would reshape the city in ways to which they were unalterably opposed. Certainly Edward Dunne himself was too upright a figure, a man who had been a respected Circuit Court Judge and would later be elected governor of the state, to merit the scurrilous attacks on him either on the basis of his personality or any ties to machine politics.

That these political tensions were more than those of reformers versus machine politicians, or matters of political personalities, is apparent too in other aspects of the Busse candidacy and campaign. Time and again, moderate Republican businessmen reformers proclaimed themselves nonpartisan, promoting only what was good for the city as a whole, claiming that if their candidates were elected there would be no more machine politicians, no more trading political patronage and political favors for votes. Many historians have accepted their claims more or less at face value, but in doing so they miss some of the inherent contradictions between these claims and actual political practices. The Republicans excoriated Dunne as a machine hack, a man engaged in vote buying and using his position to force municipal employees to work for his campaign. But Busse was also a machine politician, and the Republicans had to confront counter-accusations of Busse's vote buying. How they did so makes some interesting reading. While Dunne was accused of scandously and corruptly buying votes, Busse was a man who "just simply helps the sick and poor and lightens the load of poverty" by giving out jobs, money, and coal (he owned a coal company) to his North Side constituents. Pursuing this line of reasoning, the Republicans lauded their candidate for "more instances of the Postmaster's kindness to the needy" as told to them by Mrs. Busse, who confirmed that money and coal had been sent personally by her son to needy constituents. Letters of support sent to Busse were proffered as evidence of Busse's kindness; never was their any acknowledgment that there just might be a connection between his "gifts" and votes. In one such letter, a man wrote to Busse: "I received your letter of the 21st today. You say in your letter that a mutual friend has told you that I was friendly to your candidacy. Well I don't see how I can be otherwise. Don't you remember 3 years ago when I was going to be put out of my house . . . and I went to see you and you let me have $8.50? . . . I think this is a good reason why I should do all I can to help your election."[11] Evidently, Democrats bought votes; Republicans acted kindly towards the needy.[12]

In Chicago in 1907, Republicans of most every variety, including the liberal reformers, backed a machine politician because it suited their purposes. Better, they believed, to have a machine politician of their own who basically supported their political program, than Edward Dunne, a man who in fact was not closely aligned with machine politics, but was of the wrong party and stood on the wrong side of most municipal issues from them. Chicago Republicans were every bit as partisan as Chicago Democrats, and had been for the past decade.[13]

On election day, Dunne could not overcome the handicaps of a divided party and the uproar over the traction issue. Fred Busse was elected mayor, although not by as wide a margin as the Republicans had been predicting in the last days before the voting. While they thought a margin of 30,000 to 40,000 was a safe bet, their candidate actually won by a little over 13,000. That Dunne had won his own election by 24,000 votes two years prior, however, gives some indication of how far he had fallen in the public's esteem. Busse and the Republicans took office in a buoyant mood that, however, was not destined to last the year. They had promised to resolve with their business expertise the central issues of the time, including the traction issue. Their failure to resolve these issues would prove quickly to be their undoing because they could not understand the depth of conflict among Chicago residents.

One of these issues—a dispute that had been brewing for more than a decade—was the question of how to run the public school system. Proper Republican businessmen had been horrified by Edward Dunne's appointments to the board of education, among the most distressing of whom—from the businessmen's perspective—were Raymond Robins, a social worker, and Louis Post, newspaper publisher, member of the radical Independence League, and proponent of the single tax. Furthermore, the growing influence of the Chicago Federation of Teachers, led by Margaret Haley, had made these same businessmen apoplectic. The broad issue at stake in the school question was whether the schools were to be run by an all-powerful superintendent, hopefully a businessman who would order the system around sound business principles with finances as the highest priority, or whether the community as a whole, and the teachers, were to be given a greater measure of control by replacing the currently appointed board with an elected one, and by according the teachers' union more say in the overall educational policy of the school system. Dunne's school board pointed in the latter direction. This combined with the results of a nonbinding public policy referendum wherein the voters registered their overwhelming favor of an elected board and the increasingly vociferous rhetoric and actions of those citizens favoring an elected school board to alarm thoroughly the Chicago business community. During the mayoral campaign, the Republicans characterized the board of education as composed of "avowed single taxers and socialists," undertaking "one constant case of wild experiments and crank ideas," and run by "a preponderance of people with excessively progressive notions." What was needed, Republicans and businessmen said, was "a good, straight, hard headed businessman like Mr. Busse to straighten out the muddle."[14] But a hard-headed businessman was precisely the last person many Chicago residents wanted to see running the schools because they had spent the last several years fending off what they believed was the attempt of "business interests" to take control of the schools away from the people.[15]

Although Busse had said little on the issue of schools during the campaign, almost immediately upon taking office, he set about ousting ex-Mayor Dunne's appointees, first by requesting the resignations of twelve members (at the time there was a total of twenty-one members to the board of education) and threatening to remove them anyway if they failed to meet his demand. Among the dismissed were, of course, Raymond Robins and Louis Post, and two members of the Chicago Federation of Labor, John Sonsteby and John Harding. The *Tribune* hailed the move as one that would "give the control of the city school system into the hands of a board dominated by a practical and capable business element"; Busse, his usual reticent self, refused to comment on what he was doing or why.[16] Several of the board members refused to resign quietly, threatening legal actions against the mayor, but within two weeks Busse prevailed. His new appointees were what his opponents had expected: all business and professional men, they included John Morrow, chairman of the Merchants' Club school committee, the businessmen's group that was promoting the antithesis of what the Chicago Federation of Labor (CFL) wanted from the school system, and Severt Gunderson, "a warm, personal friend of Mayor Busse." The CFL denounced Busse's moves as a giant step toward making the public schools "a cog in the capitalistic machine, so that the children may reach manhood's estate content in a condition of abject servitude." [17]

Within days of his election, Busse had also to confront the problems posed by a proposed new municipal charter then awaiting ratification by the state legislature, which if passed would go to a referendum of Chicago voters. The Republican party, most especially its reform element, very much wanted this charter. Under its provisions, the municipal government would be reorganized administratively and fiscally in ways that they favored. They were, however, facing a stiff challenge to their charter from within the city from citizens and Mayor Dunne, who labeled it a charter designed to hand over control of the city to businessmen and the Republican party and one that failed to remove the influence of the state legislature from municipal affairs. [18] Heavy opposition was voiced also by ethnic voters in Chicago who feared the proposed charter would result in the imposition of Sunday closings of saloons and other state antiliquor laws in Chicago. This fear was especially strong among Chicago Germans, who the year previously had organized an umbrella ethnic organization, the United Societies for Local Self-Government, to help secure antiprohibition guarantees in the new charter. [19] The United Societies had not succeeded in this objective. Candidate Busse, the Republicans believed, was the right man to smooth over the difficulties. First of all, he staunchly supported the charter and the party felt it could count on him to remain firm on this issue. Beyond this, he had the distinct advantage that he was a German himself and could be expected to talk to his people in ways to allay their fears. During the mayoral campaign he did just that, promising the United Societies that if its membership voted for him he would go to the legislature and seek relief for Chicago from state liquor laws, separate from the proposed charter. [20]

Busse attempted to fulfill that pledge and journeyed to Springfield to ask the state legislature to pass separate antiprohibition bills for Chicago to accompany the new charter legislation. But when the legislature refused to consider such new liquor laws for Chicago, Busse refused to turn against the charter, and until the municipal referendum in mid-September of 1907, Busse worked to secure its ratification. In doing so, he alienated many of his German supporters, especially in the last days of the charter campaign when, in an uncharacteristic outburst for the usually quiet mayor, he accused the United Societies of being in league with the brewing industry to stop the charter and threatened to implement Sunday saloon closing himself if the charter failed. [21] A week later, he followed this blast with his pronouncement that "the best citizenship in this community approves the Charter," an insulting statement that surely won over none of the charter's opponents.[22] Despite the Republicans' hopes for success and Busse's work for the charter, the voters of Chicago rather soundly rejected it in September of 1907. For the next two years, Busse remained at odds with the United Societies and others of his former ethnic supporters on the issue of charter reform. He grew increasingly suspect in their eyes in 1909 when they believed him willing to make deals on new charter legislation with Republican state legislators who were trying to impose stricter liquor laws on Chicago.[23]

As the charter had failed in 1907, so too did attempts to revive charter reform in 1909, and Busse and his party remained linked in the minds of many voters to a measure that they had strongly opposed. Busse changed the school board, but he could not stem the continuing criticism and bitterness of which of the citizenry toward a maneuver that they believed was intended to make the schools the personal preserve of the business community. Even before the new traction franchises could be put into effect, the railway companies were saying they could not meet the terms they had negotiated with the city in these franchises,[24] an announcement that deepened the cynicism those residents favoring municipal ownership felt toward businessmen and franchises.

By running Fred Busse in 1907, the Republican party had made a practical, short-term choice: he was the man who could put them back into the mayor's office. That the reformers of the party could back a machine politician and that Busse in turn could support municipal reform measures desired by these reformers, blurs the distinctions between machine and reform politicians and turns them into ineffective categories through which to try to understand Chicago politics of the early twentieth century. Nor is it enough to assign voter behavior either to ethnic or machine sympathies. The municipal issues at stake during this time were critical factors in determining political races and the fortunes of the parties. What happened to the school system or to the public transit system were every bit as important to many voters as were the ethnic background or promises of political patronage coming from certain candidates. The "radical" Edward Dunne lost the mayoral nomination in 1911 to Harrison by only 1,500 votes and there were still those in the city urging his renomination on the basis of his support for municipal ownership.[25] The deep feelings aroused by these issues during the campaign did not disappear afterwards, and they helped insure that Busse and the Republicans would make little headway in Chicago politics at this time. Busse's continuing support of the causes of the Republican businessmen eroded much of his hitherto natural constituency. Moreover, Busse's refusal, or inability, to act the part of a politician proved as much of a liability to his party once in office as it had been an asset during the campaign. A small-time office holder and presumably capable administrator and businessman, he had not the personality nor the temperament to lead a complex urban center such as Chicago.

In the long run, then, Busse's term in office did little to enhance the party's position in municipal politics. The party itself remained split between machine factions and a liberal progressive wing, seemingly unable to find tenable ground to stand on in appealing to the voters as it fluctuated between its two wings. In early 1911, when the Republicans had to decide on a candidate, Busse was his usual uncommunicative self, saying nothing about whether he planned to put himself in for renomination. While the party leaders waited for word from him, the reform element of the party decided to put up as candidate Charles Merriam, a professor at the University of Chicago and as a member of the city council, a noted liberal reform Republican. Busse finally declared his intention to retire in a short written statement to the party, ending his mayoral career as silently as it had begun. The way was open for Merriam to win the Republican nomination. Against him, the Democrats nominated the formidable Carter Harrison. Merriam and the Republicans went down to defeat, losing to Harrison by seventeen thousand votes.[26] It was the last hurrah of the liberal progressive wing of the Republican party; the only Republican mayor for the rest of the century would be William Hale Thompson, a politician who could play the game of machine politics with the best of them.

5.

BIG BILL THOMPSON: THE "MODEL" POLITICIAN

Douglas Bukowski

The Honorable James E. Watson, Republican from Indiana, found himself in impressive company. Fellow senators William Borah, Robert LaFollette, and George Norris all were present, and, minding tradition, they consented to Watson's request to insert a magazine article into the Congressional Record. And so "Shall We Shatter the Nation's Idols in School Histories?" by Mayor William Hale Thompson of Chicago became part of the legacy of the 70th Congress. Later, the United States Printing Office made Thompson's remarks available in pamphlet form.[1]

It was fitting that the thoughts of Big Bill Thompson should reach the shelves of Harvard and the University of Chicago if only because his career thrived on contradiction. Thompson was the machine politician first elected on a harmony ticket with two Bull Moose Progressives, the nationally discredited figure courted by presidential candidates, and the alleged ally of Al Capone the Justice Department never prosecuted. After Thompson's death in 1944, the Federal Bureau of Investigation discreetly examined his safety deposit box in search of stolen securities, but J. Edgar Hoover could no more "catch" Thompson than did a generation of Chicago reformers and Democrats. When he was defeated for a fourth term in 1931, Big Bill bequeathed the electorate a final contradiction. For the next half-century, Chicagoans elected mayors who followed policies established by Thompson towards blacks, ethnics, and labor, the business and reform communities, and organized crime. Even Richard J. Daley was beholden, if not for a campaign style, then for the Thompson-fashioned image of the mayor as big builder.[2]

For the most part, critics have dismissed Thompson as a creature of the 1920s, more related to style than substance. He is the fat demagogue who appealed to the Germans and Irish with his tirades against the king of England.

His contributions are of the type cited by Daniel J. Boorstin, a member of the go-getter decade who laid the foundation for all of Capone's undertakings. The FBI, in a report on Chicago politics, was impressed enough with Harold F. Gosnell that it cited his *Machine Politics, Chicago Model* to note that Thompson was so much buffoonery. (The bureau did not read Gosnell closely; he overstated Thompson's mayoralty by eight years.) Accurate enough in themselves, these views ignore the social and political tensions Thompson exploited during his career, and they reduce the era's politics to rote stimulus-response. Rather, Thompson is best understood from the same perspective Joel Tarr used in his study of Big Bill's mentor, William Lorimer. The Blond Boss, Tarr discovered, was a politician who attracted both the laborer and the businessman. If Thompson never learned the value of precinct-level organization from Lorimer, he did grasp the importance of coalition politics.[3]

The early Thompson was a fairly conventional politician. He faced Judge Harry Olson of the Municipal Court in the 1915 Republican primary. Olson had the organizational backing of ex-Governor Charles Deneen and the support of such Progressives as Jane Addams and Charles Merriam. Still, Thompson won. Rather than a Lorimer protégé, voters saw a candidate who was physically attractive, spoke well, and knew the value of a good campaign song: "We want a cleaner city where the good can thrive and shine." In contrast, Olson came off as a drab reformer. With women about to vote in their first mayoral election, he could do no better than praise the "sense of economy" they would bring to public life. As a model of good government, he held out the meatpacking industry. Thompson won by 2,325 votes with the largely black Second Ward contributing a 6,800-vote margin, but there was more to Olson's defeat than race. With what the *Tribune* termed a "laboratory exactness and chill efficiency," Olson transformed Thompson into an attractive candidate.[4]

With the help of manager Fred Lundin, Thompson carried that new-found legitimacy through the general election. He picked his words well as he promised a "square deal" for all party factions, Progressives included, and had Deneen and Edward Brundage—a second GOP factional leader—named to his managing committee. While Merriam refused to lend support, Thompson appealed to the middle-class and reform vote by promising to fight the excessive rates charged by Peoples Gas Company. In a show of factional support, Harry Olson and Charles Deneen spoke for the party candidate.[5]

The Democrats failed to match that unity. Incumbent Carter Harrison II lost to County Clerk Robert Sweitzer in a primary one part movie, the other theatre. Harrison experimented with a campaign movie-short; Sweitzer preferred opera. He likened Harrison to Pooh-Bah from Gilbert and Sullivan's "The Mikado," as a man driven more by family pride than a sense of civic responsibility. What Sweitzer won, as Democratic leader Roger Sullivan warned him, was the right to lose. Particularly, the Democrats outwitted themselves in their appeal to the ethnic vote. During the primary, a Harrison lieutenant charged that Sweitzer was a German who chose membership in the Ancient Order of Hibernians over that of any organization from his own ethnic group. To prevent Thompson from reviving the issue and to minimize damage from the inevitable whispering campaign over his Catholicism, Sweitzer released the German Fatherland letter. The leaflet was intended for distribution in German neighborhoods, but once the Republicans discovered and reproduced it, the letter found a new audience. "You, your relatives and friends can be of great assistance to Germany and Austria next Tuesday by electing Robert M. Sweitzer . . ." took on an unintended meaning in Polish Downtown and Czech Pilsen, where sensibilities had been rubbed raw by World War I.[6]

The letter worsened ethnic friction already present in Democratic ranks. During the primary, Congressman Adolph Sabath charged that Sweitzer was an anti-Semite who called City Hall a synagogue because of the number of Jewish workers. The remark was not forgotten in the name of party unity. The leaflet was a measure of the Democrats' inability to appeal equally to all groups.[7]

Running with Progressives Charles H. Sergel for treasurer and John Siman for clerk, Thompson won by 148,000 votes. Contrary to legend, he did not begin looting the city treasury. Instead, he played the role of advocate of (relatively) good government. The emphasis remained on the middle class. In one of his first moves, Thompson thanked the *Tribune* "for the fair manner in which you gave me an opportunity" to present his candidacy and principles. Thompson chose for police chief Captain Charles C. Healey, who claimed he had never tasted liquor in his life. Thompson also acted on his promise to fight Peoples Gas by choosing a select committee of aldermen; when the committee decided on Merriam ally Donald R. Richberg as counsel, Thompson accepted. Charles Wacker was impressed—and politic—enough with the new mayor to pledge the support of the Chicago Plan Commission in furthering projects in accordance with the Burnham Plan. By the summer of 1915, the Thompson administration was promising a $3.7 million economy drive and the dismissal of one hundred overaged officers from the police department. The "new" Thompson was in full evidence after the steamship Eastland capsized in the Chicago River. The mayor left the Panama-Pacific Exposition in San Francisco to direct relief efforts, and he led a funeral procession of five thousand through Lawndale, home of many of the drowning victims.[8]

At first, Thompson was not particularly interested in the support of organized labor. His policy was shaped by middle-class interest and bias. When a traction strike shut down public transportation in June 1915, he helped mediate a quick settlement. In doing so, he realized which groups most used the els and trolleys; the page-one thanks in *Chicago Commerce* magazine could not have come as a surprise. Yet Thompson made it clear he was no friend of labor. When Sidney Hillman and a delegation representing striking garment workers went to city hall that autumn, the mayor refused to see them. The group came to protest police action against pickets. Thompson's explanation of his inaction in this labor dispute, that his participation "would set the precedent of wild agitation and murder," was not meant for a working-class audience. The strike lasted three months.[9]

Thompson was as hostile to union activity among municipal employees. At a time when officers received the same pay as they had in 1912 and were expected to work a 365-day year, Thompson's police chief suspended four officers for trying to revive a patrolmen's benefit society. It was part of the same attitude displayed for nearly two years toward the city's teachers. In August 1915, school board member Jacob Loeb, a Harrison holdover, forced passage of a measure that forbade school employees from belonging to unions. The board hoped this "Loeb Rule" would weaken if not destroy the Chicago Teachers' Federation, and Thompson gave his support. He contended, "City employees should be prohibited from organizing to operate against the municipal government. I am opposed to it for such a movement can bring no good." Instead, he urged the schools to support efficiency and the 3 Rs.[10]

Again, it was a move calculated to elicit the support of a group like the Illinois Manufacturers' Association, which approved of Thompson's stand "because the Teachers' Federation is controlled by union labor." When the federation's Margaret Haley secured an injunction against the measure, Thompson allowed the board in June 1916, under newly elected president Jacob Loeb, to pass a second antifederation rule in the guise of an employee tenure measure. The board quickly dismissed sixty-eight teachers, thirty-six of them federation members. The teachers were forced to leave the Chicago Federation of Labor in the spring of 1917 before the state would pass legislation protecting them against the Loeb measures.[11]

A mayor who settled traction strikes and fought teacher organizations naturally would move in another area of middle-class concern, the saloons. For years the city had celebrated a Continental Sunday in violation of state law. The Sunday hours of the Columbian Exposition in 1893 encouraged the practice, which was a tradition in the city's growing German and Catholic neighborhoods. From the time of his election, Thompson was pressured by temperance groups to comply with the law. On the first Sunday of October 1915, he did. There was little the estimated 7,150 establishments that were closed could do to stop him. Saloon owner and alderman Bathhouse John Coughlin tried the pen ("I never dreamed that such a day would ever come to pass/When you and I would be deprived of friendship's social glass") without success while Anton Cermak resorted to more direct action. As secretary of the United Societies, Cermak released a pledge Thompson had made to the antiprohibition group during the campaign that he would not enforce the closing laws. Cermak hoped the disclosure would make Thompson appear as a political hypocrite or weakling. Instead, it demonstrated Thompson's ability to withstand criticism when in tune with his constituency.[12]

Thompson emerged from the 1916 Republican Convention as a national committeeman from Illinois. The committeeship represented the epitome of Thompson, the conventional politician. Winning city hall, he had a power base for dealings with other party factions. Downstate political leaders soon realized the importance of Thompson's strength in Chicago. Senator Lawrence Y. Sherman needed help for his favorite son candidacy; Frank Lowden, who first supported Thompson for mayor in 1900, wanted the nomination for governor. Both figured in his election as committeemen. "Do not forget," Chicago banker and Republican leader Charles Gates Dawes wrote Sherman, "that unless it is prevented by unwise conduct in little things that Thompson, if he handles himself right, is a coming man." [13]

Ultimately, it was a series of "little things" that ended the conventional phase of Thompson's career. Critics charged that Corporation Counsel Samuel Ettleson was little more than a spokesman for the utilities while in early 1916 two city officials resigned in protest of civil service abuses. One of them, Dr. Theodore Sachs of the Municipal Tuberculosis Sanitarium, committed suicide. His suicide letter, addressed "To the People of Chicago," became a campaign staple against Thompson. With the release of a report claiming the mayor had made 9,200 temporary civil service appointments within his first five months in office, the good government forces gathered at the Auditorium for a protest rally in March 1916. [14]

Thompson knew that few elections were decided on civil service. Still, his critics understood his new image was by no means secure, and they proceeded accordingly. As early as September 1915, the press reported that the new mayor had racial problems. Blacks and Italians clashed, allegedly the result of the increased black presence on city work gangs; black employment figures were reported for the various city departments. Thompson was forced to make a public defense of his hiring practices to a rally of black supporters at the Coliseum. He spoke of "my duty to do what I can to elevate rather than degrade any class of American citizens." Blacks and whites could draw differing conclusions from the mayor's words and the size of the audience (15,000). Shortly after the rally, aldermen found bogus notices in their mail boxes for a new play, "Uncle Tom's Cabin," featuring Thompson in the lead and advisor Fred Lundin in the role of Simon Legree. The time of performance was four years. [15]

As Democratic state's attorney, Maclay Hoyne did more than satirize; he generated indictments. Running for reelection in 1916, Hoyne combined race and vice in a blow against the mayor. In the weeks before the November elections, Hoyne raided City Hall in search of evidence concerning a vice scandal. The raid led to the indictment of Police Chief Charles Healey on charges of being part of a gambling conspiracy. Two months later Hoyne lodged similar charges against Oscar DePriest, the city's first black alderman and a Thompson ally. The trials gave Hoyne the chance to portray black Chicago as most whites were inclined to see it—as a center of vice and corruption—and link Thompson to that image. Despite the use of 1,470 phone tap conversations as evidence in the Healey trial, Hoyne lost both cases to Clarence Darrow. Still, Thompson's reputation was tarnished. The middle class did not want its police chief using a private line to conduct gambling "business." [16]

If Thompson were less ambitious, he could have recovered from the Healey scandal; American participation in World War I and his desire for national office would not allow it. Ironically, until the declaration of war by Woodrow Wilson, Thompson seemed to support American foreign policy. He was the first Chicagoan to enroll in a civilian training course at Fort Sheridan, and he helped coordinate Chicago's preparedness parade, a typical Thompson production of 130,000 participants marching through downtown. [17]

In part, his stand on the war can be traced to one of the most astute observations made by a city politician: "Chicago is [in April 1917] the sixth largest German city in the world, the second largest Bohemian, the second largest Norwegian and the second largest Polish." The good mayor always trod carefully in matters of ethnicity. Yet Thompson's criticism of the war—it never reached the level of formal opposition—was based on more than simple nose-counting in the city's precincts. Thompson was a smart enough politician to sense that a majority of Chicagoans, particularly the new immigrants whose homelands were controlled by the Central Powers, would support the war, as would the city's elite. Rather than go along with that majority and in the process blunt the criticism of his administration, Thompson gambled on an issue that transformed his career. He did it because he wanted to be a United States senator, and he thought he saw something in the vote in Congress on 5 April 1917. Of the fifty votes cast against the war in the House of Representatives, six came from the Illinois delegation. [18]

The mayor intended to project himself as an Illinois LaFollette, at least to the extent his personality would allow. In one of his first moves, Thompson released a public letter warning that Chicago and the nation faced starvation if too much food was diverted to Europe. He urged Congressional action and offered his own interim solution, a city garden program. He again appealed to national self-interest in his remarks on the draft. Opposing it "until the life of the republic" itself was threatened, the mayor contended the danger would come from Mexico before it would Europe. Further comments on the war appeared in Thompson's unofficial newspaper, *The Republican*. The paper struck a Populist pose in its remarks on the war. Woodrow Wilson, Wall Street and the commercialized press, Thompson's critics, caused American involvement in the war. "The industrial and commercial rivalry between Great Britain and Germany was not our fault; and we were not especially interested in their respective pretensions to power and predominance in old world politics." It was a common *Republican* refrain. By summer 1917, Thompson and his paper together regularly cited Washington's Farewell Address, the Wilson administration's violation of free speech, and the "fat contracts" of war profiteers. [19]

Thompson balanced his wartime remarks with repeated promises of a greater Chicago. A month before the war, architect Jarvis Hunt released two plans, one for a combination monorail-subway system and the other Thompson's proposal for lakefront development. There would be offshore islands, a twenty thousand-capacity town hall set in Grant Park, and two more commercial-recreational piers, like Municipal [Navy] Pier. Although nothing came of either idea, Thompson had set a precedent with the lakefront idea: He recast a part of the Burnham Plan and offered it as his own. He would not be the last mayor to do so.[20]

Like Thompson, Charles Wacker of the plan commission publicized civic projects during the war. As a businessman and supporter of the war, Wacker had no particular affection for the mayor. Wacker fought for the continuation of public works in wartime because he was a true believer in the Chicago Plan; that Thompson held office was incidental. Wacker publicly defended his position. "How are we to develop a strong, virile and capable people?" he asked. The Wacker solution lay in better housing and more playgrounds, parks, and beaches. Wacker also helped in the fight to continue work on the Michigan Boulevard link. Writing to Frederic A. Delano—an original member of the Chicago Plan Committee—of the capital issues committee of the Federal Reserve Board, Wacker argued that the project constituted an important part of the national war effort because it facilitated traffic and, by extension, the movement of war material and because it connected the city with Fort Sheridan and the Great Lakes Naval Base.[21]

When Thompson gave his third annual message to the city council in May 1918, he avoided the war to focus on such construction projects as 12th Street and Ogden Avenue. The mayor needed these successes since his other actions, e.g., the refusal to extend a formal invitation to the visiting Marshal Joffre (on the claim that it was the duty of the city council) and the hostility shown Liberty Bond salesmen at City Hall during the first loan drive (Thompson explained he wanted to avoid the appearance of coercing city employees to buy bonds) expended political capital. Still, these were minor incidents when compared to the meeting of the People's Council of America for Democracy and Terms of Peace. Thompson allowed the antiwar group, which included Crystal Eastman and Socialist Victor Berger, to come to the city in September 1917 even though it had been denied permission throughout the Midwest. Governor Frank Lowden was unmoved by the argument of the corporation counsel that there were no grounds for barring a meeting. Lowden ordered Chicago Police Chief Herman Schulttler to stop it. After police dispersed the first meeting, representatives of the group appealed to Thompson, who again granted permission (as he avoided phone calls from Lowden). The governor dispatched a detachment of the National Guard from Springfield by train, but the People's Council held its session. It was not the only controversial appearance of antiwar spokesmen in the city. A well-known group of radicals such as Victor

Berger, Emma Goldman, Big Bill Haywood, and Morris Hillquitt all appeared without incident.[22]

The federal government did not move directly against Thompson. When the Hearst papers printed the remarks of an assistant district attorney that the Joffre snub could lead to an investigation, Assistant Attorney General Samuel Graham demanded a report; the assistant denied the statement. Rather than an investigation, the Justice Department kept a file. It included Thompson senate campaign literature and the transcript of a mayoral strategy session held in a room—which was bugged—at the LaSalle Hotel. The file did not, however, lead to any prosecution of the mayor. Rather than risk an incident, the government allowed the problem of Chicago's loyalty to work itself out, which it did. Nationalistic Poles and Bohemians helped by pressuring the school board to stop German instruction and the use of the "Kaiser-page" in the grammar school speller and to rename Bismark School. The press reported approvingly of these actions, and the *Tribune* began a Kaiser-page referendum. Those who found "The Kaiser in the Making"—the lesson on page 154 of the speller—offensive were encouraged to rip it out and mail it to the board.[23]

Self-styled patriotic organizations also joined in the cause of insuring wartime loyalty. The National Security League undertook a variety of activities, including the expulsion of Thompson from its executive committee. The American Protective League (APL) assumed a less public posture. Claiming over 6,100 active members by the Armistice, the APL provided the federal government with information that, in the words of the league's first president, "the Bureau of Investigation has generously intimated could hardly have been secured from any other source." The league helped index the names of 18,000 registered German aliens, conducted a daily average of twenty-five character checks for federal authorities, and detained some 200,000 men in a Slacker Drive conducted in July 1918. The superintendent of the Chicago division of the Bureau of Investigation credited the APL with doing 75 percent of the government's investigative work in the region during the war.[24]

Thompson accepted the constraints imposed by the prowar groups. Utilizing the school board, he found it easier to give off informal signals that he was not a dangerous politician. Immediately after the People's Council incident, the board dropped the Kaiser-page; Bismark School became Funston School in March 1918. A virtual boycott by students made German-language instruction a moot point. Mindful that his rhetoric on war profiteers would not help his Senate campaign, Thompson allowed the board to join with the Chicago Association of Commerce in 1918 to offer an adult Americanization program. These gestures could not stop criticism of Thompson—it had become a given in the newspapers—but they did succeed as damage control. The Germans could content themselves with the knowledge that Thompson had fought the good fight for them while the prowar groups had the satisfaction of getting their way on the school issue.[25]

The mayor faced Congressman Medill McCormick in the 1918 primary for the United States Senate seat. Rather than avoid it, Thompson made an issue of his own loyalty. His campaign material was intended to convince the doubting: "I love but one flag—Old Glory! I love but one country—the United States of America, which is your country and my country." To preserve it, he proposed a foreign policy guided by Washington's Farewell Address and the Monroe Doctrine; any government official sacrificing the national interest was to be impeached and removed from office. For domestic policy, Thompson promised to respect Constitutional rights and to fight for a protective tariff and an excess war profits tax. "The Truth About William Hale Thompson" included the words of Washington, Jefferson, Webster and Lincoln. On the front cover of the pamphlet were two crossed American flags; on the back, a picture of Thompson with a Shriners' pin on his lapel.[26]

Although he campaigned statewide, Thompson had little chance of victory. Primarily, he was the victim of timing. Had the election been held a year earlier, when there was still doubt over the wisdom of American participation in the war, he would have had a chance, but with the Allies close to victory, Illinois Republicans had little reason to register a protest vote. Medill McCormick exploited the mayor's vulnerability. Before a crowd at Cubs Park, he demanded the votes of loyalists against the "faint-hearted, the pacifists, the defeatists, the IWW, the Copperheads, the American Bolshevik" and all the others who intended to make the United States into another Russia. The *Tribune* contributed to the loyalist din by classifying the mayor with such Progressives as Robert LaFollette, Charles Lindbergh, Sr., and Henry Ford. They belonged together because "Bolshevism in Wisconsin, pacifism in Minnesota, peace-arkism in Michigan, [and] Thompsonism in Illinois, all have sought to divert attention from their records by shrieking against 'war profiteers.'" McCormick won by just under 60,000 votes although Thompson carried Chicago by 18,000.[27]

If the defeat frustrated Thompson and his national ambitions, it also liberated him. He no longer had to play the conventional politician. Since it was impossible for him to attempt further agreement with party leaders like Edward Brundage, Charles Deneen, and Frank Lowden, Thompson instead embraced the radical image his opponents had fashioned of him. Shriner pins and Sunday closings became irrelevant along with any semblance of the conventional. As he sought renomination for a second term as mayor in the winter of 1919, Thompson could have *The Republican* run an article on Irish independence by the president of De Paul University, or he could blame Donald Richberg, as lawyer for the city council gas committee, for the high cost of gas. It simply took an abundance of political nerve. Thompson's shift away from middle class politics also reflected a demographic change. During the 1920s, the area outside Chicago grew at a rate double the city's. Chicago was less Wasp middle class, at least politically. Reformers Harold Ickes and Donald Richberg might not have liked that change, but they were already suburbanites.[28]

Judge Harry Olson and Charles Merriam faced Thompson in the 1919 mayoral primary. Olson was as inept as before, with the promise of "an administration of good, clean and honest housekeeping" and an interest in eugenics that would not appeal to blacks or ethnics. Merriam positioned himself as the real alternative to Thompson. Returned from army service in Italy, the former Hyde Park alderman was convinced he could win without a strong organization. He cast himself as Captain Merriam, the concerned war veteran who would return democracy to local government with a platform combining business and social reform. City hall would be run efficiently and, with the use of a postwar reconstruction commission and increased home rule powers, compassionately. According to the Merriam campaign literature, Chicago had a courageous friend: "I may be standing with my back to the wall, but I do not intend to forsake the men and women who have asked me to lead this fight, nor to desert the claims of Chicago at this critical moment."[29]

If the primary constituted his critical moment, Merriam failed with a campaign that resembled that of any political opportunist. He revived the issue of Dr. Theodore Sachs' suicide, publicized the support of E. O. Hanson (a Chicagoan whose brother as mayor of Seattle had won momentary national fame for opposing a general strike), and allowed a sailors' and soldiers' vigilante club to intimidate Thompson campaign workers downtown. With a campaign speech that warned against the "Hohenzollern cult of power" in city hall, Merriam showed he could sound like Thompson if not win like him. Merriam's defeat— 67,000 votes behind Olson, 106,000 behind Thompson—ended his political career.[30]

As they had in 1915, the Democrats found party unity impossible. When Roger Sullivan slated Robert Sweitzer a second time, State's Attorney Maclay Hoyne declared an independent candidacy. His executive committee included Clarence Darrow, Donald Richberg, and the suddenly popular E. O. Hanson. Labeling his two opponents the "gasocracy" for their alleged ties to utility interests, Hoyne added a twist to the 1915 Fatherland letter. He reprinted it as a leaflet and included facsimiles of old German-language Thompson and Sweitzer campaign buttons. Between the buttons, Hoyne inserted, "This is the sort of Appeal to Race Prejudice that is a Slur on American Citizenship." The voters disagreed. Thompson, whose speeches ranged from advocating Irish independence to the free trade policies of Grover Cleveland, defeated Sweitzer by 21,000 votes, thanks in large part to the 111,000 votes Hoyne attracted.[31]

Almost half of Thompson's victory margin came from the black Second Ward. Still, the vote did not reflect an ideal relationship. Earlier 1915, the Thompson campaign claimed that Robert Sweitzer as county clerk had ignored the tearful pleas of a mother—who was white—when he issued a marriage license to boxer Jack Johnson to marry the woman's daughter. The charge failed to damage the Republicans, testament both to the strength of the South Side organization of George F. Harding and Congressman Martin B. Madden and to the inability of Democrats to attract black support. There was continued cause for dissatisfaction with Thompson. The symbolic value of Thompson's banning "Birth of a Nation" diminished as the movie managed to play in 1915 and again during the next two years. Thompson also showed himself willing to exploit race prejudice for political advantage. On the grounds that it wanted to lessen conflict at the integrated schools, the school board sent out letters in July 1918—in the middle of the mayor's senate primary campaign—to ask some 350 blacks the best means of achieving voluntary segregation. A delegation of black leaders informed Thompson there was none. He was forced to disavow the scheme, and, instead, school segregation continued along de facto lines.[32]

Yet, despite periodic reports—particularly before elections—that the "better element" in the black community was about to abandon Thompson, there was little choice for blacks in the 1920s. If a Louis B. Anderson or Robert R. Jackson wanted to run for alderman, he had to work with the mayor's white South Side allies. Had the Democrats been willing, they could have challenged that strength by cultivating the support of *Chicago Defender* publisher Robert S. Abbott. In 1926, Abbott publicly endorsed party leader George Brennan for the Senate over the Thompson choice of Frank L. Smith, and the *Defender* printed—in Polish—a speech Abbott gave that year to a Humboldt Park crowd of 50,000 on the celebration of the 150th birthday of Polish hero Thaddeus Kosciusko. Still, no change came in the Democratic attitude toward blacks until 1931.[33]

To his credit, Thompson never denied his identification with the black community. By his last term, 14 percent of the city's legal department, including six assistant corporation counsels, was black while the number of black patrolmen in the police department rose from 50 in 1914 under Carter Harrison II to 137 in 1930. If there was civil service abuse in the process, and there was, it did not end with Thompson. After Anton Cermak's election, Leonard D. White of the University of Chicago was appointed to the civil service commission. White kept his friend Charles Merriam informed of his experiences in city hall. Among White's problems was the hostility his fellow commissioners showed when he attempted to post an eligibility list for the public works department. They complained it was "full of Thompson niggers."[34]

The race riot of 1919 has been interpreted as a violent turn of the struggle over jobs, housing, and public accommodations, with the black vote in that year's mayoral election a contributing factor. The riot was that, as well as a manifestation of ethnic anxieties. Versailles did not bring peace to Central Europe or independence for Ireland. Rather, news from Warsaw, Vilnius, and Dublin brought frustration to the immigrant neighborhoods; signs of friction between ethnic groups was evident long before the riot. When a group met on south Halsted in May 1918 to urge the formation of a Polish republic which would include Poles, Lithuanians and Ruthenians, the *Dziennik Zwiazkowy* blamed the breakup of the meeting on Lithuanian Bolsheviks. In its coverage of the meeting, the *Lietuva* condemned "Polonized Liths" present who were interested in little more than imitating Polish barons; the paper found the disruption appropriate in light of Polish "intrigues against Lithuania." A year later, in June 1919, speakers at the Lithuanian National Congress meeting in Chicago charged that Polish Prime Minister Ignace Paderewski was using the Polish army to oppress Lithuania.[35]

In the case of Chicago's Poles and Jews, the argument moved from the editorial page to the streets in June and July 1919. Antagonisms arose over the issue of pogroms in Poland. The *Narod Polski* dismissed the stories; the *Jewish Courier* ran eyewitness accounts. Some 25,000 people marched downtown in late May to protest the situation in Poland. That was followed by an incident in early June, when another 8,000 people gathered around the intersection of 12th Street and Kedzie in the Jewish section of Lawndale to fend off a rumored invasion of 5,000 Poles. No onslaught occurred, but 250 police had to be stationed in Douglas Park to keep the peace. Then, in early July, Poles on the Southeast Side took to the streets. The story that a Jewish grocer had killed a Polish boy filled Buffalo Avenue with a crowd bordering on 3,000. Two days before the riot, the *Courier* reported—with satisfaction—that eighteen Poles had been fined for their part in the incident.[36]

Like the more recent immigrants, Chicago's Irish were concerned over events in the old country. In April 1919, former mayor and governor Edward F. Dunne left with a group to visit Versailles to appeal to the American peace delegation on the status of Ireland. By the time Dunne returned in early July, his efforts and his report on British atrocities against the Irish were widely covered. In the same week Jews in Lawndale prepared to fight with Poles, the Irish crowded into the Auditorium for an independence rally. Mayor Thompson and De Paul University President Rev. Francis X. McCabe both attended; the audience hissed at the mention of Woodrow Wilson's name. Later in the month, De Paul awarded an honorary degree to Irish nationalist Eamon De Valera. Visiting the city in mid-July, De Valera spoke at Cubs Park and drew a crowd of 25,000 which included Dunne and Thompson. When he presented De Valera to the city council, the mayor introduced him as the president of the Irish republic.[37]

If De Valera's visit did not hasten Irish independence, it did add to the city's emotional strain that summer. By the end of July, the situation worsened with the beginning of a series of strikes. On the eve of the riot, an estimated 250,000 workers either were threatening action, on strike or locked out by employers. Police on strike duty (500 by midmonth) weeks earlier had considered a joint walkout with firemen over salaries. When violence began on July 27, it proved impossible to contain. The rioting was fueled in part, as William Tuttle has shown, by racial tensions. Blacks also made for victims of transference. A white Chicagoan living close to the black belt could not easily prevent a pogrom, guarantee the independence of Lithuania or Poland, stop a Black and Tan, or break the British naval blockade to feed relatives in Hamburg. But if the conditions were right, as they were after the stoning and drowning of Eugene Williams off 29th Street Beach, he could find a violent release or cheer on those who had. The emotion preceding the riot was so deep and peculiar to the summer of 1919 that a similar incident the following June did not cause a repeat. Two white men, one a sailor, were shot and killed at 35th and Prairie during a parade of the black separatist Star Order of Ethiopia. In the summer of 1920, the South Side remained peaceful.[38]

Thompson's reputation survived the riot without serious damage. Critics failed to exploit the controversy over his delayed call for the National Guard, in part because Frank Lowden was in Chicago negotiating a traction strike settlement when the riot began. With the mayor and his police commissioner returning from a frontier celebration in Cheyenne, Wyoming, Lowden missed the opportunity to repay Thompson for his handling of the People's Council meeting two years earlier. Thompson came out of the riot strong enough politically to stop Lowden's favorite-son candidacy at the 1920 GOP convention. As city hall convention delegates spread stories that the governor had misspent campaign funds in Missouri, Thompson added dramatic effect by resigning as a delegate rather than vote for the "tainted" Lowden. Although he initially favored Hiram Johnson, the mayor came around to the candidacy of Warren G. Harding. After the obligatory trip to Marion, he predicted greatness for the Ohio senator.[39]

The city went Republican in the November election. The Democrats again proved themselves unable to maintain party unity. Two days before the election, the rally in Grant Park was not for James Cox but Terence McSwiney, the lord mayor of Cork who died after a seventy-five-day hunger strike; the meeting at the Coliseum, where Edward Dunne spoke and a representative for George Cardinal Mundelein gave the prayers, included cheers for "Ireland's greatest friend," William Hale Thompson. After the election, the mayor learned the advantages of having a friend in the White House. In 1921, the *Tribune* named Thompson and others in a $2.9 million suit to recover city funds paid to real estate experts who figured property values for land used in municipal construction projects. At the request of Chicago congressman and city hall ally M. A. Michaelson, President Harding instructed the Justice and Treasury Departments not to assist the newspaper in its suit. Thompson, however, received more favorable treatment from Washington in his libel suit against the *Tribune*. Asked to give a deposition in the case (which involved Thompson's treatment in the wartime press), William M. Offey, a former superintendent of the Bureau of Investigation, declined on grounds of confidentiality. Later, Attorney General Harry M. Daugherty refused to allow *Tribune* attorneys to view Bureau of Investigation files that might pertain to the paper's defense. (The suit was dismissed after a mistrial.) The Harding administration even allowed the mayor some fun at the expense of its most popular cabinet member, Secretary of Commerce Herbert Hoover. Thompson told the renowned internationalist that he should embrace a policy of "America first" and "renounce the foxhunting nobility of Europe."[40]

Despite the indictment of confidant Fred Lundin in 1922 on charges of conspiring to defraud the school system of $1 million, Thompson endured. Clarence Darrow deflected testimony on the $133 potato peelers the school board purchased under Lundin, and, for a third time, the attorney kept a Thompson ally out of prison. Thompson had to sit out the 1923 election, but his successor, the Democrat William Dever, made possible his comeback in 1927. The new mayor set out to give the city actual good government—a professional cabinet, a school board free from politics, and a police department devoted to enforcing the law. When he ran for reelection in 1927, Dever had the enthusiastic support of such Republicans as Sewell Avery, John V. Farwell and Julius Rosenwald. He also lost to Thompson by 83,000 votes. Neither Dever nor party head George Brennan understood the city as well as Thompson.[41]

The Democrat's defeat was not due solely to Prohibition. Dever did antagonize ethnics and Anton Cermak by trying to enforce the 18th Amendment, but that was not his only mistake. Dever consistently alienated his natural constituency. His appointment of A. A. Sprague was typical. Sprague had been one of the early members of the Citizens' Committee to Enforce the Landis Award. The group formed in 1921 to police an arbitration decision by federal judge Kenesaw Mountain Landis in a wage dispute between contractors and the building trades. The decision that committee members Thomas E. Donnelley and Julius Rosenwald found worth defending included a 10 to 36 percent wage cut; provisions against strikes and lockouts; and the right to use nonunion labor and materials. The committee took the decision a step further when it warned that any trade not accepting the award would be declared open shop. To force compliance, the group offered contractors and property owners insurance, guards, and, most importantly, nonunion labor. The committee declared fifteen trades to be open shop, which led to the establishment of a trade school and employment bureau. By 1925, the committee had placed seventy-five thousand workers on jobs, with twenty-five thousand brought in from outside the city. The committee was so successful that it was forced to ask participating contractors to help defray the cost of a $43,000 transportation bill, the result of paying train fare for recruits.[42]

In 1927, the citizens' committee took credit for $400 million in construction work. Landis Award projects included the Allerton Club and the Edgewater Beach Hotel, the theology and medical buildings at the University of Chicago, and the Joseph Bond Chapel and Chicago Theological Seminary, also on the university campus. As mayor, Dever could not do much to oppose the group; the open-shop drive was as much a part of the 1920s as the speakeasy. But as a card-carrying member of the tanners and curriers local of the American Federation of Labor, he did not have to appoint Sprague or be photographed breaking ground at the building site of a Landis Award contractor. To do so simply was not good politics for a Democratic mayor.[43]

Dever's efforts at reforming the schools were no better. Allowed to make seven school board appointments in his first month in office, Dever chose five members of the Chicago Association of Commerce. The board set about to select a superintendent free from politics. It chose William McAndrew from out of the New York City system. A former Chicago teacher, McAndrew reduced the advisory role of faculty by abolishing teachers councils. Popular for over a decade, the councils gave teachers a sense of participation in system policy making. Forcing through the junior high school and the "platoon" systems and the use of intelligence testing, McAndrew made little effort to explain the changes. He appeared to be another Jacob Loeb.[44]

Thompson only benefited from Dever's problems. Returning to active politics in 1926, he joined those Republican factions opposing Charles Deneen's slate in the party primaries. Thompson did not disappoint. Senator William Borah accepted his invitation to deliver a Washington birthday address against the World Court, and his own speeches helped turn a party primary into a referendum on America First and Big Bill Thompson. The anti-Deneen forces won, and Chicago Republicans knew who would be running for mayor again.[45]

Dever rested in Biloxi, Mississippi, before the February 1927 mayoral primaries. While there, he noted the polite manners of black children and complimented the schools for work well done. The remark, intentional or not, set the level of Democratic strategy in the general election. A series of vice raids on the South Side in March netted one thousand arrests, all of them black; Dever explained it was part of an effort "to give the decent colored people a chance to vote and have their votes counted properly." Party leader George Brennan predicted that voters never would allow the city to be run by the black belt or hoodlums. For music, the Democrats hired a calliope to play "Bye-Bye, Blackbird" downtown. Nor did all the independents and reformers who supported Dever avoid such race baiting. Former state's attorney Maclay Hoyne charged that Thompson caused the 1919 race riot while Raymond Robins, a veteran of the settlement house movement and Bull Moose candidate for the Senate in 1914, told listeners Thompson was "talking 'America First' and acting 'Africa First.'"[46]

A masterful campaigner, Thompson had little problem turning the Democratic attacks against Dever. He warned that the police "cossacks" who rounded up blacks could just as easily move against Jews, Poles, and Germans; these were groups that who some idea what the term meant in its European context. Where Dever posed as an upholder of the law, Thompson cast him as the head of a police force more interested in "fanning mattresses for pints or breaking in your doors" than in protecting the ordinary citizen. If Brennan wanted to label him a lawbreaker, Thompson accepted. He opened an address to a group of society women with the greeting "My hoodlum friends" and received the attention desired.[47]

Then came the classic Thompson. A rally could include charges against anyone: Sewell Avery, the "biggest tax dodger in America" and a Dever supporter; the Independent Republicans for Dever, a "gold coast committee of absentee landlords" that Thompson claimed was spending $10,000 a day in advertising against him; and Arthur Schlesinger, Sr., whose *New Viewpoints in American History* Thompson quoted to listeners as so much British propaganda taught at a disloyal University of Chicago. The demagoguery was not merely overkill; it served a vital purpose. Without a strong precinct organization, Thompson had to be outrageous enough often enough to command the respect of both party leaders and the voters. The strategy worked. After the Republican primary, the Brundage and Deneen factions had no choice but to accept him, just as Herbert Hoover, preparing for 1928, felt the necessity to visit a victorious Thompson four days after the election.[48]

With the vote counted, a group of Thompson supporters crowded the Louis XVI Room of the Hotel Sherman to sing "Bye-Bye, Dever." The ex-mayor was not the only one about to retire from local politics. He was joined by the Chicago business community. After 1927, the city's leading businessmen no longer concerned themselves greatly with local politics. They realized the voters no longer cared who business leaders endorsed for political office. The Independent Republicans for Dever Committee constituted a last stand for the business vision of good government in Chicago. The group started with a budget of $500,000 but was forced to halve that amount on two occasions. Worse, its full-page advertisements for Dever in the newspapers became unintended endorsements of Thompson, at least for labor. Seven of the twenty-four committee members whose names appeared at the bottom of the ad also belonged to the Citizens' Committee to Enforce the Landis Award. The Dever appreciation banquet held the month after the election showed how quickly Chicago businessmen were abandoning politics. The dinner did not raise enough to cover the cost of a commemorative bust and testimonial book.[49]

Thompson did not merely pay off political debts in 1927; he set precedents which endured for the next fifty years. During the election, he received the support of policemen and teachers—as well as Margaret Haley of the Teachers Federation—and the neutrality of the Chicago Federation of Labor. In return, he stopped a practice revived under Dever of surprise field checks for patrolmen, and he removed William McAndrew as school superintendent. Oscar F. Nelson, a vice-president of the federation of labor and a Republican convert, became the Thompson floor leader in the city council. Labor leaders also were appointed to positions for distributing patronage in the board of education and city hall. Where labor encountered a politician hostile to their cause in 1915, they found a mayoral ally in 1927.[50]

So too did organized crime. The estimates of the campaign contribution from Al Capone to Thompson range from $100,000 to $260,000. However, Capone was not alone in trying to buy influence with public officials during the 1920s in Chicago. Even such noted reformers as Julius Rosenwald, chairman of Sears and Roebuck, made substantial offers of stock and cash to help reform candidates reach their virtuous goals.[51]

The Capone money raises an intriguing question: Why didn't it lead to some type of prosecution? If local officials did not want to attempt it, the federal government could have intervened. Prosecution for income tax evasion seems as applicable to Thompson as Capone, yet no mention is made of the money in Thompson's Justice Department files. Regardless of the amount, though, Thompson did formalize the link between city government and organized crime when he paid off another political debt and chose Daniel A. Serritella as his city sealer. Until his death in 1967, Serritella was suspected for having ties with organized crime in the city. His trial in 1931 on charges of conspiracy to defraud the public of $54 million by shortweights did not end the relationship between criminals and Chicago officials.[52]

Thompson managed to keep attention away from crime for nearly a year after the election. His victory cruise down the Mississippi coincided with the spring floods. He quickly announced the formation of a relief committee and convened a flood control conference in Chicago in early June. The meeting attracted a number of national politicians—including Senators Smith Brookhart of Iowa and Pat Harrison of Mississippi—and helped publicize the problem. It also provided Thompson with another platform. America First took on more than King George. Farm relief, inland waterways, and national flood control all became part of the full measure of Big Bill Thompson's Americanism. During the summer of 1927, Thompson spread his message on a speaking tour that covered the Great Plains to the West Coast. By the time he reached Los Angeles, Thompson had made Boulder Dam as much a part of America First as his opposition to the World Court.[53]

Thompson's California itinerary included a rest at San Simeon. By 1927, the mayor had befriended publisher William Randolph Hearst. Although his papers had opposed Thompson in his first two elections, Hearst in time found the mayor to be something of an isolationist soulmate. They both worked for Hiram Johnson in the 1920 GOP Convention, and, by 1923, Hearst's *Herald-Examiner* was lamenting the loss of a progressive Republican the caliber of Thompson when he decided against running for a third term. Hearst's coverage of Thompson was in sharp contrast to that of the *Tribune* and *Daily News*. The mayor developed statesmanlike qualities not only in Chicago but in Hearst papers nationwide. San Franciscans reading their *Examiner* found in Thompson a "captivatingly democratic, ready witted and far visioned type" of leader the country needed. That paper and the New York *American* ran the same editorial on Thompson's 1927 victory, and both coasts were able to read how

Thompson's first two terms were a "golden age" for Chicago public works. Where other papers and the wire services reported on the Chicago textbook controversy as high—or low—comedy, Hearst accorded it serious treatment with a signed editorial, "Undermining of Patriotism Not a Cause for Laughter," to the editor of the Baltimore *American*.[54]

Thompson began the civil service proceedings against Superintendent Mc-Andrew on returning to Chicago from his speaking tour. The mayor may have gotten the idea for the showcase "trial" from an incident in 1926. The Chicago *Defender* led a protest of blacks against a school text, *Community Life and Civic Problems*, by Howard Copeland Hill of the University of Chicago. The book contained a passage which, while praising Booker T. Washington, noted his constant struggle with blacks to "change their shiftless ways and become industrious citizens." Even with a defense of the work by sociologist Robert Park, school officials agreed to changes. Still, the book continued to offend. Following the 1927 election, Victor Olander, secretary of the Illinois Federation of Labor, wrote to Thompson ally Oscar Nelson to complain of the book. Olander was no friend of the new administration; he was a leader of the Dever labor committee in the election. What offended Olander was the selection in Hill on state police, "propaganda which has no proper place in any text book except to be exposed as propaganda."[55]

By combining the proceedings against McAndrew with repeated charges that the superintendent allowed the use of school books filled with British propaganda, Thompson knew he had created an appealing issue. Chicagoans could pick and choose from the "trial" testimony and Thompson's remarks. Germans, Irishmen, and Poles might focus on the charge that the history books of the McAndrew era slighted the contributions of immigrant groups to the Revolution; teachers could enjoy McAndrew's public humiliation; and labor might smile over the charges leveled against the University of Chicago. A place that used Landis Award labor certainly could be guilty of treason. The papers cast Thompson in the worst possible role, that of book burner, but there were too many disaffected groups in the city to care. A delegation of Chippewa, Navajo, Sioux, and Winnebago Indians visited Thompson during the controversy to present him with a petition: "We ask only that our story be told in fairness." If they could not get fairness there was always revenge, and American Indians, European immigrants, blacks and organized labor did not particularly care what motivated Thompson to give them satisfaction.[56]

Thompson wanted to establish a national American First Foundation, and he played with the idea of using the radio to broadcast citizenship lessons. Both ideas died after the results of the 1928 GOP primary. The homes of Charles Deneen and his choice for state's attorney were bombed, and, the remarks of Senator James Watson notwithstanding, the press dubbed it the Pineapple Primary. The bombings and the murder of a black Deneen precinct worker were blamed on Thompson, and allies Governor Len Small and State's Attorney

Robert E. Crowe were defeated for renomination. The vote broke Thompson politically and physically. The defeat in itself was not as great as the papers made it. In 1921 a Thompson judicial ticket was rejected also, despite a careful campaign. The difference was that in 1921 Thompson defied his critics and repaired the political damage; in 1928, he suffered a nervous breakdown. He did not recover until the end of his term. Meanwhile, the city drifted through the St. Valentine's Day Massacre and the Great Crash. When he recovered, all Thompson could offer was something on the level of William Randolph Hearst Day. The October 1930 event brought fifty thousand to Soldier Field, but it did not help teachers get their paychecks on time.[57]

The 1931 election was a watershed in Chicago politics. Anton Cermak defeated Thompson and began the Democratic domination of city government. Still, Democrats changed few of those policies Thompson had established by his last term, including his hostility to the reform community. Thompson's three terms—and the identification of reformers with the unpopular William Dever—caused the political atrophy of Chicago reformers. In 1930, Donald Richberg wrote Clarence Darrow for his help in opposing a traction ordinance the mayor favored. Darrow spoke for more than himself in his response: "I couldn't go into the fight without going into it thoroughly and I don't want to undertake the work of it all. You know I am old and tired." With the election of Franklin Delano Roosevelt, the city's leading reformers found themselves welcome not in city hall but Washington. Charles Merriam went to the National Planning Board; Harold Ickes became Secretary of the Interior; and Donald Richberg joined the National Recovery Administration. Later reformers who faced the choice of political frustration at home or political reward in Washington often chose the latter.[58]

Running against Thompson, Cermak did not repeat the Democratic mistakes of 1927. Instead, he took out an ad in the *Defender* to encourage blacks to "Come and Hear the Truth" when he spoke at Wendell Phillips High School. Cermak did not appoint a black to the school board as the ad promised he would, but the rally marked the realization by Democrats that blacks would have to be included as part of the party. The later success of Edward J. Kelly in transforming blacks into Democrats may be traceable to Thompson. As president of the South Parks Board in the 1920s, Kelly had to be responsive to a black community that had become politically skilled. When he failed, he could expect to be corrected. In 1926, the park board voted against erecting a memorial to the black veterans of World War I on the grounds that it would create a traffic problem. A group of blacks, including Aldermen Louis Anderson and Robert Jackson, protested to the board. To emphasize the importance of the memorial to blacks, the group visited the board on the most revered of holidays for Chicago's Irish, St. Patrick's Day. The board changed its vote, and Kelly learned an important lesson in racial diplomacy.[59]

Thompson also instructed Democrats on matters of ethnicity. The German

Fatherland letter, Irish independence, and the McAndrew history texts all were issues that exposed the Democrats' inability to appeal adequately to the various ethnic groups. When he defeated Dever in 1927, Thompson damaged the leadership of George Brennan as Democratic party head. When Brennan died the following year, the Irish were unable to perpetuate their control of the party. Instead, it passed to the Bohemian Anton Cermak, who treated the balanced ticket as something more than a necessary evil. In 1931, Thompson promised to "load that city hall up with Poles" if he were reelected. He aimed his pitch well. Poles long had felt slighted by the Democrats despite their party loyalty. However, with Cermak in control of the party, there was no defection en masse to Thompson because Cermak had seen fit in 1930 to allow the reslating of Judge Edmund K. Jarecki, the popular but controversial Polish politician who controlled the county election machinery. Poles repaid Cermak in the mayoral election by giving him 70 percent of their vote. If Democratic party leaders failed to recognize the political aspirations of another voting bloc in 1983, it was because they either forgot or ignored the lessons Thompson and Cermak taught their predecessors.[60]

The image of mayor as big builder may be Thompson's most enduring legacy to Chicago politics. Thompson pushed through the Michigan Boulevard link, which transformed a back street into Boul Mich, and he erected enough bridges, streets, and municipal buildings to have himself compared to both Baron Haussmann and Napoleon III. The nature of the builder image has changed with administrations. For Ed Kelly, it encompassed the various Works Progress Administration projects during the Depression; for Martin Kennelly, the legal framework for urban renewal and the construction of much of the expressway system; and for Richard Daley, the master ribboncutter, the image ranged from paving new runaways at O'Hare Airport to paving the alleys of the neighborhood of Gage Park. What remained constant, however, was the realization that concrete, poured in great quantities and with equal fanfare, went a long way in silencing critics.[61]

Thompson committed an uncharacteristic blunder in 1931 when he used trucks broadcasting "canned music." Union musicians were upset to be denied work even if it was on a truckbed, and at least one Thompson truck had its signs stripped off. The Democrats were left alone because they made an agreement with the musicians' union not to use recorded music. The episode showed that the overt anti-union atmosphere of the 1920s was dead and politicians would have to treat organized labor with care. The Citizens' Committee to Enforce the Landis Award disbanded in 1929 after the state supreme court ruled against it in a suit first brought by union carpenters, whose trade had been declared open shop. The recognition Thompson granted labor in his last term and the experience of millions of Chicagoans during the Depression transformed Chicago into a real union town; later mayors treated labor with the same respect Thompson learned to use. Richard Daley's father was a sheet metal worker, another of the trades declared open shop by the Citizens' Committee. As mayor, the son made sure city hall never abused the old trade of the father or any segment of organized labor.[62]

As much as anyone, Harold Ickes had a sense of what William Hale Thompson was about. The two shared a passion for Chicago Republican politics, although from opposite sides. Of his longtime antagonist, Ickes wrote in his *Autobiography*, "He was the Huey Long of his time and locale—without Huey's brains, however." If Ickes was right, Chicago got off lucky. In his three terms, Thompson had determined how city hall would deal with blacks and ethnics, businessmen and labor leaders, gangsters and reformers. To rephrase Paddy Bauler, Chicago wasn't ready for Big Bill with brains.[63]

6.

WILLIAM E. DEVER: A CHICAGO POLITICAL FABLE

John R. Schmidt

Once there was a mayor of Chicago named William E. Dever. He built great public works, removed politics from the city schools, revitalized municipal government, cut waste, and ran the gangsters out of town. Not once was there even the hint of scandal in his administration. He became well-known throughout the land, and some spoke of him as the country's next president. At the end of four years, he was soundly defeated for reelection by a loudmouthed lout who had barely avoided imprisonment for his outrageous misconduct in the same office.

So much for good government. To anticipate Paddy Bauler, Chicago evidently wasn't ready for reform in 1927. Like any cliché, this interpretation is grounded in truth. Dever did not give the public what they wanted, so they voted him out.

There is a bit more. Dever's story is not merely the case of a naive do-gooder misreading the mind of the electorate. It is a tale of many things: the decline of personality politics, the rise of the Chicago Democratic machine, the emergence of the urban ethnic voter—and, of course, the triumphs and travails of Chicago reform. Coming as it did at the juncture of these developments, the Dever administration played a significant role in the evolution of the Chicago political tradition. Certainly it is one of the more interesting episodes in the city's public life. Even Paddy Bauler might appreciate it.

I

William Emmett Dever was born in Woburn, Massachusetts in 1862.[1] His people were what is charmingly referred to as "lace curtain Irish." Patrick Dever, his father, owned one of the area's largest tanneries; his mother, Mary, was the daughter of Martin Lynch, one of Boston's early Irish ward bosses. William was the oldest boy in a family of eight children. He attended the Woburn public schools through the ninth grade, then quit to enter the family business.

He did not want to spend his life in his father's shop. At twenty William was on the road with a friend, working his way west through various tanneries as far as Wisconsin. By twenty-five he had married a New York state girl named Kate Conway, returned to New England for awhile, then set out for Chicago, where he had heard the tanners were earning twenty-four dollars a week. He arrived in the city in August 1887.

The Devers settled in West Town, a gritty workingman's community a few miles northwest of downtown along the Milwaukee Avenue car line. William took a job at a tannery on nearby Goose Island. An ambitious young man, he also began attending night classes at the Chicago College of Law. He graduated in 1890 and began a new career as a neighborhood lawyer.

He entered politics reluctantly. During the 1890s, Dever began to participate in the political discussion groups at Chicago Commons, the local settlement house. Settlement director Graham Taylor was a leader in the Municipal Voters' League and the general clean government movement. Reverend Taylor detected potential in the young lawyer with the lantern jaw and tried to talk Dever into running for alderman. Dever put him off, pleading the press of his legal practice. But Taylor was persistent, and Dever finally agreed to run as a reform Democratic candidate in 1900. He lost. Two years later, Taylor was ready to try again. By now Dever had gotten the political itch, and was anything but the unwilling candidate. He waged a spirited campaign that attracted the attention of Mayor Carter Harrison II. Harrison liked what he saw and threw his support to Reverend Taylor's candidate. This time, Dever won easily.

Dever spent eight years as alderman from the Seventeenth Ward. Almost from the beginning, he was one of the city council's most visible and most influential members. He championed the causes of honest government, improved schools, more parks and playgrounds, bigger and better public works. When Edward Dunne won the mayoralty in 1905, Dever became floor leader of the new mayor's unsuccessful fight to achieve municipal ownership of the city's transit lines. The alderman also flirted with the idea of higher office, running for state's attorney and judge, and seriously considering a shot at the mayoralty. Through it all he kept his close ties with Chicago Commons and the reform movement, while remaining a partisan Democrat.

In 1910, he moved up another notch. The squabbling factions of the Chicago Democratic party came together to produce a "harmony ticket" that year. Alderman Dever was slated for judge of the county circuit court. The fragile party alliance broke down soon after the election, but by then Dever was safely on the bench. There he would remain for the next dozen years, still in politics, though now removed from the daily trench warfare.

Of Dever's service on the court, little need be said. His cases were a mixed lot. Probably the most publicized was the sensational fraud trial of ex-Senator Lorimer. Still, most of Dever's decisions were hardly newsworthy, and his name began to appear in the papers less and less. The periodic "Dever for Mayor" booms—heard often during his years as a fighting alderman—grew infrequent, then stopped.

As Judge Dever passed his sixtieth birthday, he was well-settled. He had built a solid, unspectacular career in local politics, not notably different from the careers of a hundred other men. His was a comfortable situation of prestigious obscurity. Dever had become an elder statesman—meaning he had reached a political dead end.

Then it all changed.

II

Some people lead events, others are led by them. Dever's emergence in 1923 was the latter case. He became mayor of Chicago by being the right person in the right place at the right time.

A bit of background is in order.[2] As far back as anyone could remember, Chicago's political parties had been fragmented. Democrats versus Republicans did not tell the story. There were Harrison Democrats, or Deneen Republicans, or Lorimer Republicans, or Dunne Democrats, or any of a half-dozen subparties at a given time. It was the age of personality politics, a decentralized arrangement based on loyalty to a factional leader. No single king reigned over this urban feudalism. The factions fought among themselves, frequently and bitterly. Alliances were only temporary. They shifted often.

Roger Sullivan had set out to make matters different. Just after 1900, this Democratic ward boss began putting together a coalition he hoped would eliminate internal strife and simplify the business of winning elections. He started with a narrow, Irish-flavored clique on the city's West Side. Very gradually, however, Sullivan was able to convince various ethnic and factional chieftains of the benefits of unity. Enlightened self-interest was a persuasive recruiting incentive, especially among the younger men who were not greatly concerned about personal fealty or national identification. Sullivan's alliance grew and prospered. By the early 1920s, most of the city's prominent Democrats had affiliated with his multiethnic organization.

Still at large was a small band of irregulars led by Carter Harrison and Edward Dunne. The two former mayors had once been on an equal footing with Roger Sullivan, each man controlling about a third of the local Democratic party. As the Sullivan organization expanded, Harrison and Dunne had seen their followings slip steadily away. They now held only a shadow of their former influence, and continued to be wary of the Sullivan brand of centralization. Yet the Harrison-Dunne group retained some importance. They held the party's pedigree for respectability. They also had an uncanny knack for attracting publicity.

The task of wooing this bloc fell to George Brennan, a genial former school-teacher who became party leader on Sullivan's death in 1920. Until the Harrison-Dunnites could be won over, the organization was incomplete, Democratic unity unconfirmed. Nor, for that matter, could the new boss's place in the center chair be secure. Brennan needed a unifying factor, something to bring his party together and cement his own position as leader. As the 1923 city elections approached, he stepped up his search for the missing piece to the puzzle.

Reform was in the air that winter. A few days before Christmas of 1922, a group of high-powered clean government advocates gathered at the City Club for a forum on the coming mayoral race. Led by Reverend Graham Taylor and Mrs. Kellogg Fairbank, a Social Register novelist who dabbled in politics, the reformers organized themselves into the Non-Partisan Citizens Mayoral Committee. Their stated purpose was to lobby the two major parties for an honest alternative to William Hale Thompson, the large Republican who had occupied the mayor's office since 1915. "Big Bill" Thompson had long captivated the city with his distinctive political style of blarney, buffoonery, and shouting; but after eight years, his act was getting stale. Worse still, Thompson's administration had grown notably corrupt. New scandals seemed to be uncovered daily. The Non-Partisan Committee was determined to be rid of Thompson. To this end, they planned to study the mayoral possibilities in each party, then issue a list of five or ten men they could support.[3]

It was at this point that George Brennan began to take an interest in the reformers' activities. Brennan had no particular mayoral candidate in mind for his party— though it was a case of having too many hopefuls, not too few. He welcomed any suggestion that might help narrow the field. So when the Non-Partisan Committee published its list of seven endorsees, Brennan was pleased to find the name of Judge William E. Dever included. Dever, he recalled, had been separately touted by such diverse people as George Sikes of the Municipal Voters' League, William L. O'Connell from the Harrison-Dunne bloc, and Harold Ickes of the Progressive Republicans. Their common argument was that Dever could unite the Democratic party while giving the city honest, efficient government. What was especially intriguing to Brennan was that Dever was being pushed forward by both the Harrison-Dunne faction within the party and the Republican/Independent reformers on the outside. He decided to have dinner with the judge.[4]

The two men hit it off well. More important from a practical standpoint, they found they could work together politically. When talk got around to the mayoral election, Brennan indicated that he was considering Dever. He said he would not attempt to unduly influence the new mayor's decisions, but did expect a promise that the mayor would not use his patronage powers to build his own political machine. Dever thought this a reasonable arrangement and said he would abide by it. The spheres of authority were thus set; other details could be worked out later. Though he made no immediate offer to Dever, Brennan was convinced he had found his man. A quick consultation with the organization hierarchy confirmed that no one had any great objection to the judge. The next day William E. Dever was officially announced as the regular Democratic candidate for mayor of Chicago.

Dever was the ideal candidate for George Brennan's purposes. The judge was intelligent, articulate, and had a reputation for honesty. As an old Harrison-Dunne man with friends among the regulars, he could bring the party together. As a sitting judge, he did not have a long, controversial political record to defend. The fact that Dever had a limited personal following was also attractive to Brennan—it was unlikely that the new man might quickly build enough power to take over the organization himself. Finally, Dever was popular with reformers and independents. He could attract these influential, well-advertised citizens into the Democratic fold.

As has been said, Dever's personal role in securing his party's nomination was minor. He had been mentioned as a possible mayor for nearly twenty years, but there was little reason to think the lightning would finally strike in 1923. His friends and admirers advanced his candidacy. When the main chance came, Dever made the necessary accommodation. He had built a career based on honesty, hard work, and good relations with all groups. Circumstances had combined to make a man with his résumé the logical Democratic candidate.

Incumbent mayor Thompson was not eager to joust with the Democrats' new champion. Within a week of Dever's slating, Thompson bowed out of the contest. The feuding Republican factions took their fight into an open primary. Finally emerging from the confusion was Arthur Lueder: businessman, federal postmaster, and favorite son of the GOP's McCormick-*Tribune* bloc. Lueder was the direct opposite of Thompson—a dignified, soft-spoken gentleman of executive skill and personal integrity. Like Dever he had been endorsed by the Non-Partisan Committee. His nomination established a scenario unique in Chicago politics. For the first time, the candidates of both parties would wear the face of reform.

Reform may make for efficient government, but it does not always provide exciting campaigns. The 1923 mayoral contest was deadly dull. The candidates agreed on nearly everything. Both men attacked the excesses of the Thompson years, vowing to give the city an honest, thrifty administration. Both promised to take the schools out of politics. Both declared for law and order. In fact, the only notable difference between the nominees appeared to be on the transit issue. Dever came out squarely in favor of municipal purchase of the traction companies, while Lueder merely promised to "study" the matter.

From the start momentum was in the Democrats' favor. The party rallied behind Dever. Carter Harrison made the keynote speech at the campaign's kickoff luncheon, and Edward Dunne cut short his Florida vacation to return home and stump for his former protegé. The Brennan regulars, meanwhile, performed with their customary professional competence. Over on the Republican side, the story was different. The GOP remained divided into at least three factions—if not hostile to one another, then surely indifferent. Thompson sulked in his tent and would not work for Lueder. As for the reformers and independents, they moved as a group to the Dever camp. Many of them took an active role in the campaign as the Independent Dever League. Though they recognized Lueder as an able man, the reformers frankly preferred Dever. Experience was the reason. As Harold Ickes put it, "Why waste time . . . educating a novice when the trained executive and experienced municipal statesman is already at hand?"[5]

The campaign moved on, with no debates, little disagreement, and few fireworks. During the last week, some of the local bigots awoke to the fact that Chicago might soon have a Catholic mayor—something of an innovation for the city—and began a whispering offensive against the Democratic nominee. Antipapist broadsides appeared in Protestant neighborhoods. By now, however, it was too late to matter.

Big Jim O'Leary, the gambling king of the stockyards, closed his election book with Dever a 1–7 favorite. Big Jim knew a winner when he saw one. Dever crushed Lueder by 105,000 votes. He carried thirty-two of the city's fifty wards. His plurality was concentrated in the Democrats' traditional stronghold, ten inner-city ethnic wards; he also made major inroads among black and Jewish voters. Lueder won the usually Republican middle-class wards on the city's rim, though Dever ran strongly in these areas as well.

In 1923 Dever had an appeal that crossed ethnic, factional, and party lines. He was not closely identified with any particular section of his party; the public vaguely viewed him as a "reformer." He had been the perfect standard-bearer around whom George Brennan could gather the diverse elements of his grand alliance. He had stayed in the spotlight, run a tight campaign, and managed to avoid any divisive controversies. Party organization did the rest. Not surprisingly, he won a great victory.

III

Dever read the election returns as a mandate. The voters were tired of the policies of the past and wanted change. The new mayor would give it to them. He saw his administration as a chance to do "something big, something worthwhile, . . . something definite in the service of the city." As one newspaper put it, Dever planned to give the people a "new deal."[6]

And so reform came to Chicago. Restoring public trust in government was a major task facing the mayor. Dever started at the top, assembling a strong cabinet of accomplished individuals. (He also treated political considerations deftly: his appointees were a nice mix of reformers, Brennan regulars, and Harrison-Dunnites.) To promote efficiency and tighten management, he initiated a complete survey of metropolitan government. Meanwhile, he revamped the city personnel system. Thompson had skirted civil service regulations by putting temporary workers into merit positions, then reappointing them each time their sixty-day commissions ran out. Dever scheduled new examinations, obtained a pool of test-qualified applicants, and fired the Thompson temporaries. Over two thousand jobs were thus restored to civil service status.

The public schools were also targeted for reform. The system had become a national disgrace under Thompson, with political interference and financial mismanagement merely the most obvious of many failings. Here Dever got lucky. Through an administrative slip, he received early resignations from eight of the eleven members of the school board. The mayor was then able to fill the board with his own people—a progressive, businesslike, independent-minded group considered one of the finest school boards in the city's history. Dever promoted education throughout his term. He backed the board's efforts to obtain more money, using his influence to promote the cause and improving tax-collection procedures to get the funds more quickly. Still, in day-to-day matters, he kept his campaign promise. He left the schools alone.

Reform came to law enforcement. For chief of police, Dever chose Morgan A. Collins, an "honest cop" who had risen from the ranks to command the tough Chicago Avenue district. The police force was in a state of near anarchy at the time. With the full backing of the mayor, Chief Collins moved swiftly to bring order and discipline back to the department. He called in district commanders, gave them their instructions, then demoted anyone who would not carry out his policies. To fight corruption, he broke up a number of suspected cliques with wholesale transfers. Collins hired hundreds of new patrolmen, many of them exservicemen whose integrity and devotion to duty he believed in. At the same time, the chief began a series of flashy raids on gambling dens and sporting houses. First reports indicated that Chief Collins's programs were succeeding.

Reform came to the public works arena. Thompson had done grand things in this field, earning the nickname "Big Bill the Builder." He had also spent lavishly, and most of his projects came in with big bills of their own. Dever shared Thompson's booster spirit; he also knew he could do the job cheaper. During Dever's four years in office, construction boomed. The mayor opened parks, beaches, public bathhouses, and more schools than any previous administration. The south branch of the Chicago River was straightened in preparation for railroad terminal consolidation and land development south of the Loop. Dever built roads: Wacker Drive, the northern extension of Ogden Avenue, a new section of Lake Shore Drive. He established the city's first full-fledged air terminal, the present Midway Airport. He also began plans for a world's fair to celebrate Chicago's "century of progress" birthday in 1933. Through it all, he kept a close watch on spending, making sure the taxpayers got their money's worth.

Finally, there was transit reform. During the campaign, Dever had declared that solving the public transport problem would be the most important job for the new mayor. Service on the Chicago Surface Lines had grown shoddy and increasingly expensive. With CSL's franchise expiring in 1927, Dever intended for the city to buy out the company; also on his shopping list was Chicago Rapid Transit, which ran the elevated lines. Twenty years after Dever had fought for it at the side of Edward Dunne, Municipal Ownership would finally become a reality. So in the first days of his administration, the mayor opened negotiations with the transit carriers. Meanwhile, he mapped plans for service extensions and the city's first subway.

Dever was still busy getting his programs off the ground when a series of events unfolded that were to have a profound effect on his administration. During the evening of 7 September 1923, two bands of bootleggers became involved in a shootout at a South Side cafe. One man was killed. Scarcely a week later, another gun-battle erupted between the same gangs, with two more men left dead. Territorial rivalries in the lucrative illegal liquor business was said to be the cause.

Although Prohibition had been part of the federal Constitution for over three years, it was widely ignored in Chicago. Most residents opposed the law; the police rarely bothered to enforce it. From the first, William E. Dever himself had been a "wet"—a person committed to the repeal of Prohibition. However, when he became mayor, Dever could see more closely that bootlegging payoffs were corrupting the police and public officials. As a former judge, he also believed that neglect of one law breeds disrespect for all laws. The South Side shootings convinced the mayor that the liquor situation had gotten out of hand. Personal feelings must be set aside. He would have to step in and set things right.[7]

Dever convened a summit conference of all the appropriate city, county, state, and federal law-enforcement officials. After securing their support, he announced an all-out drive against bootlegging. Then he unleashed Chief Collins's new shock-troops. Hundreds of violators were arrested, underground breweries smashed, and four thousand saloons padlocked. Next, the mayor moved against drugstores, soda parlors, and other legitimate businesses which sold intoxicants as a sideline. Dever lifted the licenses of 1,600 of these establishments, effectively driving them out of business. Appeals to courts or to friendly aldermen proved useless: the mayor was acting within his prescribed executive powers. The crackdown continued. By the end of 1923, barely a hundred days after the cleanup had begun, Chicago was being proclaimed the driest big city in America.

The Great Beer War made Dever a national celebrity. All over the country, journalists took time out from local affairs to examine the remarkable happenings in Chicago. The larger publications dispatched reporters to the city to observe events firsthand. Magazines printed feature articles on Dever, and the mayor was even cajoled into telling his story in a syndicated essay. At the Democratic National Convention of 1924, the new hero received a few complimentary votes for president and was seriously discussed for vice president. Though he missed on that one, the mayor was still riding high. A few months after the convention, John D. Rockefeller, Jr., and other wealthy Eastern industrialists tendered Dever a special banquet in New York. No Democrat had been honored by a similar group in that city since the days of Grover Cleveland, one writer noted. Mayor Dever had "unquestionably [become] a prominent candidate for the Democratic nomination in 1928."[8]

The mayor was always careful to state that he was "not a Prohibitionist." He said that he had begun his Beer War to preserve the integrity of the law. He told one gathering that he knew Prohibition was a bad law, but was enforcing it strictly so that the people would get fed up and force Congress to repeal it. Dever knew his stand was politically risky. Despite the large majority of Chicagoans who opposed Prohibition, the mayor was willing to gamble that the people would support his methods. They did for awhile.[9]

Trouble developed just when it appeared the cleanup had been successful. Part of the problem was that early success. Before Dever came along, there had been plenty of trade for everyone in the illegal liquor business. Violence had been rare: the South Side shootings had been an exception to the general rule of peace. Now that the city was drying up, the bootleggers were driven into more direct competition for the business that was left. Fresh bloodshed was the result. By the beginning of 1925, a major gangland war had broken out, bringing spectacular killings and lurid headlines.

Nor had enforcement worked as planned. Other politicians and government agencies were not as vigorous in carrying out the law as were Chicago's mayor and police chief. County officials had a particularly permissive attitude. As a result, many of the liquor traders simply removed themselves from Dever's jurisdiction by moving their operations past the city line—making bootlegging one of the first industries to flee the central city for the suburbs. Back in Chicago, meanwhile, Chief Collins had still not gained complete mastery over his police force. Political influence and bribery remained strong at many station houses. Ward politicians and police captains who disagreed with the enforcement program cut new deals with bootleggers. The old ways had not been unlearned.

The second half of Dever's term is a story of breakdown. Much of what he had sought to build in his first two years came crashing down around him. The mayor was reduced to conducting a holding action, trying to salvage what he could of his ruined plans. He did not accept this role meekly; he could still react to events with his customary feistiness and vigor. But the initiative no longer seemed to be his.

The grand political alliance that had swept Dever into office was showing cracks. Some strain on the coalition was to be expected—unity was an unnatural state for Chicago's factionalized, feuding parties. What was remarkable was that George Brennan's fledgling machine hung together as well as it did.

William E. Dever (1923–1927)

The Harrison-Dunnites drifted away early. Within a year of Dever's inauguration, they were fielding a rival ticket in the state primaries. They felt they were not getting a fair share of the political spoils from the regular organization. For years, Sullivan and Brennan had worked to incorporate the Harrison-Dunne bloc into their alliance. Now they were whining again, and Brennan concluded that they weren't worth the trouble. He let them go their own way.

A far more serious concern was the uneasiness within the regular ranks. Disagreement with Dever's Prohibition enforcement was the cause. Most of the Democratic committeemen were partisan, active wets; so was Brennan himself. In the first days of the mayor's Beer War, they had put aside their personal feelings and rallied behind Dever for the sake of party unity. Only Anton Cermak had spoke out against the enforcement program. But as the violence escalated and the mayor remained steadfast and the voters grew restless, more and more ward leaders were heard to grumble about the Dever crusade.

For these men, the mayor's mishandling of the Prohibition matter indicated that he was growing away from the people. Some of them believed that Dever's continuing fraternization with the reformers might be the problem. It was as if the mayor had forgotten his own roots. "It is all right for a Republican to go heavy on that reform stuff, but . . . a Democrat doesn't fit into a fanatical reform picture," one alderman observed. "Silk-hatting the LaSalle Street crowd is all right if you are one of them; but to give the impression that you've gone over to the silk-hatters after you've been raised under a fedora is fatal in politics in Chicago." [10] The mayor was losing credibility with those groups which should have formed his strongest power base.

Reflective of this mistrust is the fate of Dever's transit reform plan. By the end of 1924, the city and the two main carrier companies had reached agreement on a purchase price and method of municipal takeover. The package was to be submitted to the voters at the coming spring election. Although there was opposition to the settlement in some quarters, the referendum was rated a tossup, with the plan expected to carry. What happened was a surprise to nearly everyone. The Dever Plan was rejected by a margin of over one hundred thousand votes. The outer wards which had been cool to the transit package went against it, as expected. But the inner-city organization wards, which the mayor had counted on to carry the day, failed to deliver the votes. Some of them even voted a majority against.

Perhaps Dever had simply submitted a bad plan. Yet an analysis of the voting pattern suggests that certain committeemen may have "knifed" the Dever package. Once again, Prohibition was the reason. The ward leaders were trying to send the mayor a message. Even before the referendum, one wet politico had warned: "Now watch our smoke—if he puts his traction plan up to the people, we'll defeat it." [11] And so Dever's most treasured reform program was lost.

The Prohibition issue was not the only place where Dever's stubborn idealism cost him. The public schools had once more become involved in controversy. The mayor's board of education had hired the distinguished New York educator William McAndrew as superintendent of schools. Though the appointment was highly praised, the new superintendent soon antagonized populace, politicians, and teachers with his administrative revisions, his curriculum innovations, and his glacial personality. The teachers particularly objected to McAndrew's moves against their informal teacher councils. They enlisted several prominent labor and political chieftains in their cause and called upon the mayor for help.

Dever was in a difficult spot. The teachers had backed his candidacy in 1923; most of the party organization was sympathetic to them. The mayor realized that McAndrew was making matters worse through his personal style and had an associate privately speak to him about diplomacy, public relations, and other useful arts. However, Dever had pledged not to interfere with the schools. So he issued a statement saying as much, adding the hope that "cooler heads will prevail." This was not good enough for the teachers. Margaret Haley, leader of the largest faculty union, delivered a blistering denunciation of the mayor for his failure to intervene in the McAndrew dispute. For the rest of his term, Dever could count on the city's public school teachers as his adversaries.[12]

Despite his periodic intransigence, Dever remained a practical politician. When "moral issues" like law enforcement or keeping politics out of the schools were not involved, the mayor could compromise. His traction plan is one example of this art: though it had shortcomings, it was probably the best municipal ownership package that could have been hammered together at the time. Or when a fight was not worth the trouble, Dever could give in. Consider his attempts at budget reform. After trying to curb departmental spending by having the mayor's office draw up the city budget, it became evident that the city council would fight to keep this traditional privilege. So Dever simply allowed the old system to continue. He knew that he did not have the political clout to enforce his will. Rather than wage a symbolic war with the council over who had what power, he merely instructed his department heads to cut financial corners as best they could.

As his term entered its final year, the mayor began to express doubts about the wisdom of Prohibition enforcement. He appeared before the U.S. Senate hearings on the Volstead Act in the spring of 1926. To those who knew him only as the great enforcer of dry ordinances, his testimony must have been surprising. Dever told the senators that Prohibition had become the number one political issue in Chicago, affecting the election of aldermen, judges, and every public official. He himself had to spend too much time on the matter, time better spent on building bridges or clearing land for parks. "I find myself immersed in it . . . from morning to night," he said. "It is almost impossible to give anything approaching good government along general lines [because] this one subject presses so strongly upon our attention."[13]

He continued to make his doubts public. The liquor question was like a toothache, he told the city hall press corps—the pain makes you neglect your more important business. In a Rockford speech he compared the problems caused by the dry law to those created by slavery before the Civil War. Prohibition was a "tremendous mistake," the mayor said, and he would do "anything . . . to correct it." He also wrote another magazine article, this time for the *Atlantic Monthly*. In it Dever suggested that Congress set up a special commission to make a comprehensive, objective study of the whole liquor issue. He also made a significant concession. Once he had declared that an unpopular law could and should be enforced, if only to speed its repeal. Now he admitted that his policy had not worked. "The wise legislator in a democracy will not attempt to impose a law, however desirable in the abstract, that will not receive general support of the people," Dever wrote. "Men cannot be brought to support a policy that they believe to be oppressive and unjust." [14]

The people, it seemed, would sooner disobey a bad law than follow procedures and petition for a redress of grievance. Sometimes politics did not operate the way the textbooks said. Yet even with this knowledge, Dever still carried on his determined enforcement of the Prohibition Amendment until the day he left office. The law was the law. And there remained a good deal of strict constructionist judge in the mayor of Chicago.

IV

Dever was not anxious for a second term. He was tired of the browbeating from all sides, his health was not good, he had numerous offers of lucrative employment. Many of the wetter Democratic commitment would be glad to be rid of him. In the end, however, he agreed to run once more.

Duty was the reason—duty to his party and to his city. As George Brennan saw matters, the mayor was the Democrats' strongest candidate. Dever had the advantages of incumbency and a creditable record in office. He had the best chance of attracting independents and straying Republicans. He could also preserve his own party's unity. Although Dever was controversial, the ward lords would probably be persuaded to rally around a sitting mayor; if Dever dropped out, there might be a free-for-all primary that could rip the party apart.

At the same time, the mayor felt his work was unfinished. He had spent too much of his first term on police matters. He still had to sort out the transit mess, continue his public works projects, and move on with governmental reorganization. Perhaps a second term would be better. In any event, as business leader Julius Rosenwald warned him, he had to save the city from Big Bill Thompson.

Thompson had, indeed, emerged as the leading Republican candidate. Big Bill had spent his years of exile hatching various plots, pausing for such widely-publicized diversions as launching a safari in search of a tree-climbing fish and holding a political debate with a pair of caged rats on a Loop stage. Now he was back. The public had evidently forgiven or forgotten the scandals of Big Bill's earlier regime. He easily swept the Republican primary and squared off against Dever.

The 1927 mayoral campaign has achieved legendary status in the annals of Chicago politics. Most of this repute stems from Thompson's antics. Early in the contest, Big Bill decided to revive the splendidly vague campaign plank that had served him well in the past, the issue of "America First." Nobody could argue with him on that one—especially when he found a convenient target in school superintendent McAndrew. It seemed that McAndrew had once made some disparaging remarks about *The Spirit of '76* and other nationalistic works of art; meanwhile, his allies on the school board had promoted various "unpatriotic" history texts. There were other sins as well, too numerous to mention here. When all these facts were put together, and combined with the superintendent's curriculum innovations, a clear pattern emerged—or so Thompson claimed. A giant international conspiracy was at work. McAndrew was a British agent dispatched by King George. His purpose was to corrupt the minds of impressionable American schoolchildren, paving the way for the King's reconquest of his former colonies. Fortunately, Big Bill had uncovered the plot just in time.

Thus did William Hale Thompson embark on a crusade to save Chicago from the British monarch. Big Bill roamed from rally to rally, ranting against King George, McAndrew, and that "left-handed Irishman" Dever who had brought all this treason about. And while he moved among the voters, his sensitive political nose began to sniff out another issue: Prohibition. He began to hammer away at Dever's enforcement record, and hammer hard. He noted that the current administration had closed down "businesses" all over the city. When he was elected, Thompson pledged, he would reopen all the places Dever had closed and put in ten thousand new ones. If anyone doubted what kind of businesses Big Bill had in mind, he gave it to them straight—"I'm as wet as the Atlantic Ocean!" he roared.[15]

The Democrats fought back as best they could. Brennan called in the troops and sent them off to battle. Joining the party soldiers were many prominent independents and reform Republicans who feared the consequences of a Thompson restoration. Dever's supporters countered Big Bill's bombast with some artillery of their own. Brochures were mailed, advertisements printed, campaign orators sent into the neighborhoods. Voters were reminded of Thompson's past failures, his dubious record contrasted with Dever's honesty and accomplishment. Dark hints were also raised about Big Bill's friendship with utilities magnate Samuel Insull. Meanwhile, four of the city's six daily newspapers announced they were backing Dever.

The mayor himself came out on the stump. He appeared ready for one of his old, sedate judicial campaigns or a rerun of the bland mayoral contest of 1923. He said that he would engage in a polite debate on issues of substance, a "decent, friendly discussion without malice or sensationalism." He dismissed Thompson's pronouncements as sheer "blarney" and refused to get into a shouting match with his opponent. Nor would Dever do anything to compromise the dignity of his office. When it was discovered that the mayor still held membership in the tanners' union, some Democratic strategists suggested dressing their candidate in overalls and photographing him at one of the old tanneries on Goose Island. Dever vetoed the idea. He said that he would not descend to Thompson's level. He would win on his own terms.[16]

Most of the others involved in the election did not share Dever's ideals. In its final weeks the campaign grew more desperate and dirty. Republican bigots resurrected the anti-Catholic propaganda that had been used against Dever in 1923. The Democrats trotted out the race issue; Thompson was a great friend of the city's black community, and his opponents claimed his election would bring about "Negro supremacy." Both parties charged the other side with preparing to use chicanery and force to steal the election. It was known that gang chief Al Capone was actively supporting Thompson's cause with both money and "campaign aides."

Dever's campaign never seemed to catch fire. Thompson seized control of the contest early and did not relinquish it. The Democrats were put on the defensive. They spent much of their energy reacting to Thompson's agenda. The mayor's case got lost amid all the rhetoric. "Dever and Decency," his followers beseeched. To which one cynic replied, "Who the hell is attracted by decency?"[17]

Early newspaper and street corner polls showed Dever trailing Thompson. The election returns confirmed the predictions. Thompson won by 83,000 votes, taking nearly 52 percent of the total. Dever polled 43 percent, with third-party candidate John Dill Robertson getting the rest. The Democratic ticket suffered serious erosion in the party's stronghold: the white, working-class, inner-city wards. Though Dever captured a majority of the ethnic vote, he did worse than usual for a Democratic candidate. He also lost the black vote to Thompson by a margin of better than 10 to 1. Dever did pick up a notable number of votes in the traditionally Republican Wasp areas along the lake shore. However, these gains were not enough to overcome the other defections.

The news of Dever's defeat stunned the nation. Over the next months, the Chicago election became a hot topic for newspaper and magazine articles. How had America's best mayor been beaten? A few observers blamed the nature of the city itself: such behavior was just what could be expected from Chicago. Most analysts, however, attributed the result to Thompson's extraordinary skills as a campaigner. Big Bill had "hypnotized" the voters, one writer claimed, and Dever could not snap them out of it. Thompson knew what the people wanted: entertainment. Dever, on the other hand, had tried to jam virtue down the public throat. The mystery was not that Dever had lost, concluded Elmer Davis of *Harper's;* the mystery was how he had gotten 430,000 votes.[18]

There was also talk of conspiracy. Rumor claimed that Dever's reelection had been sabotaged by Cermak and the wetter ward bosses, with or without Brennan's complicity. Sixty years later the talk still goes on, and it is impossible to confirm or deny it. What evidence there is argues against the conspiracy scenario. Throwing the mayor to the wolves was not the practical approach. Cermak may not have liked Dever, but his own ambitions were more likely to be thwarted by putting Thompson in the mayor's chair. As for Brennan working against his own candidate for some "bipartisan deal," how could the party leader have improved on what he already had? The Democratic organization was simply better off with Dever reelected than by taking a chance on Thompson building his own machine. Dever himself never suggested he had been double-crossed; he always considered he had been treated fairly. To argue that he was beaten by Democratic turncoats is also giving the fledgling machine more power than it had at the time. The mayor lost because he was less popular than Thompson. That much is undeniable, and all else is speculation. Perhaps the party did not work especially hard for Dever in 1927. But it is more logical to assume that the lethargy was the result of voter hostility, not its cause.

Chicago Democrats had sought power in 1923 by assembling a coalition of ethnic and factional elements. Dever was slated in order to hold the party together while attracting the votes of the reform bloc. He succeeded and was elected mayor. But in reaching for the new groups, the party was pulled away from its traditional center of support. The multiethnic coalition began to come apart. By 1927, Dever's brand of politics had become a force for division, not unity. Brennan had thought Dever was the man to play it both ways, one who would be a bridge between the foreign stock and the old stock. He had miscalculated. The organization would have to try something else.

V

After his defeat, Dever retired from public life, taking a job as a bank executive. Within two years he was dead from cancer. The city mourned its former mayor with a magnificent funeral. Political associates reminisced about him. The newspapers and drugstore journals commemorated his passing with editorial testimonials on his nobility of character. There was a public school and a water-intake crib three miles out in the lake named for him, and then he was forgotten.

In the years since his death, Dever has remained unknown—or at best, imperfectly known. Putting his career in perspective requires the explosion of a few myths. For one thing, Dever was not a wide-eyed, inexperienced reformer. He was a professional politician and a party regular. He played the game well, he made deals, he got along. Dever was no hack; he retained his ideals and worked to carry them out. But first of all, he was a politician.

His election was not a grassroots uprising against an entrenched machine. In 1923, both Chicago parties were still battling their hereditary factionalism. The local clean government crowd wanted to deliver the city from the clutches of Big Bill Thompson and was inclined to accept nearly anyone who could accomplish the fete. George Brennan read the situation shrewdly, then put forward a candidate the reformers were comfortable with. When Dever won, his "reform" victory was actually part of the consolidation of the local Democratic organization. In fact, the slating of a blue-ribbon, squeaky-clean candidate worked so well that the machine would return to the practice in later years, from Martin Kennelly through Paul Douglas through two Adlai Stevensons.

Dever was a symbol of unification—the new Democratic order wrapped up in one blue serge suit. He brought together the regulars and the Harrison-Dunnites while charming the reform bloc. He was also the symbol of the new breed of urban ethnic politician. Though Dever was a straight Irish Catholic, he was a step up from the old, one-dimensional figure of "Paddy the Mick," the provincial saloonkeeper politician. Party chiefs Sullivan and Brennan had long been developing talented young men of varied background who might aspire high and go far: Catholics and Jews of many national pedigrees, and even a Bohemian Protestant. When Dever broke through in 1923, it was indication that the new peoples had achieved decisive political prominence.

Once in office, Dever recognized his role as a "respectable ethnic." He often told Knights of Columbus suppers or other such gatherings that he would show the critics a Catholic could govern wisely. He tried to avoid any hint of favoritism, and was so scrupulous that a few Catholics complained the mayor was not being fair to his own people. His Prohibition policy also reflects this concern for appearances. Dever thought the dry law was ridiculous and knew that defending it would be politically dangerous—yet he embarked on the most ambitious enforcement program in the country. He said he was preserving the dignity of the law. Once again, Dever seemed to be advertising his official scruples, demonstrating that an Irish Catholic could have the same high public standards as a Wasp Brahmin.[19]

Prohibition finished him off, of course. It cut at the heart of his party, for Dever could not get the ethnics to accept his way of dealing with the problem. "Personal Liberty" was a sacred concept to them. To have the police sniffing around for something as trivial as a glass of beer was a reminder of the oppression they had fled. This was not what America was supposed to be. In a very real sense, the mayor was betraying their dreams. No matter how much he accomplished in other areas, no matter how persistently he courted the ethnic voters, the seeds of mistrust were sewn. They would flower in 1927.

Dever should have won reelection that year—not necessarily because he was the better man, but because he had the better political apparatus behind him. Democratic unification had been accomplished by 1923, with Dever becoming the first "machine" mayor of Chicago. The infant organization was strained mightily during his administration. It hung together, and was reasonably healthy at the end of four years. Dever's defeat was a rejection of his policies and him personally, not a repudiation of the organization concept. The return of Big Bill Thompson was merely the last hurrah of the old style of personality politics. By 1931, this last vestige of Chicago's feudal age would be swept away.

What of William E. Dever himself? Studs Terkel referred to the mayor as "the Calvin Coolidge of Chicago politics." Perhaps Jimmy Carter would be a better comparison. Dever was an honorable man of fundamental decency. He helped heal old wounds when such skills were needed, and he restored public trust in his political office. He also made the people feel guilty when they wanted to feel good. He earned their admiration and probably their respect, but not their love or friendship—and in the end, not their votes. What he lacked as a political executive was showmanship and a sense of nastiness. At some other period he might have had more success in doing his elected job; but then the odd conjunction of political stars that propelled him into prominence would not have been at hand. Dever was either the right man at the wrong time, or the wrong man in the right job. Such is the comedy of our politics. And the tragedy.

7.

ANTON J. CERMAK: THE MAN AND HIS MACHINE

Paul M. Green

Anton J. Cermak was Chicago's first and only foreign-born mayor. No man in Chicago political history had a more controversial and complicated political career than "Tony" Cermak. To some Cermak was a gruff bully who consorted with mobsters and hooligans while others viewed him as a political genius and friend of the ethnic poor. Cermak's life and political style reflect the contradictions and turmoils that epitomize Chicago's political tradition. His slow and difficult rise up the city's power ladder, his transformation from slugger to statesman, make him the last street politician to reach city hall.

Cermak was the consummate ethnic politician. According to his biographer, Alex Gottfried, "Cermak made Chicago Czechs and Chicago Czechs made Cermak."[1] However, Tony Cermak was not ethnocentric in his politics. Rather, he rose above his own ethnicity and prevailing nationality conflicts to construct the city's first truly multiethnic political machine. His life story reflects in the words of H. K. Barnard the saga of a man striving to become accepted as both "The new American and the new Chicagoan."[2]

In terms of personality Cermak was not a choirboy. In Chicago political parlance he was known as an "intimidator" who was capable of unleashing a violent and terrifying temper. His large and heavy-set physique coupled with his capacity for anger made many a foe and subordinate fear Cermak's physical strength as much as his political prowess.

Cermak was a poor public speaker who "appeared to take pride in his own absence of polish."[3] Reminiscing about his experiences with the mayor, one old-timer bluntly stated "Cermak was not a very nice man."[4] Yet this man who trusted few people, who was not a good mixer or back-slapper, and who generated loyalty through ethnic attachments and shrewd political deals emerged as boss of Chicago. Why? The simple truth is that Anton J. Cermak was a political survivor who eventually outlasted his old opponents and outsmarted his new ones.

The Early Days

Cermak was born on 9 May 1873, in a Bohemian village fifty miles from Prague. His family were Hussites (followers of the early fifteenth century Czech Protestant reformer John Huss), but Cermak would eventually marry a Catholic and raise his children as Catholics. One legendary Chicago political tale reveals that Cermak, a lifelong Protestant, calculated that having a Catholic family would be a huge political benefit in the heavily Catholic Chicago Democratic party—or put another way, "how many precincts could John Huss carry?"[5]

Cermak's family immigrated to America in 1874, settling in Chicago at 15th and Canal Streets. Later they moved to Braidwood, Illinois, a small coal mining town fifty miles southwest of Chicago. Young Cermak was a big strapping lad who had a very limited elementary school education. Ironically, one of his teachers was George Brennan, a man who would precede Cermak as Chicago's Democratic leader in the 1920s.

By the turn of the century, Cermak's family moved back to Chicago finding a home in the heavily Bohemian west side. Here is where Cermak constructed a political base strong enough to support him in various political campaigns for the next three decades. In return, Cermak would identify thoroughly with his Bohemian brethren. He acted as their voice expressing their hopes and concerns on various social and political issues. Cermak, like other successful Chicago mayors, never moved from his community even as his own political and economic fortunes rose. Loyalty given/loyalty received sums up Cermak's relationship with his Bohemian constituents; he never let them down.

Cermak's move into politics was almost inevitable. After dabbling in various business enterprises—including his occupation as teamster (horse and wagon) which would give his future political enemies the ammunition to label him "Pushcart Tony"—the ambitious Cermak was elected to the Illinois state legislature. After serving four terms in Springfield, he was elected Chicago alderman in 1909, municipal court bailiff in 1912, and after shuffling back to alderman in 1919 following an unsuccessful county sheriff candidacy, he was elected president of the Cook County Board of Commissioners in 1922.

Cermak's early career illustrates not only his knack for political survival but also the quagmire known as Chicago Democratic politics. As mentioned in earlier chapters, the local Democracy was split at least three ways: Carter H. Harrison II, Roger C. Sullivan, and Edward F. Dunne were factional party leaders more intent on beating each other than in defeating Republicans. Given his ethnic and geographic situation, Cermak joined the more multinational

Harrison forces rather than the heavily Irish Sullivan troops or the reform-minded Dunneites. Aiding his choice was the fact that Harrison was mayor for much of the early part of the twentieth century—thus giving Cermak control of many of the jobs and services he needed to satisfy his constituents.

Using his organization skills, Cermak turned his Twelfth Ward into the best Harrison area in the city. In the 1911 mayoral election, Cermak's Bohemian voters gave Harrison his largest ward margin in Chicago. Cermak was rewarded for his efforts with various plums including the honor of selecting the city's new assistant prosecuting attorney—a young lawyer and fellow Czech named Otto Kerner.

Using his physical skills, Cermak quickly became known as a "stand-up guy" who would not shy away from a personal confrontation. At the 1915 Democratic party's judicial convention (the new primary law had not ended all nominations by convention), Cermak engaged in his famous one-on-one stand-off with Timothy J. Crowe, a young, tough, upcoming West Side leader. Both Cermak and Crowe were opposing factional spokesmen and following a series of personal jibes, Cermak simply told Crowe to step out into the hall to settle their differences.[6] Crowe accepted the challenge and even though they were restrained by their associates, this near battle left both men bitter rivals for the rest of their lives. This event also reveals how much of the old frontier mentality remained in Chicago politics well into the twentieth century. In Mr. Dooley's words, the city's politics "ain't bean bag"—nor was it a place for the faint of heart.

Cermak also took early command of the wet/dry issue in Chicagoland. Labeled by the Chicago *Tribune* as "the wettest man in Chicago" Cermak organized the United Societies for Local Self-Government to fight for personal liberty (the right to drink on any day, but especially on Sunday). As the movement for national prohibition gained momentum in the World War I era, Cermak led a massive pro-wet parade down Michigan Avenue. Chicago Democrats were overwhelmingly wet, and it was this issue that gave Cermak instant political entry into other ethnic circles.

The 1920s

Two themes emerged in the 1920s which aided Cermak in his quest to become both Democratic party leader and Chicago mayor. First, in the early 1920s a group of new-breed Democratic politicians exploded on the Chicago political scene. Their arrival coincided with the coming of Prohibition and the demise of the traditional saloon keeper politicians who for decades had dominated the local Democracy. The new-breed politicians were better educated and more professional in their demeanor than their roguish predecessors. These new-breeds shied away from old-style saloon, gambling house, and boodle enterprises and instead involved themselves in construction, law, real estate, banking, and insurance businesses.[7] Central to the new-breed personality was a willingness and a desire to coalesce into a unified political organization.

Cermak, already a politician with two decades of experience and a known exponent and practitioner of political unity, became a sturdy and tough bridge linking the personality-oriented, factional politics of the Sullivan, Harrison, and Dunne era with the organization-oriented, new-breed 1920 politics. Guided by his former teacher George Brennan, Cermak emerged as a political survivor who melded easily into the victorious Sullivan wing of the party by winning the Cook County Board presidency in 1922. His willingness to work openly with his former intraparty foes coupled with his loyalty to the dominant party leadership signaled an end to alternative routes of political power within the local Democratic party structure. Dissension and internal disputes would remain, but the framework was set. As one old-timer commented, "Cermak agreed that there was now only one Democratic party ballgame in Chicago— and he wanted to become its only pitcher."[8]

If new-breed politics would aid Cermak's party takeover, changing Chicago demographics in the 1920s would help his quest for city hall. From 1920 to 1930, Chicago's population rose by almost 700,000 to 3,376,438 residents. However, this growth is even more impressive when one examines the population spurts in suburban communities surrounding the city. There was a dual migration taking place in Chicago: (1) older Chicago Protestant families were beginning their short march to the suburbs, and (2) more recently arrived Catholic and Jewish families were moving into vacated Protestant neighborhoods. In short, it was a classic demographic case of departure and filling in.

Church membership roles reveal the parameters of this demographic shift. In the 1920s Protestant Chicago was moving out of its old inner and central city neighborhoods to better neighborhoods on the city's periphery and the suburbs.[9] A sizable group of traditional Republican-oriented Protestant voters would remain in Chicago, but evidence reveals that every Protestant denomination, except the Baptists because of new black migration, saw several of its churches close and its membership lists dwindle in many older Chicago communities.

On the other hand, heavily pro-Democratic Jewish residents jumped from their old Maxwell Street ghetto region to expanded new west neighborhoods in formerly Swedish and German Douglas Park and Lawndale. However, it is the Catholic church that best shows the ethnic and Democratic colonization of former Protestant neighborhoods. Between 1920 and 1930, over thirty new parishes were started on the city's northwest and southwest sides. The number of Catholic communicants in Chicago rose 8 percent even though some older inner city parishes showed a membership decrease.

All of this movement left 1930 Chicago as a city having nearly two-thirds of its population foreign-born or children of foreign-born. In short, the city was demographically ripe for a shrewd politician who could put together the right ethnic political mix—Anton Cermak was that man.

Cermak Takes Over the Chicago Democratic Party

More than any other city politician, Cermak recognized the impact of new-breed politics and changing demographics on the Chicago political scene. However, before "going for the hall" he shrewdly decided to secure and widen his city political base by running for Democratic party chairman.

Following Brennan's death in 1928, Cermak moved quickly and successfully to capture the top party post. Several authors have documented and analyzed Cermak's Democratic chairman victory. Most concur that Cermak won because he organized and mobilized city voters of eastern and southern European heritage around the slogan "get the Irish." [10]

Obviously Cermak used ethnic appeals in attracting support from Chicago's diverse population, and it's certain his main opponents for the top job were Irish. However, it is far too simplistic to label his quest for party boss as an interethnic showdown inside the Democratic party. On the contrary, Cermak found key Irish allies in his move to take over the party among several new-breed politicians. Men like Pat Nash and Joe McDonough saw Cermak as the vehicle by which the remaining old guard leadership, mainly Irish, could be replaced by them and others in a multiethnic power play. Commenting at the time, Boetius Sullivan (Roger Sullivan's son and a strong Cermak Irish ally) accused Cermak's foes in both parties of attempts to create a Cermak/Irish split: "A glance at the recent Democratic ticket on which appears the names of Sullivan, McKinley, O'Connor, McGoorty, Kavanaugh, and Finnegan . . . and the list of Democratic party leaders like Clark, Bowler, McDonough . . . is enough to convince anyone that [this charge] is as untruthful as it is malicious." [11]

Key to understanding Cermak's party maneuvers was the fact that he cloaked his efforts in the mantle of reform. He told the press, "The period of the back-room . . . is gone. From now on everybody in the organization will have a voice in its management." [12]

Cermak's commitment to political reform, as it was understood in the late 1920s, is somewhat debatable; but its use as a political tool, given his chief opposition, made a great deal of sense.

Blocking Cermak's path to political leadership was his old nemesis Timothy (T. J.) Crowe and his ally Martin J. O'Brien who through their patronage network at the Metropolitan Sanitary District and the party's managing committee refused to step aside for Cermak and his new breed. However, their political stars faded quickly when the infamous sanitary district "Whoopee Scandal" broke on the Chicago political scene. Besides the somewhat routine charges of corruption, Crowe, O'Brien, and their henchmen were accused of wild carousing during a business visit to New York's Waldorf Astoria Hotel.

Though Cermak would eventually allow Crowe to remain a committeeman (like Mayor Richard J. Daley—Cermak had opponents and not enemies), Crowe's leadership possibilities ended when the press labeled his New York behavior "as an astounding picture of political debauchery."[13]

Upon seizing party control, Cermak reorganized the existing Democratic political apparatus into his own image. Multiethnicity was the new guiding political principle of Chicago Democrats. The blueprint for assembling the country's last great political machine rested on the notion of depersonalizing politics between ethnic groups and individuals while stressing the joys and advantages of organizational unity. Cermak and his new-breed pals saw economic and political glory in having the string of Jewish, Bohemian, and Polish wards bursting with Democratic voters on the city's west side marching shoulder to shoulder with other Democratic voters spread throughout the rest of the city. Aided immeasurably by his allies Nash and McDonough, as well as the country's economic woes, Cermak led his ethnically integrated Chicago and county Democrats to an overwhelming victory in the 1930 elections. It was now clear that the former immigrant pushcart peddler was ready for the big prize—city hall.

Anton J. Cermak's March to the Mayor's Office

Luck is often the deciding variable in understanding why one person emerges from the political pack to achieve the brass ring. Anton Cermak certainly had good fortune in his lengthy climb to the top. From 1920 to 1931, issues, events, personalities, demographics, and even the sudden death of two new-breed rivals—County Sheriff Paddy Carr and Alderman and fellow Bohemian Joseph Kostner—all worked in Cermak's favor. Yet also during this time period, Cermak worked hard to make these advantages pay off. Most impressive were his efforts to change his public image as an officeholder from that of an old-fashioned political operative to a "master public executive."

Following his narrow loss in the county sheriff race of 1918, Cermak recognized the need to become more attractive to the middle-class and better-educated Chicago voters who had by and large rejected his candidacy. His election as county board president in 1922 gave Cermak the opportunity to demonstrate his administrative leadership and fiscal management to these outer ward voters. Cermak adopted many of the state-of-the-art image-changing techniques (the use of blue-ribbon commissions, the use of the latest technology, and the presenting of himself to the public as a workaholic) and began appearing before the leading good government clubs and associations in the city. His energy, intensity, and grasp of facts made up for his lack of oratorical skills as he dazzled audiences with his command of the issues. Even his unsuccessful but highly publicized U.S. Senate race in 1928 was a political plus—it demonstrated to one and all that Anton Cermak had become a serious and respected public figure who was capable of serving in high public office.

Cermak's evolution as a public administrator also included his acceptance of the leading reform notions concerning government efficiency and budget economy. Keying Cermak's image transformation was the public perception of his one remaining political obstacle to gaining city hall—Republican Mayor William Hale "Big Bill" Thompson. Big Bill's well-publicized governmental shenanigans, his highly questionable political activities, and his continuous war with the city's newspapers (especially the solidly Republican *Tribune*) was anathema to traditional GOP city voters. It was this group that Cermak wanted to win over or at least neutralize in any upcoming mayoral candidacy. The fact that Cermak was able to do this while organizing a political machine illustrates not only his own talent but the good fortune of having the discredited Thompson as his Republican opponent.

In 1931, it all came together for Anton Cermak as he swept into city hall, trouncing Thompson by almost 200,000 votes. In retrospect, Cermak's mayoral victory was anticlimactic given all the groundwork he had laid prior to the campaign. Cermak's campaign game plan was so complete that Thompson was made to look not only silly but totally out of date as the three-term mayor tried vainly to resurrect old issues. Cermak's political and governmental alliances left Thompson with only his black supporters, his city hall patronage, and some diehard Republicans to stem the Democratic challenge.

Even Big Bill's once mighty campaign skills were ineffective against Cermak's citywide onslaught. Thompson and his allies, hoping to create an old-fashioned Democratic party split brashly, charged that Cermak's candidacy was anti-Irish and an insult to the sons of Erin. Big Bill specifically attempted to make West Side Democratic Alderman John Clark part of his anti-Cermak campaign. Clark was no close Cermak friend and it was well known he wanted to be mayor, but Clark was also a new-breed organization Democrat who served on the county central committee. He and his fellow Irish new breeds were far too sophisticated to fall prey to Big Bill's ethnic baiting. At a monstrous Cermak rally in the Chicago Stadium, Clark ended any hopes for a Thompson victory when he answered the charges by simply saying "His [Big Bill's] only reason for bringing in my name was to engender intolerance." [14]

Anton J. Cermak: Mayor of Chicago

Cermak's mayoral term began during the depths of the Great Depression. Chicago and its citizens were hurting and it did not take long for Cermak to show he was the man in charge. In his inaugural speech, he told Chicagoans his first mayoral objective was to curb expenses and cut taxes. He spoke of improved government efficiency, proposed labor-saving devices for city departments, and demanded general costcutting through consolidation of overlapping city agencies and through centralized purchasing. What is important to note is that nothing Cermak advocated was a departure from what he promised as a candidate or what he had openly supported as county board president. It is of equal importance to note that none of these good government reform positions interfered with Cermak's political operation that was fine-tuning the Chicago Democratic machine. For it was Cermak and not Richard J. Daley who first recognized the enormous benefits of implementing the public policy "that good government was good politics—and good politics was good government."

Cermak intertwined the governmental and political process during his city hall reign. He was intent on providing services to all Chicagoans in the manner he knew best—as a ward committeeman. (Daley has been the only ward committeeman other than Cermak to be mayor of Chicago.) Individual loyalty to the city, loyalty to good government, loyalty to a community, church, or constituent was fostered and encouraged—as long as it was understood that it all fell under the mantle of the Cook County Democratic Central Committee or "the machine." As this complicated political mechanism began spreading its influence throughout the city, one fact became abundantly clear: Mayor Cermak's true power rested not on his ability to reward but rather on his ability to punish. Going against Cermak's political or governmental authority was considered heresy and not dissent and though it would take over twenty years to fully implement this incredible philosophy, it was Cermak who first made Chicagoans believe that his Democratic party was the only true and acceptable vehicle for one to practice local politics.

Economic issues dominated Cermak's mayoral term. Dollars to pay municipal employees, dollars to pay poor relief, discussions about taxes and budgets took up most of Cermak's time. And though some critics chastised him for maintaining friendships and associations with various undesirables from the Prohibition era and others called him "Cermak the dictator" as he fully exercised his power, the new mayor kept his eye on the target—a businesslike approach to solve the city's financial ills.

City council meetings were run for the first time in a professional manner. Cermak and his floor leader Alderman Jacob Arvey ended the practice of councilmen roaming the chambers holding private conversations. The mayor dramatically made this point at an early council session when he stopped the proceedings, telling the startled aldermen in unmistakable Cermakian tones "to keep their seats and refrain from talking while business is being transacted." [15]

His council foes balked at Cermak's iron rule but even his most bitter critic admitted that no previous mayor had ever possessed more detailed information about city issues than Cermak. Aldermen who challenged Cermak had to be prepared to debate the issue on specific terms with the mayor and his council team, for this administration did its homework. More than one council member itching for an old-fashioned fight based on personality and political innuendo were laid low by the mayor's use of outside experts, research reports, and blue-ribbon study commissions.

Cermak pressed his notion that he represented Chicago as he spoke on behalf of the city in Springfield and Washington. In a major pre-Christmas 1931 speech before the state legislature, the mayor called for passage of innovative and long-debated reform measures to deal with the economic woes of city and state. Charles Merriam, the eminent University of Chicago political scientist and former reform-minded GOP mayoral candidate, saw Cermak express his views on the evils of overlapping jurisdictions in Cook County and the need to revamp the local and state tax system. Imagine the chagrin of Cermak's Republican opponents and remaining Democratic foes on seeing the architect of a blossoming political machine earnestly advocating the leading reform ideas of the day.

How Did Cermak Do It?

Cermak's ultimate political genius rested on his ability to adopt and articulate traditional reform issues, make them his own while not hurting his political activities. Along with his trusted Irish pal Pat Nash (selected by Cermak to run the party following his 1931 mayoral victory) Cermak and his Democratic allies took the lead in advocating an end to waste and extravagance in local government. Like turn-of-the-century Progressive reformers, Cermak and Nash demanded that government become more effective, efficient, and businesslike in serving the public interest. However, whereas earlier reformers wanted to bypass or even abolish existing political party organizations to achieve their goals, Cermak and Nash advocated change through the political process—the local Democratic party.

They ran the party as they tried to run the city—as a business. One either delivered or was out; rewards equaled performance, and one was answerable to the board of directors, the central committee. More than anything else, Cermak wanted to show Chicago voters that a political party could run itself and a city like a profit-making enterprise using political victories and not financial success or reform as its overall goal. Above everything else, it must be remembered that Cermak and his machine henchmen did not trick or fool Chicago voters into accepting their style and method of governmental and political leadership. Cermak gave the people what they wanted and those who refused to follow him would eventually have to pay a price for their independence—political defeat or government exile.

As a mayor, Cermak wanted to control or influence every aspect of city life through either the mayor's office or the Democratic party. "Tony really saw himself as a corporate executive" said one old-time ward committeeman, "and he thought it was stupid for the top guy not to know everything that was happening."[16] Cermak's passion for detail and control extended to Chicago's public school system and its board of education. As has been shown in a recent study by Kip Sullivan, the Chicago Board of Education was one of the last holdouts to Cermak-style leadership.[17] Angered by the actions of the so-called "solid six" (incumbent board members previously appointed by Thompson), Cermak turned his wrath on the school system. He prepared massive educational cuts and teacher layoffs, making the schools a case study of retrenchment and reduction. Aided by another of his handy "blue-ribbon advisory committees" Cermak taught the educators a lesson of what it meant to defy his political wishes. And he did it all in the guise of reform and efficiency.

Other examples abound of Mayor Cermak using reform rhetoric and machine manipulation to build his control over the entire city. Two final case studies, one governmental, the other political, demonstrate the mastery of this political wizard.

Civil service reform is perhaps the granddaddy of all reform measures aimed at curtailing the evils of big city political machines. Government appointments based on "functional job requirements" rather than on political ties and personnel systems based on an individual's ability to perform (merit) rather than partisan party considerations (patronage) are beliefs long held by good government advocates. To the lengthy list of civil service true believers, one could add the name of Anton J. Cermak.

During his campaign against Thompson, candidate Cermak promised "a virile civil service commission" to undo the politicization of Chicago's employee hiring practices. Since 1910, the city's payroll had increased by 86 percent (41,000 jobs) while its population had grown by only 54 percent.[18] Once in city hall, Cermak immediately orchestrated a highly publicized effort to recruit the best civil service commission in Chicago history.

The mayor told the press and civic associations that the 1895 city civil service law (the Illinois legislature had forced the city to have civil service ten years before it passed the same law for themselves in 1905) had been largely ignored. To change this situation, Cermak once again offered Charles Merriam the opportunity to join his administration by suggesting him for the commission chairman post. Though Professor Merriam again declined a mayoral appointment, his University of Chicago colleague, Leonard D. White, the country's leading scholar in the blossoming field of public administration, accepted the same Cermak offer. The mayor completed the three-man commission line-up by selecting Richard Collins, a "silk-stocking businessman," and J. V. Geary, a quiet Democratic ward committeeman. Geary's qualifications in personnel matters paled compared to his two colleagues; but the publicity generated by the other two selections allowed him to slip silently into the third slot.

The *Chicago Tribune* was ecstatic over Cermak's commission choices, claiming that "the new board gives promise of integrity"; and it congratulated the mayor "for choosing its members with care." They concluded their ringing praise of Cermak by stating "there is no more important agency in the city than the Civil Service Commission," and after detailing how Thompsonism had demoralized professional public service in Chicago, the *Tribune* prophesized that Cermak's commission selections "were the best indication of his purpose to give Chicago good government."[19]

Cermak's virtuoso Civil Service Commission performance was a prime example of his mayoral style. Unlike his city hall predecessors who either sought to build political support by rejecting reform or by rejecting partisan political attachments in favor of reform, Cermak took the best from both worlds. He welcomed and even championed good government reform measures as long as it did not interfere with his political activities. He sought out governmental experts and gave them freedom to promote new ideas as long as he had final veto over their activities. Information was key to Cermak and he instituted the practice of placing one of his own men (e.g., Geary on the Civil Service Commission) on the various appointed boards and commissions to act as his unofficial spokesman. Given his passion for efficiency, Cermak accepted reform calls for government effectiveness, but he never took his eye off the overriding goal—political control.

Just as Cermak proved how reform parts could produce a political machine, he also demonstrated how a party could adopt a businesslike approach to government and elections. Under his direction, the local Democratic party became probably the first political organization in the country to use statistical analysis to evaluate political performance and devise election strategy.

Cermak published a local party newspaper, *The Public Service Leader*. Though its masthead labeled itself the official publication of the regular Democratic organization in Illinois, it was well known that its real focus was city hall and the Chicago Democratic party. Following the 1932 general election, Cermak ended some general local Democratic party jubilation by listing each ward organization's vote production performance in the *Leader*. According to the newspaper, the party's executive committee had formulated "a scientific mathematically exact grading of the vote getting machinery in each of Chicago's fifty wards."[20]

Rankings were listed by ward (1–50) for each office contested in the November election. Rating criteria included vote margins, turnout percentages, and the percentage of straight Democratic voters. Though the party had enjoyed an overwhelming victory in Chicago, Cermak hoped to avoid complacency by interjecting intraward rivalry for pecking order and patronage purposes. This political competition factor inside the party made *every* contest crucial to the fifty ward organizations and their respective committeemen. Perhaps the most revealing aspect of this new ranking practice was the *Leader's* bitter attack on some precinct captains for knifing (not supporting) two losing municipal judge candidates. Never before had Chicagoans seen a political party so organized for battle; but, then, again, the city had never seen a mayor like Anton J. Cermak.

Cermak's Death and the Chicago Political Tradition

As with most of his life, Cermak's death was analyzed for its political implications. Even as he lay dying in a Miami hospital, many Chicago politicians questioned whether his assassin, Giuseppe Zangara, was truly aiming at President-elect Franklin Roosevelt when he accidentally shot their mayor. Everything about Cermak was political.

Perhaps the best testimony to Cermak's lifelong dream to build an unshakable political organization took place during the selection process to name his successor. His multiethnic machine held firm under the guidance of his confidant Pat Nash and his organization regulars. Following Cermak's death, the council immediately appointed an interim mayor, Alderman Frank Corr, a little-known council member who was selected for his anonymity. Most of the process to find a permanent replacement for Cermak took place behind closed doors as party leaders met privately to find a suitable and acceptable mayoral successor. Choosing Edward J. Kelly as Chicago's next mayor was not an easy decision. Several names were discussed and debate often became heated; but once the designation was made, the organization rallied publicly behind their choice. Cermak would have been proud of the actual council vote as Republican and independent aldermen, recognizing the futility of contesting the nomination, joined organization Democrats in unanimously supporting Kelly 47 to 0.[21]

Cermak's place in the city's political tradition is a crucial one. His ability to link or bridge generational political change, his willingness to accept innovation and reform administratively, and his single-mindedness to reach the top changed the direction and style of Chicago politics. Often overlooked in Cermak's slow climb to city hall was his incredible public office and political background. He had worked in state, county, and local government and had run for U.S. Senate. He was knowledgeable about the court system and law enforcement (some critics would argue from both sides of the law). Politically, he had worked the precincts, run a ward organization, survived intraparty warfare and eventually was elected chairman of the party. Thus, Cermak was prepared to govern his adopted city from an experience base previously unparalleled in Chicago history.

In sum, Cermak was a winner. He demonstrated that if you were smart enough, tough enough, and lucky enough, you could have it all in Chicago politics. His vehicle for victory was a multinational Democratic machine which he created, nurtured, and fine-tuned. However, it must be remembered that little came easy to Cermak. This Bohemian immigrant also outworked all his rivals and in his own favorite phrase proved, "Only lazy precinct captains steal votes."

Joseph Medill (1871–73), Chicago's first modern mayor. Courtesy University of Illinois at Chicago

Carter H. Harrison II (1897–1905, 1911–15), the ultimate practitioner of the politics of balance in Chicago. Courtesy University of Illinois at Chicago

Edward F. Dunne (1905–7), one of a rare breed of Chicago politicians: a reformer. Courtesy University of Illinois at Chicago

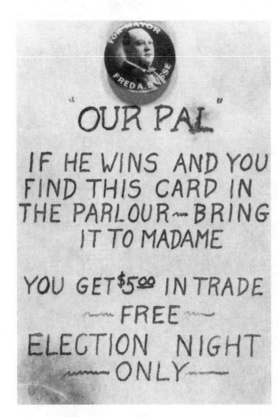

"OUR PAL"

IF HE WINS AND YOU FIND THIS CARD IN THE PARLOUR—BRING IT TO MADAME

YOU GET $5.00 IN TRADE —FREE— ELECTION NIGHT —ONLY—

Fred A. Busse (1907–11), who reflected and accepted the free and easy moral climate of turn-of-the-century Chicago. University of Illinois at Chicago, The University Library, Lawrence J. Gutter Collection of Chicagoana

William "Big Bill" Thompson (1915–23, 1927–31) at the lever of an earth-moving machine; *right,* public works commissioner Richard Wolf. Thompson began the tradition of the "builder" mayors. University of Illinois at Chicago, The University Library, Lawrence J. Gutter Collection of Chicagoana

Big Bill Thompson launching his "America First" campaign for mayor in 1927. University of Illinois at Chicago, The University Library, Lawrence J. Gutter Collection of Chicagoana

Chicago reform mayor William E. Dever (1923–27; *center*), watching his wife cast her ballot. Courtesy *Chicago Sun-Times*

Mayor Anton J. Cermak (1931–33; *left*) with presidential candidate Franklin D. Roosevelt and Roosevelt's son Jimmy at a Chicago White Sox game. Cermak was beginning to appreciate the importance of federal patronage to the Chicago machine. University of Illinois at Chicago, The University Library, Department of Special Collections

Mayor Cermak *(left)* with Alderman Charles Weber in a Havana bar during Prohibition. Cermak advertised his antiprohibition views to approving Chicago voters. Courtesy University of Illinois at Chicago, Urban Historical Collection

Mayor Edward J. Kelly (1933–47; *center*) with some members of the Kelly-Nash machine: U.S. senator J. Hamilton Lewis *(far left)* and Mathias "Paddy" Bauler, a North Side alderman *(right)*. Courtesy University of Illinois at Chicago

Carter Harrison II *(1)*, newly elected reform mayor Martin H. Kennelly *(2)*, and Edward Kelly *(3)* spanning the political generations in 1947. Courtesy *Chicago Sun-Times*

Martin H. Kennelly (1947–55), the "mugwump" reformer who could not control the machine that elected him. Courtesy University of Illinois at Chicago

Cook County clerk Richard J. Daley administering the oath of office to Mayor Martin H. Kennelly in 1951. This power relationship would be reversed four years later, when Daley would take the Democratic mayoral nomination from the incumbent Kennelly. Courtesy *Chicago Sun-Times*

A jubilant Richard J. Daley (1955–76), flushed with victory and shaking hands in 1955 with the defeated and crestfallen Kennelly. Courtesy *Chicago Sun-Times*

Richard J. Daley, "America's last boss," exuding a twinkling Irish charm even though somewhat flustered by an affectionate Hawaiian tourist representative. University of Illinois at Chicago, The University Library, Department of Special Collections

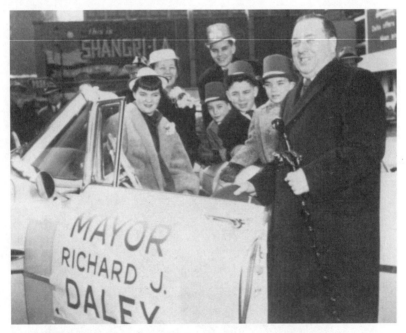

A young Richard J. Daley campaigning for mayor, always ready to demonstrate his strong commitment to family values and to the neighborhoods. Courtesy University of Illinois at Chicago

Michael A. Bilandic (1976–79), soon to be defeated by Jane Byrne and a record snowfall. Courtesy *Chicago Sun-Times*

Jane M. Byrne (1979–83) doing what she did best: campaigning among Chicago's upscale, professional women. Courtesy University of Illinois at Chicago

Mayor Byrne with the Roman Catholic auxiliary bishop of Chicago, Alfred L. Abramowicz. Raised and educated with her upper-income, "lace curtain" peers in private schools, she was an unorthodox Chicago politician. Courtesy University of Illinois at Chicago

"Fighting Jane" Byrne unleashing her campaign for the 1987 mayoral election. Courtesy Jane Byrne for Mayor, 1987

Candidate Harold Washington *(center)* celebrating his 1983 mayoral primary victory with Jesse Jackson *(left)* and Senator Alan Cranston of California. Courtesy University of Illinois at Chicago

Candidate Washington preparing to debate Republican mayoral candidate Bernard Epton. Courtesy *Chicago Sun-Times*

A smiling and photogenic Mayor Harold Washington (1983–87), no longer
an enigma to Chicago voters by 1987. Courtesy Office of the Mayor

Eugene Sawyer, acting mayor from 1987, after Harold Washington's death, until 1989, when he was defeated by Richard M. Daley. His cooler demeanor and willingness to work with others contributed toward lowering the decibel level of ethnoracial political squabbling in Chicago. Courtesy Monroe Anderson

Chicago's second Daley, Richard M., in a relaxed moment, reflecting the cooling political climate after he won the mayoralty in 1989. Courtesy Office of the Mayor

Newly reelected mayor Richard M. Daley standing proudly with his wife Maggie and their three children on election night in 1991. Also with the mayor is his mother, Eleanor "Sis" Daley, perhaps the only Chicagoan who could match her son in citywide popularity. Mayor's Press Office

Richard M. Daley attending a black history month celebration at the DuSable Museum in 1997. Like most successful Chicago mayors before him, Daley has become a master at juggling and balancing the intricacies of the city's racial and ethnic politics. Mayor's Press Office

Mayor Daley, next to his Chicago Board of Education president Gery Chico *(right)*, honoring Latino business at the annual Hispanic American Construction Industry Association dinner in 1998. Mayor's Press Office

Richard M. Daley *(second from right)* with Rod Blagojevich *(second from left)*, who was elected to the Illinois governorship in 2002, the first Democrat to assume that office in twenty-six years. In the past, conventional political wisdom in the state suggested that the mayors Daley (father and son) would rather work with a Republican governor because it made bipartisan deals easier to accomplish. Richard M. Daley went against that notion by supporting Blagojevich in both the primary and the general election. Mayor's Press Office

8.

EDWARD J. KELLY: NEW DEAL MACHINE BUILDER

Roger Biles

For fourteen critical years spanning the Great Depression and Second World War, Edward J. Kelly ruled Chicago's city hall and its Democratic party. At a time when political machines were declining in most American cities, the reverse was true of Chicago, where Ed Kelly, with the assistance of Pat Nash, not only preserved the Democratic organization but vastly expanded its power and influence. Kelly's enterprising strategy included several elements: attracting traditionally Republican black voters to the Democratic fold, allying the machine with President Franklin D. Roosevelt's New Deal, and tapping the financial resources of organized crime. Because of these changes during the 1930s and 1940s, Kelly transformed the "house for all peoples" assembled by Anton Cermak into the political leviathan commanded by Richard Daley.

To aid him in his successful quest for the mayoralty, Anton Cermak, a Czech, assembled an ethnic coalition of Chicago Democrats including the Irish, Poles, Jews, and Germans. At the time of his death, the most likely successor seemed to be the machine's second-in-command and leader of the powerful Irish faction, Twenty-eighth Ward Alderman Patrick A. Nash. But the seventy-year old Nash demurred, citing his age and lack of interest. He did, however, exercise his authority as titular head of the party to pick the new mayor. Nash used the Democratic majority in the Springfield General Assembly to pass a state law enabling the city council to go outside its membership in choosing an interim mayor. With the support of Democratic Governor Henry Horner and the majority of his party, Nash announced his selection—Chief Engineer of the Sanitary District, Edward J. Kelly.[1]

The new mayor was a familiar figure to Chicagoans, but not as an elected public official. Born and raised in the predominantly Irish neighborhood of

Bridgeport, Kelly began working for the Sanitary District at age eighteen in 1894 and remained in its employ for the next thirty-nine years. He gained more notoriety, though, in his alternate capacity as president of the South Park Board. During his triumphant years at its helm, Kelly presided over the transformation of Grant Park from a tin can dumping ground to a beautiful adjunct to downtown. During his tenure, private citizens donated the Shedd Aquarium and the Adler Planetarium, along with the Buckingham Memorial Fountain, to the newly developing civic center in Grant Park. Kelly also supervised the construction of Soldier Field and the refurbishing of what is now the Museum of Science and Industry. As a result of these efforts, he became known as the "Father of the Lakefront." More importantly, as Chief Engineer of the Sanitary District, he awarded millions of dollars in contracts to Pat Nash's sewer contracting firms and launched an enduring friendship with the Democratic leader.[2]

When Kelly took office in 1933, Chicago continued to reel from the force of the depression. The most severe economic crisis in the nation's history devastated the Windy City which, during the worst moments, virtually ceased to function. The signs of suffering and want were everywhere. As the nation's transportation hub, Chicago attracted thousands of transients to its already sizable stable of indigents and unemployed; throngs of uprooted men and women descended upon the city hoping for work and lodging, but they found only breadlines and cardboard shacks. A shantytown had appeared at the very edge of the Loop on Randolph Street. Its residents named it "Hooverville" and its streets "Prosperity Road," "Hard Times Avenue," and "Easy Street." The municipal relief agencies strained to meet the demand for shelter—they used asylums, poorhouses, and veterans homes to house the needy—but like all departments of city government, they remained incapable of dealing with such large-scale misery.[3]

Faced with forty percent unemployment, Chicago increased its relief expenditures to $35 million in 1932. But it was not enough. Private donations, though generous, proved equally inadequate. The failure of philanthropy merely heightened the dilemma, for owing to a sordid history of fiscal mismanagement, Chicago entered the depression already on the verge of bankruptcy. As a result of a real estate assessment concluded in 1929, the state reduced the city's property valuations by over $400 million. At the same time, a large number of property owners conducted a tax strike. The failure to produce revenue meant not only that the city could afford little in the way of welfare assistance, but that it could not afford to pay its employees. For a brief period, the school board issued scrip to the teachers, but the courts ruled the practice illegal. Payless paydays followed in succession. While teachers continued to work without compensation, the city discharged many of its policemen and firemen. When local banks refused to accept any more tax anticipation warrants, Chicago was flat broke.[4]

On Ed Kelly's first day in office, the tax delinquency lists filled 260 news-paper pages. Fourteen thousand schoolteachers, not having received paychecks for several months, stormed the banks and picketed the downtown financial district. The police used tear gas to disperse the crowds and arrested scores of picketers. Undaunted, the teachers broke up public meetings and heckled the city council and school board. As many as twenty thousand high school stu-dents struck on a single day to demonstrate their sympathy for the teachers. The city's unpaid workers clamored for immediate action from the new mayor; Kelly did not disappoint them. In his first official act, the mayor signed tax warrants worth $1.7 million and dispatched paychecks to the city's teachers. The city also sent checks to the other municipal payrollers, most of whom had not been paid in months. And to ensure the availability of more funds, Kelly led an entourage of Chicago politicians to the state capital to successfully lobby for legislation enabling cities to collect rents and income taxes on delinquent income-producing properties.[5]

Recognizing the need for sustained economy, Kelly set out to trim the city's budget further. He focused specifically on Chicago's white elephant, the found-ering public school system; his plan was severe in the elimination of both pro-grams and personnel. It mandated the abolition of printing, physical educa-tion, and home economics in elementary schools, as well as printing and vocational guidance in the high schools. The program also increased teaching loads by 40 percent, shortened the school year by one month, reduced all teacher's salaries 23.5 percent, and closed all special schools and special de-partments. Over thirteen hundred teachers lost their jobs. Responding to an uproar from the city's educational community, Mayor Kelly defended the ac-tion as the only alternative to closing the schools altogether. Judging by the short life of the controversy, most Chicagoans agreed.[6]

In the first few months of his administration, Ed Kelly scored a number of triumphs including meeting municipal payrolls, wiping out a significant por-tion of the city debt, establishing good relations with the state legislature, and keeping the schools open. He enjoyed good relations with the Democratic gov-ernor; and with the new Roosevelt administration more inclined than the previ-ous Republican one to commit federal monies to help the cities, he benefited from the availability of additional resources. If Kelly had not vanquished the depression, conditions had improved to the extent that the riots and confronta-tions of prior months were not being repeated. Moreover, his popularity soared as he presided over the highly successful Century of Progress Exposition and wisely extended the lucrative world's fair for a second year's run.[7]

In 1935 Kelly stood for election against an obscure Republican, Emil Wetten. The Chicago *Tribune* accurately observed: "The spirit of contest has been entirely lacking. This is recognized as the most peaceful, the most one-sided campaign since Chicago, in 1911, began naming the mayoral candidates through primaries. . . . It's all Kelly, so why talk about anything else?" On

2 April 1935, the voters elected Kelly by the greatest margin yet in Chicago. He received 799,060 votes to Wetten's 167,016 and carried all fifty wards. The defeated candidate lamented: "There isn't much to say except that the results confirm what had been repeatedly published—that the Republican party is completely disintegrated. In fact, there is no local Republican party."[8]

Pondering the 1935 election results, the New York *Times* concluded: "Why did the people of Chicago give him an unparalleled vote of confidence? Because he turned one of the worst-governed cities into one of the best-governed. . . . The floating debt has been greatly reduced and in consequence the cost of borrowed money has declined to something like a normal rate of interest. Even more dramatic has been the wiping out of the arrears in wage and salary payments of city and school employees. These are memorable achievements. . . . He is a good model of mayors and even offices of loftier title to follow." Political columnist Arthur Krock said: "Chicago still has relief problems, slums, poverty, and great groups of the unemployed. But the difference between present conditions and those in 1932 is the difference between black and white." Douglas Sutherland, director of the silk-stocking Chicago Civic Federation opined: "Mayor Kelly is giving Chicago better government than it has had in many years. He has made several strong appointments and is a man of good judgment and great strength." Indeed, praise from many quarters reflected Ed Kelly's status as one of the nation's most-heralded mayors.[9]

Along with his old friend, Democratic Committee Chairman Pat Nash, he also controlled one of the most powerful urban political machines in the nation. From the outset Kelly and Nash sought peace among the party leaders. Since a number of powerful Democrats harbored designs on the mayoralty even before Cermak's death, the prospects for amicable relations seemed dubious— especially in light of the persistent ethnic rivalries. But Kelly and Nash took immediate steps to forestall any potential difficulties by granting membership into the party's new inner circle to spokesmen for the different factions. They chose Jacob Arvey of the predominantly Jewish Twenty-fourth Ward to be chairman of the prestigious city council finance committee; Barnet Hodes, Arvey's law partner and a respected member of the Jewish community, was selected as corporation counsel for the city. The mayor appointed Polish leader M. S. Szymczak city controller and later elevated him to a seat on the Federal Reserve Board. In the city's North Side German-American community, Forty-third Ward Alderman Matthias "Paddy" Bauler and Forty-seventh Ward Alderman Charlie Weber gained increased stature in the new open-ended Kelly-Nash melting pot.[10]

Under Kelly-Nash leadership, the Chicago machine commanded the loyalty of its members because it produced at the polls and rewarded the faithful with a share of the spoils. The cobosses established clearcut standards of performance, whereby party workers advanced or were demoted according to successes or failures within their own fiefdoms. Given a certain latitutde and hope for advancement within the hierarchy, the party faithful, from ward committeemen down to precinct workers, had a reason to work hard. This system of incentives, tempered with stern discipline, was very instrumental in keeping together an uneasy alliance among disparate factions.[11]

The Democratic organization also benefited from the acceptance, if not the wholehearted endorsement, of Chicago's business community. While many of the city's wealthiest and most influential families shared a generations-old affiliation with the Republican party, they reached a comfortable arrangement with the Kelly-Nash organization. Bankers tolerated Kelly because he kept city finances in order, guaranteeing a profitable market for city bonds and tax anticipation warrants. Moreover, Kelly's dramatic success in keeping Chicago solvent between 1933 and 1935 earned him the gratitude of the LaSalle Street bankers. The mayor courted the Loop merchants by providing services for the downtown area. First-rate police and fire protection, along with prompt maintenance work on streets and sidewalks, provided everyday reminders of city hall's beneficence. Most noteworthy was the construction of the State Street subway, a boon to Loop merchants and one link in a revised transportation network designed to provide consumers with easy access to the city center. And finally, Kelly earned the plaudits of the business community through his sustained opposition to personal property and state income taxes.[12]

The Democratic machine also received the support of organized labor, despite the potentially disastrous Memorial Day Massacre of 1937. In that incident, Chicago police fired pistols into a crowd of fleeing picketers, killing ten and wounding thirty more. Kelly staunchly defended the actions of the police, but a well-publicized investigation by a U.S. Senate Committee chaired by Robert LaFollette, Jr., condemned the police action and the city's blatantly partial investigation. The Democratic leadership so feared retaliation by working-class voters that they met with CIO officials to discuss ways of improving their rapport. Kelly offered them future exemption from police interference in return for official forgiveness for Kelly's role in the Memorial Day affair. The CIO worked for the machine in subsequent elections and, amazingly, a steelworker whose eye had been shot out in the 1937 skirmish gave Kelly a radio endorsement during the 1939 mayoral campaign. Thereafter, Chicago police assumed a more circumspect stance during labor-management confrontations, and the CIO took its place among the supporters of Chicago Democracy.[13]

To a great degree the ability of the Kelly-Nash organization to command the allegiance of the various Democratic factions and the goodwill of both business and labor constituted a continuance of Anton Cermak's policies. If these had been the only accomplishments of the fourteen-year Kelly stewardship, his sole claim would have been that he preserved the status quo for his successor. However, the machine not only survived but expanded during the Kelly years as a result of three new resources tapped by his machine. The additional revenue and votes supplied by blacks, organized crime, and the New Deal enabled Chicago Democracy to thrive in the 1930s and 1940s.

Prior to the depression decade, blacks voted Republican in overwhelming numbers, but that changed dramatically during the Roosevelt years. Contrary to the belief that urban blacks switched to the Democratic party solely because of New Deal generosity, in Chicago local factors contributed significantly as well. Kelly's popularity in the black community existed independently of, and indeed preceded, Roosevelt's. Kelly set out to capture the black vote and did so by appointing blacks to an increasing number of municipal posts, by selecting them as candidates for elective offices, and by distributing government aid—first municipal and later, in much larger quantities, federal—to the ravaged South Side. Moreover, the mayor intervened on several occasions to defend the principals of desegregated housing and education.[14]

Kelly worked assiduously to present a good image to black voters and succeeded in establishing a reputation as a friend of "the Race." The mayor censored the showing of the film "Birth of a Nation" in Chicago because of its explicit racism. He honored successful black Americans for their accomplishments—making Joe Louis "mayor for ten minutes" in an elaborate city hall ceremony, for example—and made numerous personal appearances at South Side functions. "Big Red," as blacks affectionately called the mayor, attended the annual Tuskegee-Wilberforce football games at Soldier Field and endorsed Governor Horner's refusal to extradite a fugitive black man to an almost certain lynching in Arkansas. As a result of these concerted efforts, blacks supported the Democratic ticket in all elections, consistently giving Kelly a greater percentage of the vote than he received citywide.[15]

Kelly's soaring popularity in the black community first became evident in 1934 when the Democrats selected a black candidate, Arthur W. Mitchell, to contest Oscar DePriest's congressional seat from Illinois's 1st District. The popular DePriest, a three-term incumbent who was nationally renowned as the first black Republican to sit in Congress since 1901, had the endorsement of the black press, including the influential Chicago *Defender*. But with the aid of the Kelly-Nash machine, Mitchell won a narrow victory and became the first black Democratic U.S. congressman.[16]

The man who ultimately came to rule the black Democratic "submachine" was former-Republican Alderman William L. Dawson. Kelly did not start out to choose a subordinate to whom he could entrust the administration of the party's interests in the black community; he initially chose Dawson for a very specific purpose, to assume control of the troublesome Second Ward. In the words of a politician close to Dawson: "Kelly did not build Dawson by prearranged plan into the South Side boss; he made him head of the second ward, and after that Dawson just grew. In each showdown, Dawson was seen to be the better man and was supported." Eventually, his domain included not only the Second Ward but also the Third, Fourth, Sixth, and Twentieth on the South Side; as a result, he controlled an estimated quarter-of-a-million votes.[17]

Kelly's capture of the black vote proved to be a monumental contribution to the Chicago Democratic machine. Beginning in the 1930s, with the city's black population increasing and whites fleeing to the suburbs, the black vote became a precious commodity to the white politicians seeking to maintain control. The importance of Kelly's feat became evident years later, during the Daley era. In 1963, for instance, Daley lost the white vote in the city—Benjamin Adamowski gained 51 percent of the votes cast in the white wards—but carried the black vote by such an overwhelming margin that he managed to retain the office of mayor.[18]

While the black community provided votes in substantial quantities for the machine, its modest economic resources precluded contribution of another essential need, money. For that factor, the Kelly-Nash organization turned to organized crime. The mayor deplored the publicity that attended gangland killings, and to a great degree his administration restrained the rampant lawlessness of the Roaring Twenties, but gambling revenue was so important to the ward organizations that no genuine effort was launched to enforce the anti-gambling statutes. Tribute paid to the organization by the vice lords in return for protection became a vital source of funds, variously estimated at $12 to $20 million annually. A particularly prosperous handbook operator might pay up to $1000 a month, whereas for a more modest hole-in-the-wall crap game the fee might have commanded $300 per month. While rates varied by wards, gambling proprietors typically had to split their profits equally with the local political representative.[19]

The Kelly-Nash machine entrusted the supervision of the gambling revenue to each ward committeeman. A portion of the money collected went to the Democratic offices downtown, while the rest stayed in the ward to defray the expenses of campaigning and electioneering. (In the Forty-second Ward, for example, 40 percent of the money collected stayed in the ward organization, and the remaining amount went to party headquarters in the Morrison Hotel.) Ward committeemen chose police captains, who were usually placed in charge of collections. If a ward committeeman became troublesome to the organization, a new police captain would be dispatched to that district with orders to enforce the gambling laws. Thus cut off from his source of revenue, the penitent committeeman would get back in line and gambling would again flourish in the area.[20]

The Chicago *Daily News*, mindful of the vast sums of money available to the Kelly administration by virtue of its toleration of gambling, touched on an even more important factor in the mayor's decision to sanction protection for the underworld:

Cynics, viewing the mixed picture of the mayor's good financial administration in contrast with his tolerance of protected vice and gambling, are tempted to ask whether the two are not somehow related. The question arises whether it is not because the mayor has courageously denied his henchmen the opportunity to exploit the city's finances directly that he allows them to exploit vice and gambling on so lucrative a scale.[21]

But while Kelly presided over an organization saturated with graft and corruption, there is little evidence to suggest that he profited personally—at least after his elevation to the mayoralty. His apparent decision to spurn emoluments from gambling may have been the result of several considerations. Having fallen victim to an Internal Revenue Service investigation in 1933 for which he paid over $100,000 in penalties and interest, he cautiously avoided any hint of fiscal impropriety. Another explanation lay in the mayor's already healthy financial state. Since he allegedly stockpiled a fortune during the infamous "Whoopee Era" at the Sanitary District years before, he could bypass this second wave of graft. (In the sensational Whoopee Era scandal, over seven hundred witnesses testified that Sanitary District officials had stockpiled sizable fortunes from payoffs, bribes, and kickbacks. Of the eleven men indicted, several served jail sentences, and only Kelly went unpunished.) In the parlance of Chicago politics, "Big Ed already had his." Some observers suggested that Kelly's abstinence reflected a change in his character triggered by exposure to New Deal principles; this seems unlikely. Though the money generated from gambling seemed too important to the party organization to refuse, Kelly, with one eye on what would go on his gravestone, insisted upon a higher standard for himself. As one student of Chicago politics wrote, Kelly tolerated the corruption around him "in the familiar style of Irish Catholic politicians who went to mass, led lives of personal fidelity, and were not scandalized by an imperfect world." In all likelihood, all of these factors contributed.[22]

Under the aegis of Roosevelt's New Deal, the federal government also provided desperately needed financial assistance to depression-stricken Chicago. After Kelly established himself as the most powerful Democrat in Illinois with his landslide 1935 victory, federal relief czar Harry Hopkins turned his back on the mayor's rivals. Governor Horner, with whom Kelly frequently quarreled in the second half of the decade, complained that Hopkins ignored him, even refusing to return his telephone calls. Secretary of the Interior and native-Chicagoan Harold Ickes bemoaned Hopkins's "blind worship" of Kelly to President Roosevelt, but to no avail. Ickes called the Kelly-Nash organization "the rottenest crowd in any section of the United States today" and toyed with returning to his native city to run against the mayor in 1939, but his attacks failed to sever the strong ties between the Chicago machine and Washington. Hopkins went out of his way to support the Kelly administration, funneling extra money to the Chicago WPA office; in 1936, for example, he phoned that office to say, "the Treasury has suddenly found a little more money, and I don't want to put you and Ed in a hot spot. If there is any money here and it will do some good, I want you to have it." [23]

Along with Hopkins, Kelly could count on the support of Roosevelt's political right hand, Postmaster General Jim Farley. Like Hopkins, Farley ignored other Illinois politicos to focus all his attention on Chicago's mayor. One disgruntled politician told Ickes that "Farley never talks with anyone in Chicago except Mayor Kelly." To affirm their exclusive contact, Farley wrote Kelly that the Democratic National Committee would "do nothing in your County with reference to speakers or meetings without consulting Pat [Nash]." With these members of Roosevelt's inner circle favorably disposed toward him, Kelly enjoyed an enviable position. At the same time, he also benefited from a favored position with the president himself. [24]

Kelly frequently regaled Roosevelt with results of public opinion polls he conducted in Chicago and advised him on topics ranging from practical politics to foreign affairs. According to Samuel Rosenman, one of the president's speech writers, Roosevelt valued Kelly's opinions because he knew the mayor to be totally candid. Besides establishing his reputation as a sagacious politician, Kelly also made himself a worthy Roosevelt lieutenant by performing some sensitive tasks for the Democratic party. He championed administrative measures in Illinois and frequently aided WPA chief Hopkins in his struggle to compel Governor Horner and the General Assembly to assume greater financial responsibility for the state's relief program. Furthermore, Kelly used his influence on other Illinois politicians to force them into line with presidential initiatives. [25]

There also developed between the president and the mayor a mutual respect and friendship. Roosevelt not only thought enough of Kelly's political prowess to rely upon his counsel. He also socialized with him, inviting him to luncheons at the Roosevelt estate in Hyde Park, New York, and at the White House. While the president stayed on the good side of many big city bosses whose support he coveted, men like Ed Crump of Memphis and Frank Hague of Jersey City, Kelly was one of a select few who penetrated into the inner circle. Even Eleanor Roosevelt, who looked upon the urban bosses as anathema, thought enough of Kelly to defend him publicly when journalists labeled him a corrupt boss of the Frank Hague–Tom Pendergast stripe. [26]

As for Kelly, he could not have been more effusive in his praise of the president. He made "Roosevelt Is My Religion" the title of his standard campaign speech in the thirties. Privately, Kelly called Roosevelt one of the greatest Americans of all time, not to mention the country's finest chief executive. According to many Kelly intimates, the mayor became so enamored of Roosevelt Democracy that he became an avid New Dealer himself. It appears logical that a man in his position would at least pay lip service to New Deal tenets—urban bosses profited from both the nationwide success of the Democratic party and the provision of large quantities of federal funds—but Kelly genuinely seemed to embrace the spirit of liberal reform. This, of course, made the president's association with the boss more palatable.[27]

Most important, though, in explaining Roosevelt's esteem for Mayor Kelly was the power wielded by Illinois's political kingpin. Chicago was the key to carrying Illinois at election time, and the Kelly-Nash machine could deliver the necessary votes. Kelly's political achievements contrasted sharply with the stubborn recalcitrance of Governor Horner, whose relations with Washington New Dealers were as strained as the mayor's were excellent. Roosevelt cast his administration's lot with the Chicago Democrats and often opposed antimachine reformers in the prairie state. (He supported Kelly's bid to unseat Horner in the 1936 gubernatorial contest, for example.) And because of the huge Democratic vote turned out in Chicago throughout the thirties—most notably in 1936 when Roosevelt carried the Windy City by over 500,000 votes—the president's decision to back Kelly paid off handsomely.[28]

Good relations with the federal government aided the city of Chicago as well. The largess made available to Mayor Kelly enabled him to provide jobs and a modicum of relief for the city's destitute; it also made possible a number of long-overdue physical improvements in Chicago. As a result of WPA and PWA funds, the city's transportation network came to maturity with the completion of Lake Shore Drive from Foster Avenue to Jackson Park, including the Outer Drive Bridge, and the opening of the State Street Subway. Thanks to PWA funds, thirty new schools opened in the years from 1933 to 1940, and three housing projects (Jane Addams, Julia Lathrop, and Trumbull Park Homes) were constructed. Later in Kelly's mayoralty, funding from the U.S. Housing Authority resulted in the construction of several other housing projects, including the Ida B. Wells Homes, Altgeld Gardens, Frances Cabrini Homes, Bridgeport Homes, Lawndale Homes, and Brooks Homes. Kelly enlarged Chicago's antiquated municipal airport, adding four sets of dual runways so that for the first time, two planes could land simultaneously, and installed the most modern lighting system in the nation. Equally advantageous were the acres of beautiful new parks landscaped by WPA labor and the ubiquitous road and sewerage improvements. The partnership between Kelly and the New Deal indeed resulted in a major facelift for Chicago.[29]

A savvy politician, Kelly became a master at reaping political capital from the machine's New Deal alliance. In the words of one historian, "Kelly and his organization clung so tightly to the New Deal that the two seemed to be one." For federally financed work projects the mayor chose items of a highly visible and enduring nature, such as construction projects, usually with no special assessments required. The premium placed on labor inevitably resulted in overmanning at project sites, so much so that the state admitted that the use of excessive numbers of workers constituted a serious problem in Chicago. Other complaints arose about Kelly's "exploitation" of New Deal programs: critics charged that machine hacks administered federal agencies, needy citizens were threatened with the loss of relief if they failed to vote Democratic, and WPA workers had to contribute portions of their paychecks to the machine coffers. In short, good government advocates feared that the expanded federal power would be abused by the unsavory political machine wielding it in Chicago.[30]

Without question, some measure of graft existed in the implementation of the New Deal in Chicago. It could not be said, however, that the local Democratic machine received carte blanche authority to manipulate federal programs in any manner. From all indications, WPA officials insisted that the relief certification process be free from political influence. Though many party workers received WPA jobs, federal officials denied that any consideration other than need had been used to certify employment recipients. Harry Hopkins's top troubleshooter, Lorena Hickok, toured WPA projects in Chicago to see "if we were being made victims of the political spoils system." She found no evidence of widespread nepotism, and concluded that "someone apparently had put up a fight to keep politics out of this Chicago show—and pretty successfully too." Similarly, the administration of relief was relatively immune from spoils politics. While machine operatives tried to penetrate the relief apparatus, the county agencies designated to award stipends, staffed by trained social workers, maintained their independence. Director Leo Lyons wrote of his agency: "At no time has the mayor or other city officials attempted to direct the formulation of policies or the selection of personnel by the Chicago Relief Administration."[31]

In fact, the primary contribution of the New Deal lay in the financial largess it provided for the Kelly administration during the threadbare depression years. Set afloat with federal money, the city saved its own slender resources and spent great sums of federal money for the support of the indigent and unemployed. With this working capital, neither patronage nor city services needed to be trimmed. At a time when the gravest threat to the Democratic machine came from financial disaster rather than from a robust opposition party, New Deal largess assured Chicago's solvency.

Kelly's assiduous labors for Roosevelt and the special perquisites that the president granted to the Chicago machine do indeed make it seem indisputable that the Democratic organization thrived as a result of its association with the New Deal. In fact, the operation of the New Deal in Chicago contradicts many of the tenets of the "Last Hurrah" thesis, which attempts to explain the demise of big city political machines. Based upon Edwin O'Conner's novel, *The Last Hurrah,* this thesis suggests that the New Deal destroyed urban political machines by terminating the dependence of the poor upon city hall and substituting federal suzerainty. Kelly's experiences called into question the notion that the bosses were at odds with Roosevelt; clearly, the relationship between the mayor and the president was both cordial and mutually beneficial. No evidence indicates that Roosevelt set out to subvert the influence of the Chicago politicians, nor did he attempt to deemphasize the achievements of the local Democrats in favor of his own federal programs. In the 1936 battle between a "reformist governor" and a corrupt local boss, Roosevelt sided with the latter. Clearly, the ties between Chicago and Washington grew stronger, not weaker, during the 1930s. For a variety of reasons, the Kelly-Nash machine enjoyed a much more secure position than had .Cermak's fledgling model on the eve of Roosevelt's inauguration.[32]

As the Democratic machine enjoyed continued good fortune, so too did its leading figure. Mayor Kelly successfully sought reelection in 1939 and 1943, making his the longest administration in Chicago history to that time. In the 1939 contest, dissident Democrats united behind the candidacy of state's attorney Tom Courtney but failed to derail the incumbent in the party primary. In the general election, the resurgent Republican party, enervated by their strong statewide showing the previous year, put forward an attractive, dynamic candidate to challenge Kelly. Dwight H. Green, an able young lawyer and reformer, had as an assistant district attorney helped build the income tax evasion case against notorious gangster Al Capone that resulted in his imprisonment. Green conducted an aggressive campaign, hammering away at the machine's underworld connections and "exorbitant" increases in the municipal tax rate. Nonetheless, Kelly managed to hold the Democratic party together— even Courtney grudgingly supported the mayor—and won by a comfortable margin.[33]

In 1943 reform-minded Democrats again attempted to unseat the mayor, but the candidacy of Alderman John S. Boyle excited even less support than had Courtney's crusade four years earlier. Lackluster Republican standard-bearer George W. McKibbin, like Wetten and Green before him, based his campaign on an all-out attack on bossism and machine politics. "Pendergast is out in K.C.," he proclaimed. "Hague, in Jersey, and Tammany, in New York, have been cleaned out. Now it is time to clean out the Kelly-Nash machine." And like his unsuccessful predecessors, McKibbin returned repeatedly to the theme of the underworld-politics connection. Despite machine apathy and overconfidence, Kelly's refusal to campaign, and the outbreak of some untimely scandals shortly before election day, the incumbent bested the challenger by a plurality of 114,000 in a very light voter turnout. The Chicago *Sun* observed:

> The reduction of the mayor's majority from that which he attained against Governor Green in 1939 thus seems no more than legitimate wear and tear, chargeable to the four years in office which intervened. In view of the heavy artillery which the Republicans leveled against him, his 54.5 percent looks pretty solid.[34]

Following his reelection Kelly devoted much of his time to grappling with the problem of the city's antiquated mass transportation system. The traction situation had plagued not only Kelly but his predecessors as well, hailing back to the first decade of the twentieth century. When Kelly became mayor in 1933 he faced a disastrous situation: Bankrupt companies had no capital to make structural improvements; streetcars averaged twenty-five years old and suffered from disrepair; and elevated trains varied in age from twelve to forty years. In all, the public transportation system, once the pride of Chicago, paled in comparison with its counterparts in virtually every other large American city.[35]

Kelly consistently affirmed his commitment to the city's purchase of a unified transit facility but balked at the asking prices of the companies. As the years passed, the mayor's unwillingness to compromise the city's bargaining position meant that a lingering problem went unsolved, and Chicago's straphangers chafed at the inaction. Finally, in 1945 Kelly offered a plan to the state which provided for a privately financed Chicago transit authority empowered to buy up all existing facilities and operate them as an independent agency. Authorized to operate in eighty-one municipalities in Cook County, the supporting agency could issue bonds, payable solely out of its own revenues, but not levy taxes. Following legislative action by the state, the city council granted the newly created Chicago Transit Authority (CTA) an exclusive franchise for fifty years. In October 1947, after selling $105 million worth of bonds, the CTA began operation in metropolitan Chicago.[36]

The creation of the CTA, a landmark in the city's development and decidedly one of the most notable achievements of the Kelly mayoralty, came at what should have been a politically propitious moment for the Democratic machine, just before the 1947 mayoral election. But the traction settlement was largely overlooked in the preelection atmosphere—unfortunately so for Kelly, who found himself in a bitter struggle to maintain control of a fractious Democratic party and to secure for himself the party's nomination for yet another term.

For years Kelly and Nash ruled effectively through a clearcut division of labor: the mayor maintained high visibility, giving speeches, cutting ribbons, kissing babies, and keeping reporters abreast of party affairs as well as city business. The reclusive Nash shunned publicity and limited himself to behind-the-scenes administrative work. More importantly, Nash occupied the role of beloved patriarch. With the trust of the politicians and a reputation for fairness and scrupulous honesty, Nash served as the great harmonizer for the party—a task he often had to undertake due to the impulsive Kelly's fiery temper. As one contemporary noted: "Pat Nash was revered by the committeemen. They adored him. . . . Had it not been for Pat Nash, Kelly would have been in trouble nine times out of ten." Nash died in 1943, and without his mediating skills to calm the tensions between rival factions, party discipline faltered as seldom before. For the first time, Democratic aldermen dared to criticize Kelly in city council sessions, and talk that the mayor did an inadequate job as party chairman since Nash's death became widespread. Arguing that doing both jobs demanded too much from the seventy-year-old Kelly, the malcontents called for a new party leader.[37]

The man chosen was Jacob Arvey. Shortly after assuming control he began conducting public opinion polls in Chicago movie theaters and commissioned one of Kelly's speech writers to canvass by telephone in order to gauge the mayor's popularity. Arvey summarized: "Well, we were still solid with the Jews, we could see, and better than even with the Negroes, but everywhere else—the Poles, the Irish even, the Germans—we were in trouble. 'Him?' they'd say. 'Are you kidding? We'd sooner vote for a Chinaman.'" The once popular Kelly had seen his esteem crumble under the weight of several damaging scandals and the failure of his administration to deliver services to the citizenry. Defalcations in the public schools, official tolerance of organized crime, an ineffective and corrupt police department, haphazard garbage collection and street cleaning, high taxes with no apparent return in municipal services—all of these shortcomings surfaced in Arvey's canvassing.[38]

Chicago's civic leaders also called for Kelly's removal, but the opposition of the better government advocates, the reformers, independents, and "goo-goos," had surfaced in each of Kelly's election campaigns. Scandals of every variety plagued the Democratic machine over the years, yet it always managed to survive. In the opinion of Arvey, however, one new issue that arose in the mid-forties crystallized public opinion against Kelly: the open housing controversy. Jealously guarding their turf, South Side whites braced to resist racial "blockbusting" and sneeringly referred to neighborhood swimming pools which blacks seemed to monopolize as "Kelly's inkwells." The mayor's repeated pledge to guarantee the availability of housing citywide to blacks galvanized the public and helped to explain the findings of Arvey's polls; the Germans, Irish, and Poles shared one thing in common—an opposition to Kelly's stand on open housing.[39]

Ultimately, the opposition within the party, not just public indignation, which had been transcended repeatedly in the past, persuaded Arvey to dump Kelly. Supporting the incumbent mayor, hazardous enough on the basis of his record, would have been disastrous without the united support of the party leadership, and Arvey, vulnerable in his new post at the head of the machine, was in no position to alienate other party dignitaries while possibly losing his first election. Kelly had to go. Ironically, Kelly's efforts to strengthen the Democratic party led to his own demise. The machine he helped make became so powerful that the mayor was no longer in complete control, and it unmade him. The days of personality politics as personified by Big Bill Thompson and others had passed.[40]

Though clearly crestfallen, Kelly remained a good soldier and campaigned strenuously, if infrequently, for the Democratic candidate, moving-van magnate Martin H. Kennelly. After fourteen years in city hall, Kelly lapsed into the role of elder statesman. Stripped of the mayoralty and the county committee chairmanship, he continued to serve in the largely symbolic role of Illinois Democratic national committeeman until his death in 1950.[41]

A few hours after Kelly passed away, Illinois governor Adlai Stevenson eulogized the former-mayor on a statewide radio broadcast. He said: "Here was a leader! Strong, adroit, and tireless, he guided the destiny of Chicago as its Mayor longer than anyone in history. . . . And he will be studied by students of American politics as a leader who was never afraid to lead." Kelly was without question an aggressive, self-confident leader. He boasted to a reporter, "I tell a million people what to think, and they listen to me because they vote for me." He exercised nearly complete control over the city council, so much so that until the last year of his tenure, never more than ten of the fifty aldermen ever dared to oppose a measure he favored. To those who railed against the Kelly autocracy, he replied: "These people look to me for leadership. To be a real mayor you've got to have control of the party. You've got to be a potent political factor. You've gotta be a boss!"[42]

As boss of the Chicago Democratic machine, Kelly not only dominated local politics and government for fourteen years but greatly expanded the strength of the organization. To a great extent, the amazing resiliency of what came to be known as the "Daley machine" was nurtured, shaped, and enlarged under Kelly's leadership. Unfortunately for Kelly, the political "monster" that he had developed turned on its master and destroyed him—thus making good on the old Chicago machine axiom: "don't make anyone who can unmake you."

9.

MARTIN H. KENNELLY: THE MUGWUMP AND THE MACHINE

Arnold R. Hirsch

He was a nice man. It is not the sort of thing one usually says about Chicago's mayors, but the description suits Mayor Martin H. Kennelly. The incongruity stems not from his personality, but rather from his accidental occupation of city hall. Unlike those who clambered to the top of Chicago's political heap by stepping on the fallen bodies of their rivals, Kennelly ascended the ladder of business success and simply found himself the most "available" candidate as the Cook County Democratic organization desperately sought respectability after Ed Kelly's forced retirement in 1947. He was thrust into a political maelstrom for which he was ill-prepared, and yet he was, most notably, the Chicago machine's political savior. His fresh face and clean image saved the Democrats from almost certain defeat. The organization subsequently survived its postwar electoral scare, utilized the time and freedom bestowed upon it by Kennelly's lax administration, seized the credit for the mayor's achievements, and finally dumped him when he no longer served its purposes.

Popular legend portrays Kennelly as a naive reformer. It is a label that flows out of the inevitable comparisons with both his immediate predecessor and his successor. Next to Edward Kelly and Richard Daley, he *did* appear to be a political babe-in-the-woods. But there is more to it than that. His emphasis on civil service reform, his crackdown on open gambling, and his frequently expressed desire to upgrade the moral tone of Chicago's government all contributed to his squeaky-clean image. And it was a portrayal that was trumpeted in the contemporary press. Not only was he the darling of Chicago's media, but after a year in office even national publications such as the *Saturday Evening Post* marveled at the city's "new moral climate." [1]

Martin H. Kennelly was as close as the Chicago machine could come to Puritan respectability. A Bridgeport-born Irish-Catholic, Kennelly could cite

126

only his poor background as a reason for his otherwise ill-fitting Democratic affiliation; indeed, he remained a Democrat more out of inertia than conviction. He was a self-made businessman and millionaire who had left the old neighborhood for the North Side's Gold Coast. A bachelor, he lived with his widowed sister in a posh apartment that belied his humble origins. In his connections with Chicago's business community, his concerns for efficiency and respectability, and his circumspect personal life—he took only an occasional drink and that often only to prove that he was "one of the boys"—he seemed a mugwump out of season. Even sympathetic observers believed him to be, personally, a "cold fish," and if Kennelly fit any popular stereotype at all, it was not that of the glad-handing, back-slapping ward politician, but rather than of the distant, proper, civic leader.[2]

The image, however, obscures reality. Kennelly was neither naive nor a reformer. There is no question that he struck an apolitical pose, content to leave party matters in the hands of chairman Jake Arvey, while cultivating the image of an administrator concerned only with the broader public interest. If he remained aloof from politics, though, it was not out of naivete or ignorance, but because of the certain knowledge that he would be soiled if he descended into that arena. "All I have in the world is my reputation," Kennelly declared as he accepted the party's nomination for mayor, "and I don't propose to have it dirtied up in politics."[3] He had no taste for that kind of action, and his refusal to engage in the rough-and-tumble of everyday politics thus suited his inclination, philosophy, personality, and talents. And on social issues he was, simply, quite conservative, displaying none of the New Deal activism that animated Ed Kelly's administration.

Moreover, the sharp division between political and governmental authority meant that Kennelly—despite some good intentions—accomplished a good deal less than he might have desired. It also left him exposed and vulnerable to those political professionals who respected neither his intentions nor his personal attributes. Forty-third Ward Alderman Mathias "Paddy" Bauler derisively dubbed him "Fartin' Martin," and other regulars, even more indelicately, referred to his large, round features, his lifestyle, and, perhaps, his habitual flight from political combat, and christened him "the capon."[4] Obviously, Kennelly's dalliance with Chicago's Democrats was a mutually unsatisfying marriage of convenience; but it was an accommodation that each party entered with open eyes. Ultimately, Kennelly gave more to the organization than vice versa. If he received eight years worth of ribbons to cut and banquets to attend, he helped trigger a spurt of postwar development that redounded to the favor of the man who yanked the newly polished throne out from under him in 1955.

Martin Kennelly was born in 1887 in that cradle of Chicago mayors on the near Southwest Side, "practically in the shadow of the packing plants," according to his campaign biography. His father, Jeremiah, a packinghouse worker who came to Chicago from Wisconsin, died when Kennelly was two years old. His mother, Margaret, a migrant from Vermont, subsequently raised five children; Martin was the youngest. Kennelly graduated from the Holden Public School at 31st and Troop in 1901 and quickly went to work for Marshall Field and Company as a stockboy, earning $2.50 per week, including overtime. In little more than a year he left that job ("He did his work well and we found him honest," his employer wrote) and, benefiting from the tuition raised by a brother's packinghouse labor, entered De La Salle Institute, the "poor man's college" in Bridgeport. Taking the three-year commercial course that attracted many of the area's upwardly mobile Irish, he learned the ways of the counting-house rather than the slaughterhouse. After graduation in 1905, Kennelly took a job with the Becklenberg Warehouse Company, and made the moving and storage business his career. With the coming of World War I, he enlisted, served in the Quartermaster Corps, and emerged in 1919 as a captain, with enough capital to start a partnership with an older brother. With the aid of his twenty-year-old letter of recommendation, Kennelly won the Field's contract to move exhibits to the new Grant Park museum of natural history, and within a few years he presided over one of the largest storage companies in the midwest. By 1929 he helped organize a nationwide moving cooperative, Allied Van Lines, and by 1931 he assumed the presidency of the National Furniture Warehouseman's Association. Financially successful beyond his wildest dreams, Kennelly had reached the pinnacle of his professional world.[5]

Politically, Kennelly was a fringe player, generally assuming the role of silk-stocking contributor and supporter of individual candidates of his own choosing. When he took on a public role, it was usually as the concerned civic leader performing a disinterested service. Still active in local business groups such as the Chicago Association of Commerce and Industry and the Illinois Furniture Warehouseman's Association, Kennelly made his greatest civic impression during World War II. He served as president of the Army Emergency Relief Auxiliary and, most notably, chaired the American Red Cross campaign in Chicago. He raised some $44 million, refused compensation for his services, and greatly enhanced his reputation.[6]

In the narrower political realm Kennelly held only minor appointive offices on the Lincoln Park Board and the reorganized Chicago Park District. His only real political notoriety came from his support of anti-Kelly Democrats during the depression. Kennelly backed the independent Henry Horner in the bitter gubernatorial primary of 1936 and helped thwart Kelly's attempted purge of County Judge Edmund K. Jarecki two years later. Less successful, but equally telling, was Kennelly's support of state's attorney Tom Courtney in the 1939 mayoral primary against Kelly himself. But when initially presented with the opportunity to hold office himself—the mayor asked Kennelly to fill out the unexpired term of the recently expired Cook County Sheriff in 1943— Kennelly wisely declined.[7] Little did either of those Bridgeport Irishmen suspect that, within four years, the Cook County Democratic organization would again ask Kennelly to lend his beaming visage to a campaign to retain yet another tainted office—this time Kelly's own.

After fourteen years as mayor, Ed Kelly found himself on the ropes as he contemplated running for reelection in late 1946. His administration's undeniable connection to Chicago's underworld, the deterioration of the city's schools, and Kelly's aggressive efforts to bring blacks into the Democratic party had alienated Republicans, independents, and machine adherents alike—each could find something to vote against in the Kelly record. When the organization's own polls raised grave doubts about another Kelly campaign, the party leadership convinced him to step down and tabbed Martin Kennelly as his replacement.[8]

It is unclear whether Kelly himself selected his successor, although Kennelly's biographer (Biles), Jake Arvey, and the mayor's 1943 offer to the moving van executive suggest so.[9] What is abundantly clear, however, is that Martin Kennelly offered what Chicago Democrats desperately needed: respectability. Kennelly's integrity was unquestioned, his image was nonpartisan, and his independence was a matter of public record. And if, as the *Daily News* believed, the machine's embrace of Kennelly was a "desperate political necessity," Kennelly took full advantage of that desperation and accepted the mayoral nomination with no strings attached.[10]

Kennelly's statement to the slatemakers of the Cook County Democratic Central Committee on 20 December 1946 went beyond the sort of posturing that even hardened politicians could be expected to tolerate with equanimity. It was a measure of their distress that the party leaders sat quietly and handed the mayoral nomination to a man who assaulted their political faith. Displaying no sense of party loyalty, recognizing no commitment to the organization, and acknowledging no sense of reciprocity, Kennelly laid down the terms on which he would become the party's standard bearer. "I am a Democrat but I have never had any connection with your organization," Kennelly informed the central committee. "My political experience," he continued in a phrase that surely made the party regulars squirm, "has been confined to the several occasions when I supported such fine Democratic officials as the late Governor Horner, Judge Jarecki, and Thomas J. Courtney." Reaffirming his independence, Kennelly concluded, "I will have only the interest of the people at heart. If there is a conflict between personal or political considerations . . . I will decide the matter on the basis of what is good for the city and its citizens. We must get away from the idea that government belongs to a party and realize it belongs to the people. . . . I do not subscribe to the principle of "to the victor belongs the spoils." If Kennelly was pleased at receiving the Democratic mayoral nomination without encumbrances, however, he was rash in assuming that the organization was "willing to follow" his lead.[11] Indeed, the rejection of reciprocity cut both ways. The party's commitment to its candidate extended no further than his election and the denial of the feared Republican takeover. After that, all bets were off.

The Republicans exposed the tension in the civic leader/machine coalition and attacked it mercilessly. Kennelly's nomination, according to his opponent, Russell Root, was nothing more than a "deathbed repentance act" put on by a "divided and discredited" group that had "adopted a plea of 'Guilty' as its platform." Former Republican mayoral candidate George McKibben agreed and noted that even though the Democrats had put forward a new candidate, he had been selected in the "usual manner, at a secret meeting of the same old Democratic City Hall gang." Such charges might have been more effective had they not been tied to the undistinguished candidacy of a nominee foisted on Chicagoans by Governor Dwight Green's statewide Republican organization. If anyone were open to the charge of being a party hack, it was Root, not Kennelly.[12]

For his part, Kennelly parried the Republican jabs and enunciated a set of principles that was lifted whole out of the Progressive era in which he matured. He spoke of efficiency, of economy, of curbing waste, of running the city on a nonpartisan basis, and of treating public offices as public trusts. For Kennelly—as for the antimachine politicians of an earlier age—his allegiance was to the city as a whole and he viewed Chicago as a "cooperatively owned municipal corporation" in which the voters were shareholders and the alderman served as so many directors.[13] And when Republicans tried to tarnish Kennelly's image by accusing him of profiteering in the public contracts let to store polling place materials, Kennelly simply replied that he charged the city no more in 1947 than he did initially in 1923; he performed that service as a civic duty and not as a profit-making venture. Kennelly was, as his precinct workers contended with a mixture of awe and disdain, "running on his sainthood."[14]

When the dust had settled, Kennelly won nearly 920,000 votes and 59 percent of the ballots cast. "Our first concern must be Chicago's progress," he affirmed in his inaugural; "an objective which must exclude partisan politics. Let our record for the public good be our only politics."[15] The irony was that Kennelly's attempt to be nothing more than a city manager in an intensely political city government hamstrung his administration. His most lasting legacy, consequently, was not the blow he delivered to the machine, but rather the breathing space he provided for it. He saved the Cook County Democratic organization from itself, warmed the mayor's chair until a revitalized machine could safely reclaim it for one of its own, and left himself vulnerable enough so that the party had little trouble in dispatching him once his usefulness had ended. Certainly not an eager front for the organization, Kennelly, in fact, became one as he found himself besieged and out of his depth. The man who had no use for politics could not outmaneuver those who lived and breathed it.

Kennelly's administration, though, was not without a record of achievement. Indeed, in early 1954, in a speech before the State Street Council, Kennelly eyed a third term by looking back over his first seven years in office. He pointed with pride to the financial and administrative reforms enacted under his tutelage. The installation of a centralized purchasing department that met "every possible standard of efficiency and integrity" replaced the chaotic practices of earlier years. A Home Rule Commission laid the groundwork for the city's future development, and a host of other mayor-appointed committees likewise proved their value. A commission on municipal finances under civic leader Frank Sims, particularly, issued a report that independent alderman Leon Despres used "over and over again" after he was elected to the city council in 1955; it was a "fabulous job" according to Despres.[16]

Nor was the modernization of the city's administration confined to its financial affairs. The police department was similarly "streamlined and reorganized." The department brought its crime laboratory up-to-date, improved its motorized equipment, and developed contingency plans to meet every emergency. Kennelly improved record-keeping procedures and installed a new traffic system that unquestionably saved lives. And the mayor's transfer of district captains and his well-publicized crackdown on open gambling drove the most notorious operations underground or to the suburbs early in his first term.[17]

The two areas, however, that provided the most substantial support for Kennelly's reputation as a "reformer" involved the public schools and the city's civil service system. A series of investigations during Kelly's last term exposed the Chicago Board of Education as a political wasteland. Indeed, in the mid-1940s the school system served primarily as a source of jobs and contracts for the faithful and a safe haven for precinct workers between elections. The atrophy of its educational mission was so pronounced the North Central Association of Schools and Colleges threatened to revoke the accreditation of local high schools. Even before he left office, Ed Kelly consequently appointed a nonpolitical citizen's advisory committee that recommended the resignation of the board president and the superintendent of schools, and the appointment of a new board of education. Six new faces, in fact, already graced the eleven-member board and the superintendent had resigned when Kennelly was elected.[18]

Two tasks confronted the new mayor. The first involved the revision of the state law that set the school superintendent's term of office but left control of the system's business and legal affairs in the hands of the heretofore politicized board; it was a situation that made it impossible to lure a competent and independent educator to the superintendent's position. The proposal to centralize authority in the superintendent's office subsequently attracted strong opposition from those who profited from the existing arrangement, and it was one of the mayor's first jobs to smooth its passage. Margaret Hancock, vice president of the Citizens' School Committee, recalled that Kennelly brought both sides to his office and that he impressed her with his "poise and persistent good humor, and withal, the gentleness with which . . . [he] dominated the group which gradually came to terms, with concessions on both sides."[19] The bill eventually sailed through both houses of the legislature without a dissenting vote. In the appointment of Herold C. Hunt as superintendent, Kennelly fulfilled his second task. A first-rate administrator, Hunt "practically stopped" the trafficking in politically dictated contracts and jobs, greatly improved teacher morale, and directed a spurt of new capital improvements that were financed with a succession of Kennelly-backed bond issues.[20] It was a remarkable turnaround.

The appointment of a tough, efficient, nonpolitical administrator also characterized Kennelly's approach to civil service. The mayor's selection of Stephen E. Hurley, a former director of the Chicago Bar Association, to head the Civil Service Commission aroused the "bitterest kind of opposition from ward bosses who [gave] up patronage about as cheerfully as they sacrifice an arm or an eye," according to the *Tribune*.[21] While there was no wholesale firing of city workers, there was a constant, gradual erosion of politically sponsored jobs. Before he was through, Hurley's persistence and tenacity transferred some ten thousand jobs from the patronage rolls to the merit system and earned the undying enmity of the machine. One precinct captain, in an almost hysterical 1951 assessment, warned Kennelly that "Hurley . . . has wrecked the working Democrat organization" by "calling more examinations and laying off Temporary workers" on the eve of important municipal elections. The mayor, however, remained true to his mugwump faith, allowed Hurley his freedom, and raised an irreconcilable conflict of interest between his administration and the organization that gave it life. The city's progress on civil service was, in the *Tribune*'s estimation, "the brightest star in Mr. Kennelly's crown."[22]

Finally, Kennelly had the good fortune to preside over the city as it stood poised on the edge of a postwar boom. The history of his administration would also, consequently, be read in bricks and mortar. Responding to the tug of decentralization, the city provided greater access into, around, and through the Loop; the Dearborn Street subway, the Congress Street Superhighway, the Northwest Expressway, the Calumet Skyway, and the extensions of the North Outer Drive and Wacker Drive all gave evidence of that priority. Within the business district itself, the Grant Park underground garage helped accommodate the Loop to the automobile and the construction of the Prudential building heralded a new round of downtown development.[23] And in terms of the city's most pressing need—new housing—the Kennelly administration began a massive urban renewal program. The New York Life Insurance Company's investment in Lake Meadows, the planning of Prairie Shores, and the beginning of the University of Chicago's reconstruction of Hyde Park gave further proof that the city would not be willingly stripped of its middle-class population. It is not surprising that Kennelly began his 1954 "State of the City" address with a detailed recitation of his physical accomplishments.[24]

But the edifice of achievement rested on a rotten foundation. The mayor's accomplishments were weakened at every stage by political ineptitude. Kennelly's record, in fact, exemplified the abdication, not the delegation, of authority; and where the executive vacuum was filled by powerful, active forces, things did get done. But the limits and possibilities of Kennelly's administration were determined by the needs of others, particularly the Cook County Democratic organization and aggressive downtown business interests.

Kennelly's police reforms provide a striking case in point. He may have brought the department into the twentieth century technologically, but its politics remained rooted in an earlier era. Whether due to a prior, unspoken agreement with organization leaders, or simply a reflection of his political weakness, Kennelly did not touch its command structure—the network of political influence that dominated it—nor did he challenge its ties to the underworld. In part, his refusal to deal with the department's most fundamental problems may have been linked to a world view that acknowledged the inescapable reality of human frailty and elevated the habit of "looking the other way" to a local art form. It is also possible that Kennelly embodied the city's political ethos—one that defined democracy as being the open and equal access to "the fix"—although this is less likely given his frequently expressed beliefs on public morality. The bottom line, however, was that there were limits that the mayor either understood and accepted or was too weak to overcome. Before Senator Estes Kefauver's peripatetic committee on organized crime and, indeed, before the public at large, Kennelly played the comfortable role of civic booster and, however reluctantly, defended the machine's interests.

The results were the eruption of repeated scandals during Kennelly's tenure, the demonstration of his inability to maintain order, and a series of public embarrassments that undermined his administration. Payoff scandals involving Thomas Harrison and Redmond Gibbons, police captains in the notorious Hudson Avenue district in Paddy Bauler's Forty-third Ward, belied Kennelly's protestations and exposed, it appears, not his naivete, but rather his mendacity.[25] The sensational 1952 murder of Republican committeeman Charlie Gross (who was a Republican in name only) and the mob's successful expulsion of Democratic alderman and committeeman George Kells from the Twenty-eighth Ward the previous year (Kells's lieutenant, Big Jim Martin, had been gunned down to emphasize the criminals' desire that Kells not run for office again) similarly revealed the city's inability to control its own streets. The *Tribune* could only denounce the fact that Kells was "Kennelly's man" and that the mayor could not "protect him from the hoodlums."[26] Under such circumstances, Kennelly's denial of the existence of organized criminal influence in Chicago prior to the Kefauver hearings and his dogged defense of Police Commissioner John C. Prendergast proved major public embarrassments.[27]

Having rebuffed repeated calls for Prendergast's removal before the Kefauver investigation, Kennelly merely dramatized his lack of independence by his later retreat. Reacting to the prospect of selecting a new police commissioner,

Kennelly earlier had curtly rejected the Chicago Crime Commission's suggestion that candidates should be selected by a blue-ribbon citizens' committee. "The Mayor alone is responsible to the people for the police department," Kennelly asserted; and, he added, "[t]he statute makes no provision for sharing this authority with anyone." Yet the same statutory responsibility governed the mayor's selection of a new school board; and, in that case at least, Kennelly did not hesitate to share his power in order to end political "meddling." The police department, Kennelly explained—making a distinction that required a sophisticated eye wise in the ways of Chicago politics—"is an integral part of the city government administered by the Mayor." [28] It could perhaps also be added that, in 1947, the machine could no longer ignore the clamor for school reform while control of the police department occupied a more insulated position closer to the organization's heart—which, in this case, was located next to its wallet. Kennelly consequently refused to look outside the department and named Timothy O'Connor as Prendergast's successor. An honest cop, O'Connor was noted, as was Prendergast and the mayor himself, for his uncanny ability to look the other way and represented a safe choice for the organization. [29]

Kennelly's great reluctance to confront the Cook County Democratic organization could even be detected in the one area he did directly challenge it—on patronage. If Stephen Hurley's actions met Kennelly's expectations, the new civil service commissioner was hardly sustained by the mayor's willingness to do battle for him. Harassed, insulted, and repeatedly investigated by a hostile city council, Hurley resigned at one point, only to be cajoled into returning by Kennelly. Even then, however, the mayor refused to defend Hurley before the council and stood aside as the aldermen held his budget hostage. When independent alderman Robert Merriam championed Hurley's cause in budget hearings, rather than receiving praise from the mayor, Merriam caught only Kennelly's queasy lament that he "wished Steve wouldn't get into all these jams." Merriam subsequently concluded that the mayor was "a very delightful person but with no real backbone, and no real desire to fight with the organization." [30]

The Hurley episode not only revealed Kennelly's distaste, if not outright fear, of confrontation, but also his failure to support members of his own administration when they crossed swords with Democratic regulars. Both qualities surfaced again when Kennelly and a group of aldermen surveyed prospective public housing sites by bus in 1950. Met, at one point, by an angry West Side crowd, Kennelly simply told the bus driver not to make the scheduled stop; even neighborhood women in "babushkas" set the mayor to flight. [31] It was, in fact, shortly after this incident that Kennelly's corporation counsel, Benjamin Adamowski, tendered his resignation and—unlike Hurley's later recantation—this time there was no retraction. Adamowski was "shocked" by Kennelly's close cooperation with the machine-dominated council on public housing and, something of a maverick himself, he was further disappointed that the mayor did not support independent members of his own administration in their clashes with top party leaders. Adamowski said later that Kennelly "never should have been mayor of Chicago. He should have been a cardinal or monseigneur."[32]

Even more important, however, was Kennelly's willingness to let the city council—and, consequently, the Cook County Democratic organization—run its own affairs. Kelly had said earlier that, as mayor, "either you run the machine or the machine runs you." Kennelly proved his point. The budgetary squabble over Hurley's civil service commission was only symptomatic of the larger problem. In leaving the city's budget in the hands of the council's "Big Boys"—people like Tom Keane, John Duffy, and Clarence Wagner—Kennelly guaranteed that the political initiative remained with the regular Democrats. As expected, they used their power to harass their enemies and reward their friends. At one point, Stephen Hurley had to dig $1,500 out of his own pocket to cover the salaries of the "intellectuals" on his staff; on another occasion, the mayor had to dip into his private fund to sustain the Commission on Human Relations (CHR). On the other hand, Kennelly's budgetary green light and his refusal to trample on the council's domain ushered in a "golden era of mayoral permissiveness," according to Len O'Connor. Republican John Hoellen, first elected in 1947, said simply that it "was a sickening and terrifying experience to be involved in the city council in that period. Graft was rampant." Insider Paddy Bauler confirmed Hoellen's minority assessment when he told Robert Merriam that he could find but two honest aldermen at the time. The first, Bauler admitted, was young Merriam, the independent Democrat; the second, according to the forty-third Ward saloon owner, was himself—unlike the other "fakers" in the council, Bauler claimed the integrity to admit being a crook.[33] There was, in sum, no shortage of "grease" for a machine in sore need of lubrication during the Kennelly years.

Kennelly's candidacy was, of course, an open admission that the machine was in dire need of repair. And Chicago's voters turned not only to the "clean" Kennelly, but they simultaneously elected seventeen Republicans and an independent Democrat to the city council. There were enough nonorganization votes, in other words, to sustain mayoral vetoes and challenge the machine (which was itself deeply divided and factionalized) if that was the mayor's inclination. Clearly, it was not. Kennelly offered no direction to the regulars (who would have rejected it in any case) or their opposition, and meekly stood aside as machine stalwarts seized committee assignments and chairmanships. Except for Adamowski's ill-fated appointment as corporation counsel, Kennelly also generally retained Kelly's department heads and offered few alternatives there, either.[34] It was a precarious moment for the machine; one that found it fragmented, vulnerable, out of public favor, and potentially confronted with significant opposition. But the final blows never came. The "anti-machine" mayor provided the time, freedom, and wherewithal for the organization to regroup and emerge stronger than before.

If Kennelly's unique style of nongovernance proved helpful to the Cook County Democratic organization, it was also a boon for the downtown business community. Indeed, the mayor had little to do with either the conception or the execution of Chicago's urban renewal program. As was the case with the regulars in the political arena, Kennelly simply got out of the way of the Loop's economic giants and powerful institutional interests and merely lent his name to their endeavors.

Chicago's postwar reconstruction proceeded under the Illinois Blighted Areas Redevelopment Act of 1947, the Illinois Urban Community Conservation Act of 1953, and the federal legislation that was modeled on these pioneer measures: the Housing Acts of 1949 and 1954. Coming out of Chicago during the Kennelly administration, the Illinois laws were the products of years of private concern and activity. The Chicago Title and Trust Company, directed by Holman Pettibone, and Marshall Field and Company, which provided the services of Milton C. Mumford, had been working since World War II on plans to revitalize the central city. They had, in fact, drafted their own legislation before Kennelly assumed office and steered it through the legislature with the mayor's blessing shortly thereafter. When some controversial aspects of the law created a public uproar, however, Kennelly's reaction revealed how poorly he understood the measure and, indeed, Mumford concluded that the mayor "did not really know what was involved" when he agreed to its essential features. Similarly, the Urban Community Conservation Act was the product of the University of Chicago's desire to restructure Hyde Park and was the legislative handiwork of the Metropolitan Housing and Planning Council, Julian Levi, and the South East Chicago Commission. Levi recalled "dumping" the plan on the mayor's desk, and, though the conservative Kennelly remained "lukewarm" toward a law that entailed a significance expansion of government power, he did not oppose private interests he found philosophically congenial, socially acceptable, and politically useful.[35]

The mayor did little more to see the plans through. It was Pettibone and Mumford who brought in the New York Life Insurance Company to develop Lake Meadows, and, in a telling episode, the businessmen themselves had to deal directly with the city council when it threatened their designs. Ira Bach, director of the Chicago Land Clearance Commission, remembered that the chairman of a key council committee demanded a bribe as the price of his cooperation in closing a section of Cottage Grove Avenue that was vital to the project. The mayor, in Bach's words, said he "couldn't do anything about it," and Bach instead turned to Pettibone, who somehow broke the logjam in the council. Ultimately, Bach relied less on Kennelly ("who was not the strongest kind of mayor") than he did on the Republican businessman who "knew how to wheel and deal with the aldermen."[36] Little more could be expected from a chief executive who went so far as to refuse to read housing authority recommendations and related newspaper stories so that he might honestly claim ignorance when asked for an opinion.[37] Such practices were testimony both to his integrity and to the quality of his leadership.

If Kennelly had any direct impact on Chicago's postwar development, it was, perhaps, to slow its pace. Chicago's finances were strained throughout the period, and, despite the presence of a Democratic governor in Springfield after 1948, the state hardly opened its coffers to the beleaguered urbanites. Much of the coolness in the Adlai Stevenson–Kennelly relationship apparently stemmed from personal pique as the mayor resented both Stevenson's privileged background and his slating at the expense of longtime Kennelly friend Tom Courtney. And when the governor called a special session of the legislature to deal with Chicago's financial problems and convened a meeting of legislative leaders to hear Kennelly's proposals, Stevenson was appalled to learn that the mayor had none to offer. Left to his own devices, Kennelly simply "talked aimlessly" and informed the legislators that they had to develop their own plans for Chicago's benefit. After such a performance, the governor concluded that Kennelly was "hopelessly inept" and offered him little future assistance.[38]

Party chairman Jake Arvey echoed Stevenson's use of the word "inept" when assessing Kennelly's political acumen. The mayor's evident lack of skill undoubtedly flowed both from his inexperience and from his barely episodic attention to such details once in office. It was not that Kennelly ignored politics as a matter of principle as his campaign rhetoric suggested, but rather that he played the game only intermittently, usually poorly, and almost exclusively in conjunction with his own electoral fortunes. Thus it was with a transparent heavy-handedness that the "reform" mayor overrode the recommendations of his citizens' committee and retained Kelly-holdover and heavy party contributor Bernard Majewski on the school board in 1951 for fear of alienating both regulars and the Polish vote on the eve of his reelection. And in a futile attempt to impress the new party chairman, Richard J. Daley, in his hunt for a third term, Kennelly tried unsuccessfully to pressure the Chicago Housing Authority into appointing the chairman's cousin, John Daley, as its new counsel. It apparently mattered little to Kennelly that John Daley ranked 183rd out of 191 in his law school class or that he lacked the requisite experience specified by CHA guidelines. Even worse than the proposed appointment itself was Kennelly's failure to make it stick and the public embarrassment that caused the young attorney to withdraw his name. Such spasmodic attention to personal politics would prove no match for the man who spent his whole life preparing to seize the prize that had earlier fallen fortuitously into Kennelly's lap.[39]

Kennelly's subversion of the CHA for political purposes also exposed a weakness on racial issues that eventually helped to engulf his administration. Where Kelly insulated the housing authority from the political demands of the ward committeemen, encouraged its experiments in integration, and offered unswerving support to executive secretary Elizabeth Wood, Kennelly backtracked and dashed the hopes of those who believed the local Democratic party could become a truly multiracial (and not just a multiethnic) organization. His administration represented a turning point in the machine's relationship to blacks. After Ed Kelly's symbolic and substantive overtures to the black community, party leaders, with Kennelly's acquiescence and support, made certain that blacks occupied a subordinate and "safe" position within the local Democratic coalition.[40] If the full implications of that decision only became apparent during Richard J. Daley's long tenure, it was Kennelly's administration that set the course. Indeed, it was only in this context that Kennelly's billing as "white knight" had any real meaning.

None of this, of course, was apparent in Kennelly's 1947 campaign. Riding his predecessor's long coattails in the black community, Kennelly won the *Defender*'s endorsement because blacks felt it important to "continue and expand the progressive and far-reaching racial policies" of Kelly.[41] The bright hopes for Kennelly's administration, however, withered under the twin pressures of rapid black population growth and white resistance to change.

The first signs of trouble came as violence erupted in changing neighborhoods. White assaults on the black pioneers homesteading on the city's racial frontier began during World War II and plagued Kelly's last years. It was, in fact, Kelly's use of the police to protect blacks and his unqualified assertion of the blacks' right to move wherever they wished that destroyed his support within the organization and guaranteed that the machine would not reslate him.[42] The hit-and-run attacks that bedeviled Kelly, however, evolved into massive mob violence in the postwar era. Large scale rioting surrounded the CHA's Fernwood Park Homes just months after Kennelly took office in 1947, and erupted again in Park Manor and Englewood in 1949. When confronted with this reaction to black expansion, the mayor refused to reaffirm his predecessor's stand on nondiscrimination. His reaction to recurrent disorder, according to a Commission on Human Relations that openly longed for Kelly's firmer hand, consisted of little more than "appeasement and persuasion." Relations between the CHR and the mayor subsequently remained cool until the Englewood riot, when they broke down completely. Blaming the uprising on subversives, Kennelly did little to end the violence or assuage black feelings.[43]

In the aftermath of that explosion, Urban League executive Sidney Williams attacked the Kennelly administration's "inepitude" and its "shameful failure" to protect blacks. He also called for the mayor's impeachment and organized the Committee to End Mob Violence to prod the city into greater action. Kennelly's response, it was rumored in the black community, was to use his influence in Chicago's business community to dry up white contributions to the Urban League. While it is impossible to confirm Kennelly's alleged role, the Urban League's subsequent financial distress forced it to shut down for six months and fire its entire staff, including Sidney Williams. When it opened its doors again, it had the support of the city's business leaders and, not coincidentally, a more conservative leadership.[44]

When Kennelly finally did take a stand on housing discrimination, it was to oppose an ordinance that would have banned it. Black Republican alderman Archibald Carey, Jr., introduced the measure to assure blacks that they would not be displaced by the city's slum clearance program and that they would have access to all publicly assisted housing. After its proposal, Kennelly maintained a silence that was, according to the Chicago Council against Discrimination, "interpreted not only as opposition to the Ordinance, but also as a tactic repudiation of the platform commitments of the [Democratic] party." Opposed to the architects of the city's redevelopment plans and denounced by whites fearful of any expression of black political power, Loop business elites and machine politicians stood together to defeat the Carey Ordinance. With such solid support, the debate over the measure provided one of the rare occasions when Kennelly stepped entirely out of character and took the council floor to speak against pending legislation.[45]

Ultimately, however, it was not Kennelly's leadership but the lack of it that was of the greatest significance. Under his regime the ward bosses were able to reassert themselves and, most tellingly, exploit the vacuum at the top to attack the CHA. Bereft of Kelly's protective shield, the authority was now vulnerable, and before Kennelly left office in 1955, it was transformed into a bulwark of segregation.

The process began just weeks into Kennelly's first term when the state, at the city council's request, passed a redevelopment program that gave the council a veto over locally funded projects. The legislation threw the authority into a "new relationship" with the city, and led Elizabeth Wood to anticipate "profound difficulties . . . due to the Authority's racial policy." Indeed, within months that policy led to the passage of additional state legislation that granted the city a veto over all CHA projects, even those supported by federal funds. The result was that the precedent-setting first slate of public housing sites selected under the Housing Act of 1949 was chosen by a handful of council leaders whose chief desires were to contain the city's black population and bring the CHA's building program to a halt. By the fall of 1952, Elizabeth Wood acknowledged their success and characterized the CHA as a "captive Authority." Those who looked to the mayor for help found that he had "forsaken" their goals, and was incapable of the "aggressive leadership" missing since "Mayor Kelly left office."[46]

Wood vowed to fight on, but realized that she had become a controversial figure. It was because, she said, she "made every effort to run an honest enterprise" and "tried not to discriminate." When the Trumbull Park Homes exploded in yet another racial confrontation in the summer of 1953, she found herself unable to withstand a final political assault on her independence. Demoted and rendered powerless in a reorganization inspired by one of Kennelly's "efficiency" studies. Wood attacked the hypocrisy of her superiors and their lack of resolve on racial issues. Dismissed by the authority's commissioners in 1954, Wood's removal ended the CHA's resistance to the racial demands of the city's white ward leaders. It also set the agency on the road to becoming one of the "worst" managed authorities in the country, according to a 1982 federal study, and one whose sole purpose was the "acquisition of as many Federal . . . dollars as possible for the creation of patronage jobs and financial opportunities."[47] Scandal-free under Elizabeth Wood, the CHA became a bastion of segregation and a trough for the machine.

Kennelly's difficulties were compounded by the mayor's disastrous relationship with William Levi Dawson, political overlord of the black South Side. Kennelly, who was clearly uncomfortable with blacks, never developed a political strategy to deal with them, and had no basis for communicating with Dawson who was both black and a "boss." Instead, when Kennelly dealt with blacks at all, it was through more "respectable" leaders such as the *Defender*'s John Sengstacke, the housing authority's Robert R. Taylor, and Rev. J. L. Jackson—all individuals with strong ties to the white business community. The mayor consequently isolated himself not only from the black ward organizations, but also from the black labor movement as well—despite repeated overtures from the CIO's Willard Townsend. And in his 1951 reelection bid, Kennelly kept even those blacks friendly to him at a chilly distance, organizing a committee of black leaders only in the campaign's final weeks. Dawson could not understand Kennelly's "disregard" for him or the mayor's willingness, in Dawson's view, to work with "opportunists who would go either way."[48]

Kennelly's much publicized crackdown on gambling also infuriated Dawson. The embarrassment of the Kefauver hearings in late 1950 and Kennelly's campaign for reelection in early 1951 led the mayor to prove he was "tough on crime" by raiding South Side policy wheels that were nominally under Dawson's protection. Police conducted 11,562 raids that netted 24,476 individual arrests between January 1951 and the end of March 1955. Even Kennelly's friendly biographer noted that such operations simply "became a satisfactory way for creating favorable headlines without upsetting [the larger] system of payoffs." And when Dawson tried to negotiate their differences by offering to support Kennelly's redevelopment plans, Ira Bach—who served as Dawson's intermediary in this instance—received nothing more than the mayor's characteristic "blank stare" in return. The raids continued, Dawson's opposition slowed progress on Lake Meadows, and the mayor fashioned yet another loop on his own political noose.[49]

There was also more to the gambling raids than met the eye. C. C. Wimbish, Dawson's Third Ward committeeman, was embroiled in a bitter dispute with the one-legged congressman over the division of the ward's spoils. Dawson kept a tight rein on South Side operations despite Wimbish's expectation that, as committeeman, he would rake in the "goodies." The success of Kennelly's raids subsequently owed a great deal to information provided by Wimbish, and the mayor's actions projected him squarely into the middle of an internecine political battle that challenged Dawson's dominance on the South Side. The Cook County Democratic Organization—at Dawson's insistence—later purged Wimbish and Kennelly succeeded only in alienating Dawson beyond redemption.[50]

The mayor's problems in the black community, and elsewhere, surfaced during his 1951 campaign, but they were not yet enough to deny him victory even if they did manifest themselves clearly in the returns. Kennelly lost sixteen wards in 1951, doubling the number he dropped four years before. Significantly, not only did he lose traditionally Republican wards on the far Northwest and Southwest sides, but defections could be detected in the black belt and those white wards threatened with racial transition.[51] The tally graphically revealed the racial-political dilemma of postwar Chicago: Kennelly could not protect blacks without alienating the still-dominant whites, nor could he ignore black concerns without losing the support of the most rapidly growing group in the city. Eager for a third term in 1955, Kennelly proved only that he lacked the considerable skill necessary to handle, balance, or negate the forces at work. He never had a chance.

Going into the campaign, Kennelly was burdened by a number of debilitating problems. First, his inability to defuse the city's gnawing racial tensions left both blacks and whites dissatisfied. Second, the mayor's stance on civil service and his estrangement from organized labor made his removal from office a virtual necessity for organization Democrats; indeed, party leaders decided back in November 1952 that Kennelly had to go.[52] Finally, there was the consuming personal ambition of the new party chairman, Richard J. Daley. Any one of these factors could have dashed Kennelly's third-term hopes. Any two of them would have caused certain political death. All three together produced a perfunctory four-minute interview for the two-term incumbent mayor before the organization's slatemakers and his unanimous rejection. It was a swift and sure political beheading executed by Daley's hand-picked committee. Stripped of the party's support, Kennelly was left virtually alone to face Daley and onetime ally Ben Adamowski in a three-cornered primary.

The white siege of the Trumbull Park Homes on the far South Side entered its second year in 1955 and provided the backdrop for the campaign. Violently protesting the presence of a handful of black families, the whites in South Deering faced a housing authority forced to take a public stand against discrimination, but one fearful of disorder and eager to avoid the appearance that policy was being made in the streets. The CHA consequently "froze" the number of black families in the project and watched helplessly as recurrent violence lashed the community. Kennelly, doing what he did best, stood on the sidelines and ignored black protests. Believing that the "mob violence at the project was sanctioned and stimulated by the willful failure of the city administration to end it," blacks rejected Kennelly's candidacy. Indeed, not only did the *Defender* claim that Kennelly's "cowardly handling" of the Trumbull Park disorders cost him black support, but white strategists mapping Democrat-turned-Republican Robert Merriam's race in the general election also concluded that blacks deserted Kennelly because he "failed them in the Trumbull Park situation."[53]

Faced with such dim prospects in the black community, Kennelly turned his imminent defeat there into a rout by running a campaign that openly courted white backlash voters. Having the sophistication to use stereotypes rather than slurs, Kennelly claimed that it was the vicelord Dawson who "pushed the controls in the 'Dump Kennelly' project." The daily press dutifully echoed the charges, claiming that "the notorious Bill Dawson" was the "chief architect" of the nefarious "plot." If Kennelly campaigned against "bossism" in general, he was counting on a white reaction to the prospect of being dominated by a black boss in particular. The *Defender* denounced Kennelly's transparent "race baiting" and attacked his strategy as "both dirty and dangerous." Even Claude A. Barnett of the Associated Negro Press, hardly a Dawson supporter, believed the campaign coverage in the white press "fanned racial hate," made the mayor's dumping a "racial issue," and merely served to rally even unsympathetic blacks to Dawson's cause.[54] And while there is no question that Dawson played an important role in the mayor's defeat, the perception that it was an angry Bill Dawson—stung into action by the mayor's attack on policy—who was primarily responsible for an outpouring of pliable black votes that denied Kennelly renomination merely reflects the lasting legacy of the incumbent's rhetoric and the white dailies' election coverage. The black community's dissatisfaction with Kennelly was much deeper, and its rejection of him far more profound, than such self-serving interpretations suggest.

Mobilized by the mayor's vituperative campaign and the deadly drone of disorder that echoed not only from South Deering, but from Fernwood, Park Manor, and Englewood as well, black voters marched to the polls not to vote for Richard J. Daley, but to bring down Martin H. Kennelly. The distinction is important, for Daley was able to win their support with no more than the assurance that he would place the solution of Trumbull Park's troubles "at the head of his program" and the promise that he would defeat the incumbent. Indeed, it was a measure not of Daley's political skill, but of Kennelly's, that the challenger was able to pick up endorsements from both the Chicago *Defender* and the South Deering Improvement Association at the same time. With the regular organization solidly behind him (forty-eight of the fifty ward committeemen backed Daley), the party chairman left the mayor in an impossible situation. When it was all over, Bill Dawson's five wards turned nearly 82 percent of their votes over to Daley (58,999 to 13,437) and the rest of Daley's 100,000 vote plurality came largely from a handful of inner city, machine-controlled "river" wards.[55]

Kennelly, however, still had one arrow left in his quiver. The general election between Robert Merriam and Daley would, the *Sun-Times* indicated in an article that projected hyperbole beyond the primary, be a showdown "between the forces of civic righteousness and the nefarious political bosses." Kennelly's endorsement in such a contest was potentially of great value, and it offered one last chance for the mayor to deliver a blow to those who had ended his career. It never came. Told by machine operatives that Merriam sought his indictment in earlier criminal investigations, Kennelly rejected Merriam's personal denial and sat out the election. If the press had little trouble distinguishing between the forces of light and darkness, Martin H. Kennelly was not similarly blessed—or, if he was, it made little difference.[56]

On the night of his primary defeat, Kennelly watched the vote roll in, shook his head, and muttered, "They're unbeatable, just unbeatable, aren't they?" It was not a thought that would have occurred to anyone just eight years before. But by 1955, with Richard J. Daley in control, they were. And they would remain so for another twenty-five years.

10.

MAYOR RICHARD J. DALEY AND THE POLITICS OF GOOD GOVERNMENT

Paul M. Green

Richard J. Daley was Chicago's mayor from 1955 to 1976. His lasting legacy and reputation are filled with political and governmental contradictions. To some current political scientists he was "the last of the urban machine bosses"; a friendly biographer called him "an Irish warrior"; *Time* magazine in 1963 labeled Daley "the first of the new bosses . . . the first of the new leaders"; a contemporary Chicago commentator described Daley as being "unmovable as a bucket of ten-penny nails . . . and sentimental to the point of being maudlin . . ."; while one of his old mayoral consultants summed up his boss by stating simply that "he [Daley] was the hardest working man I ever met."[1] Who is right? They all are.

Like Chicago itself, Richard J. Daley fits no single description. A world-class city in architecture, the arts, transportation, and commerce and industry, Chicago is also a city that has been on the front lines of those social and economic urban problems that remain stubbornly unsolvable. At times larger than life, Daley could also be petty and petulant and though known for his cold, stoneface demeanor he also often wore his heart on his sleeve.

This chapter will take an admittedly controversial look at this man on whom very few Chicagoans or political observers are neutral. In short I will argue that Daley, the stereotypical political machine boss to most analysts, was in fact antipolitics. Moreover, Daley's famous dictum that "good government is good politics" was more than a slogan; rather, it was his operational strategy of public administration.

The key to this argument is the distinction between apolitical and antipolitical. Daley knew and practiced politics at the highest and lowest levels. He was an observer and participant in some of the toughest and most bruis-

144

ing political battles in American urban history. Yet from the day he won his first public office in the 1930s to his death in 1976, Daley was more comfortable, more able, and more at ease managing government than managing campaigns.

In my view, Daley used politics to protect his governmental activities. He was deeply committed to modernizing, organizing, and streamlining bloated and nonfunctioning governmental agencies whether he was serving in city, county, or state government. He combined these views with his unabashed faith in the Democratic party's commitment to helping working-class people and over the years developed an accommodation between these two beliefs. This personal adjustment thesis is the only logical explanation for a man who could rail against government waste and extravagance while supporting an army of patronage workers within his political ranks. Admittedly this distinction is not always neat and consistent, but neither was Daley's life as public servant and political boss.

Much of the accepted criticism of Daley reflects mostly anecdotal assumptions about his post-1963 activities when the mayor underwent a dramatic political and personal change. As will be seen in this chapter in his third mayoral campaign (1963) Richard J. Daley's often spoken and demonstrated liberalism ran headlong into the harsh political reality of his city. Civil rights and race were issues that Daley could not overcome, and his last thirteen years as Chicago's mayor would prove to be far different than his first eight.

Finally, this analysis must be understood in the context of Chicago politics. Daley served in a city whose political tradition ranged from First Ward Alderman Bathhouse John Coughlin's turn of the century battle cry "hobo-floto-voto" to Forty-third Ward Alderman Paddy Bauler's gleeful comment "Chicago ain't ready for reform" following Daley's 1955 mayoral victory. What is not often remembered is that in that same election Bauler gave an even more insightful overview of Chicago politics saying "the proof of the puddin' is in the votin'."

Richard J. Daley was no policy saint, but he was also far from a machine sinner. He understood politics and government better than any of his allies or opponents. In his long climb up the ladder, Daley quietly garnered encyclopedic knowledge of men, their ambitions, and how things worked. Like one of his great mentors former mayor Anton J. Cermak, Daley would accept and even seek governmental reforms and then implement them within the political process. He trusted few individuals, especially aldermen and ward committeemen, and whenever possible tried to prevent these alleged allies from hindering governmental operations by either a slick finesse or if need be straightforward muscle.

Mr. Dooley said it best: "Chicago politics ain't bean bag"—and Daley working in such an environment needed to maintain control. Obviously this control would guarantee him personal political success, but it also would allow him to bring new ideas and innovations into government. And that was his true love. As I was told by several old Daley colleagues and acquaintances, "The mayor avoided all political talk in his city hall office . . . party matters had to be discussed across the street at headquarters," usually a downtown hotel office suite. Misplaced moralism, perhaps, but it also reflected a man determined to alter the political environment that had so long dominated Chicago.

This chapter will have four parts. First, a brief discussion of Daley's mileu, Chicago; second, a short overview of the man's life; third, an analysis of the political process in Chicago; and fourth, Daley the mayor—especially his first two terms—and how in that time span he became Chicago's first "totally modern mayor."

I. Chicago

In early 1952 writer A. J. Liebling captured the essence of Chicago when he wrote, "The city is less one town than a loose confederacy of 50 wards. Communication between the residents of the different wards is limited by the pronounced tendency of immigrant groups . . . to coagulate geographically".[2] No major American city was as ethnicly diverse or as segregated as Chicago. What many historians and commentators overlook is that the city's recognized ranking as the nation's most racially segregated city was in fact a carryover from its traditional ethnic segregation days. Obviously racial segregation eased ethnic segregation making the issue of separation more a case of white and black.

Foreign born and children of foreign born poured into the city late in the nineteenth century looking for jobs. These newcomers fitted perfectly into Ira Katznelson's theory of the separation of "the politics of work from the politics of community" in most American cities.[3] Though a strong union city, true loyalty was given to one's neighbors, not ones' coworkers. A national identification was critical to enter both public or private service. At the same time the Anglo-Saxon establishment (aided by its allies in German and Scandinavian neighborhoods) set up a "Wasp wall" around downtown to limit ethnic political, business, and social advancement. Most young ethnics learned early that loyalty to a neighborhood (which almost always meant loyalty to a nationality) was far more important to them than any citywide attachment. In few cities did an individual's parish name, his ward number, or his street corner carry as much weight or socioeconomic information than in Chicago. And though much changed during the first half of the twentieth century, traditional stereotypes remained vivid to Richard J. Daley as he matured from a youngster to a middle-aged man. In his mayoral years he personified every scar and slight ever heaped on ethnic Chicago, and his determination to succeed was reflected in the hopes and dreams of his second-generation ethnic contemporaries.

Starting as a 10-square-mile settlement of 4,000 persons in 1837 Chicago had grown to a 212-square mile city of over 3.6 million inhabitants by 1950. In the nineteenth century Chicago had parlayed its entrepreneurial energy in such commercial activities as grain, lumber, and meat with its geo-transportation location to become a dominant urban center. The industrial age brought factory and service jobs along with civic "giants" who owned the biggest companies and who despite the brawling local political scene influenced important public policy actions. The so-called city of "big shoulders" had in the words of longtime political observer Len O'Connor developed "a high tolerance for sin and scandal; as long as the city functioned in an orderly way an enterprising man could make money."[4]

As Daley came into power in 1955, Chicago's population growth and economic energy began to ebb. Building had stopped within the city's central business district (the Loop). "Investors were turning to the cheaper land of the suburbs . . . [causing] several of the major downtown landholders and commercial interests . . . [to] organize to restore its competitive standing as a business site."[5]

Migration of southern blacks to Chicagoland spurred a suburban white housing market and major socioeconomic changes in several traditional ethnic neighborhoods. The 1950 United States census revealed that of Chicago's 1.1 million housing units, "64,000 were dilapidated and should be demolished; some 180,000 [other] units lacked essential sanitary facilities, and about 300,000 dwelling units were in structures built in or before 1895."[6] Though still a city on the make and with vast resources, Chicago's incredible competitive will seemed stuck in neutral—thus, enter Richard J. Daley.

II. Richard J. Daley, the Man

Richard J. Daley was born 15 May 1902, at 3602 S. Lowe—a half block from where he would live most of his life. Baptized at the nearby Nativity of Our Lord parish church, Daley's home turf would always remain the working-class Bridgeport neighborhood on the city's southwest side. The only son of a sheet metal worker father, Michael, and an extraordinary, demanding mother, Lillian, Daley received a fine Catholic school education. Like many of his community, Daley saw public service as a way to economic betterment, but unlike most of his pals young Daley also saw the value of an education. In 1923 he would start an eleven-year odyssey to complete a law degree program at De Paul University. Going to law school part-time at night forced Daley to discipline his lifestyle and activities, thereby giving him a lifelong edge over actual and potential political rivals.

A shy and polite young man, Daley worked at several minor city and county jobs during his law school days. Perhaps his most interesting post was "aldermanic scribe" to ten city council members during the late 1920s. Many Chicago aldermen during this time were barely literate, so young men like Daley were hired to read and write proposed legislation. This council experience would stay with Daley all through his life, and though publicly as mayor he would praise his aldermanic allies, in reality he had a very low opinion of the city council.

Daley rose slowly up the public service ladder. He attached his early political fortunes to the career of "Big Joe" McDonough who brought Daley into the county treasurer's office as his chief assistant. The astute and conscientious Daley also became active in his neighborhood's social club, the Hamburg Athletic Association. The "Hamburgers" gave Daley status in the community and though the club's reputation was at times unsavory (some have labeled it an original street gang) Daley was never personally involved in any illegality. Like his political associations in later years, young Daley gained control of the Hamburgers without being tainted by the worst elements of the group.

In 1936 Daley married Eleanor Guilfoyle and was elected state representative as a Republican (an identification he quickly changed in Springfield). For the next two decades Daley held several governmental and political posts. He was elected state senator and county clerk and also served as the first budget director for Illinois Governor Adlai Stevenson. Through a series of moves Daley also emerged as Democratic political leader (ward committeeman) of his Bridgeport-dominated Eleventh Ward. At the same time, Daley dedicated his nonworking hours to his family, avoiding the social pitfalls that would afflict many of his political colleagues.

In the mid-1950s Daley had become in the words of Milton Rakove the creature of "six wellsprings" that had shaped and guided his life.[7] First was his faith. A daily mass-goer Daley was proud and open about his devout belief in the Catholic church. Second was Daley's strong belief in family. Third was his ethnicity. Unlike previous Irish politicians Daley could out-Irish his Erin rivals while maintaining strong ties to other ethnic leaders. Fourth was his love of his Bridgeport neighborhood. Not even his severest critics could claim that Daley was not of his community, and no one believed that any reward or glory would ever make him leave his ancestral roots. Fifth was his connection with the Democratic party. Daley believed that only through a strong party could working people achieve upward mobility. Sixth was his city. Daley was Chicago's greatest booster. Like his relationship with the Democratic party, identifying with the city was good politics.

Daley's six wellsprings propelled him to the forefront of many valuable political symbols. No opponent could out-Catholic, -family, -Irish, -neighborhood, -Democratic party, or -Chicago Daley. He was the ultimate in every wellspring area as mayor of Chicago. In the fifty-three years it took him to reach city hall his personality and behavior were molded by these six factors. Given city demographics this gave him incredible advantages over all opponents both Democrat and Republican. Without a media advisor or public relations consultant constituency in Chicago. It was not an easy struggle, but once in City Hall Daley was the unchallenged leader of ethnic Chicago. It was a perfect fit for the time.

III. Chicago Politics

For nearly the first century of Chicago's existence individuals not party organizations dominated city politics. Chicago's rapid growth, its ethnic diversity, and its belief in neighborhood solidarity made it virtually impossible to establish a citywide organization or political machine. Instead, factions developed around dynamic local leaders who would trade off support between rival groups in both parties. In this type of atmosphere "rule or ruin" politics reigned. Primary losers would simply "trim" or "knife" primary winners in general elections by voting for opposing party candidates.

At the turn of the twentieth century each major political party in the city had three factions. The Republicans pushed by immigrant newcomers more and more to the huge wards on the city's periphery were dominant in national and state elections but were roundly defeated in mayoral contests. Philosophically there was little difference between the three GOP groups until William Hale "Big Bill" Thompson rose to mayoral power. Thompson, a three-term mayor, controlled City Hall from 1915 to 1923 and 1927 to 1931 (the last year Chicago had a Republican mayor) and during this time consolidated his control over the local GOP.

Thompson was an unscrupulous political manipulator who shoved and bullied his foes into compliance. His often-bizarre and unpredictable political behavior made Thompson a formidable campaigner while his unsavory personal and administrative ethics gave him political leverage and allies with like-minded aldermen from both parties. However, his questionable political associates (Al Capone, etc.), his well-documented tainted and corrupt governmental practices, and his general demeanor made him a pariah in respectable Republican circles. A key factor for the Democratic machine takeover of Chicago in the early 1930s was a bipartisan belief of many city dwellers that Thompson had to go. Unfortunately for Chicago Republicans, they are still looking for a Big Bill mayoral successor sixty years later.

The Democratic story is much more complicated than the Republican saga. In the first three decades of the century their three factions merged into a single political organization under the leadership of Anton J. Cermak. No man in Chicago history had a more controversial political life than Tony Cermak. Elected mayor in 1931 after a long political career, Cermak used party discipline based on a multinational appeal to many ethnic groups to take over the party and then the city. A gruff bully in appearance but a political genius behind closed doors, Cermak saw the party apparatus as his vehicle to power.

His chief allies were so-called new breed Democrats who were better educated and more sophisticated than traditional Democratic ward bosses. Under Cermak's leadership the party turned away from its saloon keeper and rogue image to the more acceptable (and lucrative) pursuits in law, banking, insurance, and construction businesses.

One of Cermak's key political allies was Joe McDonough who disregarded old-fashioned overt ethnic appeals (Cermak's last party foes constituted a faction of mainly Irish pols unwilling to submit to Cermak's leadership or party discipline) and wholeheartedly supported the new mayor. Watching closely was McDonough's prize protege, Richard J. Daley.

Young Daley saw Cermak and his party chairman Pat Nash (Cermak gave up the party post on becoming mayor—something Daley would not do) run the party as a business. One either delivered or was out; rewards equaled performance, and one was answerable to the Board of Directors, the central committee. Governmentally Cermak and Nash demanded that government become more efficient, effective, and businesslike in serving the public interest. However, whereas many reformers wanted to bypass or even abolish existing political party organizations to achieve their goals, Cermak and Nash advocated change through the local Democratic party. Much history needs to be written about the governmental changes instituted by Cermak as he consolidated control over the city with his machine.

Cermak's assassination in 1933 left the Democratic party leaderless for twenty years. The martyred mayor's successor, Edward Kelly, benefited enormously from the system Cermak had put into place and along with the old warhorse Pat Nash established the infamous Kelly-Nash machine. Without any real political opposition Kelly-Nash ran roughshod over the city. After Nash's death in the early 1940s Kelly proved utterly incompetent to run the city or the party by himself. Forgetting Cermak's businesslike governmental message, Kelly corrupted a process that though far from pure at the outset had lost direction and most of its effectiveness.

By 1946 Chicago's governmental structure and its politics were in chaos. "The truth is," wrote Harry Barnard, "Chicago's municipal affairs are shot through with political knavery, overt and concealed corruption. . . inefficiency and fakery." What is needed is a municipal administration, topped by a man with political guts and unquestioned personal and political integrity, which will devote itself completely and energetically to the one task of rebuilding and reorganizing the municipal services of Chicago. . . . [8]

Ironically Barnard would have to wait nine more years for such a man to take over City Hall. The discredited Kelley was dumped by party leaders in 1947 in favor of businessman and political amateur Martin J. Kennelly.

Kennelly was an amiable but incompetent administrator. Unfortunately for him he was not nearly tough enough to deal with a city council that was often out of control. Moreover, Chicagoland's historic governmental fragmentation had produced numerous local governmental bailiwicks that many local political leaders used as patronage safe havens for their important workers. Kennelly's avoidance of politics (he often said "I am a public servant first and a party member second") left him little political leverage to deal with powerful local pols. Though elected in 1947 and reelected in 1951, Kennelly was more a spectator than a player in the ever-degenerating Chicago political scene.

Kennelly's mayoral weakness was noted in Chicago and around the country. In late 1951 the *Nation* claimed that under Kennelly "adequate housing, real civil-service reform and trimming of unnecessary city expenditures are no closer today than they were at the end of the Kelly administration."[9] In mid-1953 the *New Republic* labeled Kennelly as being "affable and ineffectual . . . [as well as] being numbed by an inability to take firm action for fear of hurting someone's feelings".[10] It was during this period of political instability and leadership vacuum in the city that Richard J. Daley made his move.

In 1950 Daley left Governor Stevenson's cabinet to fill out the term of Cook County Clerk Michael Flynn who died in office. Daley's credentials were impressive but so was his political backing from Stevenson, United State's Senator Paul Douglas, and party chairman Jacob Arvey. Later in 1950 Daley was elected to the clerk's position on his own, and he quickly joined the leadership of the liberal wing of the local Democracy. He became a contact man for the Stevenson-Douglas-Arvey forces who were being challenged inside the party by powerful local Democrats who openly called themselves conservatives.

In July 1953 Daley, supported by the liberal wing of his party, sought the party chairmanship against alderman Clarence Wagner, the leader of the city Council. Though little is known about the actual proceedings, Daley and Wagner slugged it out behind closed doors in perhaps the most vicious internal party battle in the city's history. Unable to pick a winner the Democratic central committee recessed for two weeks, Wagner went on a vacation to the north woods, and unfortunately died in a fatal car crash. Following a short mourning period the central committee reconvened and Richard J. Daley was elected county chairman.

Like Cermak a generation earlier Daley moved quickly to consolidate party control. He engaged in no bloodletting against party foes, presented a united front in the party's successful 1954 general elections, and kept his own counsel about a possible 1955 mayoral run. Kennelly was an outsider in his own party, and though he would claim this aloofness was a sign of independence it more accurately reflected his indifference to politics and public affairs.

Daley's decision to challenge Kennelly in 1955 was a logical move for the chairman. Publicly he stated that the city lacked leadership and direction under Kennelly, but it was the internal forces and his own ambition that catapulted Daley to City Hall.

Governmentally and politically Chicago was a mess, and Daley was seen by many party leaders as the choice to challenge the bumbling Kennelly. Within his own heart Daley saw himself as the true successor to Cermak. Like the martyred mayor, Daley was also a ward committeeman and a believer in both efficient government and effective politics. It was in the 1955 Democratic mayoral primary and general election that all of Daley's wellsprings erupted, and when the dust settled Chicago would have its first real mayor in twenty-two years.

Much has been written about Daley's primary victory over Kennelly and a third candidate Benjamin Adamowski (a longtime legislative friend of Daley who also saw the political opportunity of a lifetime) but unfortunately it has been mainly one-sided. Indeed Kennelly received endorsements from (1) all four major daily newspapers (2) business and industrial interests, and (3) many good-government groups. And Daley was portrayed as a hack, a machine lackey, and painted in evil colors by many commentators throughout the campaign. However, what is seldom mentioned is that Senator Douglas openly and forcefully endorsed Daley, the Independent Voters of Illinois (a leading independent, liberal citywide organization) had its membership splinter on their endorsement with leading liberals like Leo Lerner supporting Daley, and even former governor and presidential candidate Adlai Stevenson lent his support to Daley.

Perhaps the best indicator of both the problems facing Chicago and its need for leadership came from the Independent Voters of Illinois (IVI) executive director James Cunningham. During the primary campaign Cunningham wrote a major article for *Commonweal* in which he lamented the fact that "Chicago has never produced a local administration able to solve the city's complex problems." Cunningham claimed that Chicagoans wanted simple things from local government like "regular garbage collection, safety on the streets, adequate schools . . . fair taxes, blight free neighborhoods, a place to park and peaceful race relations." At the end of his wish list for Chicago, Cunningham suggested "a few mayors have been successful in a couple of these areas, but there has never come forth a Fiorello LaGuardia to begin setting the whole house in order." Cunningham concluded his article with a frank and favorable assessment of candidate Daley by praising his progressive state legislative record and commenting that "some liberal leaders believe he [Daley] represents a healthy new force, able to clean things up from within the party." [11]

Daley parlayed the split in the liberal-independent political ranks, his strong inner-city ethnic organization support, and alliance with black leader William Dawson to defeat Kennelly in the primary and Republican Robert Merriam in the general election. On 20 April 1955 Richard J. Daley was sworn in as Chicago's fortieth mayor. In his little-remembered inaugural speech Mayor Daley told the city and its aldermen that government and politics as usual were about to end. "I have no intention of interfering," said Daley, "in any way with the functions of the city council. But as mayor of Chicago, it is my duty to provide leadership for those measures which are essential to the interest of all the people and if necessary to exercise the power of veto against any measures which would be harmful to the people."[12] Neither Kelly or Kennelly had vetoed a council ordinance during the past twenty-two years. Daley finished his address with a demand that the council adopt the recommendations of the blue-ribbon home-rule commission, especially the proposal to strip the council of executive functions (including budget making) and transfer administrative powers to the mayor's office. Clearly Mayor Richard J. Daley was taking charge of the city and bringing order to the city council.

IV. Richard J. Daley, the Modern Mayor

From 1955 to 1963 Richard J. Daley was the best mayor in Chicago's history. However, an examination of his governmental innovations, operations, and accomplishments cannot be undertaken until one first comes to grips with his mayoral politics—especially the well-documented "Daley machine." Without getting into a theoretical debate about either political machine formation or its morality it is important to see the political playing field from Daley's perspective. First, corruption in the city was open and rampant. Second, an economic development policy did not exist. Third, the city council was filled with individuals determined to continue running roughshod over mayoral programs and prerogatives. Fourth, Chicago's incredible governmental fragmentation had created lucrative safe havens for lazy and crooked politicians. Fifth, the city's demographics were changing and more poor people were piling into the city. Lastly, a whole generation of political lightweights had for years gotten fat on Cermak's original game plan. Thus, in order for Daley to get things done governmentally he had to crack the whip politically.

Somewhat forgotten in the rush of post-1963 psychobiographies and moralistic musings about Daley and machine politics was Edward Banfield's contemporary analysis of 1950s city politics that said, "The Chicago area from a purely formal standpoint can hardly be said to have a government at all . . . nothing can be done if anyone opposes."[13] To counter this stagnation Banfield argued, "the mayor of Chicago can pursue a course of action only so far as the formal decentralization is . . . overcome by informal centralization . . . [and that] the political party or machine [was] the most important mechanism that over[came] formal decentralization."[14]

Banfield's thesis made Daley more a broker than a boss. As political leader Daley traded influence and favors to gain authority and leverage needed to make governmental things happen. Given Chicago's political history, economic position, and the players involved Daley could not succeed by playing the role of a naive "goo goo." Chicago was not Madison or Minneapolis. Banfield even recognized the reality that if it were to survive "the machine must tolerate a certain amount of corruption at least until such time as competent precinct captains [could] be induced to work from other motives than personal gain."[15]

A generation later another political scientist, Paul Peterson, writing from a different perspective called Daley's machine behavior "institutionalized bargaining."[16] Peterson believed correctly that Daley's pragmatic ideology "did not always include mechanics for handling new forces [blacks, street demonstrations or antiwar protesters] in the traditional way."[17] Indeed the post-1963 Daley saw his well-organized ideas about how to run things come apart because the could not "pragmatically bargain" with civil rights activists or Vietnam protestors. Though he would maintain strength in the black community due to his unique alliance with Dawson, it would continually wither in the post-1963 period. To counter this vote falloff, Daley would restructure his organization, push it into the peripheral wards, make it more middle class and race conscious, and fight Democratic party reformers for control of the city and the party. (This intraparty action nearly made the GOP irrelevant in local affairs.) It was not always pretty politics or morally justifiable politics, but through it all an aging Daley fought his foes to maintain or regain an age and an era that existed in his first two mayoral terms. Back in April 1956 the New York *Times* columnist Cabell Phillips had suggested "there [was] a world of difference between the boss of old and the leader of today [and that] young Richard J. Daley, Chicago's new mayor, though brought up in the Kelly-Nash machine . . . was a reformer at heart rather than a boss."[18] Throughout all of his mayoral years Daley clung to these types of words and images written about him during the 1950s.

Even Daley's harshest critic had to admit that the new mayor's first term "would be four of the busiest, most frantic years City Hall had ever seen without people being indicted."[19] Daley's incredible governmental experience and knowledge allowed him to attack the status quo and incompetency everywhere. According to a Daley confident at the time "the city council hated Dick for the first two years . . . in part because not a single city employee was hired without the mayor's personal approval."[20] Daley took away the council finance committee's budget-making authority by turning this critical activity over to his comptroller's and budget director's offices. In less than two years Daley's executive budget process and personnel hiring practices smashed a generation of council superiority over the mayor. Even his eventual choice of council leader, Thomas Keane, was based on the latter's recognizing his number two status in the council to Daley. This eventual longtime Daley-Keane relationship was from the start not based on friendship but on professionalism, for the mayor recognized that "Keane was [governmentally] the smartest 'M.F.' in the valley and Keane knew who was in charge."[21]

Daley's administrative reorganization went well beyond taking over the budget. The new mayor stripped the council of its long-standing ability to issue city contracts and placed this critical function in the hands of the city purchasing agent. Other council losses were the issuance of politically lucrative driveway permits, routine personnel appointments, and the establishment of the

Chicago Department of Planning. The latter was crucial. Since the 1930s planning in the city had been a hodgepodge of red tape and special-interest payoffs that involved the city council in all aspects of the process. On 12 July 1956 the aldermen under severe pressure from the mayor passed the city's first comprehensive planning bill that gave the new planning commissioner cabinet rank and also placed him in charge of capital improvement projects.

Daley also had to deal with a business elite that was skeptical of his personal and political background. Ironically it was Daley's unabashed Chicago boosterism that allowed him to break down the socioeconomic "Wasp wall" in the city. Fairfax Cone, senior partner in the advertising firm of Foote, Cone and Belding and the epitome of the Protestant establishment that had so long stayed aloof from total city involvement, symbolized Daley's breakthrough to the business community. "Before mayor Daley came along," Cone told an interviewer, "Chicago was stalled. From 1929 to 1946 not a single major building went up."[22] Cone, anti-Dailey in the heated 1955 mayoral campaign, described the new mayor as "the most serious man I have ever met" and one who has quickly convinced business leaders that his one main desire is "to make Chicago a good place for children to grow up in." Men like Cone were surprised by Daley's governmental knowledge and businesslike attitude toward public service, but most were even more shocked by Daley's ability to transcend ethnic and religious stereotypes. In language more fitting to the 1850s than the 1950s Cone summed up Daley by stating "now lets be frank, people brought up as I was in a completely Protestant atmosphere can't help having a certain feeling about Catholics. You know they stick together . . . but Daley breaks both party and church lines."[23]

Daley's governmental moves were backed by his inflexible political muscle. Unlike Cermak he refused to resign from the party chairmanship after winning City Hall. Following his victory Democratic national committeeman and longtime Daley ally Jacob Arvey visited Daley urging him to resign and thus fulfill his pledge to the party's central committee. Daley in no uncertain terms told his friend Arvey no. The new mayor was not about to become a potential hostage to certain political leaders angered over Daley's surge to power. Daley needed the political clout to reinforce his governmental changes, and after watching and witnessing so much political intrigue throughout his adult life he was not about to break one of the cardinal political rules of Chicago politics which he had learned very well, "Don't make anyone who can unmake you."

To reinvigorate government and professionalize procedures, Daley brought into high levels of his administration his so-called whiz kids. Most were political outsiders, young and ambitious. Daley would protect these policy professionals from all political influencers except one—himself. Daley demanded loyalty to himself and what he represented—political and policy control. Not exactly textbook democracy, but no other major American city at the time created as much public policy enthusiasm as Chicago. Nowhere else was the path to modernizing governmental practices longer than in Chicago, and nowhere were there as many entrenched barriers to effective service delivery than in the often balkanized interward rivalries of Chicago.

Daley also recruited a few older professionals to take command of the whiz kids and take charge of critical governmental responsibilities—especially the budget. Alvin Weber had been a statistician and accountant for Cook County government since 1930. Daley had worked with Weber while serving as county clerk and after becoming mayor named Weber city budget director. A nononsense pro, Weber attacked Chicago's arcane financial situation by drafting a new performance budget and winning respect and awards from the Chicago Civic Federation and Municipal Finance Officers Association.

Carl Chatters was a nationally known municipal finance expert before coming to Chicago to work for the city and Mayor Daley. Prior to Chicago he served as executive director of the American Municipal Association, comptroller for the New York Port Authority, and executive director of the Municipal Finance Officers Association. One month after Daley's election he was named city comptroller of Chicago. To some, Chatters was a somewhat remarkable choice for a high post in Daley's cabinet since through the years he had written extensively attacking city political organizations that were "built on the dispensation of favors for cash or votes or power." Yet after two months as city comptroller Chatters could respond to an inquiring letter from Atlanta mayor William Hartsfield (who wanted the lowdown on Daley) and say. "He [Daley] has unlimited energy, an unusual sense of decency and great decisiveness."[24]

What impressed most of the older incoming professionals and young policy-oriented newcomers about Daley was his businesslike approach to his job. His day was planned, his suit always pressed, his desk always clear, and his demeanor almost always friendly but with a strong edge to get down to business. Tom Jacobs claims "Daley would have outshined any city manager on knowledge of government operations. He knew the business and mechanics of garbage collection to budget-making."[25] A Daley secretary claims she "never heard the mayor ever raise his voice to any of his staff . . . screaming was for the politicians."[26] Frank Sullivan, his one-time press aide, suggests that Daley intentionally walked briskly into a room with certainty and confidence to demonstrate both his power and his willingness to take command. And through it all he separated policy actions from political actions by shifting the latter talks over to a separate political office. As former mayor Jane Byrne relates from her days as an aide to Daley, "It never ceased to amaze me how he would cut off political conversation in room 507 City Hall [mayor's office] and then move everybody over to the Bismarck Hotel [party headquarters] and continue the conversation."[27]

While Daley trumpeted his policy accomplishments, it was in the political arena where he caught the most heat. Jack Sperling, one of the city's few Republican alderman left in the council after Daley's first two terms, conceded the mayor had done many good things but that Daley also "used the government as a means of furthering the Democratic party which he heads." To Daley taking command meant controlling the city and the party and though he worked hard to separate them in his own mind he knew political control insured policy action. As he grew older Daley's sense of balance would weaken, and as new threats challenged him he would unfortunately reverse the roles of politics and policy.

Daley won an easy reelection victory in 1959. His All Chicago Committee for Daley included the biggest guns in the city's business arsenal. His three cochairmen were William Patterson, president of United Air Lines; Clair Roddewig, president of the Association of Western Railroads; and Lawrence Kimpton, chancellor of the University of Chicago. At the same time he kept big labor and his multiracial political organization firmly in his corner. In spite of his political control Daley supporters praised their boss as a reformer and often during the campaign referred to a *Harper's* article of the previous year which said in part, "Daley has upset some cynical expectations. He has chosen able and honest department heads and he has been running the city council as effectively as he controlled his ward committeemen."[28]

Daley's mastery of the political process in Chicago can be seen in the final party rallies held before his 1959 mayoral reelection. At the Democratic gathering Daley spoke a mere three minutes. His remarks came near the end of an hour-long parade of Democratic dignitaries who praised his public record, his party leadership, and his commitment to family values. Former Governor Stevenson captured the moment when closing the rally he said, "I dare say that seldom if ever have we been served by such a combination of politician and idealist, who by the arts of one could achieve the objectives of the other."[29]

As for the GOP their amiable but sacrificial candidate Tim Sheehan was almost ignored by his allies at his own rally. Illinois Governor William Stratton, the state's leading Republican, concentrated his speech almost entirely on Daley as he referred to the mayor as "the mortal enemy of our party." And perhaps showing greater insight than he realized, he summed up Daley's nearly inseparable identification with the city stating, "He has perverted pride in Chicago to make it seem that any criticism of Daley is an aspersion of the city itself."[30] Few mayors in American history have ever during their first terms woven themselves deeper into the fabric of their city with as much ease or speed than Richard J. Daley.

Daley's second term saw scandal and race overshadow the ongoing innovations from his first term. Though he continued to revamp and professionalize government practices the incredible energy demonstrated in the late 1950s was replaced by more caution and intransigence in the early 1960s. Blockbuster building programs, sweeping transportation and industrial policy pronouncements, an expanding city that worked mentality, and his all-out effort to elect John Kennedy president in 1960 added luster to his governing and political prowess. Yet the man who gloried in describing himself a "liberal" and who saw politics as a vehicle for policy control saw forces moving against his seemingly perfect situation. By eliminating all potential rivals Daley stood alone to defend both his city and his party. The council had been beaten into submission, department heads ran the city with Daley's approval, and Daley's political control gave him a patronage pot of jobs to reward and punish. However, by 1963 Daley was forced to make a choice he did not want to make, and play in a game in which he did not want to participate. Race and racial politics would alter Daley's policy choices, political moves, and mayoral decisions for the rest of his life.

Unlike every other remaining big city, political boss Daley had been able to integrate his organization. Rapid racial change in the 1950s only slightly modified Daley's inner-city ward numbers on election night. By balancing racial interests and promoting black candidates, especially black Catholics, Daley was able to maintain unity within the party and the city. This was the politics he understood and where he could be the unbeatable master broker.

What is seldom discussed about Daley is that the original revolt in his tight organization did not come from city's blacks but rather from his own white ethnics. In 1963 Daley's old nemesis Ben Adamowski challenged his former friend once again for mayor. Adamowski appealed to the city's huge Polish community, but more importantly he painted Daley as a liberal, big taxer who was doing too much for the city's poor, especially the fast-growing black population. The tripwire issue was "open housing" which in Chicago meant simply racial integration.

During the campaign Daley tried to finesse the issue by refusing to answer reporters' questions directly on whether he was for or against open housing. Time and time again he told the press "everyone knows my record on adequate housing for all people," and when that response was deemed inadequate he merely shortened his answer to "you know my record." Adamowski, on the other hand was clear on the issue of open housing. "I am opposed to so-called open occupancy legislation," said Adamowski over and over again during the campaign, "because like patriotism it cannot be legislated. I would oppose it because it creates tense situations and can't be enforced." [31]

The 1963 mayoral returns revealed that Daley was the first victim of white voter backlash in Chicago. Unbelievably Daley lost the white ethnic wards by a three to two margin and beat Adamowski only because black voters overwhelmingly supported the mayor. In fact over one-half of Daley's mayoral vote came from black Chicagoans. Faced with a revolt in his core ranks and struggling with his own wellsprings that saw him becoming isolated from his natural constituency, Daley glumly turned conservative on race and other urban issues to preserve both his mayoralty and his political organization.

From 1963 to 1976 race would dominate city politics and Daley would be swept along by events. Though elected Chicago mayor three more times (1967,

1971 and 1975) Daley, after 1967, would face a liberal challenge from the GOP in 1971 and within his own party in 1975. The aging Daley, especially after the disastrous 1968 Democratic National Convention, would tighten his circle of advisors, no longer reach out to new people, and would become contemptuous of the very governmental professionals he had sought out in his first two terms. Most sadly he would become a caricature of the type of government he had abhorred most of his public life. Few today remember the administrative revolution he brought to Chicago government and how in his own way he modernized decayed and rusted public service delivery systems. Ironically, to most people Daley's legacy is more in tune with the government style he replaced then with the type of progressive changes he actually brought to Chicago.

II.

MICHAEL A. BILANDIC: THE LAST OF THE MACHINE REGULARS

Paul M. Green

Unlike most Chicago mayors, Michael Bilandic is most remembered for how he entered and exited office and not for what he accomplished as the city's chief executive. Under any circumstance, the mayor succeeding Richard J. Daley would have found the task of governing the city difficult. Daley was Chicago, and for many citizens the office of mayor died with him. Daley's genius of intertwining government and politics under his sole control left his political survivors the unenviable task of finding a replacement either to handle both tasks or two individuals who would share power. As Chicago's mayor and Cook County Democratic committee chairman, Daley had followed the old Chicago political axiom to his grave: "Don't make anyone who can unmake you." On both the governmental and political levels there was no logical heir apparent to fill the "Old Man's" shoes. However, there were many pols with itchy feet eager to assume power.

On 21 December 1976, one day after Daley's death, Michael Bilandic was one of four aldermen to meet in Daley's city hall office to discuss succession. The other three council members present were Edward Vrdolyak, Tenth Ward; Edward Burke, Fourteenth Ward; and Wilson Frost, Thirty-fourth Ward. These men, along with several key Daley aides—Tom Donovon, the city's patronage chief being the most important—would guide the mayoral replacement process. Vrdolyak, Burke, and Frost (the only black) were all powerful Democratic ward committeemen who combined personal ambition with hard-nosed political moxie in pushing themselves to the forefront of city politics. Yet it would be Bilandic who would receive the honor of replacing Daley and the responsibility of maintaining the Chicago political tradition.

Who was Michael Bilandic? A lifelong Chicago resident of Croatian descent,

Bilandic earned a law degree and settled in the Near Southwest Side, blue-collar Bridgeport community. What Eton's playing fields were to the English war effort, Bridgeport's streets and alleys were to Chicago's governmental leadership. Bridgeport was Daley's neighborhood, the backbone of "Hizzoner's" famous Eleventh Ward Democratic organization and the city's bungalow version of "God's Country." In 1969, Daley selected Bilandic to fill an Eleventh Ward aldermanic vacancy, thereby elevating the middle-aged bachelor attorney to instant political prominence. In the council, Bilandic, a shy and careful politician, demonstrated a sound mind and a willingness to work hard, and with Daley's approval assumed the powerful post of finance committee chairman in 1975. In his meteoric rise to political power, Bilandic was never tested politically or challenged in a fair political fight. In the end, this lack of political experience and acumen would cut short his mayoral career.

Potent political forces collided during the urgent and secret negotiations to determine Daley's successor. Frost, the council president pro tempore, asserted he was the city's acting mayor. Backing Frost's mayoral claim was the city's huge black community whose activist leaders, like the Reverend Jesse Jackson, overlooked Frost's nearly impeccable regular Democratic organization credentials. Also openly angling for the mayor's job was Northwest Side Polish alderman Roman C. Pucinski. Chicago's huge Polish community, like the black community, was frustrated at its inability to capture real power in the world's second largest Polish city. Also moving quickly into the mayoral sweepstakes was Ed Vrdolyak, a youngish, tough, and smart Southeast Side alderman. Vrdolyak—called by some the Che Guevara of Chicago politics for his leadership in orchestrating the so-called "Young Turk" aldermanic "Coffee Rebellion" against Daley's iron-fisted council control—was working the hardest and fastest to line up council support.

Beyond the constantly shifting political scenarios, two other factors complicated the mayoral selection process. First, who would fill Daley's other crucial position, party chairman? Most political players wanted to avoid a Daley-style replay where one man was both party boss and mayor. Cook County Board President George Dunne, a recognized old pro, was the leading contender for the chair—in part due to his pledge not to seek the mayoralty. Second, the city council could only select an interim mayor since state law required a special mayoral election within six months[1]—thereby raising the issue of whether the council's acting mayoral choice would be a candidate in the special election. Obviously, if the interim mayor became a special election candidate, he would have a huge advantage, for in effect he would be the incumbent mayor. Into this labyrinth of Chicago political intrigue entered Michael Bilandic, whose strengths and weaknesses combined to make him Daley's mayoral successor.

Not only was Bilandic from the right neighborhood and a Daley disciple, he was also not Irish (some ward committeemen and aldermen wanted to break the four-decade Irish hold on city hall), and he was admittedly not a very able politician. On Christmas Eve, two events cemented Bilandic's selection as interim mayor. First, he told his fellow aldermen and other city hall leaders that he would *not* be a special election mayoral candidate. Second, he and his old guard advisors (Daley's key administrative aides) worked out a council compromise with his potential rivals. Frost was made chairman of the crucial council finance committee (Bilandic's old job); Vrdolyak was made council president pro tempore (Frost's old job); and Burke retained his important police and fire committee chairmanship and was given credit for putting the deal together. As for Pucinski, he announced his special election mayoral candidacy relieved that the interim mayor, Bilandic, would not be his mayoral challenger.

The Bilandic selection as interim mayor was perhaps the old machine's "last hurrah." It was done easily and quickly, with style and old-fashioned crispness, and few Chicagoans raised any objections. The *Chicago Tribune* editorialized that Bilandic was "technically well qualified to serve as acting mayor."[2] The council vote on his selection was 45–2, with only the lakefront independent aldermen Dick Simpson and Martin Oberman questioning the process. Finally, the strength of the machine's muscle was illustrated in Frost's closing comments following the council vote. He told his black supporters who had wanted other black aldermen to nominate Frost without his consent, "Why should I be the one who takes the suicide job. I've been the mayor for eight days and it's been a difficult task. The only way I could sit in that chair is to have 25 council votes and I didn't have them."[3]

One week into his interim administration, Bilandic reversed his field with a move that would have made Chicago Bears halfback Gale Sayers proud.[4] The acting mayor suddenly announced he was open to a mayoral draft for the upcoming special election. Old-timers thought it was déjà vu as they recalled that a generation earlier Richard Daley had reneged on his promise that if he was elected party chairman, he would not seek the mayor's office. Bilandic's pledge, like Daley's promise, was quickly forgotten: an integral party of the Chicago political tradition is "never admit that you ever said never."

Bilandic's surprise announcement, coupled with Dunne's easy election as party chairman, conjured up thoughts that a new Kelly-Nash machine was on the horizon.[5] However, Chicago in 1977 was no longer an ethnic/Catholic dominated city. Its citizens and voters reflected the changing lifestyle and demographics of the previous two decades. The civil rights movement, antipatronage court decisions, the decline of political involvement, and simple white flight had eroded traditional organization power. The old pols had been lulled and misled by the ease of the Bilandic appointment. Their fight to retain power would never again go unchallenged.

Bilandic soon found himself in a mayoral primary campaign. An outraged Pucinski scoffed at the well-staged "draft Bilandic movement" that led to a party central committee endorsement. Pucinski rejected intense party organization pressure to be a team player as he told his largely Polish supporters that he was in the race to stay. The Northwest Side alderman unleashed a bitter barrage against Bilandic and the entire process as he boldly challenged the acting mayor to a series of campaign debates (Bilandic refused).

Soon another major mayoral contestant entered the arena. State Senator Harold Washington—like Bilandic, a middle-aged, bachelor lawyer—became the black community's new champion. Under-financed and under-organized and suffering from the effects of personal legal problems, Washington campaigned largely in South Side black wards. Late in the primary campaign, he told the congregation of Ebeneezer Missionary Baptist Church that "there is a sleeping giant in Chicago. And if this sleeping giant, the potential black vote, ever woke up, we'd control the city."[6] Washington's prophetic words would have to wait two more mayoral primary elections before they would become reality.

Bilandic campaigned leisurely for mayor. He ignored his primary opponents, was cool with the press, and refused to be drawn into any controversy. Bilandic wanted Chicagoans to recognize him as a competent administrator and a solid, if somewhat dull, chief executive. When a third primary opponent, the discredited former State's Attorney Edward Hanrahan, told voters to reject Bilandic because "there (was) no pepper in the city . . . (only) a b(i)land(ic) diet,"[7] the acting mayor responded by addressing a meeting of professional public administrators. Bilandic, like a suddenly crowned Prince of Wales, had to prove to all that he was a worthy successor to the departed king.

At first glance, the April Democratic special mayoral primary election was an easy Bilandic victory. He captured slightly over 50 percent of the vote, carried thirty-eight of fifty wards, and won by a comfortable 130,000 vote margin. Yet on closer scrutiny, the vote returns revealed severe cracks in the once omnipotent machine. Pucinski won seven North and Northwest Side wards while receiving over 32 percent of all the votes cast. Most interesting was the fact that his total citywide vote was almost identical to the final numbers of 1975 Daley mayoral primary challenger William Singer, a reform-minded, former alderman. Thus, in two consecutive elections, an independent lakefront liberal alderman (Singer) and a regular, northwest side ethnic alderman (Pucinski) were able to attract one-third of the Democratic primary vote. Singer and Pucinski had different power bases—thus revealing the potential for a meaningful future organization challenge by a candidate who could unite supporters from both rebel camps.

Also foreboding to organization Democrats were the Washington vote totals. The state senator won five middle-class, black Southside wards while capturing 10 percent of the citywide primary vote. His numbers, when combined with Pucinski's totals, exposed the future possibilities of a real mayoral horserace.

Three groups, Poles, blacks, and lakefront liberals, were upset with the machine, and they had demonstrated this displeasure at the most vital part of the Democratic organization's life-support system—the ballot box.

Bilandic accepted his primary triumph in a businesslike manner. He gave traditional thank-yous to the party workers, business and labor organizations, and Chicago's various ethnic communities. Though nominated under his own name, Bilandic paid special homage to the Daley family for their support as he expressed his hopes to follow in the footsteps of "hizzoner." According to Bilandic, "the standards of (city) leadership, in the past 21 years would be a great challenge for anyone." As mayor, Bilandic would never truly find an adequate method of freeing himself from Daley's memory while maintaining the proper respect for the man who was his chief patron. In almost every comparison between the two, Bilandic came out second best, thus leaving the impression in the minds of most Chicagoans that the new mayor was a stand-in and not a successor.

In the April general mayoral election, Bilandic wiped out his hapless Republican opponent, Forty-Eighth Ward alderman Dennis Block—the last GOP city council member remaining in Chicago.[8] The machine's main opponents were Democrats, not Republicans. Thus, Bilandic's easy victory was a low-turnout, low-interest affair.

What kind of mayor was Michael Bilandic? According to one public official, "Bilandic put the job of mayor on—like a comfortable bathrobe."[9]

Some years after he left office, Bilandic admitted that as mayor, "I didn't rearrange the administrative furniture."[10] In little over two years in city hall, Bilandic never overcame the notion that he was a caretaker and not the man in charge.

Administratively, Bilandic's term was not without its achievements. His good friend and eminent political scientist, the late Milton Rakove, summarized Bilandic's record as one "of accomplishment, continuity, and some forward motion."[11]

Bilandic maintained a balanced city budget, kept the city's bond rating high, and, until late in his term, reinforced the public service city tradition that "Chicago was the city that worked." Bilandic also maintained peace in the city council by using a strategy that relegated all controversies and fights behind closed doors. Years later, Bilandic refused to call the council during his term a rubber stamp. Rather he claimed it "had the opportunity to perform its tasks . . . but they did it backstage."[12]

Politically, Mayor Bilandic walked a tenuous narrow line. Unlike his predecessor, he could not consolidate his power in the county central committee. In simple terms, Bilandic was not a committeeman, and his future prospects of joining this elite, ruling party hierarchy were bleak. Blocking his political progress was the incumbent Eleventh Ward Democratic committeeman, State Senator Richard M. Daley—the eldest son of the "Mayor." Thus, Bilandic was forced to become a political broker who worked with (1) the traditional "old guard" (Daley's entrenched administrators and the party's warhorses like Alderman Vito Marzullo, County Commissioner Matthew Bieszczat, and Sewer Commissioner Edward Quigley); (2) the hungry "Young Turks" (led by Vrdolyak, Burke, Frost, and Chicago Park District Superintendent Edmund Kelly); and (3) the emerging dissidents (Poles, blacks, and lakefront liberals). It was to Bilandic's credit that in late 1978 few political commentators thought his upcoming 1979 reelection bid was in jeopardy.[13] Indeed, most praised Bilandic for keeping the city together and for successfully navigating the political tightrope that had appeared so slippery at the outset of his term.

How did Bilandic lose? Jane Byrne beat him. She combined an incredible streak of good luck with several costly Bilandic blunders to eke out a narrow 16,675 vote victory in the 1979 Democratic mayoral primary.

The overriding factors in Bilandic's defeat were threefold. First, Jane Byrne was his sole opponent. Second, she was able to unite the disenchanted behind her candidacy because, third, the now famous Chicago January snowstorms that closed down and covered the city also buried for the moment the divisive race issue. Unquestionably the blizzards eased and accelerated the movement of the divergent machine antagonists behind Byrne's candidacy, and she was also smart enough to take advantage of this heavenly gift and use it as entry into snow-clogged neighborhoods. Yet, with all her cleverness and the incumbent's ineptness, Bilandic still almost beat her one on one.

Bilandic's tale of woe following the record January snowstorms reveals a careful man finding himself suddenly in unknown territory. The city that supposedly worked stopped working. Garbage cluttered the alleys and remained uncollected, streets continued to be impassable, and parking spaces became prime real estate. Bilandic's public policy response to the snow was administratively inadequate and politically disastrous. His so-called snow removal plan, written by a former city-hall crony, turned out to be a joke. He alienated the black working class by having CTA (Chicago Transit Authority) commuter trains skip several large South and West Side stations; and perhaps most damaging, at the campaign's end Bilandic seemed out of control.

On St. Valentine's Day, two weeks before the primary, Bilandic spoke before a huge meeting of precinct captains at the downtown Bismarck Hotel. Under Daley, these traditional lunch gatherings were used both to fuel the organization's troops and to discourage the mayor's foes. Bilandic's performance on this occasion was described as bizarre and zany. Under a huge banner that read, "Keep Chicago Strong," the mayor for a time rattled off his accomplishments, then suddenly shifted gears and began answering critics of his snow-removal policy and mayoral performance. He compared the recent criticism of his administration to the crucifixion of Christ, the Nazi's persecution of the Jews, and the decline of democracy around the world. He concluded his rambling speech with a final astounding outburst: "In the early history of Christianity, you see a leader starting with twelve disciples. They crucified the leader and made martyrs of the others. It is our turn to be in the trenches and see if we are made of the same stuff as the early Christians, the persecuted Jews, the proud Poles, the Blacks and Latinos." [14]

Some in the audience listening to Bilandic giggled at his comments. Most were embarrassed. Few knew that the pressure of the campaign was not the only factor taking a toll on the mayor. A day before the meeting, Bilandic's elderly mother was rushed to the hospital; her death seemed imminent. His mother's illness, the unceasing criticism from the media, and the two-month battle against the unmeltable snow pushed Bilandic into reacting emotionally to his opponents.

Lost in the campaign's closing days was any mention of Bilandic's political strengths and election advantages. First, he had received strong newspaper endorsements from the Chicago *Tribune* and the Chicago *Sun-Times*. Both papers applauded the mayor's record and praised his efforts "to expand the city's economic base." [15] Second, nearly forgotten was the fact that his opponent, Jane Byrne, was an untested former city hall department head who had never held an elective office and whose philosophy and personality were virtually unknown to most Chicagoans. Finally, Bilandic had the Democratic organization; though admittedly it was not in the best condition, it still had not lost a contested mayoral primary since 1911. All of these Bilandic plus factors received scant public attention: the campaign ended as it began, centering on the snow and the mayor's snow-removal policy.

The blizzard of 1979 gave the three dissident voting groups in Chicago the leverage to beat the machine. Byrne won fourteen of the sixteen city's black wards, all seven independent lakefront wards, and several Northwest Side Polish wards. She won a total of twenty-nine city wards, leaving Bilandic the inner city and Southwest Side ethnic wards and a few remaining organization strongholds scattered throughout Chicago.

Bilandic's loss to the city's first woman mayor (for the record, Byrne did have to defeat another hapless Republican, Wallace Johnson, six weeks later to assume office) was a Chicago political revolution. The tradition of Democratic machine invincibility was broken. Four years later, another revolution would take place and a black would lead another successful battle against the once mighty machine.

In 1979, meteorological and political forces combined to oust Michael Bilandic. Chicago was receptive to these forces because it was undergoing dramatic demographic and lifestyle changes. Yet the question was and is still asked, "Could Bilandic have won even with the snow?"

The narrowness of his loss suggests an obvious yes answer to the above question. However, Bilandic's defeat was caused by more than just bad political luck and inclement weather. In retrospect, Bilandic was the wrong choice to carry on the policies of Cermak, Kelly, and Daley. Each of these organization legends reflected the city and the political machine they led. Bilandic did not. Wilson Frost or Cecil Partee (a long-time black organization stalwart and currently Chicago city treasurer) would have been much wiser choices than Bilandic. To be sure, their selection would have altered organization rule, but it would have been an evolutionary change that would have prevented the Byrne and Washington revolutions. Instead, the organization went with Bilandic, a shrewd and decent man, whose lasting legacy in the Chicago political tradition is that he was the last of the card-carrying machine regulars to serve as mayor.

12.

JANE M. BYRNE: TO THINK THE UNTHINKABLE AND DO THE UNDOABLE

Melvin G. Holli

When Jane M. Byrne won the Democratic Party's primary nomination for mayor in February 1979 in a stunning upset over incumbent mayor Michael Bilandic, a power surge of euphoria went through her. "I beat the whole god-damn Machine singlehanded," she uttered in an ecstatic moment.[1] It had been a David-and-Goliath contest pitting a diminutive, five-foot-three-inch, scrappy blonde against the political heavyweights and machine overlords who had not lost such a contest for half a century. The mighty had fallen, and most of Chicago cheered. The general election which followed in April was a cakewalk by comparison, for in one-party Chicago, winning the nomination in February has been tantamount to winning the general election in April. Jane Byrne handily beat her Republican opponent Wallace Johnson with the largest major-ity in Chicago's mayoral history, an astonishing 82 percent of the vote. Even Richard J. Daley in his peerless triumphs at the polls had never matched that percentage. From all appearances the new mayor had been put into office by a powerful, but evanescent mandate. This study of Jane Byrne is not intended to be a comprehensive story of every event of her four-year mayoral career, but rather a selective effort to separate the substance from the style and to take a hard look at the administration's record and the political meaning of Byrne's mayoralty.

Why the Machine?

Jane Byrne in her campaign caviled endlessly about the evils of machine poli-tics and about the "cabal of evil men" who ran the city. She seemed to promise a new deal in politics and a reshuffling of the structure of power, at least in the city council. Don Rose, a political liberal and her consultant, ran her low budget, high decibel campaign, and he produced more bang for the buck than most of his high-priced rivals.

Martin Oberman, a lakeshore liberal councilman and certified reformer, was showered with flattery by the nominee during the interregnum between the February primary and the April general elections. According to Oberman, Byrne attributed her primary victory partly to the work of reform independents such as Oberman, Dick Simpson, and Bill Singer. Northwestern University Professor Louis Masotti, at Jane Byrne's behest, assembled a topnotch, blue-ribbon panel which authored the "transition report"—a voluminous four-year blueprint for reform and change that promised to do for Chicago what the first five-year plan did for a ramshackle Russia. Seldom had Chicago reformers been so sanguine. Like the spring tulips, hope for reform blossomed forth that April from the cold unyielding soil of twenty-five years of machine domination. It seemed almost too good to be true. On the eve of her election, candidate Jane Byrne paid a visit to independent leader Martin Oberman and congratulated him and a small band of liberals, saying that the people wanted an open, honest system. Oberman busied himself with the delightful prospects of organizing a new reformed committee structure in the council.[2]

Unexpectedly, immediately after her election, the new mayor slowly began to shift into a state of studied and uncharacteristic mayoral inaction. Masotti was treated with benign neglect, and his phone calls went unanswered. He and his committee, all volunteers and *pro bono*, were left to wither on the vine. Even the distilled wisdom of their "transition report" went unread. Mayor Jane's masterful inaction let the machine politicians and the "evil cabal," led by councilmen Edward "Fast Eddie" Vrdolyak and Edward Burke, organize the council committees and select their chairman. Oberman and the reformers had been left out in the cold seemingly without influence. The hopes for political reform died at the starting gate.[3]

Why did Jane Byrne abandon reform at such a critical moment? Many of her detractors later wrote it off as simply another example of her fickleness, her "battiness," or her biology (it's a woman's prerogative to change her mind). Former mayoral aide Paul McGrath and the late Professor Milton Rakove argued on rational grounds that Mayor Byrne had nowhere else to turn. The reformers lacked the numbers and power to govern the council effectively, and no other public constituency was available in sufficient numbers and with passion enough to follow the mayor and turn the council into a popular assembly goaded to a reform agenda by a raging mob at its doors. The only plausible alternative was the machine regulars led by the "evil cabal." Thus Jane Byrne made a pragmatic compromise with Chicago's political reality. Seeing it somewhat differently, city budget director Donald Haider attributed Byrne's political about-face and her abandonment of her reformist ideas to the progressive deterioration of the city's financial situation. The period of high hopes and reform, according to Haider, lasted until about September 1979. When the financial crisis worsened, Byrne turned to the "evil cabal," the Old Guard, to tap their financial savvy and political potency. As Haider remembered it: "The Vrdolyaks and Burkes and others from the old regime returned. Suddenly the ins were out and the outs were in." About a year after the rapprochement with the machine, Mayor Byrne explained her actions or lack thereof in this manner: "I will have to work with these people. If I don't, nothing will move in the city council."[4]

In a more involved explanation of that turning point, Byrne explained in a 1986 interview that her single-handed toppling of the machine's mayor had sent seismic shock through the entire business-banking-labor nexus of city hall politics. Her aide, Don Rose, had warned her that her victory had threatened long-standing agreements, understandings, and ways of doing business dating to the Daley era. Unpredictability and destabilization are the nemesis of the banking and business world. Apparently, the newly elected mayor met with representatives of the banking community to calm their fears and may have sent similar assurances to Loop business interests and big labor. At this critical juncture, according to Byrne, an unrelated event occurred. Representatives of Richard M. Daley rudely intruded and began pushing Byrne to appoint a rival slate of Daley loyalists into key chairmanships (with the implied understanding that Daley junior was running the show). Evidently annoyed at Daley's cheekiness and aware of the weakness of the Byrne-backed group, she permitted the "evil cabal" to appoint the committees and chairman. Presumably this act symbolized that something less than radical reform was in the wings and that the machine Humpty Dumpty had been put back together again. Stability and predictability had been restored to their time-honored and rightful places in Chicago politics.[5]

When Jane Byrne assumed office in 1979, the second destructive wave of OPEC-driven inflation was lashing at the nation's vitals with 15 to 20 percent interest rates. Cities on the high-risk list had difficulty in selling their bonds, sometimes absorbing massive losses through deep discounts, and some bankers were even looking askance at short-term tax anticipation warrants which all cities needed to tide them over until taxes were paid. The doubling of interest rates meant that a massive transfer of money that formerly might have gone for raises to city workers would now be needed to borrow money from the bank. No or slow growth and the loss of industrial jobs and plants, a rustbelt-wide phenomenon, was felt most acutely at the time and aggravated Chicago's ability to pay its bills.

These were the grim fiscal realities that the vibrant new mayor faced during her first year in office. Unfortunately for Byrne, inflation as an objective measure of the consumer price index and as a built-in and emotional expectation would peak in 1980, calling forth escalating demands from the municipal unions and a time of troubles for the mayor.

In December 1979, Byrne became the first mayor to challenge the demands of the transit union. She entered into negotiations with the city's transit union hoping to pare back the expensive cost of living adjustments, high wage settlements, and overgenerous benefits package which neither the system nor the city could afford any longer. She also hoped to introduce other efficiencies which would moderate future fare increases and direct subsidies which the system regularly absorbed. The union's response was a threat to strike during the peak of the downtown and Loop Christmas shopping season. When Byrne refused to back down and announced a contingency plan which she said would keep the trains and buses running, the union struck. Byrne had no contingency backup plan to keep shoppers and workers moving into the Loop, and the downtown business community protested vehemently, placing fierce pressures on both the administration and the union to settle. The union returned to work. Some observers blamed the mayor and called her a union buster, and her rhetorical behavior lent some credence to that line of reasoning. Yet behind the smoke and fury lay the inescapable fact that Chicago simply could not afford the handshake giveaways to labor of former days.[6]

A second labor problem followed in January 1980 when the teachers' union went out on strike to recapture the jobs it had bargained away in the fall 1979 school talks. The school crisis which emerged in November 1979 had revealed that the board of education had illegally invaded capital funds to meet operating expenses and was nearing the end of its illicit resources. An audit showed that the board had misspent $47 million in school bond proceeds. The cumulative education deficit at the end of 1979 was $101 million. Moody's bond rating service dropped the Chicago schools from Municipal Investment Grade 2 to an unmarketable MIG 4, and the First National would no longer buy its bonds. School superintendent Joseph Hannon resigned in the middle of the revelations.

The city, with its own newly discovered deficit of $102 million, was drowning in its own red ink and was in no position to rescue the schools with a straight bailout. An agreement had to be worked out with the city putting in $50 million and the state putting in $50 million to meet the January payrolls and back pay for the teachers. The city then committed itself to interim financing until a new School Finance Authority—set up by the state and with powers over the budget—could straighten out the mess and sell $500 million in new bond issues. The board and the union also agreed to trim $60 million, to eliminate more than a thousand jobs from the budget, and to grant the Finance Authority veto power over the budget. In January, the teachers' union reneged on the spending cuts and job trimming and struck for two weeks, forcing the board to accept higher costs and to cut the losses out of the succeeding year's budget. Mayor Byrne took a large role in the final settlement; although it diminished the city's autonomy over its school and the mayor's influence over education matters, it did rescue the system from near-bankruptcy. And without the mayor's backing, the bailout could not have been achieved.[7]

The administration was on a strike-a-month schedule. A few weeks later on 14 February, Chicago firefighters went out on strike in what became an incredibly messy and nasty affair. The firemen, who had been promised union contracts by candidate Byrne, struck to force the issue. Since taking the oath of office, Mayor Byrne had apparently changed her mind on the issue of union contracts for public employees, but had never said so publicly. The editor of the Chicago *Tribune* upbraided her for this apparent duplicity and told her to come clean. The firefighters had chosen the dead of winter and the peak of the heating season when citizens are most likely to need fire protection. The union also brought in an "outside agitator" to lay out strategy and to call the tactics for the local union chief, who took a consistently belligerent, bellicose, and public-be-damned attitude on the nightly television news. The firemen won surprisingly little sympathy from the public for they were hardly charity cases, earning $21,000 for a 91-day year of 24-hour shifts. Many held second jobs, managed small businesses, and doubled their city income. Aggravating the issue in what appeared to be a bargaining ploy to make the union back down, the mayor promised as she had in the transit strike, that the firehalls would be fully staffed and fire protection would be available as usual in the city. Meanwhile nasty exchanges continued for several days between the mayor and the union. Some city hall aides openly suggested that some striking firemen were actually sabotaging fire protection and perhaps even engaging in arson. By the end of the winter, public opinion switched massively against the firefighters and over to the mayor, forcing the firemen to capitulate and return to work, but without a face-saving contract. The strike had taken a heavy toll on the close relationship that had long existed between the firemen and city hall.[8]

Although Byrne had beaten one of the toughest municipal unions in the city, she both then and later lamented that the strike was one of her biggest errors. Even though the mayor later agreed to a contract, the strike caused an irreparable tear in the municipal service fabric and would cost her future political support in one of the city's more politically active service units. Byrne later called it a "perceptual error," saying that she had intended to grant them a union contract all along.[9] It is difficult to follow the evidence trail of this incident and concur with that view. Jane Byrne's postmayoral remarks seem to be an effort to put the best face possible on the strike.

Yet in the long run her three major public employee strikes may have been necessary and possibly even unavoidable. The urban gravy train which had richly rewarded public employees such as transit workers and skilled craftsmen in the inflation ridden 1960s and 1970s had come to a halt in the austere, cash-short, and deflation-prone 1980s. Unions accustomed to riding the inflation escalator upward were not prepared psychologically and emotionally to adjust to the tax-conscious fiscal crunch of the 1980s. To her credit Jane Byrne faced this new reality. With few prospects for new transit money or to pay firefighters, she took two strikes. A third strike by the Chicago teachers' union, although a governmental unit less directly under her control was resolved only through her bargaining powers with the state government. To her discredit, Byrne handled all three strikes—transit, teachers, and firemen—in what to the public seemed to be a vacillating, then vindictive, and sometimes mean and small-minded manner. In all three affairs newsmen and the unions unflatteringly referred to her as "Attila the Hen" or "Calamity Jane" and a person who "shot from the lip." Her bombastic rhetoric and her oversell on preparedness to take on the strikes, tarnished and diminished somewhat the magnitude of her victory over the firefighters union.

In a larger sense and behind the smokescreen of rhetoric and verbal pyrotechnics, Byrne had shown a sense of fiscal responsibility in facing down powerful municipal unions and interest groups that no previous administration in modern times in Chicago had dared take on. Thereafter municipal unions and employee groups became more attentive to the burdens that their demands placed on taxpayers and more amenable to compromises, such as the transit workers agreements to slim down their fat cost-of-living adjustments and permit parttime drivers and other efficiencies. Politically Mayor Byrne had embarked on a high risk strategy in taking on three powerful employee groups and lost political support in all three. Whether the tradeoff of support in the public opinion polls was worth the loss of these interest groups would remain to be seen.

Budget and Fiscal Matters

On the fiscal front the mayor showed herself equally ready to bloody her lance. Fiscal policy is ultimately the lifeblood of any administration. Those dull numbers, that blizzard of figures that festoon the account books and ledgers, may numb the mind and glaze over the vision and certainly do lack political sex appeal. Yet ultimately they have the awesome power to topple the most popular mayoral regimes, as the political demise of New York City's John Lindsay so aptly illustrates, or to evoke huzzahs of praise as did Mayor Richard Daley's solid management in the mid-1970s when urban bankruptcies were threatening other big cities.

Candidate Byrne, during the twilight of Michael Bilandic's caretaker term (1976–79) and during her campaign for the Democratic nomination for mayor had been hinting that "hidden deficits," creative bookkeeping, and other irregularities were damaging the city's fiscal health. On 16 April 1979, only a few days after she took office, the city comptroller notified her that the city would have a cash storage of $64 million by the end of May. Instead of calling the chairman of the First National Bank of Chicago and the president of the Continental Illinois Bank, which had been standard operating procedure in the past, and quietly arranging to rollover the debt with another loan, Mayor Byrne called a press conference and blasted her spendthrift predecessors, and then went to the banks for loans.

Byrne brought in as budget director Donald H. Haider, a Northwestern University professor, who had spent the previous year monitoring the finances of near-bankrupt New York City and Cleveland. Haider was to work out a plan to liquidate whatever deficits a probing audit would reveal. An examination of the city's books uncovered a deficit of $102 million and the fact that previous administrations had dipped into specially marked state and federal funds and "trust and agency accounts" earmarked for special uses, such as neighborhood development, and had used such funds to pay ordinary city expenses. Mayors Daley and Bilandic had delayed payments to vendors, and as early as 1972 Daley began to use the trust and agency accounts as an "all purpose emergency fund," as well as using capital funds, such as bond proceeds, to meet ordinary expenses. Bilandic continued these practices and Chicago's peculiar bookkeeping methods kept the deficits from being noticed. Chicago meanwhile had a high bond rating.[10]

Mayor Byrne publicly damned the "political cowardice" of past administrations and vowed that as long as she was mayor, the city would not waste the "public money like a profligate welfare queen." She blistered her predecessors, charging that "good politics and good economics were at war in City Hall" and that the "city that worked was working largely—and surreptitiously—on next year's money, juggled books, and taxes on the next generation." These revelations caused Chicago's bond ratings to drop twice. Byrne put in an austerity budget for 1980 with a mere 1 percent spending increase, eliminated 1,500 jobs in city hall, raised taxes by $150 million, restructured $180 million in short-term debt, and vowed to run a tight ship and exert an iron grip on the city's purse strings. Meanwhile a falling out between the mayor and her budget director caused Donald Haider to quit, and the mayor brutalized him, publicly blaming him for an error that raised an extra $29 million in taxes. Byrne and her new budget director decided to keep the extra $29 million which persuaded Moody's bond rating service then to raise Chicago's rating. The higher ratings not only helped the city through its cash crises, but also enabled the School Finance Authority to now sell its bonds as well. Former budget director Donald Haider later claimed that Mayor Byrne had overdramatized the original crisis, that the actual inherited deficit was not more than $50 million, and furthermore that it could have been handled with less fanfare through some internal economies and modest tax increases.[11]

Whatever the case may be, Mayor Byrne did follow through with her promised fiscal responsibility and balanced the budget not only for 1980, but also for 1981, 1982, and finished up in 1983 with a small deficit (or surplus, depending on how one interprets the numbers.) Mayor Byrne's 1983 budget, although initiated by her, would be carried out by Harold Washington who assumed office in April of that year. Washington, in his campaign, in what now has become standard political rhetoric, lashed out at Byrne for reckless spending, giving away the store, and handing him a debt-ridden city with deficits that Washington feared would range into the high millions. The later budget figures showed only a $15 million deficit for 1983. And according to Byrne advisors, if Washington would have followed through on the city sale of cable franchises and parking garages as intended in the 1983 budget, there would have been a surplus of about $12 million.

Achievements

The measure of accomplishment for any mayoral administration is somewhat difficult to gauge, partly because no administration is completed within its formal office holding period and partly because of hostile successor administration. Since Jane Byrne's reign (1979–83) was an administration of motion and movement, perhaps her record should be looked at in motion or as it unfolded. At the end of her first year in 1980, when the honeymoon period had just drawn to a close, some observers perceived solid achievements. A Chicago *Tribune* review in June 1980, although deploring Byrne's "revolving door" policy of much hiring and firing of top staff, nonetheless cited as her "record of achievement": (1) trying to balance the budget, (2) increasing minority representation in government, (3) cracking down on worker inefficiency, and (4) making her administration more accountable to the public. The mayor had fired or laid off hundreds of employees (mostly from streets and sanitation) where, according to the "transition team" report, "bloated" street cleaning and pothole-patching crews operated without effective supervision. "Other reform areas," according to this first year report card included: changing the school board membership and giving minority representatives a majority voice, shaking up the Chicago Transit Authority leadership and appointing black Eugene Barnes as chairman, consolidating various categories of building inspectors, reorganizing the department of health with a new commissioner, an Hispanic, Dr. Hugo Muriel, and expanding special entertainment events including Chicagofest. The assessment concluded with "for better or worse, Mrs. Byrne has been more available to the media and the public than her predecessors."[13]

Jane Byrne's second year report card issued at the midpoint of her mayoralty was considerably less glowing. According to *Tribune* writer Robert Davis, friends and foes alternately described her administration as "creative, chaotic, dramatic, devastating, exciting, excrutiating . . . historic," although some claimed it was "hysteric." Mayor Byrne listed as her main accomplishments the restoration of financial and fiscal integrity to the city government. Her school rescue package, new taxes, and straightening of city bookkeeping had rescued the city's slumping bond ratings. She had also raised some $300 million in new taxes and fees and helped bring to the Chicago budget "user fee" real-ism. The mayor also pointed to her first year and the continuing austerity program that lopped off hundreds of superfluous workers from the city payroll. She announced, in 1981, plans to professionalize the upper levels of the bureaucracy by raising salaries to entice quality administrators, new initiatives for her "North Loop project," a massive O'Hare International Airport renovation and building program, and a new entertainment-business complex at Navy Pier. In closing, Davis lamented in his article that with few exceptions her "own staff of advisors is undistinguished at best and woefully inadequate at worst." Furthermore her substantive projects had been obscured by her "image as a mind-changing, impulse-directed chief administrator." Nevertheless the turmoil in the mayor's office had been much less in the preceeding few months and, as Davis saw it, "city government has quieted down." [14]

On the political side many negatives had accumulated. As *Tribune* reporter David Axelrod saw it, the administration was plagued with "errors in style— imprudent remarks and reversals, ill-conceived appointments, open battling within the administration, and heavy-handed attempts to derail her opponents or punish the news media." These had "obscured the mayor's substantive accomplishments." In 1979 she won kudos for appointing a majority black and minority school board and in 1980 incurred the wrath of the black community for dumping two blacks in favor of two white opponents of busing. Byrne's former campaign aide, Don Rose averred: "It's absolutely amazing how she managed in such a short time to antagonize both the black and whites." "There's just no way around the fact that the first two years have been a political disaster," added Rose who had masterminded her election. [15]

Part of the "battiness" and three-ring circus atmosphere derived from first husband Jay McMullen whom the press referred to as the "Rasputin in a turtleneck" and who needlessly inflamed relations with the press. He once banished a *Tribune* representative from the city press room and threatened a group of reporters that he would "bloody their noses." He referred to unfavorable coverage of his wife's administration as "more skunk juice from the Chicago *Tribune*." [16]

Moving on to Mayor Byrne's last year in office, 1983, Harry Golden of the *Sun-Times* summed up her record as a grand mix of public works, executive shakeups, civic celebrations, spats with the press, and some solid achievements. She started a $1 billion expansion project at O'Hare Airport, completed a new rapid transit system to the airport, positioned the city to consider bids for a new hotel-office complex in the North Loop, worked a redevelopment project for Navy Pier into the planning stages, was repairing the city's infrastructure of sewers and water mains at 15 to 20 miles per year, laid out plans for a new Southwest Side rapid transit system, reorganized the school board and set its finances on a firmer footing, installed a new personnel code that ended "temporary employment" of patronage works in civil service but exempted some 10,500 less skilled jobs from merit tests, reorganized the Chicago Housing Authority, took steps to convert Goldblatt's deserted downtown department store into a new public library, raised city revenues of some $400 million in new taxes and fees annually; rolled back real estate taxes by $30 million and turned in a balanced budget for each year of her administration (with the possible exception of 1983). To that list might be added a projected World's Fair for 1992.[17]

Political Socialization

Yet Jane Byrne's achievements were all but blurred and nearly erased by her peculiar mayoral style. Part of the answer to the enigma of Jane Byrne's mayoral career is to be found in her ability to think the unthinkable and to do the undoable. To understand this ability takes us to an odyssey of her political socialization. She was not the daughter of a working-class stiff or an aspiring precinct captain from the bungalow belt, but a debutante from a wealthy lace-curtain family from the Far Northwest Side. Unlike those who have carefully picked their way through the local political minefields, cajoled and dodged irate voters for years, spent most of their political lives as supplicants to some ward lord or boss, Jane Byrne had come through St. Scholastica, Barat College, J. F. Kennedy's football box at the Army Navy game,[18] and within less time than the normal politician takes to make it from ward heeler to precinct captain, landed an administrative appointment in the Daley family and a cochairmanship of the Cook County Democratic Committee. Starting more than two-thirds of the way up may not be as comforting as starting at the top, but it spares one those years of ankle busting, doorbell ringing, attending endless ward parties and minor events, and shelling out a goodly portion of a small pay each year to support your patron. It also spares the soul from that demeaning grovelling that political underlings put up with for most of their young working lives—unrecognized, unsung heroes whose most heroic acts are getting aging widows and disgruntled housewives to vote. None of the hurts, admonishments, and limitations that the lowly live through and which ultimately shape their adult character into what has become the quintessential Chicago politician—cautious, deferential to his political and economic betters (at least on the surface)—none of that long conditioning, soul-searing discipline, and humiliation was part of Jane Byrne's heritage. Jane Byrne did not fit the mold. She had sprung, as it were, in full political armament from the brow of Zeus (read Daley). She even looked different. She was physically small and shapely and had "gorgeous legs" (according to Jay McMullen), whereas most Chicago politicians looked like overstuffed armchairs or furniture movers.

Jane Byrne was *sui generis* in Chicago's recent mayoral history. She had no parallel in the half century following the Democratic machine's accession to power with Anton Cermak in 1933. Jane Byrne was *sui generis* because she could think the unthinkable (gambling casinos and world-class stock-car racing in the streets or rescuing an abandoned department store for a public library) and do the undoable (moving into crime-infested Cabrini-Green or taking on the toughest municipal unions such as the firefighters to restore fiscal soundness.)[19] She had not been subjected to the socializing of regular Chicago Democratic politicians. Unorthodox and not brought up with the table manners and courting rituals of Democratic machine politics, she was refreshingly free not only of its restraints and its decorum, but also of its limitations. She was in some ways a political free spirit, a burning ember waiting to alight on the dry prairie grass, a stormy Robespierre ready to chop off heads, encouraged by her husband Jay McMullen.

In the end she obscured many of her achievements by giving way to that powerful impulse that Chicago politics ultimately is at its heart—street theater. Sometimes farce, sometimes high drama, and occasionally mere comic opera, Jane Byrne lightened the civic mood. She clearly had the best act in town. Few politicians in Chicago's history could match Byrne for her zaniness, madcap, and daring acts that were to mar the solid and substantive acts of her administration. Unfortunately for her, too many Chicagoans mistook her style for her substance.

13.

HAROLD WASHINGTON: THE ENIGMA OF THE BLACK POLITICAL TRADITION

William J. Grimshaw

Mayor Harold Washington is described in a biographical sketch by Robert McClory as "a remarkable man of paradoxes and enigmas."[1] McClory, a former reporter for the Chicago *Defender,* the principal black newspaper, certainly knows his way around black political circles; but he admits that Washington baffles him. Says McClory: "At times he seems as wise as a serpent and at others as simple as a dove."[2] I will argue that the paradoxical imagery of the serpent and the dove provides illuminating insight into the enigmatic Harold Washington and the equally perplexing black political tradition.

Since the Chicago Democratic machine's inception over a half century ago, blacks have been torn between a cultural antipathy to the machine's style of politics and a devastating array of social and economic circumstances which drive blacks into supporting the machine. The paradox is not well understood by students of Chicago's politics because no other ethnic group in the city's modern history has experienced the conflict to the extent blacks have. To speak of the black political tradition, then, is to speak of a unique political tradition in the city's recent history. It is a complex tradition to comprehend because it is at odds with itself; cultural values pull blacks in one direction while social and economic needs push them in an opposing direction. The tradition also is difficult to understand because it is so at odds with the political machine tradition which has so thoroughly dominated Chicago's politics until just recently.

Harold Washington personifies the torn black political tradition. His roots are deeply embedded in an intensely personal way in the torn tradition. Washington's own father, Roy, for many years had to manage the paradoxical roles of serving his community as a Protestant minister while serving the Democratic machine as one of its ward leaders, combining, as it were, the roles of the serpent and the dove.

179

The personal heritage is profoundly important because the bond between Washington and his father was extraordinarily warm and firm. The mayor had a relationship with his father that many fathers dream of but few achieve. He has described his father as his "one and only hero in life," as "a real man, a good man," and "my role model."[3] Thus, the path Washington has followed in his political career is essentially the footsteps his father laid down years ago in the Third Ward: to be a good man while working in the serpentine world of Chicago's politics.

At the cultural core of the torn black political tradition is the elemental fact that black politics is deeply rooted in the teachings of the church. During a long and arduous history of economic, social, and political segregation and discrimination, the one critical institution to which blacks had access was the church. The church was the sanctuary; it nurtured, and it instructed. The instruction included an extraordinary set of premises for political action. An elementary aspect of the creed is that action ought to be based on principle. Another basic aspect is the belief in universal brotherhood. These principles stand in the sharpest opposition to the machine tradition of politics. The machine tradition dictates that action ought to be taken on the basis of expediency. This requires a calculation of self-interest and consequences, instead of adherence to principle and leaving the outcome in ethereal hands. The machine is no less fundamentally committed to inequality. Those who support the machine are rewarded, while those who oppose it are punished.

It is a simple matter to see how the black community's social isolation and poverty figure in the machine's success. Machine politics has been described as a "system of organized bribery,"[4] an exchange of benefits for votes, and in communities of high need and low resources, the machine finds the largest number of takers. Yet for blacks, schooled politically by the church, machine politics presents a dilemma; cultural antipathy wrestles with economic necessity for control.

A compelling case can be made for the torn black political tradition by examining black political behavior over the past fifty years, beginning with the creation of the machine in 1931 and culminating in Mayor Washington's election in 1983. The evidence will be presented in terms of four distinctive stages of black political behavior.

Stage one is entitled Transformation and Contradiction, which encompasses the first twenty years of the political machine's hegemony, from 1931 through 1954. The second stage is called Exodus and Domination; it runs from 1955 through 1965, spanning the first decade of Daley's mayoralty. Stage three covers the second decade of Daley's reign and the succeeding mayoralties of Michael Bilandic and Jane Byrne; this stage runs from 1966 through 1982 and is entitled Disillusion and Revolt. The final stage, Victory and Resolution, covers the Washington mayoralty.

Some commentary on Harold Washington's progression and development as

a politician will be woven into the four sections of the analysis. T
to identify certain critical junctures which have served to shape
character and political career.

Two basic conclusions emerge from the analysis. First, the torn black political tradition has existed since the Democratic machine's inception, and while
the shape of the paradox changed over the years, the content remained un-
changed until the 1983 mayoral election. Thus, Washington's election represents a watershed in the black political tradition. It resolved the paradoxical
character of black political behavior. For the first time, blacks stood in unified
opposition to the political machine. The compelling question, of course, is
whether the novel resolution can hold. In the balance swings the black political
tradition: the new against the old.

Transformation and Contradiction

The conventional interpretation of why low-income voters readily support
political machines rests upon a rational economic theory of motivation.[5] Because of their high degree of material need and social disorganization, the poor
willingly give their votes to the machine in exchange for a combination of material and affectual benefits. This is the well-known favors-for-votes explanation which is said to account for the machine's high level of success in poor
communities.

The ascendancy of the Democratic party during the Great Depression offers
a valuable test of the conventional interpretation. President Franklin Roosevelt's Democratic New Deal established the modern welfare state, and it took
the Republican party twenty years to regain the presidency. In Chicago, the
Democratic machine rode Roosevelt's long coattails to victory and thoroughly
eliminated the Republican party as a factor in the city's politics. Accordingly,
we would expect to find a prompt and substantial shift of black voters in Chicago to the ascendant Democratic party.

Initially, the predicted shift occurred. After nearly a decade of Democratic
dominance, Chicago's black wards cast 57 percent of their ballots for Democratic Mayor Edward Kelly in 1939, and President Roosevelt secured 53 percent of the black vote in 1940.[6] This constitutes a decisive shift inasmuch as
Chicago's black voters had been overwhelmingly favorable to the Republican
party just a decade earlier.

At this point, however, a wholly unanticipated development occurred. The
black Democratic tide continued to rise at the national level. But at the local
level, black support for the Democratic machine began to recede.

Mayor Kelly's black vote fell from 57 to 53 percent in 1943. His successor,
the reform-minded Martin Kennelly, who received the largest popular vote of
any mayoral candidate in the city's history, barely survived in the black wards.
In both 1947 and 1951, Kennelly's black vote amounted to less than 51 per-

cent. No less remarkable, the Republicans regained control over one of the two black wards. In 1943 the aged and once all-powerful Oscar DePriest was elected alderman of the Third Ward, and he was succeeded by Archibald Carey, a reform-oriented minister, who held the post for the Republicans until the great Democratic landslide of 1955 swept him under. Thus, even though the Democratic machine had thoroughly controlled the city's politics for two decades, the black vote was still altogether up for grabs.

What makes the situation even more perplexing is that at the national level the black Democratic vote continued to soar. Roosevelt's black vote reached 64 percent in 1944, and his successors did even better. Harry Truman picked up just over 70 percent of the vote in Chicago's black wards in 1948, and Adlai Stevenson raised the black Democratic margin to a record 75 percent four years later. Thus, Chicago's black voters were drawing a compelling distinction between the national Democratic party's New Deal and what many black voters perceived as the local Democratic machine's "raw deal."

Figure 13.1 capsulizes the black Democratic transformation and indicates the

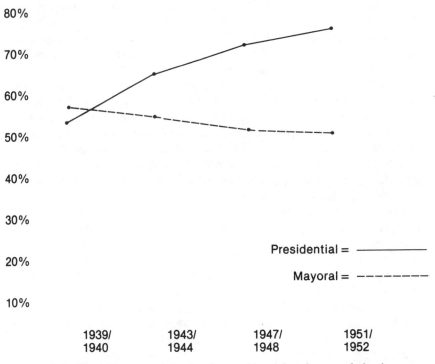

Figure 13.1. Black Democratic voting in presidential and mayoral elections, Chicago, 1939–1952

magnitude of the contradiction between national and local voting in the black wards during this period.

The massive electoral contradiction represents a strong piece of evidence for the existence of a torn black political tradition. Despite the Democratic machine's clear dominance and the black community's dire poverty, a substantial and rising proportion of the black electorate was unwilling to support the machine. There was a powerful countervailing force afoot in the black wards, which was sufficiently strong to overcome the Democratic machine's material inducements.

The core of the countervailing force is the cultural antipathy to the machine's style of politics.[7] The cultural antipathy was reinforced by the machine's racism. The machine honored the minor political quid pro quo in dealing with black voters, exchanging small favors for votes. But the machine did very little to ameliorate the racial segregation and discrimination which devastated the black community. Quite the contrary. The machine played a leading role in confining blacks to a second-class level of citizenship.

Ironically, the key to understanding the black rejection of the machine during this period is the machine's commitment to segregated housing. Over 70 percent of the black population was confined to a small, narrow, black belt, a patently illegal situation that nevertheless was enforced by the machine-controlled local courts.[8] The confinement created a community unlike any other in the city because it required the middle class to live among the poor, and this gave the generally poor black wards a decisive political advantage over their low-income white counterparts.

The unique social composition and structure of the black wards produced the unique political behavior. The middle class, being less dependent upon the machine's material inducements, was able to provide the poor with alternative political goals and leadership, and it possessed the wherewithal to construct organizations to counter the machine's ward organizations. Thus, the black wards, critically leavened by a politically active middle class, fought the powerful Democratic machine to a standoff.

Washington's Political Baptism

Harold Washington's first major campaign was not his own, but his father Roy's Third Ward aldermanic campaign in 1947.[9] Even by Chicago standards, it was an extraordinary political baptism for the twenty-five-year-old son. The campaign was befouled by layers of duplicity, eerily presaging Washington's mayoral campaign against Bernard Epton years later.

Roy Washington secured the nomination of the Third Ward Democratic organization; but the committeeman, Edward "Mike" Sneed, double-crossed Washington by quietly throwing the support of his forces to the Republican candidate, Archibald Carey, Jr. Sneed feared that if Washington won, he would use the aldermanic post as a launching pad to challenge Sneed for committeeman. Sneed's treachery paid off. Although Washington came in first, he lacked a majority of votes, and in a runoff election, he lost by just over two thousand votes to Carey.

In the following year, however, the tables were turned on Sneed. The committeemen were up for reelection, and Sneed was dumped. To begin with, his effectiveness was deplorable. He had twice failed to elect a Democratic alderman, and he committed the cardinal sin of failing to carry the machine's mayoral candidate in 1947, Martin Kennelly. The rumor of his double-dealing in the Washington election had also become widespread, making Sneed an acute embarrassment. Thus, while Sneed had won the aldermanic battle, he wound up losing the committeeman's war.

Washington was the reported frontrunner for the committeeman post; but the long arms of "Boss" Bill Dawson, committeeman of the neighboring Second Ward, reached into the Third Ward and grabbed the post. Dawson's chief aide, Christopher Wimbish, was slated. Dawson had gone before the slate-makers to argue that with the deep rift between the Sneed and Washington forces, an outside party was needed to restore order, and the slatemakers went along with his suggestion that Wimbish was the man for the job.

As it happened, Dawson had actually helped set Sneed up. Sneed had gone to Dawson for help in his aldermanic battle against Washington, and Dawson had discreetly sent over some of his best precinct captains to work for Carey.[10] The "policy wheels" tied to Dawson also assisted Sneed. Their wealth and array of "runners" (bet collectors) made them a potent campaign force. Needless to say, Dawson did not divulge his role in the conspiracy when he asked the slatemakers to dump Sneed and put in Wimbish.

With Wimbish in, Dawson became the de facto boss of two of the three black wards. At least, that was Dawson's intention; but Wimbish had other plans. He wanted to go into business for himself, dealing directly with the downtown bosses, instead of taking his orders from Dawson. The two conspirators promptly fell out, setting the Third Ward up for four more years of turmoil.

During the 1951 mayoral and aldermanic elections, Dawson once again crossed the political aisle, discreetly aiding Carey and Mayor Kennelly's Republican challenger, and Wimbish's Third Ward organization lost both elections. The turmoil and twin defeats set Wimbish up for the same fate Sneed had suffered four years earlier; he was dumped as committeeman.

This time a new figure on the scene designated the Third Ward committeeman. Carefully staging his run for party chairman, Richard Daley selected a political novice for the Third Ward post, Ralph Metcalfe.[11] Daley anticipated that Metcalfe would return the favor by backing him for chairman. Within the space of a few years, all of the black committeemen began dealing directly with

Daley, which left Dawson as little more than the ceremonial leader of the black wards.

The internecine warfare and duplicity had a profound impact on the young Harold Washington. Despite the ambiguity and treachery, the bottom line was easy to read. What the machine gave, it could just as easily take away, and the only way to combat it was to become a force in the community. Thus, while Washington worked hard within the machine, he also worked hard to develop ties outside the organization, with labor, church, and community groups. As it turned out, the hard-won knowledge and his high standing in the community saved him on more than one occasion when the machine sought to contain and destroy him.

Exodus and Domination

The 1955 mayoral election produced a critical political realignment in Chicago's black wards. Running in his first mayoral campaign, Richard Daley secured an unprecedented 72 percent of the vote in the black wards. Thus, the election finally resolved the massive electoral contradiction that had come to characterize black voting behavior. Under Daley, the black wards became so firmly Democratic that they displaced the poor white ethnic wards, which had carried the machine to success since its inception, as the machine's principal electoral stronghold. It would be wrong to assume, however, that the strong black Democratic shift was produced by either the machine's material resources or Daley's popularity. To borrow a distinction from Shakespeare, the machine did not achieve victory in the black wards so much as it had victory thrust upon it by two critical developments.

The first development was produced by the U.S. Supreme Court. In 1948 it overturned the racially restrictive housing covenants that had been used to confine black residents within a small and densely populated black belt. The decision opened a floodgate through which thousands of housing-hungry blacks poured. Within just two years the black belt, which had contained over 70 percent of the city's black population for decades, held less than half the population, and by 1960 the figure fell to 20 percent.[12] Yet it was not the exodus as such that produced the black political realignment. The realignment resulted from the class differentiation that was produced by the exodus. The vast proportion of those who fled the black belt were the economically able, the ones who could afford to take advantage of the new housing opportunities.[13] Thus, the poor remained in the black belt, and bereft of their middle-class political mentors, they quickly succumbed to the machine's material blandishments.

A second development augmented the political impact of the exodus and ensuing class differentiation. The volatile issue of race was injected into the 1955 mayoral campaign. The issue was used by Mayor Kennelly in an effort to develop a white backlash against Daley's candidacy. The racist ploy boomeranged, however. Not much of a backlash developed. But black opposition to the machine collapsed, losing its sense of purpose and legitimacy in the community through guilt-by-assocation with the racist forces. Consequently, Daley became the prime beneficiary of Kennelly's strategy.

After he was dumped by the machine, Kennelly realized that he needed a potent issue if he was going to successfully combat the machine's strong organizational edge; given his predilections, he seized the race issue. Kennelly charged that the notorious black ward boss Congressman William Dawson had been the chief architect of his dumping. He linked this charge to a characterization of Daley as a well-meaning but weak and naive fellow. Thus, Daley would be a puppet mayor and Dawson and the other venal ward bosses would be the ones jerking his strings.

Needless to say, the charge was electrifying, and the media, strongly committed to the reform-minded Kennelly, gave Kennelly's accusations extensive coverage. The newspapers competed with each other to see which one could produce the most sensational descriptions of the unsavory puppeteers, and Dawson received the most prominent coverage. Shortly after the dumping, the Chicago *Sun-Times*, in an editorial entitled "Policy, Narcotics, and Mayoral Politics," had this to say:

> While Dawson did not singlehandedly execute the coup, there is no doubt that he wielded more influence than any other one man in the organization's decision to deny Kennelly the Democratic machine's support in the February 22 mayoral primary. Dawson has long been a force for evil within the local Democratic organization. He is a political overlord of a district where policy rackets and narcotics peddling flourish as they do nowhere else in the city.[14]

The chief weakness of Kennelly's strategy was that the black media, notably the Chicago *Defender,* which was heavily committed to the Democratic cause, used the attack on Dawson to rally the black community around Dawson and the Democratic machine. In a long and passionate front-page editorial, the *Defender* defended Dawson, called Mayor Kennelly a racist, and made Kennelly's rejection a civic obligation.

> The tactics being used by Mayor Martin H. Kennelly to win the Democratic nomination for mayor are both dirty and dangerous. He charges that Rep. William L. Dawson, a Negro and a powerful Congressman, is primarily responsible for the fact that he has been dumped by the Democratic Party. Moreover, the Kennelly forces and the daily newspapers have found Congressman Dawson "guilty" of many crimes without benefit of any court of law. Congressman Dawson has not been indicted nor convicted for any crime by any judicial body. Kennelly's strategy is clearly designed to arouse the in-

dignation of whites against a powerful Negro leader and influence them to vote their prejudices rather than their well-founded convictions. After eight years as mayor with the entire police force at his command, Kennelly has suddenly discovered the policy racket. His own police department will tell him that this racket is owned and operated by the same syndicate gangsters who have been assassinating citizens on Chicago streets ever since the rise of Al Capone. Congressman Dawson does not now nor ever has had the power to prevent Mayor Kennelly from wiping out policy. The basic issue is not policy—it is politics. The majority of Negro voters are the same as voters in other wards: hardworking, law abiding citizens who want a clean, decent city, and who want, above all, to avoid racial bitterness. Hitler rose to power in Germany by accusing high-placed Jews of treason and whipping up anti-Semitism. Race-baiting in our own country has won victories in such states as Georgia and Mississippi. By building up a powerful Negro Congressman as a symbol of hatred, the Kennelly forces can exploit racial prejudice for all it is worth, while at the same time pretending to be crusading against corruption. This is a greater crime than any attributed to Dawson. It is the responsibility of all decent citizens of both races to make certain that race-baiting will produce no victories in Chicago.[15]

It is not difficult to imagine that with material such as this to distribute, the black Democratic ward organizations became the *Defender*'s best delivery boys. The message the black machine precinct captains conveyed was simple and potent: Reject Racism, Dump Kennelly. The black antimachine forces, which had always relied on moral suasion to move voters against the machine, had the tables turned on them. The 1955 mayoral campaign turned politics in the black wards into a one-party affair. Table 13.1 indicates how radically the middle-class exodus and the race issue affected the performance of the three black-belt wards.

While the Daley machine was establishing its dominance in the old black-belt wards, it also was leaving nothing to chance in the new black areas. The new territory was carefully gerrymandered in order to minimize the political impact of the black middle class. Thus, while the city's black population stood

TABLE 13.1

Democratic Pluralities in the Black Belt Wards: Mayoral Elections, 1943–1963

Ward	1943	1947	1951	1955	1959	1963
2	1,134	1,325	2,110	13,416	13,733	12,890
3	2,804	− 35	−248	11,860	12,739	18,852
20	——	——	−795	10,459	12,652	15,020
Total	3,938	1,290	1,067	35,735	39,124	46,762

SOURCE: Chicago Board of Election Commissioners

at 23 percent in 1960, only six of the city's fifty wards—12 percent—had black representation in the city council.

The only dark cloud on the Daley machine's horizon did not appear until the end of Daley's first decade in office. In 1963 the six black wards gave Daley the largest black vote he had ever received, and it was instrumental in putting Daley over the top against the Polish Democratic renegade, Benjamin Ada-mowski. At the same time, however, a seventh black ward, the Seventeenth Ward, elected a black independent alderman, Charles Chew. Running against a white Democratic incumbent, the flamboyant Chew tore into the machine, making its "plantation style" of politics—denying representation to blacks— the centerpiece of his campaign.

Chew's victory marked a critical breakthrough because it represented the first crack in the Daley machine's seemingly invincible armor.[16] The impossible suddenly seemed possible, and black independents across the city drew hope from Chew's win. In the ensuing years, many black independent campaigns were launched against the machine, and several were successful. But at this point a critical distinction must be drawn. Virtually all of the significant black antimachine activity and success came in the new, more affluent black areas. South 63rd Street, which had once marked the southern border of the black belt, now marked the black community's class divide. The torn black political tradition was now torn along the new class divide. To the north of 63rd Street, where the poor resided, the machine prevailed. In the more affluent wards south of 63rd Street, the machine faced increasingly stiff opposition.

Washington's Entry into the Machine

Harold Washington was weaned on politics; but it was an odd style of poli-tics. His allegiance was personal instead of political or organizational. He learned the craft from his father, Roy, by working as his assistant in the pre-cincts in one campaign after another. He worked hard, and he was always around; but he was "Roy's boy" to those who knew him then, not a member of the organization. The organizational bond did not form until after his father's death in 1953. He joined the Third Ward Democratic organization in the fall of 1954, taking over his father's precinct and inheriting his city job in the corpora-tion counsel's office.

Washington not only entered the machine late, he brought an unusual set of credentials with him. He had more practical experience than many of the orga-nization's precinct captains, yet he was also a graduate of Northwestern Univer-sity's prestigious law school. The Third Ward's newly elected ward commit-teeman, Ralph Metcalfe, a political novice appointed by Daley, knew just what to do with the unusual recruit. He gave Washington the responsibility for re-suscitating the moribund Young Democrats organization.

The Young Democrats was an auxiliary of the Cook County Democratic organization, organized like the machine on a ward and township Young Democrats represented the high-minded side of the machine. ... ... cipal purpose was to attract young businessmen and professionals into the machine by providing a forum for debating the issues of the times, raising money, and sponsoring various programs and activities. For those who were willing to "dirty their hands," the organization also conducted training sessions on how to work a precinct and win elections. Mayor Daley had asked the black committeemen to reestablish the Young Democrats as a means of containing and coopting the disaffected black middle class.

Washington made the most of the opportunity. He got the jump on the other black ward organizations, and the Third Ward Young Democrats organization was drawing young blacks from across the city and even the suburbs. By 1960 the auxiliary organization had grown twice as large as Metcalfe's parent ward organization, and the Young Democrats was by no means merely a debating society. By the mid-1960s, over half of Metcalfe's precinct captains had come up through the Young Democrats. Thus, when the Third Ward emerged during the 1960s as one of the crack ward organizations in the city—it gave Mayor Daley his largest plurality in the critical 1963 election—a large part of the Third Ward's success was attributable to Washington's efforts.

But Washington wound up reaping a peculiar reward for his success. In 1962 Mayor Daley sent word down to disband the Young Democrats. The civil rights movement was rearing its head, and the cautious Daley, fearful that the high-minded black Young Democrats might become a fifth column within the machine, decided to get rid of the Young Democrats before the movement fire swept north. When Metcalfe gave Washington the word to disband the Young Democrats, Washington straddled the line. Disinclined to draw Metcalfe's wrath, Washington formally withdrew from the organization. But he continued to serve informally as the Young Democrats' advisor, reluctant to give up the strong base he had developed outside the ward organization. The decision paid a handsome dividend. When the Third Ward's state representative, Kenneth Wilson, was elevated to a seat on the Cook County Board in 1963, the leadership of the Young Democrats recommended to Metcalfe that Washington be slated for the state legislative post. Metcalfe responded with alacrity for a couple of reasons. It would be easier to contain and coopt the Young Democrats with Washington in Springfield, and Springfield was a good place for Washington. The state legislature would occupy Washington's time and energy, and for Metcalfe, who had come to view Washington as a potential rival because of his success with the Young Democrats, this was no minor consideration.

Thus, Washington launched his legislative career by straddling the torn black political tradition. He played a major role in establishing the Third Ward Democratic organization as a dominant force in the increasingly lower-income old black belt. Here, as one of the organization's leading precinct captains, Washington became a master at trading on friendship and dispensing favors to secure votes. At the same time, as the principal leader of the Young Democrats, Washington had a solid foot in the black middle-class political camp. Here the issues were not merely favors and jobs, but racial equality, representation, and power. These were the issues on which the machine was willing to concede little ground.

Disillusion and Revolt

A third stage in black political behavior emerged during Mayor Daley's second decade in office. Once again, a critical external event—this time the civil rights movement—coupled with another outbreak of virulent racism at the local level, profoundly changed black political behavior.

The civil rights movement's dramatic moment in Chicago came when Dr. Martin Luther King's forces swept into the city in 1966 seeking open housing. King selected Chicago for his first northern foray because Chicago represented the greatest bastion of racism in the north. Thus, if King could bring Daley to heel, the movement would be established on a national instead of merely a southern regional basis. But Daley thoroughly outfoxed King. The movement depended upon confrontation; Daley artfully dodged King's grasp, offering co-operation instead of antagonism, greeting King by saying "Your goals are our goals." [17] Daley arranged summit conferences, publicly put his good offices at King's disposal, and deplored the violence that dogged King in the white ethnic areas. King seethed—"The people of Mississippi ought to come to Chicago to learn how to hate" [18]—but Daley's dancing trashed the movement's strategy and momentum.

Yet the outcome of the confrontation was not nearly so one-sided as it seemed at the time. King certainly did lose the open-housing battle to Daley. However, the movement won the political war by exposing the Daley machine's intransigent racism to the black community. One of Mayor Daley's aides, Earl Bush, recently summed it up this way: "What Daley did was smother King. What Daley couldn't smother was the civil rights movement." [19]

The movement's political impact turned up on the heels of King's foray into the city. The poor black wards, which had become the machine's electoral stronghold during Daley's first decade as mayor, displayed their first sign of disillusion with the machine in 1967, and the disenchantment grew progressively deeper during the 1970s. The political shift in the poor black wards from dominance by the machine to disillusion with it is indicated in table 13.2.

While the new disillusionment was festering in the poor black wards, the revolt was proceeding apace south of the 63rd Street class divide in the more affluent black wards. In 1967, two more black independent candidates defeated the machine: "Sammy" Rayner in the Sixth Ward and William Cousins in the Eighth Ward. Then in 1971 the revolt began spilling over the class divide. Anna Langford's independent candidacy was successful in the Sixteenth Ward,

TABLE 13.2

Dominance and Disillusion in the Poor Black Wards:
Citywide Ranking in Mayoral Elections, 1955–1975

Wards	1955	1959	1963	1967	1971	1975
Near South Side						
2	4	7	5	26	36	30
3	8	10	1	3	23	31
4	16	6	7	18	16	23
6	19	16	10	28	43	35
20	11	11	3	12	31	32
West Side						
24	1	1	2	7	4	25
28	7	23	20	37	40	44
29	6	4	4	6	24	41
Proportion in top ten wards for Daley	63%	63%	88%	38%	13%	none

SOURCE: Chicago Board of Election Commissioners. Ranking is based on the plurality for Daley in each of his six mayoral elections.

a ward straddling the class divide; and the once unthinkable happened in the Second Ward, the legendary "Boss" Dawson's ward. Dawson's organization, in a shambles following his death in 1970, was defeated by an ambitious social worker turned politician, Fred Hubbard.

There was trouble of sorts along the machine's mayoral front as well. Daley was confronted by two liberal independents in the 1975 primary: Alderman William Singer and a black state senator from the Hyde Park area, Richard Newhouse. Daley easily turned back both challenges; but the election revealed that black discontent with the machine had become pervasive. In the fourteen black wards, the combined Singer-Newhouse vote actually exceeded Daley's vote by a small margin. The greatest discontent was, of course, expressed by the more affluent black wards. However, Daley also trailed the combined Singer-Newhouse vote in two of the five poor Near South Side wards and in one of the three West Side wards. The black revolt was clearly running over the political demarcation lines of the social class divide.

The machine's downward spiral in the black community continued following Daley's death in 1976. The intriguing thing about Mayors Michael Bilandic and Jane Byrne is they both appear to have patterned their behavior after the aged and arrogant Daley in decline, instead of using the earlier, wily Daley as their model. Daley's dangerous arrogance was displayed, for example, in his lengthy feud with Congressman Ralph Metcalfe during the 1970s, a confrontation that transformed Metcalfe from a machine hack into an antimachine hero in the black community's eyes. Instead of seeing Daley's action for what it was, petulant personal politics, Bilandic and Byrne seem to have adopted it as their standard for dealing with the black political leadership.

Bilandic's arrogance was revealed shortly after he became mayor. He allowed some of the committeemen to work against Harold Washington's reelection to the state senate. This was widely seen as Washington's punishment for having challenged Bilandic in the 1977 mayoral election. When Bilandic's other challenger, Roman Pucinski, went unpunished, the black community viewed the discrimination as being racially motivated. Once Washington defeated the machine challenge, he emerged as the new champion of the black antimachine movement, and, more important, Washington himself became convinced that he had no future left in the machine. Thus, he stepped out, as Metcalfe never really had, to lead the black assault on the machine.

Bilandic compounded his problem in the black community by designating a notorious black hack, Bennett Stewart, to take the place of the deceased folk hero, Ralph Metcalfe, in Congress. The move drove the antimachine activists into a frenzy, and even some of the normally complacent black committeemen were offended by the decision. Congress was the highest office to which blacks could aspire, and Stewart did not begin to measure up to his predecessors: Oscar DePriest, William Dawson, and Ralph Metcalfe.

Bilandic's final display of insensitivity cost him the mayoralty. His fatal rash step came during the great snow storm that crashed down on his reelection bid. In an effort to speed the flow of traffic into the Loop during the storm, several black train stops along the Dan Ryan El were closed. The black hue and cry that ensued caused Bilandic to rescind the closings; but the damage could not be undone. Jane Byrne rode the crest of the black protest into the mayor's office.

Jane Byrne's mayoralty sated Chicago's gargantuan appetite for political folly as it had not been satisfied since the zany Roaring Twenties regime of "Big Bill" Thompson. Fear drove Byrne from the first days to the bitter end. The ghost of Mayor Daley always hovered around her: could she measure up? The mayoral aspirations of young Richard Daley dogged her: would she survive? The fears compelled her to get rid of the "dreamers"—Rose, Masotti, Haider, and finally McGrath—and embrace the "schemers" she had campaigned against—Vrdolyak, Burke, Roti, and Swibel. Blacks became her pawns in the match against young Daley for the white ethnic vote. Time and again she pitted black against white ethnic representation—in school, police, public housing, and ward boundary disputes—and came down heavily on the white ethnic side. The strategy was simple and brutal, and it openly divided the city along racial lines as it had not been divided since the 1960s.

Byrne apparently believed that two factors would keep a sufficient number of black votes behind her candidacy in 1983. The black Democratic ward organizations and their satellites, heavily dependent upon her good will and patronage, would work hard for her reelection, regardless of her racist actions. As well, no strong black mayoral candidate would emerge to challenge her. History supported the Byrne strategy. But her fears drove Byrne too far. The racial pot she had so furiously stirred spilled over, swamping both her expectations and her mayoralty.

Washington's Disillusionment and Revolt

Whatever high hopes Washington harbored on his way down to Springfield were soon dashed by the harsh realities of the general assembly. Chicago's legislators danced strictly to Mayor Daley's music. "Boss" William Dawson, a tireless dancer for Daley and the Democratic party in congress, explained why. "We must play the game according to the rules. I always play it that way and I play with my team. If you are on a baseball team you stick with your team or you may not be able to play much longer." [20] So the freshman legislator danced; but he kept falling out of step. Generally the missteps were minor. Yet by his second term he showed that he had both the skill and temerity to go beyond the pale. He assaulted the machine head-on by getting a bill out of committee calling for a civilian review board for the Chicago Police Department. Daley sent word down through Metcalfe that Washington had to be dumped. But before the ax fell, Washington appealed to Jack Touhy, the wily West Side ward boss who ran Daley's Springfield operation. Touhy had taken an avuncular interest in the bright, brash Washington, and he managed to pull Washington's neck off Daley's chopping block.

The near execution did not have the salutary effect on Washington that Daley expected. Instead, Washington started stepping out even further on his own. He developed a code of divided loyalty that he hoped would enable him to survive in the machine while operating outside of it when he had to. On legislative affairs, he insisted on being his own man when the occasion called for it. On electoral matters, he played strictly by the machine's rules. He managed Metcalfe's aldermanic and congressional campaigns, ran the Third Ward's training program, and supported the machine's ticket from top to bottom.

Washington's extraordinary code of honor did not endear him to the iron-willed Metcalfe. But Metcalfe's supreme caution—Washington once described him in a moment of pique as "a man who plotted every step in advance before he decided to cross a street" [21]—made him heavily dependent on Washington's electoral skill, and this bridged the breach between the two men. The fragile bridge finally collapsed, however, under the weight of the 1975 mayoral primary election. Washington saw the black community breaking away from the machine, pushed along in large part by the celebrated Metcalfe-Daley feud, and he urged Metcalfe to seize the momentum by running for mayor. He managed to push Metcalfe to the precipice; but all the cautious Metcalfe saw when he peered over the edge was few troops, little money, and no hope of winning. He pulled back, and the decision severed the thin bond that had held the two men together for twenty years.

Still, Washington was able to capitalize on the Daley-Metcalfe feud the following year and move up to the state senate. In a set of state elections that had more twists than a John LeCarré plot, Daley dumped Metcalfe for congress; Metcalfe then allied himself with the machine's arch enemy, Governor Dan Walker. Daley countered by putting up the black president of the state senate, Cecil Partee, as his candidate for Illinois attorney general. This was a classic Daley move. It appeared as if Daley was moving Partee up; but Partee stood no chance against the popular Republican incumbent William Scott. Daley was moving him out of the senate and out of the presidency.

Washington wanted Partee's senate seat; but getting it was no simple matter. Daley despised Washington's independence and he thought even less of his committeeman, Metcalfe. But by this time Washington had become a master at slipping through the few cracks in the monolithic machine. He asked his labor allies to intercede with Daley on his behalf, and the leadership of the United Auto Workers approached Daley with two compelling arguments. Washington had a superior labor record, and if he did not get Partee's seat, he was going over to the Walker-Metcalfe ticket. Revealing his fear and loathing of Walker and Metcalfe, Daley reluctantly agreed to slate Washington.

Washington sailed easily to victory; but the campaign convinced him that he was going to have to make a clean break with the machine. Despite his backing by the machine, his poorly organized and financed opponent still managed to get 43 percent of the vote merely by waving the independent flag and castigating Washington as a machine hack. The characterization infuriated Washington; but he understood its effect. Many voters simply did not know what to make of him, half in and half out of the machine.

The maverick went a long way toward clarifying his image by challenging Michael Bilandic in the 1977 special mayoral election. Washington did not renounce the machine; but he tore into it for failing to give blacks their due rewards for long years of support. At the same time, Washington was tearing into the machine in the state senate, working with the Black Caucus and the "Crazy Eight"—an independent band of legislators—and the media began to give recognition to his skill and independence.[22] Once again, Washington's neck was perilously close to the chopping block.

The chop came in his 1978 reelection campaign. In a hotly argued slating session, Washington won a bare majority of support; but two of the committeemen in his senatorial district were nevertheless allowed to oppose him. In an election settled by a few hundred votes, a strong independent force of volunteers proved to be the difference for Washington.

Washington's first full-blown independent campaign came in 1980 when he challenged Bennett Stewart for congress in the First District. Washington picked up the victory handily; but he also picked up a remarkable message during the course of the campaign. Everywhere he went word was coming up about a black mayor. An aide conducted straw polls, and the results were staggeringly positive. Washington spread the word, and other black organizations—which were springing up like mushrooms in response to Byrne's may-oralty—began polling and coming up with the same remarkable results.

A second set of polls was conducted to find the man to match the moment, and Washington's name invariably came out on top. But he proved to be a re-markably reluctant candidate. If he ran, he was determined that it would not be another symbolic gesture of black protest. It had to be a serious campaign, one that was well organized and well financed. Thus, the next step was a mas-sive voter registration drive, and black businessmen for the first time were brought into the independent political movement in a large way. The prospect of a black mayor was remote. But, on the other hand, the momentum was there and building, and never before had the black community been as united be-hind one man and one issue.

Victory and Resolution

The two most remarkable aspects of Washington's mayoral bid were the ex-ceptional prominence of religious symbolism in the campaign—reflecting the religious roots of the black political tradition—and the extraordinary sup-port Washington received from the traditionally machine-oriented poor black wards—an unprecedented phenomenon in mayoral politics.

Religious symbolism was present at the launching of the campaign. Washing-ton threw his hat into the ring surrounded by a host of black ministers who offered up prayers for the candidate's success. One of the political reporters covering the event remarked that he had never seen a campaign kicked off this way; it resembled a religious revival meeting.[23]

During the course of the primary campaign, a "truth squad" of Washington supporters emerged to prevent Mayor Byrne from using black churches for campaign appearances, contending that the conventional political practice desecrated the black church. Meanwhile, Washington rode the black church circuit hard, drawing upon the extensive clerical network he had formed over the years as a legislator.

Then came the mammoth rally at the University of Illinois Pavilion. Thir-teen thousand Washington supporters rocked for four hours to the politico-religious cadences of a group of black elected officials from across the country. Organized by Sid Ordower, who had hosted a black gospel music show on local television for many years, the rally resembled nothing less than a religious re-vival meeting at full swing.

On the day of the primary election, the Chicago *Sun-Times* carried a photo of the candidate that evoked the campaign's religious crusade dimension. Wash-ington was shown bowed down before his minister receiving a blessing before heading off to the final day of battle. From beginning to end, then, the Wash-ington campaign displayed a meld of the political and religious. It was a reli-gious movement as well as a political campaign, and the moral dimension of the crusade resonated throughout the black community, producing an unprecedented number of campaign workers as well as voters. A majority of the Washington campaign workers in the poor Near South Side wards, where the author coordinated election day activities, had never before worked in a political campaign.

The extraordinary transformation of the poor black wards was unprecedented in mayoral politics. Yet there was a clear basis for the political shift. During Daley's first decade as mayor, the poor black wards had been the machine's principal electoral stronghold. But, as we saw, a profound disillusion set in during the late 1960s, transforming the poor black wards into a lazy backwater of the machine; the machine was still supported by those who voted, but fewer and fewer blacks turned out to vote.

Thus, the problem for Washington was not so much to pull poor black voters away from the machine as to rekindle their faith in politics. This involved passing a qualification test—demonstrating that Washington possessed the capacity to govern—and a "win-ability" test—demonstrating that he could actually win.

The first test was essentially passed during the widely watched first television debate, which by virtually all accounts Washington won handily. Washington continued to demonstrate his superiority in the second debate, and he held his own in the other two debates. The debates were critically important because they transformed Washington from the black protest candidate into the most qualified candidate. His standing in the polls rose steadily throughout the debates period.[24]

The second test was not actually passed until the waning days of the primary campaign. The turning point came at the huge and wild rally at the Pavilion. The rally was an extraordinary gamble that paid off. It violated the political advance man's basic rule that events should always be held in the smallest room insurance against a low turnout. But the momentum from the debates was flagging, and the gamble had to be taken in order to catch the front-running Byrne.

The rally struck like a thunderbolt, convincing those who were there and those who saw it on television and read about it in the newspapers that the impossible had suddenly become possible. Washington could actually win. His standing in the polls began to soar once again as the last of the doubters were swept up by the enthusiasm displayed at the rally.

A simple comparison indicates the revolutionary effect that Washington's campaign had in the poor black wards. In 1977 Washington had carried four black wards (plus the racially mixed Fifth Ward), all of which were affluent wards south of the 63rd Street class divide. He fared poorly in all of the poor black wards, particularly in the so-called "plantation" wards on the West Side. Thus, we can gain a clear sense of the transformation that occurred in 1983 by seeing how Washington performed in these two areas (see table 13.3).

TABLE 13

Victory and Resolution: The Washington '

Wards	Primary Election		
	Vote	Turnout	
Affluent			
6	87%	79%	
8	86%	76%	9.
9*	80%	75%	94%
21	88%	78%	99%
Poor			
24	79%	73%	99%
27*	72%	71%	93%
28	81%	69%	99%	7.
29*	76%	71%	93%	80%

*A small white population resides in these three wards, accounting for the lower levels of support for Washington

SOURCE: Chicago Board of Election Commissioners

The campaign did not entirely remove the effects of social class and attendant ties to the machine in the poor black wards; but it came remarkably close to doing just that. Turnout in the poor wards was lower in both elections, and Washington received a lower vote in the primary election in the poor wards. Yet when the voting pattern is viewed in historical terms, the differences become trivial. For the first time black voters, affluent and poor, spoke with virtually one voice. The election resolved the long-standing torn black political tradition.

One election does not, of course, constitute a political realignment, and so the big question is what the future holds. Can the new unified black political tradition hold in the new maelstrom that has engulfed Chicago's politics since Washington's election? Washington has thus far—three years into his first term—remained true to the reform convictions he expressed during his campaign for office, and the voters approve. His black support remains firm across the board, and white opposition has subsided, according to both the private and public polls that have been conducted. Thus, if Washington can continue to avoid the serpents snapping at his heels, the political realignment should hold, affirming both the new black political tradition and a new course for Chicago politics.

14.

THE SAWYER SAGA: A JOURNALIST, WHO JUST HAPPENED TO BE THE MAYOR'S PRESS SECRETARY, SPEAKS

Monroe Anderson

So there will be no doubt about where I am coming from or where I am going, let me say this first: Eugene Sawyer got a bum rap and a blunt shaft.

This is not the voice of Acting Mayor Sawyer's press secretary speaking, mind you, although there is the distinct possibility that you will hear it from time to time later on. But rather, this is the opinion of a veteran Chicago journalist who studied and covered Chicago politics for sixteen years before curiously crossing over to the other side. By time the particular but peculiar political process of selecting Mayor Harold Washington's successor began on Thanksgiving Eve of 1987, I knew, either professionally or by reputation, quite a few of those cast in the background, many of those waiting in the wings, and most of the central players.

As a matter of record, I was the first reporter to predict publicly that the next mayor of Chicago could—contrary to the prevailing political wisdom—be black. I made that prediction in an op-ed page opinion piece I wrote in late September of 1982. The op-ed article ran in the Chicago *Tribune* on November 8th. On the same day, on the front page of the same issue of the *Tribune*, coincidentally, I also scooped every other reporter in town by breaking the story that Harold Washington was in the mayoral race.

I mention this only as a matter of background before attempting to sort out the Sawyer administration dilemma and the black political debacle that followed. Let me begin at the beginning, which, as everyone knows by now, actually was the end of the Washington era and African-American political power in Chicago. Oh, one last thing first. As an African-American in Chicago, attempting to speak to African-Americans in Chicago, I am compelled to state the obvious: No one did anything to us, but us. We fell on the sword—and, as I write this—continue to complete our self-inflicted political disembowelment.

* * *

On 2 December 1987, I was a Midwest bureau correspondent for *Newsweek* magazine. Somewhere around 1:30 A.M., I turned off my television set and called it a night. That was some time after the Evans faction began playing parliamentary procedure. I covered City Hall for the *Tribune* for a short stint right after Washington became mayor and, for nearly a year and a half, wrote a weekly political column on the *Tribune*'s op-ed page. Therefore I knew those kinds of parliamentary maneuvers for what they were—stalling tactics. It was all over except for the speechmaking, the name-calling, and the final roll call. "Sawyer," I thought to myself as I began drifting off into a fitful, too-short night's sleep. "I can't believe it's Sawyer. Mayor Sawyer."

As was the case for an overwhelming majority of African-Americans in Chicago, Mayor Washington had taken on a larger-than-life persona for me. Early on, as the first black member of the *Tribune*'s City Hall bureau. I closely followed and duly reported Mayor Washington's trials and tribulations during what political satirist Aaron Freeman dubbed "council wars." It was during that period that I first met Eugene Sawyer. Washington was on one of his many super-celebrity-mayor excursions. This time it was to Oakland, California. For reasons that were not explained, and did not seem to matter to any of Chicago's traveling press corps, Sixth Ward Alderman Sawyer was part of the mayor's entourage. During a reception there, Sawyer introduced himself to me. We had cocktail conversation for about three or four minutes. I do not recall what we discussed. However, I do remember my initial impression at that time: Eugene Sawyer was a nice man. A little quiet, but very nice. And somewhat boring.

Maybe it was because I found Sawyer so nice, so quiet, and so subdued that he did not immediately come to my mind as the natural successor to the wily warrior, the man with the quick tongue and the disarming shrug, Harold Washington. But, in retrospect, I realize that I too fell victim to the images, lies, and propaganda born out of Mayor Washington's untimely death. When Washington died at his desk the day before Thanksgiving, I, like most Chicagoans, was startled and stunned. I was also captivated by news accounts of the political maneuvers to replace him. Like so many thousands of Chicagoans who had listened carefully to those media reports and the word on the street, I thought the next mayor of Chicago would be none other than Fourth Ward Alderman Timothy Evans.

As I would later learn, the impression that Evans was the gatekeeper of the Washington legacy was no more than a notion—and a misleading one at that. In politics, public perception and what is really going on are twains that seldom meet. So while Evans enjoyed the public persona of being Harold's right-hand man, in reality the inside story featured someone else. It was Eugene Sawyer who functioned as Washington's key alderman. "Gene was the invisible senior statesman among the Washington 21," recalls Grayson Mitchell, the mayor's first press secretary.

Sawyer, a dependable, knowledgeable, nuts-and-bolts legislator, was the linchpin in Washington's council machinery. The Sixth Ward alderman was the first committeeman to bolt from the Regular Democratic Ward bloc to support Washington's candidacy for mayor, risking considerable political retaliation from Jane Byrne. Sawyer, who was president pro tem of the city council at the time of the mayor's death, was the one who usually forged a consensus among the black and progressive aldermen so that the mayor enjoyed a united front on the council floor. And Sawyer was a valued consultant to Washington, whose political experience was rooted in the Illinois state legislature and the United States Congress, not in municipal government. It was Sawyer who tutored the newly inaugurated mayor on how the council floor worked, giving him a practical rundown on the players while telling him the score. And it was Sawyer who, from the floor, signaled Washington on the podium to indicate how many more votes the mayor needed to pass a motion. "Harold had a lot of respect for Gene's judgment," Mitchell said. "It was always solid."

Eugene Sawyer had two glaring weaknesses, however. He was media shy and too soft-spoken for his own good.

Tim Evans was something else. Tim Evans was an illusion. Shortly after the council wars erupted, Mayor Washington needed a point man to carry on the fight from the floor. Evans was articulate, photogenic, and eager to bask in the glow of the television cameras. He became the designated face and voice of the new Washington administration but never the brains nor the heart and soul. Evans served as a public prop but seldom as a behind-the-scenes support. Although Evans was bright and capable, he lacked one crucial ingredient: follow-through. Tim Evans, Washington administration insiders sighed, was not reliable. Not dependable. Evans had a reputation for not being on time. Politically, Evans was thought to be too cautious and conservative by many of the Washington progressives. And Evans was not known for doing his homework. On a number of occasions, according to Washington administration insiders, Evans's floor speeches had to be written for him because he had not prepared himself well enough to discuss the issues without prompting.

It was because of Sawyer's strengths and Evans's weaknesses that Jacky Grimshaw, Ernest Barefield, and their aldermanic allies, Bobby Rush and Dorothy Tillman, sought to exploit the public perception rather than the political reality. "Tim was controllable," says a former Washington administration insider. "He was a complete captive of their 'movement.'"

To be fair, I would like to mention one tangential factor that obviously played a part in the Washington coalition schism. For the first three and a half years of its existence, the Washington administration was under siege. Naturally, a bunker mentality took hold. A talented, all-pro politician, Washington understood that after his reelection the prudent thing to do was to make peace with the loyal opposition. Operating on the theory that, in politics, "There are no permanent friends. No permanent enemies. Only permanent interests," he buried the hatchet in the same resting place where patronage lay dead and danced upon. After Washington's death, many of his supporters experienced post–council wars traumatic flashbacks. An automatic reflex of theirs returned. If those of the 29 mentality went left, then those with the 21 philosophy had better look to the right. The 29 whispered Sawyer, so some of the 21 got the irresistible urge to shout Evans.

Before Washington's death, few voters beyond the boundaries of their respective wards, knew—or cared—much about either Evans or Sawyer. Within hours after Washington's burial, that was no longer true. Thanks to an instant burst of revisionist history coupled with a not-so-spontaneous combustion of modern myth, the twin creations of the Washington legacy and the Sawyer sellout were conceived. Or, to be more accurate, ill-conceived. Tim Evans became "the heir apparent," a designation that a week earlier was neither in the air nor apparent. Gene Sawyer became, in Alderman Tillman's disingenuous words, Monty Hall, out to make a closed-door deal at his people's expense. The Evans transformation gave credence to the old axiom about possession being nine-tenths of the law. Motivated by fear and selfishness, those in power— the Washington administration without Washington—decided that an Evans succession to the mayor's seat was in their best interest. Once that self-serving decision was made, making fiction look like fact hinged on their skills in telling the big lie, staging the big event, and organizing the big demonstration.

But before those relatively easy pieces could be put into place in this political chess game, the king had to be put in check.

If there was anyone big enough to fill Washington's shoes and assume the Washington legacy, it was the Reverend Jesse Jackson and only the Reverend Jesse Jackson. The civil rights leader was drum major and chief cheerleader in the black political movement that led to Washington's election as mayor of Chicago. The night of the primary victory, a sharp split developed between Washington and Jackson after the latter commandeered the mike and shouted the battle cry, "It's our turn." Washington, who wisely waited in his hotel suite for definite election results before making a victory speech, was furious with Jackson for a couple of reasons. The first one had to do with Jackson's bad habit of stealing the spotlight any time and every time he got the chance. The second and more substantive one was based on Jackson's action alienating almost every white voter in the City of Chicago. Washington put Jackson at arm's length after that. Once he won (narrowly) the general election, his star eclipsed Jackson's as the king of the black leadership hill in Chicago—and challenged it on a national level. Overnight, the nation's third-largest city became too small to nurture the substantial political egos of both men. For about a decade, Jackson had been the 800-pound gorilla among Chicago's black politicians and the big, bad wolf to the city's white power structure. Suddenly, Jackson found himself playing Tonto to Mayor Washington's Lone Ranger. It didn't take long before Jackson acted on a urge to move up and out—shooting for the American presidency as a consolation prize. To nearly no one's surprise, Jackson's quest for the presidency failed. But the African-American preacher did so much better than anyone—with the possible exception of his most fervent followers—expected that he became the undisputed champion and spokesman for black America. An uneasy accommodation between the newly elected black mayor of Chicago and the newly crowned leader of black America followed.

Jackson, who chronically was a prophet without honor in his own city, even managed to take on the aura of national black statesman at home. So much so that Washington, who was late and reluctant in endorsing Jackson during his first presidential run, was quick and emphatic in endorsing the civil rights leader the second time around, describing Jackson as "a force for good."

Had Jackson been around when Washington died, it is unthinkable that he would have let the division occur, let alone unwittingly precipitate it. But, as fate would have it, Jackson was out of the country and therefore out of the loop on 25 November 1987. When he learned of the mayor's death, Jackson was nearly halfway around the world at the Kuwait Hilton, where he was attempting to shore up his presidential timber. He immediately headed back home. All of Jackson's information on the political wheelings and dealings in selecting Washington's successor was spoon-fed to him by Grimshaw and Barefield, who warned the civil rights leader that the African-American community was about to lose City Hall in his absence. By the time Jackson returned to O'Hare Airport, he was a one-man disinformation campaign waiting to happen.

With Washington dead, Jackson once again was unquestionably the best and the brightest black politico in town. But this was one time that the best man could not win: Illinois state law decreed that the fifty members of the Chicago City Council must select a mayoral successor from among their own. Jackson was not a member of the city council and therefore not eligible for consideration. Unable to assume the mayoralty, Jackson opted for the post of kingmaker. Proclaiming himself a peacemaker, Jackson obviously had heard the big lie and took it to heart. Although his public posture was that of the neutral negotiator attempting to forge a consensus candidate for the Washington coalition, he clearly favored Evans. During the regular PUSH meeting the Saturday following the mayor's death, Jackson stood at the podium, flanked by Evans and Sawyer. Although Jackson thrust both men's extended arms upwards, he thrust Evans's hand upwards with much more enthusiasm. Jackson's body English spoke volumes to volumes. Jackson had been suckered into believing that Evans truly was the heir apparent who had the tacit support of the black community at large. Using the full force of his overt popularity and implied authority in subtle ways, Jackson's misinformed understanding became the African-American community-at-large's misled conviction. It was a full year later, when he returned to Chicago after taking another stab at winning the Democratic party presidential nomination, that Jackson concluded that he was bamboozled. He tried to right the wrongs. But by then it was much too late. The African-American community's nihilistic political course was set and not about to be altered.

In the days following the mayor's death, Chicago's African-American community was so thoroughly in the throes of shock and disbelief that anything but the truth seemed feasible to a large portion of it. Rumors, lies, and conspiracy theories, anything that gave comfort while placing blame, were desperately embraced. I visited City Hall the last day that Washington's body lay in state. As I viewed the open casket, a weeping African-American woman in her early fifties stood beside me. She shook her head and moaned, "It's a shame the way they murdered that man." On WVON, the black talk radio station, where conversation stopped making sense the day the mayor died, all sorts of conspiracy theories were voiced about how he was killed. More than one member of the mayor's security force—almost all of whom came from the ranks of the black nationalistic Afro-American Police League—were admonished by an anguished black for allowing "them" to murder Mayor Washington. One theory had him poisoned. Another had him dead from a cocaine hotshot (there has never been any report or evidence of drug use by the mayor). Perhaps the most bizarre theory attributed the suspected "murder" to the mayor's press secretary and confidant, Alton Miller, who happened to be the only person in the inner office with Washington when he suffered the heart attack on November 25th. And who happens to be white.

In that perversely paranoid atmosphere, lies stood on their own, developing legs and racing forward as "the word on the street." The next logical move in this topsy-turvy tall tale was to stage the big event. Hours after Washington's remains were laid to rest on Monday afternoon, a "memorial" for the late mayor was held at the Pavilion of the University of Illinois' Chicago campus. In the wake of a legitimate memorial for the late mayor, an Evans-for-Mayor rally was grafted. As a journalist with more than a passing interest in the Chicago political scene, I planned to attend the gathering. However, when I discovered it would be broadcast live on WBEZ, the local public radio station, I opted to listen instead. What I heard, I found disquieting. Conspiracy theories hung in the air like so many funeral buntings. The principal conspiracy, warned speaker after speaker, was to disenfranchise the black-Hispanic-progressive coalition that had fought so hard to reform City Hall. These maleficent conspirators planned to deny Tim Evans, Harold's right-hand man, his rightful role as heir to the fifth floor of City Hall. Harold had to be spinning in his grave.

And so spiel after spiel was spun. Then Vernon Jarrett took hold of the mike. If anyone could be classified as a one-man black journalist conglomerate, it was Vernon Jarrett. He was a columnist for the Chicago *Sun-Times* and a member of that newspaper's editorial board; a commentator on WLS-TV, the Capital Cities/ABC-owned and -operated station in Chicago, as well as the talk show host for "Vernon Jarrett: Face to Face," a public service program there; and a major stockholder at WVON-AM radio. Jarrett also had served as a sort of professional mentor and role model to me. It was this name I used, when I was an assistant editor at *Ebony* magazine, to get a job interview at the Chicago *Tribune*. And it was his Friday slot on the *Tribune*'s op-ed page that I inherited when Jarrett quit as a columnist at the *Tribune* to go across the street to the *Sun-Times*. Although the "memorial" had taken a decidedly pro-Evans political tack, I expected a different direction from Jarrett, who had been a close friend of Harold Washington. I thought an honest-to-goodness eulogy would come at last. I expected that although Vernon would pepper his remembrance with politics, any such observations would not be buried hip-deep in unfounded conspiracy theories and fabricated fables.

My expectations went unmet. Ten minutes into a diatribe that was so hysterical that I feared that Jarrett was experiencing a nervous breakdown, I needed a reality check. I left the radio to find my wife. "Joyce," I shouted in amazement, "come here. You've got to hear this. Vernon has gone over the edge."

Just how far Jarrett had gone became increasingly clear as time went by. Jarrett's strident town crier role the night of the Pavilion rally became his public persona, replacing his well-respected identity as a crusading advocacy journalist. Paul King, an African-American contractor who is president of the Chicago Business Council, likens Jarrett's transformation to that of the Howard Beale character in the 1976 movie *Network*. Shouting, "I'm mad as hell and I'm not going to take it anymore," the Beale character, a television news anchor, went from giving the news to being the news. Eventually the Beale character, who was plays by actor Peter Finch, went so far off the deep end that he ended up encouraging viewers to throw their TV sets out the window.

Columnist Jarrett played the Pied Piper in a real-life political drama, ushering six years of African-American progress in Chicago politics out the window. It was Jarrett, more than anyone else, who managed to keep the invention of the Washington legacy and Evans as the heir apparent in the public domain. It was Jarrett, as much as anybody else, who created the impression in Chicago's African-American community that the mayoralty competition was exclusively between Sawyer and Evans—no white candidate need apply. It was and remains a mystery to me just how Jarrett became so mired in his own fiction. The only sense I can make of it is that Jarrett is a staunch traditionalist. His columns frequently start with historical references or quotes from earlier decades and slowly work their way to current events. Keeping that in mind, perhaps Jarrett was set on the traditional line of succession, where the second in command follows a fallen leader. It was this sort of thinking that called for

Ralph David Abernathy, rather than the younger, more energetic, and talented Jesse Jackson, to succeed the slain Dr. Martin Luther King, Jr. Because Evans was Washington's floor leader, Jarrett must have persuaded himself that this was the only proper progression.

Whatever thought process Jarrett may have gone through, once his mind was made up, it got stuck on that one note. Jarrett served as the unofficial minister of misinformation for the Evans faction. His radio station, WVON, day in and day out played a key role in allowing unquestioned assertions and half-truths to mold community opinion, fostering the effigy of Acting Mayor Sawyer and ministering to the phantasm of should-be mayor Evans. Column after column, Jarrett praised Evans while damning Sawyer. The acting mayor did nothing right, while the Fourth Ward alderman could do no wrong. There were no shades of gray applied to either man. There is no doubt in my mind that if Jarrett had not constantly and consistently beaten the anti-Sawyer drum, the rift in the African-American community would have stood a remote possibility of healing.

A lot of young African-American journalists looked up to Jarrett because he was a pioneer who not only succeeded against all odds but exacted the best revenge by living well. So many, such as the Chicago *Defender*'s Chinta Strausberg, WVON's Ty Wansley, and WVAZ's Debra Scott, followed his lead down that slippery slope into partisan journalism. They played the same politics he played and contributed to the loss for the African-American community. There was no pretense of the journalistic staples of objectively or fairness with Jarrett and little from them. There is a lesson to be learned from this. Had these journalists played it straight rather than choosing sides and toeing a party line, the one thing they thought they were trying to prevent—the loss of Harold Washington's seat to his white political adversaries—could have been prevented. It was their good intentions that paved the road to the eventual outcome. It was Jarrett's fiery, misguided speech that set the stage during the Monday, November 30th, rally for much of what was to follow.

By the time the roll was called for the special council meeting on Tuesday, the memorial rally had influenced passions to a flashpoint. The city's Department of Human Services, at taxpayers' expense, generously provided transportation for busloads of demonstrators destined to clog City Hall. Before the council could get around to doing its business, there was barely any room in which to do it. The big protest was raging according to the blueprint. Concerned citizens, mostly black, were here, there, and everywhere. The crowd of thousands, packed inside and out, had no understanding of the required procedure in selecting a mayoral successor. But, thanks to the disinformation campaign that had been waged the day before, it "knew" a deal had been made to cut the Washington coalition out.

As early as Thanksgiving Day, Sawyer had enough council votes to become the next mayor of the City of Chicago. Although the bloc of white ethnic aldermen who had staunchly opposed Washington for three and a half years sought vainly to select one of their own, mainly Thirty-second Ward Alderman Terry Gabinski, for the post, Cook County Democratic party Chairman George Dunne would have none of that. Dunne was politically astute enough to know that choosing anyone but an African-American to fill Washington's seat would mean political suicide for the local party and possibly rioting in the streets. Once the white ethnic aldermanic bloc came to accept that political reality, Sawyer was their obvious choice. Besides being well liked by his aldermanic colleagues and well schooled in council affairs. Sawyer had two other attractive attributes as far as the white ethnic members were concerned: He was not particularly ambitious and even less articulate. Sawyer suited the likes of the old anti-Washington 29 well because they believed he could either be controlled or, if not controlled, then defeated in a special election.

In the thick of the fight over the succession, Sawyer offered Evans his personal council vote, if the Fourth Ward alderman could muster the other twenty-five. That was not about to happen. Evans was not especially loved or respected by most of his colleagues in the council.

The greatest irony, I believe, is that the system worked. The better man was, in fact, chosen. Washington, without a doubt, was what the African-American community needed as its first mayor, a razzle-dazzle warrior with a clear vision of the big picture. Sawyer was the perfect person to succeed Washington. He was a bridge for a city that was attempting to heal itself racially. A peacemaker. A doer. Someone who knew what it took to get the garbage picked up, to keep the streets cleaned, and to get the potholes filled.

By Thanksgiving Day, Sawyer knew he had enough votes to lock up the post. But in the days that followed, the Sixth Ward alderman watched in dismay as the propaganda machine transformed him from the guy who was liked by everybody who knew him to the man who was hated by everybody who did not know him. He watched as his support among African-American aldermen was stripped away. At one point he had the signatures of fourteen of the council's sixteen African-American aldermen on a resolution calling for him to be elected as Washington's successor. That number shrank to six as an organized terror campaign ripped its way through the black community. African-American aldermen who supported Sawyer started receiving profane calls laced with death threats. The threats, the calls, those targeted, followed a pattern so plain that there could be little doubt that it was all orchestrated.

Dismayed by the crowd of 3,000 inside the council chambers and the crowd of nearly that many out on LaSalle Street, Sawyer, who is by nature reticent, easygoing, and noncommittal, wanted to postpone the vote for a couple of days. The delay, he hoped, would give the crowd—and the community it came to represent—time to get some understanding of the legislated process that was destined to take place.

No one doubts that Sawyer felt the heat from the passionate protesters. There is some question, however, about how he reacted. Wendell Peete, a six-foot-three-inch 320-pounder who was chief of police for Cook County Hospital and a member of Sawyer's ward organization, acted as a bodyguard to the man who would be mayor that night. Peete, who has since parted ways with the former acting mayor, says Sawyer may have fainted or his knees may have buckled. Peete says that although the mayoralty was Sawyer's for the taking, the alderman was badly affected by the intense hostility of the crowd. "He kept saying he needed some time," Peete recalls. "He kept saying, the perspective is wrong. The community's perspective is wrong." Sawyer readily admits that he believed that the African-American community misunderstood what was happening. However, he is adamant in insisting neither of two things happened: He did not faint; his knees did not buckle. As he was maneuvered through the throng back to his council seat, Sawyer says the crush of the crowd literally lifted him off his feet; he was physically carried through the swarm. At the point where the crowd thinned out, Sawyer came crashing to the ground. In other words, his knees did not give out; his people let him down. Assuming it happened as Sawyer says it did, it was a prophetic occurrence.

From that decisive moment forward, whether he dropped or was dropped really did not matter. The image of Eugene Sawyer as a weak-kneed, tender-footed stumbler was fixed permanently in too many minds. The 10:00 P.M. nightly news on December 1st turned into expanded live coverage of the city council proceedings, and by then television reporters already were making references to and quips about Sawyer's knee-buckling episode. Later in the live coverage, Fourteeth Ward alderman Ed Burke, a seasoned electronic media performer who surely must have known the cameras were rolling, ostentatiously pointed his finger in Sawyer's face as the two men met behind glass walls. If the walls had ears, they would have heard Burke warning Sawyer that his opportunity for succeeding to the mayor's seat was now or never; that the existing voting bloc would not hold during a two- or three-day waiting period. That, in essence, Sawyer was the not-so-great black hope. It did not, of course, play that way on the tube. It was Boss Burke telling Tom Sawyer, in articulate body English, what to do. That silent image, broadcast to scores of thousands of television viewers, was the coup de grace. Eugene Sawyer was Humpty-Dumpty. Millions of dollars in television campaign ads, iron-jock political ploys, and staunch human decency aside, Sawyer could not overcome the image of the meek, weak, plantation-raised pol being ordered around by Burke, the zealous, vitriolic lieutenant of the anti-Washington council war.

Sawyer's mayoral race was over, long before it started. (My 20/20 vision on this, I must admit, is greatly enhanced by hindsight.)

There was other bad symbolism. Sawyer was sworn in as mayor at four o'clock in the morning, "like a thief in the night," to borrow a phrase from Washington. Unfortunately for Sawyer, hundreds of thousands of viewer-voters were still watching the live broadcasts, and many were turned off by what they saw.

As the newly sworn-in acting mayor, Sawyer found himself being shuttled from a bad situation to a worse one. The government, and its department heads, were not his. They were Harold Washington's. Many of them believed the images and propaganda being spread, and therefore operated openly as Evans sympathizers and Sawyer saboteurs. Worst of all, there was nothing the acting mayor could do about it. Those classical clichés, "caught between a rock and a hard place," and "damned if you do, damned if you don't," became Sawyer's watchwords. There could be no housecleaning during his watch. To fire the saboteurs, malcontents, and misfits would have given some credence to the Evans-Tillman-Grimshaw-Rush combine's smear that he as a puppet of Burke and the boys. Not to fire them left him open to sabotage, with even high-ranking officials in his employ working furiously against him. It also played into the public perception that Sawyer was too weak-willed to take charge. To say it was a no-win situation is to speak in understatement.

The end result cannot be emphasized enough: Sawyer wore the mantle of loser, long before he lost.

Knowing that Sawyer's support was soft, if not nearly nonexistent, among his natural constituency, the white ethnic aldermen applied pressure from the other side. The recurrent pitch went like this: Gene didn't frighten Chicago's white ethnics the way Harold had. Gene was somebody they could sell to the voters in their wards. All Gene had to do was stop listening to the Tillmans and Rushes of the city and do the right thing. Fire the gaggles of city workers who were working against him. They named names. Hire a gaggle of their people to work for him. They had names. If he cooperated, he would be mayor for as long as he wished. But if he did not play ball, they were going to run one of their guys against him. And that would be that.

Being caught in that Catch-22 position was the bane of the Sawyer mayoralty. Sawyer was savvy enough to know he could not and should not trust the siren song that the white ethnic aldermen sang. Yet there was another irony here. Washington, whose base was in the integrated Fifth Ward, was a semistrange bedfellow to the so-called lakefront liberals. Sawyer, whose base was in the solidly black middle-class Sixth Ward, was firmly rooted in African-American political philosophy. Had Sawyer survived the Evans-Daley double-team, the Sixth Ward could have become to African-Americans what the Eleventh Ward had been (and currently is) for Irish-Americans. Unfortunately for Sawyer, he did not have the luxury of contemplating political dynasties. Instead, he had to focus on political survival. If he was to continue as Chicago's second black mayor, he had to shore up and broaden his base. That was no simple task with the Evans faction working overtime at undermining his efforts, his accomplishments, and his good intentions.

The most serious crisis of the Sawyer administration sprang from the trick bag in which the acting mayor found himself. The day before a Chicago *Tribune* story broke reporting that a member of the Sawyer administration, Steve Cokely, had made anti-Semitic statements, I was warned by a friend at the newspaper. I called the mayor to explain to him what was going into the May 1st Sunday *Tribune* and what sort of media hounding and pounding would follow. Before I completed my rundown, the mayor stopped me. Jumping to the logical conclusion I was leading to, Sawyer blurted: "I'm not firing Stevie." Steve Cokely had been a special charity case of Alderman Sawyer's for the better part of two and a half years. Cokely, who was one of those people who never seemed able to connect all the dots when going through an extended thought process, had attracted bad press nearly three years earlier when, while serving as an aide to Eighth Ward Alderman Marion Humes, he attacked Columbus Day as a racist holiday that did not deserve celebrating in America. Humes dropped Cokely like the hot potato he was. Good Samaritan Sawyer picked him up and set out to try to rehabilitate him. When Alderman Sawyer became acting mayor, he gave Cokely the low-level administrative post of community liaison. Cokely's new job called for him to be Mayor Sawyer's eyes and ears in the more radical grass-roots segments of the African-American community. Media reports, predictably, made Cokely sound as if he were an integral cog in the policy-making machinery. By implication, one of Sawyer's top administrative aides was a wild-eyed, harebrained, anti-Semitic bigot.

The Cokely story broke early Saturday afternoon. By late Saturday night, Sharon Gist Gilliam, the mayor's chief operating officer, Erwin France, his most reliable advisor, and I all had talked to Mayor Sawyer at home, attempting to persuade him to get rid of Cokely. He either did not listen or did not hear. Those who had his ear on the Cokely issue whispered wrongheaded advice. Several key members of his security detail and some of the black aldermen in his camp did not see the issue as the anti-Semitic, hateful episode it was. To them it was simply a black-and-white issue. If Sawyer was seen as siding with whites against a black, once again it would seem to his natural constituency that he was a tool of the anti-Washington whites. Meanwhile, Sawyer's traveling aide, Derek Shelton, was telling the mayor that the brouhaha would blow over. It was obvious to me that it was only going to blow us away if we did not hurry up and get it behind us.

That weekend was long and punishing. Monday was just as bad. Chief Counsel Judson Miner, Commissioners Joan Harris and Liz Hollander, and other Jewish members of the Sawyer administration were on the verge of open revolt. Chicago *Sun-Times* columnist Irv Kupcinet mysteriously and uncharacteristically cancelled a private, one-on-one lunch appointment with the mayor. By noon, I had had one of my staff writers prepare a short, to-the-point press release announcing Cokely's resignation. Cokely was summoned to the mayor's office. My understanding was that the mayor would ask Cokely to tender his resignation. Should he refuse, he would be fired. After a twenty-minute closed-door private meeting with the mayor, Cokely emerged wearing a smug smirk. When I entered the mayor's office, I was told that Cokely would issue an apology. I shuddered and handed Sawyer the "Cokely resigns" press release.

"Okay, Your Honor. But sooner or later, we're going to have to release this."

Politics aside, there were personal reasons for Sawyer's aversion to canning Cokely. Rather than viewing Cokely strictly as the political liability he was, Sawyer saw him as his charge and as the father of two small children who had to be clothed, housed, and fed. There was also a cultural element at work here. From childhood on, African-Americans are lectured constantly on the importance of having a job. In a community where unemployment is discriminantly disproportionate, having a job takes on iconic preeminence. Therefore, firing people does not come easily to an African-American in a position to do so. Harold Washington had a hard time doing it. So did Eugene Sawyer.

There was one other striking similarity between the two African-American mayors. Both men were legislators, not executives. They were in the practice of seeking consensus rather than bossing people around. By the time he died, Washington understood that as mayor, as the city's chief executive, he sometimes had to utilize the surgeon's scalpel and wield the butcher's axe. That was a lesson Sawyer was waiting to learn. "Sawyer's style of hearing everybody but not stopping anybody worked to his detriment," observes Erwin France, Sawyer's brilliant, city-contract-laden advisor.

Cokely's Monday apology failed to ameliorate anything. By Tuesday, it was becoming increasingly clear that government was screeching to a standstill. The media became an angry mob on a self-righteous mission, intent on tarring and feathering Mayor Sawyer. Cokely had to go. Arrangements were made for Sawyer to meet with Cokely at the McCormick Hotel. That meeting turned into a meeting with the Mau-Maus, a bittersweet nickname given to the most vocal, most aggressive, and most doctrinaire of the African-American grass-roots leadership. After a long, stormy session with them, it was agreed that Cokely would be allowed to resign. The next morning, Cokely met with the mayor again. Cokely was in tears as he told Sawyer that he could not resign because his manhood was on the line. His nationalist brothers would think he had punked out. That he was not black enough. Later that day, a press release came out of my office announcing the firing of Steve Cokely. But by then irreparable damage had been done. The Jewish community and a healthy portion of the liberal white community was lost. However, the equation in the black community changed very little—if any at all.

Except for taking it on the chin in the Cokely fiasco, Mayor Sawyer was weathering relatively well. Considering how things started out and how things were going, the first six months were much better for the Sawyer administration than anyone would have predicted. A newspaper story about a $30,000 finder's fee paid to Sawyer proved to be too dense, too complicated, too far in the past, and too void of sex appeal and visuals to stimulate much television coverage and therefore much public outrage.

With no executive experience and little popular support, Sawyer managed to keep the government not only going, but going smoothly. That is particularly significant, I think, when you stop to consider that Sawyer literally was thrust into the job without any aspiration or preparation, and that he did not get one day of the customary honeymoon accorded newly elected public officials by the news media. An appreciable amount of his early success had to do with the efforts of Erwin France, his much-maligned one-man transition team. France held Sawyer's hand and guided him through troubled waters for the first three months or so of the new administration, until the neophyte mayor had developed his administrative sea legs.

That Sawyer was such a quick study should come as no surprise. His sixteen years of council experience and the relationships he had developed over the years with his fellow aldermen worked to his advantage. And he had served as the chairman of the crucially important rules committee after Washington finally gained numerical advantage in the council. Thus, the Sixth Ward alderman knew how to move things through the council. He knew which buttons to push—and when—to get things done. And that is exactly what he did.

Acting Mayor Sawyer had enacted the late Mayor Washington's 1988 budget and a needed $66 million tax increase before he had been in office a month. In January 1988, he got council approval for legislation that broke the taxi monopoly in the city, something that Mayor Washington had not been able to do. In February, Sawyer managed to round up enough aldermanic support to get a bill passed allowing lights in Wrigley Field so that the Chicago Cubs would no longer be the only team in major league baseball unable to play night games at home—a feat his five predecessors were either unwilling or unable to accomplish. Sawyer got the ball rolling for private development of land around O'Hare Airport. During the Sawyer administration, an unprecedented agreement was reached with the firemen's union, guaranteeing labor peace for four-year chunks of time. And, after a number of failed attempts, under Sawyer's leadership the city council finally passed a long-overdue human rights ordinance that protected gay and handicapped citizens from discrimination in employment and housing.

Seeing how well Sawyer performed under the most adverse conditions, I convinced myself that he could become another legendary Chicago mayor if only the shackles were stripped away. In the long run, I believed, an election in 1989 would work to the acting mayor's advantage, because after winning, he would have the necessary mandate to put his imprint on city government. I probably was the only person in the entire administration who felt that way; everyone else seemed to think that Sawyer needed Harold Washington's full term in order to build a toutable record while letting the wounds in the African-American community heal.

I innocently believed that an actual mayoral election—and all there was at stake—would serve as a wake-up call to the African-American community. That this selfish Evans ego trip would be exposed for what it was and that the community would rally to the common cause. That the African-American community would embrace the "bird in the hand" principle and come to understand that holding the mayor's seat was critical in both real and symbolic terms to its economic and political development. But there was one small piece of the puzzle I overlooked: There was not enough time for the benefits of having one of your own running city hall to trickle down.

Michael Scott, who has held positions in the Byrne, Washington, Sawyer, and Daley administrations, points out that the average African-American in Chicago never got a sense of what having power at the top meant. Washington never had the chance to get many of the services down to the little people. For the first three and a half years of his administration, Scott notes, Washington did not have a majority vote in the city council. After the court ruled that key wards had been gerrymandered and called for special aldermanic elections, the balance changed. But by that time, Washington was running for reelection, and all his energies and resources went toward that end. Seven months after his second term got under way, the mayor died. The African-American community did not fully realize the benefits of having one of their own in the fifth-floor seat. That and the protracted family feud took their toll. The 1989 election found many African-Americans apathetic again.

My own political shortsightedness was surpassed by that of those in the Evans camp. They envisioned a crusade clone mirroring the one that swept Congressman Washington into city hall. They failed to realize that a passionate crusade, like the loss of one's virginity, happens only once. That same emotional excitement can never be experienced twice; a copycat crusade was an impossible dream. But in its quixotic folly, the Evans faction went to court, brandishing a lawsuit, forcing an early election and its unavoidable ending. Had it not done that, I would not be writing this. The white ethnic pols were not about to risk a heated political backlash by seeking a 1989 election. Had the Evans camp not forced a legal showdown, an African-American would be sitting in the seat Harold Washington was elected to hold until the term expired in 1991. A singular-minded white Chicago, which never stopped believing that the black mayoral victory in 1983 was a fluke, merely seized the time by taking advantage of an inopportune split in the African-American community.

Even if the December 1st and 2nd fiasco and the resulting community cleavage had not been so maledictive from the beginning, the Sawyer mayoralty definitely was doomed in the end because the special election campaign effort turned out to be a tragedy of errors. It had the wrong man with the wrong strategy reporting to the wrong people for the wrong reasons.

There are obvious reasons why things occurred the way they did. First and foremost, the campaign fund-raising arm also was the political think tank. As a general rule, fund raisers know how to raise money but know little about political strategy. If fund raisers and strategists are commingled, the result is bad politics. All during the campaign, for example, Al Johnson, a retired millionaire Cadillac salesman who could best be described as a political dilettante, used his ties to the purse strings to influence or put a stop to ideas, people, or positions.

With the bean counters at the helm, the campaign committee went down South and downscale to select Louisiana accountant Reynard Rochon to manage the effort to make Acting Mayor Sawyer the mayor. Had the Daley and Evans camps conspired together, they could not have found a worse man. Rochon was an outsider who had little interest in and less appreciation for the subtleties and nuances of Chicago politics. His philosophy on municipal election campaigns aped former Vice-President Spiro Agnew's viewpoint on ghettoes: if you've seen one, you've seen them all. In a mayoral campaign, according to the Rochon paint-by-the-numbers scenario, all cities had community groups that had to be co-opted, a few key reporters who could be seduced, and commonplace political problems that called for simple political solutions. Thus, any big-city mayor had to be against drugs, for law and order, and against tax increases. Though this obviously was a cookie-cutter approach, Rochon implied that it had a proof-in-the-pudding credibility because he had managed the successful second campaign of Philadelphia Mayor Wilson Goode. As I saw it, it was Frank Rizzo, not Reynard Rochon, who won that race for the incumbent mayor. Had anyone except the overtly racist Rizzo run against Mayor Goode, who allowed the Philadelphia police to bomb an entire block in an African-American neighborhood, the outcome would have been decidedly different.

Larry Horist, the veteran Republican political consultant who became the Sawyer campaign's second political press secretary, notes that Rochon had a penchant for taking press opportunities that should have been executed by the mayor or one of his two media spokesmen—Horist or me. Although Rochon's media forays were sometimes blatantly self-promotional, no one in the Sawyer campaign seemed to notice or care. Further complicating the matter, Rochon was an absentee campaign manager who spent nearly as much time at home in New Orleans as he did on the battlefront in Chicago.

Rochon did, however, have a few workable strategies. The best among them was his push, from the beginning, to seal Evans's political coffin by any means necessary. As long as Evans was perceived as a political factor, Sawyer would not be able to rally all the troops for a victory. At first there was the carrot approach. Sawyer assured Evans that should an accord be reached, Sawyer would use his mayoral clout to ensure that Evans was the second most powerful man in Chicago. It was a no go. Later on, Sawyer offered to pull some behind-the-scene strings that would lead to Alderman Evans becoming Congressman Evans. No good. Finally, Sawyer reminded Evans that he (Sawyer) was not the type who would want to be mayor for twenty years and that he would be willing to step down after a term or two and throw his full support behind Evans. No deal. Unwilling to work it out, Evans and those calling his shots had a fight-to-the-death wish.

Believing its own concocted press clippings, the Evans camp operated under the illusion that Sawyer was the one who could be knocked out of contention. But this time, reality slapped the Evans campaign in the face as it tried futilely to line up some support from the African-American business community while Sawyer racked up one fruitful fund raiser after another.

Because the Evans campaign never had any evidence to support the bill of goods it had sold people about the Sawyer "sell-out," it grasped at the tactics it knew best: dirty deeds. Alderman Tillman turned up the volume on her name-calling tactics, declaring that the mayor was "an Uncle Tom." Borrowing a page from its successful initial strategy of fostering false images, the Evans gang resorted to orchestrating a boo campaign. Everywhere the mayor went, Evans operatives would start booing, giving the impression that Sawyer had gone beyond being unpopular to being reviled. This time the Evans faction was tripped up by its own tired tricks. Tillman's name calling, the constant booing, and the pimping of the late mayor's name fueled a steady climb in the polls for Sawyer.

However, the nastiness took its toll. Sawyer, who by nature is someone who loves to be loved, frequently was immobilized by the virulent hatred he encountered from the Evans faction. Many of Sawyer's supporters began to wonder whether the mayor really wanted to continue as mayor. That impression, naturally, was exploited by the Evans camp, which spread rumors that Sawyer did not want the job but merely was holding it for someone from the anti-Washington side.

Unfortunately, the acting mayor did not do enough to dispel those rumors. Those closest to him recalled how, just months before fate pulled him into the mayoral maelstrom, Sawyer was floating the idea of not running again for his aldermanic seat. Now that he was mayor, they sometimes wondered whether he still harbored a secret desire to get away from the madding crowd and settle comfortably in his easy chair, because he seemed to take little interest in the running of his special election campaign. Although there definitely was an air of indifference, much of it may have resulted from the unending gauntlet of political opposition and the accompanying obstacles that Sawyer had to face day after day.

One situation was constant throughout the Sawyer mayoralty and special election campaign. During all of his lengthy political life, Sawyer was a low-key, low-visibility public servant. Political analyst Bruce DuMont recalls a number of occasions when Sawyer accompanied then Alderman Clifford Kelley to WBEZ studios, where the Twentieth Ward alderman was scheduled to appear on the radio show "Inside Politics." DuMont says he frequently invited Alderman Sawyer to participate on the program. Each time, Sawyer declined. Not much changed once the alderman became the mayor. Although he saw to it that he was as open and as available to the media as any Chicago mayor, the shy Sawyer did so while heaving a deep sigh. Because Sawyer was not a media creature, and because his maiden media excursion on December 1st had turned him into a bogeyman to his natural constituency, the challenge was to change him from being unknown and unpopular to being as familiar and comfortable as a pair of old shoes.

Rochon's effort to achieve this impossible mission boiled down to a one-two punch of TV commercial clips and community coffee sips. A slick media consultant was brought in from Boston to film the mayor's campaign commercials. With the exception of the dumb-dumb Daley spots, in which the state's attorney was portrayed as being unable to complete a full sentence without cue cards, these commercials were of the pretty-picture, feel-good genre, giving a rundown of what had been accomplished in a short amount of time. The coffee sips, on the other hand, were off-limits to the media. That was just one of many Rochon mistakes. Sawyer was at his best in small, intimate groups.

But the greatest shortcoming of the campaign was that aside from its media efforts, it had little going for it. The campaign overbought media while failing to put enough financial resources early on in such essentials as placards, buttons, campaign literature, and field offices. As a result, there was little evidence of a field operation. In the end, the Sawyer campaign proved to be top-heavy with generals and lacking crucial foot soldiers. When campaign posters were finally bought, there was no one to distribute them to supporters who would put them in the windows of their homes. Most of the time the campaign headquarters had two, only two, secretaries answering the telephone, so when those who were interested in volunteering called, it was almost impossible for them to get through. Those who managed to get through seldom were lucky enough to have anyone get back to them.

During the campaign, on more than one occasion Larry Horist and I commiserated about the lack of a cohesive campaign strategy. There was no theme. No vision. No position papers were published. Although the campaign was selling Sawyer as the mayor for all the people, too much time was spent securing his base. One critical campaign worker grumbled, "We keep sending him back to the same black churches over and over again." The mayor was a victim of his campaign's scheduling in other ways as well. So many stops would be jammed into a single day that some had to be dropped along the way. The mayor found himself outrunning the media assigned to cover him. "It was an island of things," says Horist of the campaign, "that never connected."

I am going to make one other related point. The 1983, 1987, and 1989 Chicago mayoral races all were miscast. Although they were not reported that way, those contests were nothing more than a variation on an old American theme: an emerging ethnic group exercising its political muscle to make its way further into the mainstream. Irish-Americans did it a century ago. Other hyphenated American groups have done it in other parts of the nation at other times. Our skin color and our unique history in this nation do not allow African-Americans the luxury of being just another developing ethnic group. We always are dealt the race card. Granted, sometimes we ask for it, but often we do not. It does not matter. We are dealt it whether we want it or not. So, rather than being an American ethnic group, we are a racial group. Rather than being recognized as the largest ethnic group in this nation, we are classified as a minority in white America. It follows naturally that the mayoral contests, rather than being covered along the lines of an African-American against an Irish-American, were reported and voted along racial lines. White against black. Although it was not articulated that way, I do not believe that African-Americans were voting skin color so much as they were voting ethnicity. However, the lion's share of the European-Americans voted race, regardless of creed or national origin. In Chicago in 1989, a united white racial front prevailed over a divided African-American ethnic bloc.

As early as July of 1988, Alderman Burke proved to be clairvoyant. After months of anti-Sawyer political games from Evans and his small band of aldermanic allies, the acting mayor reluctantly moved on the long-overdue council reorganization. Evans, Tillman, Rush, and others in their rump group finally were stripped of their council committee chairmanships, their clout, their patronage, and the enormous discretionary funds that accompanied the posts. With the vote over and the Evans contingent out, Burke and Thirty-third Ward Alderman Richard Mell stood in the men's room off the council chambers, gloating as they washed their hands. A non-African-American television reporter, who was also in the council men's room at the time, alleges that he overheard Burke make this omniscient observation to Mell: "The niggers will never get together after this."

Enough said.

15.

THE DALEY ERA: RICHARD J. TO RICHARD M.

Melvin G. Holli

The story of Chicago politics during the last half century is that of a father-and-son team, the Daleys. Father Richard J. served as Chicago's mayor from 1955 to 1976, and son Richard M. was elected first in 1989 for a short term and in 1991, 1995, 1999, and 2003 for full four-year terms. The six-term father and thus far five-times son rival Chicago's other famous father-and-son team, the Carter Harrisons, who served five mayoralties each between 1879 and 1915.

Political Stability, 1955–1976

What historic and other factors help to account for Richard J. Daley's long tenure as mayor? The times certainly were inauspicious for elected public leaders.[1] The last decade and a half of Daley's career, until his death in 1976, was a troubled and turbulent period in American history in which the rate of change was faster than normal and the types of change were greater than ever before. The dynamics of the period were race, gender, ethnicity, a liberal political culture, urban obsolescence, and an economic transformation that rendered many cities nearly ungovernable. The 1960s—and the aftershocks in the 1970s—were perilous times for big-city mayors. Ghetto rioters, black power activists, protesters against urban renewal and expressway building, welfare rights groups, the Gray Panthers, and a myriad of other groups, all fighting for some special interest, were turning urban government into one of the most perilous political jobs in America. The afflictions wrought by that age were fatal to the careers of some of the best-known and most promising big-city mayors. The political achievement of Detroit's "golden boy" mayor

Jerome Cavanaugh, for example, was crushed by a 1967 riot. The nation's first big-city black mayor, Carl Stokes, experienced a career-shattering black riot and "shoot-out" in Cleveland in 1968. New York City's handsome jet-setter, John Lindsay, was ambushed by racial and ethnic conflict over housing and schools that destroyed his career both as mayor and as a presidential hopeful. Although wily Los Angeles mayor Sam Yorty survived the 1964 riots in Watts, he did not survive the decade politically and—like his urban counterpart, Lindsay—saw his attempt for the presidency collapse ignominiously. Daley, almost alone among the prominent big-city mayors, survived that career-killing decade.[2]

Why did Daley not only survive but thrive? One factor important to his survival was that he managed a city that actually worked. As *Newsweek* put it in 1971,

> Chicago is that most wondrous of exceptions—a major American city that actually works. While breakdowns in essential services have become almost a daily event elsewhere, Chicagoans enjoy virtually an uninterrupted supply of urban amenities. They commute to work on the nation's most ingeniously integrated transportation system. . . . Chicago's streets are probably the cleanest and best-illuminated on the metropolitan scene; its police and fire departments are ranked by professionals as among the most effective in the world.

Finally, under Daley, liberal zoning laws and flexible tax policies prevented the "corporate exodus" then "plaguing New York."[3]

Perhaps even more important, Daley brought a sense of stability to his city during a time of deep troubles in urban America. He projected and often lived up to the image of a strong leader whose firm hand on the throttle permitted only orderly and slow change, if it permitted change at all. This effort to slow change to a manageable and controllable pace had a deep and profound appeal to Chicagoans. Chicago's voters—who were heavily Catholic, "corporate" in social outlook, ethnic, blue collar and often hard-hat in occupation, and politically conservative, were deeply troubled by the long-haired leaders of an ill-mannered generation that ridiculed their occupations, religion, politics, and lifestyles and, furthermore, threatened the existing order of things.

Stability and order above all became Daley's stock in trade for a troubled electorate. "Huge numbers of people in every corner of the city," observed Chicago television newsman Walter Jacobson, "regard Mayor Daley as a father. He had weathered all the winds of change, and his people look to him for safekeeping." Even Daley's political enemies recognized this devotion. Daley's 1959 GOP opponent, Timothy Sheehan, said he had always got a rise out of any downstate or suburban audience by referring to "Boss Daley" or "Dictator Daley." "That always worked them up." But after the 1968 riots, that strategy did not work anymore. "They liked Daley in the most conservative areas and they should. Nobody did the job he did. He didn't let the minority groups have whatever they wanted. He took a stand." A Sindlinger public opinion poll conducted immediately after the 1968 Democratic national convention riots confirmed Sheehan's judgment: Some 71 percent of the public polled found no fault with Chicago's hard-hitting police, and 61 percent said Mayor Daley was doing a good job. Another one of Daley's Republican mayoral opponents, Benjamin Adamowski (1963), warned in the 1970s that Chicago was sitting "on a keg of dynamite" and that only Daley, who worked with the black, white, and Hispanic communities, could prevent an explosion. Daley's 1975 vanquished challenger, John Hoellen, after much criticism of Daley's insensitivity, conceded that "he [Daley] has been able to avoid the worst riots, and probably kept the lid on the city from exploding."[4]

Keeping the lid on and maintaining stability were also the refrains heard from William Singer, an independent Democrat and challenger in the 1975 primary. In a retrospective on his primary defeat, Singer said that people voted for Daley "not because the precinct captain forced or cajoled them, but because they made a decision that they were for Daley. They felt a great sense of stability in knowledge of what they had. . . . It was an incredible thing. There was an enormous stability factor." Certified reformer and professor William Grimshaw conceded the same with his remark that Daley in his later years was a "rock of stability. And he was holding the whole thing together."[5] Undoubtedly Daley's ability to control some of the threatening changes and runaway events accounts for much of his popularity during more than a decade of turbulence and unpredictability for Chicagoans. Stability and order, alongside slow or no change, played great roles in Daley's lengthy tenure in a time of national and urban political troubles.

Political Instability

Enter, Exit Michael Bilandic, 1976–1979

On 20 December 1976, Mayor Richard J. Daley died. What would follow Daley was a dozen years of political instability and near chaos in the Chicago political system. Richard J. Daley, a six-time elected mayor who served twenty-one years, would be followed by four different mayors who went through four hotly contested elections and served only twelve years. Daley's death in 1976 saw the system destabilize and ushered in unpredictable election outcomes and an opportunistic smash-and-grab political style accompanied by seemingly endless and rancorous ethnic and racial squabbling. The slow slide into an interregnum of political disorder began with a racial tiff over who should be interim, or acting, mayor: a black alderman, Wilson Frost, or a white alderman from Daley's Eleventh Ward, Michael Bilandic. Unlike most mayors, Bilandic is remembered mostly for his stormy entrance into office and his even stormier exit.

Potent political forces collided during the urgent, and secret, negotiations just after Daley's death, in the days before Christmas 1976, to pick a successor. Frost, the council president, asserted that he was the acting mayor. Backing Frost's mayoral claim was the city's huge black community and its loud-voiced leaders, such as the Reverend Jesse Jackson. Also looking for the city's top job was Northwest Side alderman Roman C. Pucinski, a sterling son of Polish Chicago, which was irritated over its inability to capture real power in the world's second-largest Polish city. Also entering into the acting-mayor fray was Edward Vrdolyak, a tough, smart Southeast Side alderman. Bilandic was quickly picked as interim mayor by a lopsided 45-2 city council vote. Only two lakefront independents opposed the choice, but many in the black community were affronted by what they considered a political snub. The appointed black champion Wilson Frost sheepishly explained to his African American supporters that it would have been suicide to go up against a done deal by the remnants of the machine. Bilandic's selection as interim mayor was the old guard's last hurrah.

The Chicago of 1977 was a city different from the one in which a young "Boss" Daley had first come to power in 1955. The black community had swelled by a record-breaking five hundred thousand people, mostly from southern migration, and their percentage of the city's population had shot from about 20 percent to 35 percent and was still growing. In addition, the civil rights movement, antipatronage court decisions, the decline of party loyalty, and white flight were steadily eroding the bases of traditional organizational power. The old boys in the organization had been lulled into a false sense of security by the ease with which they had put Bilandic over on the city. In the future, they would face stiff resistance to such decisions.

In the mayoral primary scheduled for February 1977, candidate Pucinski unleashed a bitter attack on both Acting Mayor Bilandic and the entire closed-door selection process, challenging the mayor to a public debate, which he refused. Then another mayoral contestant jumped into the ring. Underfinanced and underorganized but with overpowering rhetoric, Harold Washington began campaigning vigorously on the South Side, threatening to draw black voters away from the Democratic slate makers' choice, Bilandic. "There is a sleeping black giant in Chicago," Washington told a South Side Baptist church congregation, "and if this sleeping giant, the potential black vote, ever woke up, we'd control this city."[6] Prophetic words for future elections. Things really got out of hand when a third Democratic candidate waded in—discredited state's attorney Edward Hanrahan (tainted by the 1969 raid on the Black

Panthers and the shooting of two Panther leaders). The easy entry of loose cannons such as Hanrahan into the Democratic primary indicated how enfeebled Democratic machine control had become.

Even so, Bilandic went on to an easy victory in the general election. He carried slightly more than 50 percent of the vote, losing seven North and Northwest Side wards and 32 percent of the vote to Pucinski, and five middle-class black South Side wards to Washington, results that clearly signified a weakening of party discipline. Three groups—Poles, blacks, and lakefront liberals—had shown their displeasure with the old way of doing things.

Bilandic's short two-year term was not without its achievements. As political scientist Milton Rakove saw it, Bilandic's tenure was one of "accomplishment, continuity, and some forward motion."[7] Bilandic had balanced the city budget, kept the bond rating high, and continued the public service tradition that made the "city that worked." He had also maintained peace in the city council with backroom bargaining and by avoiding the public appearance of conflict. Few political commentators foresaw any threats to the 1979 reelection of Bilandic.

How then did Bilandic lose with the last big-city machine backing him? Bilandic's tale of woe began with a record January snowstorm that left the mayor bogged hip-deep in problems he was unprepared to face. The city that supposedly worked stopped working. Garbage piled up in the alleyways and remained uncollected, streets remained impassable, and parking spaces that had been carved out of glacial snowbanks were guarded like prime real estate. A cold snap froze the heavy snow in the streets to a concretelike hardness that not even snowplows could dent. Bilandic's response was to assure the city that all was well. But the city's snow plan, which had been written by a city hall crony, turned into a bad joke. The black community was outraged when the Chicago Transit Authority, which had a limited number of already overcrowded trains, began skipping South and West Side stops as white commuters whizzed by, Loop-bound. Other trains ran sporadically, their electric power shorting out on mountains of ice and snow. Buses ran hours behind schedule. Side streets went unplowed. The outrage was widespread and white hot, just the kind of catalyst needed to dump an incumbent.

On Valentine's Day, a beleaguered Mayor Bilandic spoke before a huge meeting of precinct captains at a downtown hotel and lapsed into a bizarre, off-the-wall performance. The struggling mayor compared recent criticism of his administration to the crucifixion of Christ, the Nazi persecution of the Jews, and the decline of democracy around the world. His rambling speech concluded with an astonishing outburst: "In the early history of Christianity, you see a leader starting with twelve disciples. They crucified the leader and made martyrs of the others. It is our turn to be in the trenches and see if we are made of the same stuff as the early Christians, the persecuted Jews, the proud Poles, the blacks and Latinos."[8] Some of the audience giggled. Most were embarrassed. The strain was showing.

Even though the Democratic Party has not lost a contested primary election since 1911, it was going to lose this one. An outsider named Jane Byrne, diminutive but a bombshell campaigner, unleashed a slam-bang, hell-raising campaign that caught the old boys with their guard down. The anger over the blizzard of 1979 and Bilandic's fumbled handling of it gave three dissident groups the leverage to beat the machine. Byrne won fourteen of the city's sixteen black wards, all seven independent lakefront wards, and several Northwest Side Polish wards.

The tradition of the invincible Democratic machine had been broken. The long and hoary practice whereby machine Democrat begat machine Democrat and Chicago voters queued up at the ballot box like somnambulist proles thumping for the peerless leader was over. Predictability and stability, the great Democratic cynosures built into the system over a half century of careful cultivation and polishing, were over. No longer was the Democratic party's choice automatically the people's choice for mayor.

Jane Byrne, 1979–1983

"I beat the whole goddamn Machine singlehanded," crowed Jane Byrne after her stunning upset of incumbent Mayor Bilandic in the party's February 1979 primary election.[9] It had been a David-and-Goliath contest, pitting a five-foot, three-inch scrappy woman against the machine political heavyweights and overlords who had not lost such a contest for half a century. The mighty had fallen, and most of Chicago cheered. The general election that followed in April was a cakewalk by comparison, for in one-party Chicago, winning the nomination in February had been tantamount to winning the general election in April. Jane Byrne handily beat her Republican opponent, Wallace Johnson, with the largest majority in Chicago's mayoral history, an astounding 82 percent of the vote. Even Richard J. Daley in his masterful triumphs at the polls had never matched that percentage. From all appearances, the new mayor had been put into office by a powerful but evanescent mandate.

In her campaign, Jane Byrne had caviled endlessly about the evils of machine politics and about the "cabal of evil men" who ran the city. She seemed to promise a new deal in politics and a reshuffling of the structure of power, at least in the city council. Then, in a stunning reversal, she deserted the reformers who had helped her win and linked up with the "evil cabal" of the council, including Edward "Fast Eddie" Vrdolyak and Edward Burke, permitting them to organize the council and select committee chairmen. Disarray, confusion, and gloom descended upon the dissident communities that had helped elect her. Hopes for political reform had died again at the starting gate.[10]

Grim fiscal realities faced the vibrant new mayor. When Byrne assumed office in 1979, the second destructive wave of higher prices for oil and gas from OPEC drove up the inflation that was soon gnawing at the nation's vitals with 15 to 20 percent interest rates. Cities on the high-risk list had difficulty selling their bonds, sometimes absorbing massive losses through deep discounts, and some bankers were looking askance at even short-term tax anticipation warrants, which all cities needed to tide them over until taxes were paid. The doubling of interest rates meant that a massive transfer of money that formerly might have gone for raises for city workers would now have to be borrowed. No or slow growth, accompanied by the loss of industrial jobs and plants, a rust belt–wide phenomenon, was felt acutely and exacerbated Chicago's inability to pay its bills.

With the municipal cupboard bare, Byrne resisted the costly demands of public service employees and took on three publicly disruptive and emotionally wrenching strikes. In December 1979, it was the transit workers union that struck at the peak of the downtown and Loop Christmas shopping season. In January 1980, the teachers union reneged on agreed-upon spending cuts and job trimming and walked out. And in February, in the dead of winter and at the height of the heating season, when citizens most need fire protection, the city's firefighters struck. Byrne was on a strike-a-month schedule. The firefighters' walkout was a nasty and messy affair. To help lay out strategy, the union brought in an "outside agitator" who consistently took a belligerent, public-be-damned attitude on the nightly television news. Into this volatile mess Byrne brought strikebreakers, some of whom were black. City hall aides to the mayor suggested publicly that some firefighters were sabotaging fire protection and even engaging in arson. The union capitulated, but the strike disrupted permanently the chummy relationship that had existed between the mayor's office and the firefighters.[11]

The urban gravy train, which had richly rewarded such public employees as transit workers and firefighters in the inflation-ridden 1960s and 1970s, had come to a halt in the austere, cash-short, deflation-prone 1980s. To her credit, Byrne faced this reality and took on three difficult strikes. To her discredit, she handled all three strikes in what to the public seemed to be a vacillating, then vindictive, sometimes mean, and small-minded manner. News reporters and the unions unflatteringly referred to her as "Good Jane, Bad Jane," and "Attila the Hen." Her bombastic rhetoric and her oversell on preparedness to take on the strikes tarnished and diminished the magnitude of her victory over the firefighters union.

Part of the circuslike atmosphere of Byrne's administration derived from "first husband" Jay McMullen, whom the press took to referring to as "Rasputin in a turtleneck" and who needlessly inflamed relations with the media. He once banished a *Tribune* correspondent from the city hall pressroom and threatened another group that he would "bloody their noses" if they did not give Mayor Byrne better copy. He referred to unfavorable coverage of his wife's administration as "more skunk juice from the Chicago *Tribune*." Part of the media's perception of battiness also came from Byrne's personal style with the press. She was so feisty and combative with reporters that they took to calling their meetings "gang-bang" press conferences. She played fire-away-Flanagan and hurled half-thought-out bombshells at them before disappearing behind an elevator door or exiting in a chauffeured car. She offended friend and foe alike, and her administration was, as Robert Davis of the *Tribune* described it, "creative, chaotic, dramatic, devastating, exciting, excruciating . . . historic," although some claimed it was "hysteric."[12]

Fighting Jane had committed fatal blunders during her one-term administration by turning former black supporters against her. She replaced black appointees with whites on the housing authority board and the board of education, and petulantly attacked a popular black alderman, targeting him for defeat. She soon became known as "Calamity Jane" who "shot from the lip" and kept Chicago in a state of turmoil with her helter-skelter hiring and firing policies, which became known as the "revolving door" policy.

Byrne was in some ways a free spirit, setting Chicago politics afire, a stormy Robespierre ready to chop heads, egged on by her husband, Jay. Few politicians in Chicago's history could match Byrne for her zaniness and madcap acts of derring-do. The larger meaning of the Byrne administration was that the political system had failed to settle down into a comfortable coalition with predictable political outcomes. A smash-and-grab style and opportunistic politics thrived in the political disequilibrium that prevailed.

Chicago's Ugly Racial Election, 1983

The open and unblushing use of racial, ethnic, and religious slurs reached an all-time high in the 1983 Chicago mayoral campaign. That blowout featured incumbent mayor Jane Byrne opposed by black challenger Congressman Harold Washington and States Attorney Richard M. Daley in the February Democratic primary. For States Attorney Daley to oppose the incumbent and Democratic party's choice made Daley look greedy, reckless, and contemptuous of political stability. The primary winner, Harold Washington, went up against Republican Bernard Epton in the general election for mayor. Both campaigns unloosed an overload of emotional blockbusters, racial code words, and slurs. Tocsin calls to action such as "It's our turn now. . . . We want it all, we want it now. . . . It's a racial thing, don't kid yourself. . . . Ditch the bitch and vote for Rich. . . . Go get 'em, Jewboy. . . . Epton! Epton! He's our man; we don't want no Af-ri-can," punctured the heady contest.[13] Harold Washington won the election to become Chicago's first black mayor.

During the four years before the next mayoral election, the new mayor Harold Washington went through a baptism of fire called "council wars" that amounted to three years of nonstop verbal fisticuffs and rat-a-tat-tat repartee with his white opponents. Bad feelings between the mayor and his white council opponents ran deep. And the conflict was so inflammatory and racially volatile that the eastern press took to calling Chicago "Beirut on the lake." Washington lashed out at his opponents in the language and tone of an irate southern preacher or an Old Testament prophet as he levied a writ of rhetorical fire and sword on the blasphemers who blocked his path or otherwise vexed him by disagreeing with him. The mayor spewed forth barrels of bile and wrath on gainsayers who crossed him. His principal council opponent, Edward Vrdolyak, was known in inner circles as the "Prince of Darkness," "Darth Vader," or "Mr. V.D." Fast Eddie's twin council commander, Edward Burke, was socked with such epithets as "draft dodger," "twerp," "the pits," and "a pimple on an elephant's butt." The mayoral wrath even reached downstate and arraigned Governor James Thompson for playing "hocus pocus, dominocus" with the voters and for being "a South Africanite," "an apartheidite," a "no good," a "disaster," and, occasionally, a "nincompoop" and an "SOB." For the late mayor Richard J. Daley, Washington employed a special lexicon of insult, calling him "a racist to the core, from head to toe, from hip to hip," adding, "I give no hosannas to a racist, nor do I appreciate or respect his son. . . . He is an insult to common sense and decency." Mayor Washington was an articulate abuser of his real and perceived enemies and got off some of the most intemperate verbal pyrotechnics and ad hominem attacks of any mayor in Chicago since Big Bill Thompson, the champion declaimer of bombast, who left office in 1931. The binge of political name-calling exceeded even that of the Byrne administration.[14]

When Washington sought reelection in 1987, the campaign (as hindsight would later show) reached a crest in ethnic, racial, and religious slandering. A new group on the scene, CONDUCT (Committee on Decent, Unbiased Campaign Tactics), directed by John McDermott, helped cool down the smoldering embers of racial conflict. Even so, it was not a squeaky clean, high school–style debate. CONDUCT issued thirteen reprimands related to the mayoral campaign, nine to Washington and his supporters, two to Byrne, and two to Vrdolyak. Ironically, CONDUCT had been set up by liberal types to fight 1983-style white racism but spent more time in 1987 denouncing black racism. The prize for the most inflammatory remark probably belonged to the former appellate court judge R. Eugene Pincham, who unleashed an emotional blockbuster at an Operation PUSH meeting in which he threatened, "Any man south of Madison who casts a vote in the February 24 primary and who doesn't cast a vote for Harold Washington ought to be hung. We know who you are." Despite such egregious blasts, city watchers and campaign observers generally agreed that the free and open use of racial and ethnic attacks had cooled somewhat, probably because of CONDUCT's monitoring.[15]

Harold Washington was reelected in April 1987 and turned over a new leaf in the book of Chicago mayoral politics. Instead of rubbing salt in the wounds of the vanquished as he had in his 1983 inaugural, he began his term in 1987 on a kinder and gentler note, speaking of a "new spirit of Chicago," the need to work together, and even going out of his way to compliment his hard-working mayoral predecessors who had helped build the downtown. He also excised a section of his campaign speech that cast aspersions on the Democratic machine, and his aldermanic ally David Orr noted that the mayor "didn't challenge them to fight. . . . The mayor's message was we should lower our voices." In October Washington extended an olive branch to his erstwhile enemies, white ethnics, by slating for countywide office a multiethnic, multiracial, gender-diverse slate that included Richard M. Daley; a Polish candidate, Aurelia Pucinski (daughter of Roman Pucinski, one of his bitterest council opponents); and Carol Moseley Braun, a black. This slate "tells people we've gone too far with this acrimony, this negativism, this inability to get along," Washington told the press.[16] This was his famous "dream ticket." But before a racial conciliation could be effected and before Washington could recast Chicago politics in this new rational and pacific mold, he died on November 25. With no faction sufficiently powerful enough to assert easy control, the political system ran wild again with a variety of pretenders posturing as the legitimate successors to the dead mayor.

But like Richard J. Daley before him, Mayor Washington had neither named a successor nor groomed an understudy to take his place. There was no heir apparent. The result was another fight for succession. Beginning on Thursday, Thanksgiving Day, the struggle was on for a new mayor. Jesse Jackson jetted in from a world-class trouble spot, the Persian Gulf, where he had been nursing his presidential ambitions, to support an A.B.C. (anybody but a Caucasian) successor. In one of the more astute political engineering jobs in recent memory, a white near-majority bloc of twenty-three aldermen joined with a minority black bloc of six aldermen to put over Eugene Sawyer as acting mayor. The event was a stormy one, with the black "movement" posturing alternately like French revolutionaries and bullyboys. The spectacular all-night pep rally ended at 4 a.m. After all of the insults had been exchanged, the movement people lost to the newly formed black-white alliance of convenience. The new acting mayor, Eugene Sawyer, was a soft-spoken conciliator (so soft-spoken that the press called him "Mayor Mumbles.") A former alderman, Sawyer, who had worked both sides of the street—machine and reform—was acceptable to the ethnics and a small circle of black aldermen.[17]

Acting Mayor Sawyer, who served from December 1987 through April 1989, was an excellent transition figure to ease Chicago out of its brawling past of racial politics and into a new, less rancorous, low-key era in which low-decibel politics did not count against you. The new mayor also was a good object lesson in two ways: he demonstrated (1) that a mayor did not have to keep the emotional throttle wide open, always revving up his core constituency with racial politics and thinly disguised honky bashing; and (2) that a mayor whose soft-spoken style was not threatening to white and ethnic Chicagoans could effect cooperation between seemingly irreconcilable whites and recalcitrant blacks.

But "gentleman Gene's" grip on the office began to slip. The movement people insisted that Mayor Washington's unexpired term could be completed only by a regularly elected mayor. The courts agreed. Elections were scheduled for February and April 1989. Then African American alderman Timothy Evans, the black movement candidate, dropped out of the Democratic mayoral primary in December 1988. This exit permitted two low-key moderates, Richard M. Daley and Eugene Sawyer, to move to center stage. A third candidate, Lawrence Bloom, entered, and when he tried to resurrect the strident tones and polemics of his late friend Harold Washington, the strategy backfired. After Bloom's intelligently drawn position paper failed to ignite the public, he became more visceral in his attacks, belittling Daley's intelligence and flaunting his own not inconsiderable abilities. A tactic that had worked for Washington and Byrne flopped badly when reformer Bloom tried it. However, its failure was a commentary less on Bloom than on the changing political climate of Chicago. A decade of "chaos-fest," council wars, Beirut on the lake, and smash-and-grab politics was over. The public had tired of the circus of insult, racial screaming, ghetto ranting, and white demagoguery, and was fed up with the politics of emotionalism and racial battling. Sawyer and Daley were refreshing changes. The overheated and overwrought racial politics of the Byrne-Epton-Washington wars were coming to an end, only Lawrence Bloom and Timothy Evans were not aware of it. When they tried even tentatively to revive the old "us versus them" style, they appeared to be mean-spirited and anachronistic throwbacks to a little-lamented, conflict-filled racial past. Whites "had learned in their unsuccessful campaigns to stop Washington in 1983 and 1987 that racial campaigns don't work where neither race holds a majority," columnist Clarence Page wrote. "Perhaps now black leaders will learn the same lesson."[18]

The Cooling Political Climate

Richard M. Daley was ideally suited to exploit the cooling political climate. He campaigned on the argument that the electorate was fed up with racial polarizers such as Representative Gus Savage, who liked to scream "racist" and shout "Dumb, dumb Daley" when the TV cameras were rolling; black alderwoman Dorothy Tillman, who attacked Acting Mayor Sawyer as a "shuffling Uncle Tom" for cooperating with whites; and Afronationalist Steve Cokely, who poisoned race relations with his venomous slurs that Jewish doctors were injecting the AIDS virus into black babies.

Richard M. promised to calm the troubled waters of Chicago politics. He asked for lowered voices and increased reason. He attacked none of his opponents—only the problems that he identified as needing mayoral attention. Daley stood up to insult, race baiting, and honky bashing and, following his handlers' advice, returned none in kind. Daley rejected the time-tested strategy of the outsider (which had been followed by Byrne, Washington, Vrdolyak, and even Tim Evans) of lambasting the person in power and delivering every other day a bill of particulars about the incumbent mayor's failings. Instead, and ironically, Daley ran like an incumbent rather than an outsider—cool and positive, releasing position papers on numerous subjects and, above all, underscoring again and again that the city was tired of racial extremism and that he would bring racial healing to Chicago. In addition, he promised stability and steady leadership. He was businesslike and city-manager-like in tone and substance. He offered no pie-in-the-sky cornucopia of goodies to his followers; in fact, he hinted at austerity and economy in government. Daley did not say to his followers, as the challengers had in 1983, "It's our turn now. . . . We want it all, we want it now!" Missing was any hint of a classical reward-your-friends–punish-your-enemies sentiment.[19]

By the time the low-key primary ended in February 1989 with Daley's victory, several things had happened. The tone of the campaign had been civil. The only strident voice in the primary, that of Lawrence Bloom, had faded out before the vote was taken. No verbal bomb throwers or flaming incendiaries had excited the campaign. The exchanges were dull, if not boring, and sounded as though they had been prescribed by a League of Women Voters manual on campaign etiquette. Seldom had Chicago seen such well-behaved candidates. There was no eye gouging, ear biting, or hitting below the belt.[20]

The general election campaign was only a tad more exciting, pitting Democrat Daley against Timothy Evans of the Harold Washington party. Underfinanced and poorly directed, Evans was so ineffectual he looked like a rabbit caught in the headlights of a car on a country road. He did not know which way to run; his campaign tried to exploit the "Son of Boss" theme and "plantation politics," but it floundered and got nowhere. When Evans tried to resurrect the stridency of his mentor, that too fell flat. He failed to rev up the black community, where he did most of his campaigning. When race baiters and honky bashers such as Tillman and Savage tarnished his candidacy, he seemed genuinely surprised over his loss of liberal lakefront supporters.

By election time in April, it seemed clear that the old Byrne-Washington-Vrdolyak venom and vinegar had been drained, at least temporarily, out of

Chicago politics. The twelve-year interregnum of nasty racial code words, harsh honky bashing, and Jew baiting was drawing to a close. The curtain was ringing down on racial battling, council wars, and high-decibel name-calling, in addition to the political chaos unleashed by a system that had gone into disequilibrium for more than a decade. The city had passed through violent contradictions, and now in 1989 was experiencing the birth pangs of a new political equilibrium slowly rising from the ashes of no-holds-barred racial battling. The rediscovery of political moderation was novelty to a political generation that came of age during turbulent times. But Chicagoans not only rediscovered moderation, they voted for it. Low-key Rich Daley took 55 percent of the vote, the biggest majority since 1979, when political disorder had begun in earnest. But Daley in some ways was only the agent of the need to return to a saner, less shrill, lowered-voice campaign and governance style. If Rich Daley had not been on the scene, most likely someone else of a similar political temperament would have been. Chicago could not have gone on much longer with its smash-mouth, in-your-face ethnically explosive politics. The city and the electorate had grown exhausted and weary of what a *Newsweek* cover story in May 1983 called "ugly racial" elections. Daley, albeit somewhat timorously, throttled down the runaway locomotive called Chicago politics. Repeating his 1989 short-term victory, Daley won again in 1991 for a full four-year term. The Bilandic-Byrne-Washington years were over. A rediscovered age of political moderation was dawning, as was a new political equilibrium.

Richard II

During his campaign for mayor, Rich Daley dismissed the need for an urban industrial policy as a modern-day version of cargo culting (a reference to South Pacific primitives who hoped to bring down big shiny birds, airplanes, and their goods by grubbing out mock airstrips in the jungle). But by his re-election in 1991, Daley had flip-flopped completely and came out in support of "planned manufacturing districts." Why? Young Rich saw how new businesses and industries were moving into cleared spaces of a one-mile-square rubble heap that had once been the city's fabled stockyards and how they had begun a phoenixlike revitalization of the individual region. Seeing was believing for Rich, who then lived in the nearby neighborhood of Bridgeport.

The new Daley is a hands-on, action-oriented leader more in the CEO or city manager mold than an old-style boss-politician. His passion for management is such that a few insiders label him a "policy nerd." He told *Chicago Enterprise* in February 1991 that he wanted to "get control" of the bureaucracy and achieve "better productivity" and "accountability of the work force." Rich Daley knows how the new Chicago works. Old-time bossism is gone.

Mayor Harold Washington read its obituary in 1983, observing, "Patronage is dead. I walked around its grave. I called out 'patronage where are you?' Patronage did not answer. Why? Because patronage is dead, dead, dead!" Dead indeed. Like his predecessor, Daley signed a court-decreed Shakman order that forbids patronage hiring and firing in the city's work ranks. No-show jobs for precinct captains were becoming a thing of the past. Daley cut payrolls in departments such as housing and job training, deemed to be inefficient and unproductive, and expanded them in planning and economic development, where he hoped for future payoffs for the city in jobs and business growth.[21]

Daley pushed administrative reforms, such as taking parking tickets out of traffic court and putting them before administrative hearing officers, achieved a new ethics code through the city council, and brought in a new system to locate slumlords who were hiding their ownership behind blind trusts. He has also privatized some public works such as janitorial services, drug counseling, and the removal of abandoned cars from the streets. All of these initiatives appeared to be bureaucratically efficient and saved the tax-payers money. It amounted to tearing a page out of dad Richard J.'s book of keeping government spending under control, holding down tax rates, and keeping the city's credit rating high.

The central aim of the Daley administration was economic growth and job expansion. The mayor pushed redevelopment of the long-shuttered Navy Pier, which was undergoing a multimillion-dollar facelift in 1993 aimed at restoring its recreational and entertainment value to Chicagoans and tourists. In addition, he wanted a trolley car connection to the hotels and the Loop. Expansion of the city's convention center, McCormick Place, was high on his priority list, along with support for a privately financed West Side sports arena. Both were under way by Daley's second term.[22]

Yet the pièce de résistance of all of young Daley's dreams is a multibillion-dollar airport, which the mayor hoped would be constructed on the Southeast Side on a shallow backwater known as Lake Calumet. From it Daley anticipated thousands of new jobs and an economic renewal for the rundown rust belt district—an idea straight from Dad's "builder mayor" book. But an unfriendly governor, a lukewarm legislature, and a lot of loud vocal opposition stymied Daley's program. Then, a half-hearted effort by the Republican governor to build his own airport under state, instead of city, control complicated and stalled the whole third airport idea. Finally, the Clinton administration in Washington, perceiving city-state stalemate, killed the whole idea by withdrawing planning funds in October 1993.[23]

Another builder project advanced by Daley was the construction of a two-billion-dollar land-based gambling casino near the downtown lakefront. This plan, reasoned the mayor, would provide thousands of construction jobs that would make the unions happy, big financial deals that the bankers and real estate moguls would welcome, more hotel and restaurant construction, and in the long term, several thousand additional casino jobs and new tax revenue to the hard-pressed city budget. This formula had worked marvels for his father and brought astonishing amounts of money and support to the city Democrats from the well-heeled Republican business community. Unlike dad Daley, young Daley lacked the powerful influence needed in the Springfield legislature to pass the enabling legislation to make such a megabuck project possible. Again the mayor met head-on the opposition of the legislature's upper house and a Republican governor who resolutely opposed land-based casino gambling, even though he had approved, and was then in the process of approving more, riverboat gambling in the state. This setback forced the mayor to consider a scaled-down gambling enterprise in Chicago—possibly with a few riverboats near the central business district. Later when Daley ran for his fifth term in 2003, he had sidelined and shelved his support for a Chicago gambling casino, possibly because of the steady growth of public and press opposition to it. Such reversals cut to the quick of a mayor who had hoped to make large-scale projects a major prop in his economic recovery and jobs program.[24]

Facing his third-term reelection campaign in 1995, the mayor did not want to come before the voters with a builder's cupboard empty. He did, of course, have an expanded McCormick Place convention center, a new rapid transit system (albeit started by his predecessors), and a rehabbed Navy Pier but no riverboats to parade before the voters. He would also be able to show off his relatively good record as a city manager, his efficiencies brought about by privatization, and his tolerable record as a political leader. In addition, a public opinion poll taken at midterm, in May 1993, showed public support running deep and wide for Daley. Two-thirds of the registered voters in Chicago approved of the job he was doing as mayor, while only 29 percent disapproved. Support for Daley crossed political party, gender, and racial lines, with three-fourths of the white voters, more than half of the black voters, and six out of ten Republicans liking the job he was doing as mayor. Despite a string of disappointments on his builder projects, a surprising 55 percent approved of Daley's efforts to bring economic development to the city. Even on the sensitive issue of taxes, which Daley had once raised, some 52 percent of all registered voters approved of his performance. Finally, Market Shares polling discovered that Daley's name recognition was incredible even for a politician, for he was known to virtually every registered voter in the state, with 53 percent holding a favorable view and only 18 percent disapproving. All of this evidence suggested that Daley was well positioned for the mayoral election of 1995, in which he overran an African American opponent, winning 56 percent of the vote and increasing his share of the black vote from 7 percent in his first election to 28 percent. Subsequent elections followed the same pattern, in which incumbent Mayor Daley won the 1999 election with 72 percent of the vote and the 2003 race with 79 percent of the city's vote and nearly 60 percent of the black vote.[25]

There was more good news for Daley on the political front, where black leadership remained divided between what analyst Jacky Grimshaw called "the blacks only need apply" radical nationalist wing and the realists who worked with the mayor. Daley in 1989 had been the first big-city white mayor to turn a black incumbent out of office. Since Mayor Washington's death, Daley has defeated several black challengers, including Eugene Sawyer, Timothy Evans, Danny Davis, Eugene Pincham, and Bobby Rush. In addition, demography was no longer running favorably for black nationalists, for the great South-to-city migration had ended and the African American share of Chicago's population stopped growing, as Hispanics became the fastest growing new population group. Along the way, Hispanics had moved en masse into the Daley camp. Finally, as Grimshaw pointed out earlier in the summer of 1993, the lesson of four defeated black contenders was that a blacks-only ticket was doomed and that "there is no black candidate on the horizon" with the vision and skills to mount a credible multiracial campaign.[26]

With no viable coalition opponent on the horizon, and an electorate with no stomach for returning to the sour politics of the ethnoracial battling of the 1980s, Daley was the beneficiary and partly the cause of a public satisfied to see the return of some degree of predictability and a calmer political mood. After his 1991 primary, Daley told the voters that "we have proven that we can have an election in Chicago without tearing our city apart just as we have proven in the past two years that we can discuss issues without tearing each other apart."[27] As the election returns and the public opinion polls showed for the next decade, the electorate agreed. A diminished racial friction brought a cooling political climate, and a saner balance had returned to politics. The political system was back in equilibrium with a Daley, as it had been under the Carter Harrisons and the long half-century reign of the Kelly-Nash-Daley political organization.[28]

But it was Daley's programs and policies that also played a vital role in attracting a majority of Chicago's voters to support his five terms in office. The Daley administration has strongly supported minority set-asides and preferences for city contracts, and awarded some to key families of politically prominent African American families. The mayor's policies paid dividends for the Black Contractors Association. The city's black congressman, Jesse Jackson Jr., endorsed Daley's reelection in 2003, as did the leader of the Southern Christian Leadership Conference, Martin Luther King III.[29]

Some of the mayoral incumbent's critics in the 2003 campaign accused the mayor of cronyism and of rewarding his support groups and individuals, including the first openly gay aldermanic candidate in Chicago history, whom the mayor endorsed. Even so, Daley has declined preferential treatment for gays as minority group contractors. Daley also won public endorsement during his 2003 reelection from two long-time foes of Daley mayors, city council member Helen Schiller (Forty-sixth Ward) and councilwoman Dorothy Tillman (Third Ward). *Tribune* reporter Andrew Martin observed that Tillman had benefited from major projects in her ward funded by the city and that the "flow of money into neighborhoods had effectively muzzled former critics." Political writer Mark Brown concurred, asserting that with the mayor's winning over Helen Schiller, "the last squeaky wheel in the council had been greased." Brown concluded that Daley's political strategy is to give "them what they want until they no longer see themselves as opponents."[30]

Daley's citywide appeal was also enhanced by the 1995 Illinois School Reform Act, by which the mayor took over control of the Chicago public schools, allocated more money for classroom teaching, raised academic standards, ended social promotions, and provided summer school and after-school remedial instruction for failed students. The result was that the test scores of Chicago pupils began to rise, while truancy and dropout rates went down.

In the tradition of his father, Richard J., the "builder mayor," Richard M. Daley brought about the rehabilitation and remodeling of Navy Pier, which by the century's turn was attracting nine million visitors a year and increasing city income and tax revenue. The administration also worked hard to attract new business like the national office of Boeing Aircraft and other companies to locate in Chicago. The Windy City gained some 470,000 new jobs in the Daley decade. In addition, the administration had pushed expansion of convention center McCormick Place, Midway Airport, and Soldier Field stadium; encouraged private builders to clear out dilapidated slum housing; and moved to downsize crime-ridden, rundown public housing projects such as Cabrini Green and the Robert Taylor Homes. The mayor also directed the spending of billions on building and improving community schools, public parks, libraries, and fire and police stations. He also used federal funds to increase the size of the Chicago police force, although the move did not bring down homicide rates, which had increased to a record level in 2002.[31]

Some of the administration's programs are being or have been emulated by other governmental bodies. Mayor Daley continued Chicago's Community Action Program, which aimed at crime prevention, and which the U.S. Justice Department used as a model for its national crime prevention program in funding local agencies. In addition, the mayor's role as education czar, made possible by the 1995 Illinois School Reform Act, had also become a model for cities such as New York, which did the same. Finally, Daley helped clean up the city with an antigraffiti program begun in 1993, whereby "graffiti blasters" used high-powered blasts of baking soda and water to cleanse private and public buildings of hate messages, smeared walls, and gangland graffiti that marked neighborhood gangs' territorial claims. The "blasters" often responded to up to two hundred thousand requests a year by individuals and corporations to remove criminal marking off soiled walls. "It sends a message that the neighborhood belongs to the people, not the gangs," asserted streets and sanitation commissioner Al Sanchez. He also noted that "folks come in from other cities, and the first thing they tell us is how clean the city is." Government representatives from Milan, Italy; Prague, Czech Republic; Warsaw; and the Israeli town of Petach Tikva have traveled to Chicago to study its anti-graffiti program.[32]

Daley's big win in the 2003 election was a confirmation of strong public support, as was the glad-handing of America's Republican president George Bush, who made an effort to be friendly with Chicago's Democratic chief executive. With his fifth-term victory, Mayor Richard M. was on the road to challenging his father's twenty-one-year record as the longest-serving mayor in Chicago's history.[33]

16.

RANKING CHICAGO'S MAYORS: MIRROR, MIRROR ON THE WALL, WHO IS THE GREATEST OF THEM ALL?—AN UPDATED POLL

Melvin G. Holli

Who is number one? Who has been the best mayor in Chicago's history? The age-old question was addressed in a new survey completed in fall 2002. The poll asked Chicago experts in history and politics to rank all of Chicago's mayors from the very first in 1837 down through the 2002 incumbent, Richard M. Daley.

Expert rankings of political leaders date back to a 1948 poll conducted by Professor Arthur M. Schlesinger Sr., who asked fifty-five expert historians to rate U.S. presidents on a scale from "failure" to "great," with each historian using his own criteria. Schlesinger repeated his exercise in 1962, with results largely confirming his earlier findings. More recently, a Murray-Blessing poll asked American historians to rate presidents, and in 1982, a Steve Neal– Chicago *Tribune* survey queried some forty-nine prominent historians and authors, all of whom had published some germinal work on the presidency, for the purpose of ranking American presidents. Neal, the Chicago *Sun-Times*, the University of Illinois at Chicago in 2000 conducted similar surveys, and so did C-SPAN television. The findings, with a few exceptions, were very similar to those of the earlier Schlesinger polls.[1]

One surprising result of these national surveys is that in most cases, the ranking of a president appears to become fixed within a relatively short period after he leaves office. Whether the same pattern will obtain for our mayors was a question we raised in the first-ever expert poll about Chicago mayors in 1985 (published in the first edition of this book) and one that this survey will speak to later. For the moment, it is important to note there exist a body of research and a methodology for grading elected political leaders.

Methodology

The second effort to rate Chicago's forty-three elected mayors who served since the city's incorporation in 1837 relied on the same methodology used in the 1985 Chicago survey, was conducted in 1994, and was published in the Roper Center's *The Public Perspective* journal. The results of the 1994 survey were similar to those of the first expert poll conducted in 1985.

Now we are reporting on the third expert poll to rank Chicago's mayors. There are some similarities: Retrospectively, poll number two in 1994 had fifty-five respondents. By the time expert poll number three was conducted in the summer and fall of 2002, a few of the earlier poll respondents were deceased and several had retired or moved from the Chicago metro area and Illinois. The result was a total of thirty-two expert respondents. Even though this number is substantially smaller than that of the earlier survey, the new poll is a good representative sample of Chicago political experts, as shown in the variety of disciplines, articles, books, and other publications represented by these men and women. Also, twenty-eight of the thirty-two experts had been respondents in the first two Chicago mayor rankings.[2]

Rankings were solicited by means of a questionnaire mailed between June and November 2002 to sixty potential respondents. This mailing elicited a response from thirty-two, for a rate of return of 53 percent. A one-half or greater response level is considered reliable for mail surveys and compares favorably to other polls of this type.[3] Repeated mailings were made to non-respondents and to those who had changed addresses. That twenty-eight of the respondents in the new poll had also been respondents in the first polls in 1985 and 1994 accounts for a repeat percentage that is very high for such a survey. The thirty-two experts who returned questionnaires clearly seemed qualified for the task, for as a group they had published fifty-eight books and more than 150 articles related to Chicago and its politics. On average, each expert has published five articles and one book. Only one had not published print articles or books but had delivered analyses through electronic broadcast media and in lecture forums. Our expert respondents seemed well qualified by their formal credentials to rate Chicago mayors.

The survey instrument had three components. The first question asked each respondent to rank Chicago's eight mayors who served since 1933 and to judge them on three different dimensions, namely, leadership, accomplishments, and political skill. A second asked the respondents to rank the ten best of the forty-three mayors elected since the office was established in 1837 (including Eugene Sawyer, who was elected by the city council). A third sought to identify each respondent by residence, occupation, and publications related to the Chicago mayoralty.

Ranking Mayors since 1933

Table 16.1, which ranks mayors since 1933, covered all eight elected mayors, excluding Anton Cermak, who was assassinated in 1933. As the table shows, Richard J. Daley (1955–76) was ranked by the experts as the best mayor and had the highest mean rank and the highest mode of the group. (The mean is the arithmetic average of all the respondents' rankings and is determined by adding all of the scores and dividing by the number of respondents, and the mode is the most frequent value in a set of data.) The senior Daley was rated highest among the eight mayors by fifteen voters, for a frequency greater than that for any other mayor in the since-1933 group.

TABLE 16.1
Ranking of Mayors since 1933

Mayors	Mean Rank	Mode	Times Ranked First	Times Ranked Second
1. Richard J. Daley 1955–76	1.75	1	15	7
2. Richard M. Daley 1989–	2.60	2	7	8
3. Harold Washington 1983–87	2.89	3, 4	6	2
4. Edward Kelly 1933–47	3.00	3	1	4
5. Martin Kennelly 1947–55	4.00	5	1	0
6. Jane Byrne 1979–83	5.53	5	0	0

NOTE: N = 32. Ranking averages were based on 1 for the highest and 5 for the lowest. Mayors Michael Bilandic, 1977–79, and Eugene Sawyer, 1987–89, were ranked among the top six by only four and two voters, respectively.

Moving into an impressive second place is the first-ranked mayor's son, Richard M. Daley (1989–), who had a mean rank in the 2-to-3 range, a similar mode, and a first-place rating only half as frequently as his father but an equivalent number in the times-ranked-second column. In third place is the city's first African American mayor, Harold Washington (1983–87), with a mean rank in the 2-to-3 range. Having prevailed through two stormy elections and won recognition as the city's first black mayor, he attracted favorable votes from many of our experts.

Fourth is Mayor Edward Kelly (1933–47), with a mean rank slightly below that of Washington and a mode of 3. The three-term Kelly garnered only one-fifth as many times-ranked-first votes as Washington but drew four second-place votes. Kelly was well known to Chicagoans as a cofounder of the Kelly-Nash political machine, which got into trouble over education and other scandals in 1946. Kelly's replacement was blue-ribbon reform mayor Martin H. Kennelly (1947–55), rated fifth by the experts, with a mean rank of 4.00 and only one first-place vote. The two-term Kennelly began the city's first large-scale federal public housing project to clear away some of the worst slums. Following in sixth place is the city's first female mayor, Jane Byrne. Known for her stormy entrance into office after a record snowfall in 1979, she had an equally stormy exit in what the press dubbed "Chicago's ugly racial election" in 1983. She pulled no first-place or second-place votes. The other two mayors who were elected to office during the post-1933 period, Michael Bilandic and Eugene Sawyer, drew too few votes to be ranked.[4]

The question about three dimensions of the mayoralty—leadership, accomplishment, and political skill—did not prove especially revealing, since it produced rank orders similar to that in table 16.1, with only a few minor changes: Washington ranking second in the leadership dimension, pushing Richard M. Daley into third; and Kelly replacing Washington in the accomplishment category, pushing Harold down to fourth place. The difference between the two tables is that the question reflected in table 16.1 asked the experts to rank mayors with no limit on the number of dimensions or criteria considered, whereas that for table 16.2 asked each respondent to focus specifically on only three dimensions of the mayoralty. The three-dimensions table then should be perceived as showing criteria-specific rankings.

Ranking Mayors from 1837 to 2003

The question and responses used to create table 16.3, which ranks Chicago mayors who served between 1837 and 2003, increased fivefold the number of mayors considered, from eight to forty-three, and more than doubled the size of the historic hunting ground from 70 to approximately 165 years. We might hypothesize that expanding the number of potential choices should statistically diminish the strength of the leaders in tables 16.1 and 16.2, because we have provided the expert voters with so many more choices. To some extent, diminishment of the rankings of the more contemporary mayors did occur. For example, Richard J. Daley's mean rank of 1.75 in the since-1933 test slipped to 3.00 in the since-1837 list, and Harold Washington's slipped from a mean of 2.89 to 4.23, lowering his rank from third place to fourth. Moving into second place on the since-1837 list is Carter Harrison II (1897–1905, 1911–15), a five-term mayor whose tenure spanned the turn of the century.

TABLE 16.2
Mayors since 1933 Ranked on Three Dimensions

Leadership	Mean Rank	No. of Times Ranked	Score
Richard J. Daley 1955–76	4.14	29	116
Harold Washington 1983–87	3.89	29	109
Richard M. Daley 1989–	3.89	29	109
Edward Kelly 1933–47	3.42	26	89
Martin Kennelly 1947–55	3.00	8	24
Jane Byrne 1979–83	1.76	13	23

Accomplishments	Mean Rank	No. of Times Ranked	Score
Richard J. Daley 1955–76	4.14	29	119
Richard M. Daley 1989–	3.71	29	104
Edward Kelly 1933–47	3.26	26	85
Harold Washington 1983–87	3.17	29	89
Martin Kennelly 1947–55	2.37	8	23
Jane Byrne 1979–83	1.84	13	24

Political Skill	Mean Rank	No. of Times Ranked	Score
Richard J. Daley 1955–76	4.89	29	137
Richard M. Daley 1989–	4.07	29	114
Harold Washington 1983–87	3.89	29	109
Edward Kelly 1933–47	3.46	26	90
Martin Kennelly 1947–55	2.62	8	21
Jane Byrne 1979–83	1.84	13	24

NOTE: Mean rankings and total scores are based on a value of 5 given to a respondent's highest-ranked mayor and 1 to the lowest-ranked in each category.

TABLE 16.3

Ranking of Mayors since 1837

Mayors	Mean	Mode	Times Ranked First	Times Ranked Second
1. Richard J. Daley 1955–76	3.00	1	10	3
2. Carter Harrison II 1897–1905, 1911–15	3.70	3	3	3
3. Richard M. Daley 1989–	4.08	2	4	9
4. Harold Washington 1983–87	4.23	7	6	1
5. Carter Harrison I 1879–87, 1893	4.63	4	2	3
6. Edward Kelly 1933–1947	4.95	3, 7	1	0
7. Joseph Medill 1871–73	6.10	9	0	1
8. Anton Cermak 1931–33	6.23	6	0	1
9. William Dever 1923–27	6.33	8	1	0
10. William Ogden 1937–38	6.38	10	1	1
11. Edward Dunne 1905–7	6.60	6, 8	0	1
12. John Wentworth 1857–58, 1860–61	7.61	9	0	1

NOTE: Ranking based on 1 for the highest and 10 for the lowest.

In third place is Richard M. Daley (1989–), who slipped down a notch from second place in the since-1933 table. In fourth place is the city's first African American mayor, who also slipped a notch, from third in table 16.1 to fourth in table 16.3. Even so, both mayors retained high rankings among the city's forty-three elected mayors. In fifth place is Carter Harrison I (1879–87, 1893), another five-term mayor and the father of Carter II. In sixth place is Ed Kelly (1933–47), who is credited with honing the political skills of the Kelly-Nash machine and beginning a long half-century run of Irish American mayors for Chicago. Ranking seventh is Chicago's post–1871 fire mayor, Republican Joseph Medill, who had helped to nominate Abraham Lincoln for the presidency in 1860 and who took over ownership of the Chicago *Tribune* newspaper in 1874. In eighth place we find Chicago's only foreign-born mayor. Bohemian Anton Cermak (1931–33), a rough-and-ready bruiser and anti-Prohibitionist, put together a multiethnic political organization that would, over time, bring about Democratic dominance of Chicago. Ninth best is reform mayor William Dever (1923–27), a law-and-order leader who tried to enforce the Prohibition laws, fought organized crime, and drove the chief of such crime, Al Capone, out of Chicago. The city's first mayor, William B. Ogden (1837–38), won a solid tenth place, securing one ranked-first vote and a goodly number elsewhere in the top ten. Being the first mayor and putting his personal credit on the line to save the young city's fiscal reputation were achievements that doubtless put Ogden among the ten best. The city's only progressive reform-era mayor, Edward Dunne (1905–7), came in eleventh, missing the top ten by a fraction of a point. Dunne was notable as a clean-election, civic-minded reformer at a time when Irish Catholic politicians excelled in running political machines. He was also the only mayor in Chicago's history to move up from city hall. Dunne was elected to the Illinois governorship in 1912. Finally, Civil War mayor Long John Wentworth (1857–58, 1860–61) garnered twelfth place. Known as a pro-Union and War Democrat, he eventually switched parties and guided the city through the turbulent times of the secession crisis of 1861.[5]

Overall, the most striking finding is that Richard J. Daley's high ranking in both the since-1933 (table 16.1) and since-1837 (table 16.3) lists almost isolates him into a class by himself—sui generis. In the since-1837 list, the elder Daley also had the lowest standard deviations of both rankings, suggesting there is more agreement by the experts on his ranking than on any of the others in the list. The close clustering in ranks of the elder Daley's son, Richard M., and Harold Washington suggests that the two are perceived as more alike and closer in achievements to each other than to the elder Daley.

Other interesting observations can be made of the top-twelve list. Seven of the twelve served more than one term. Long-term officeholders include the two father-and-son teams: the Harrisons served five terms each, and the elder Daley was elected six times, the younger Daley five times thus far. Holding office for multiple terms is clearly an advantage in attaining high rank in this survey. For starters, multiple terms in office probably indicates that the mayor is doing a pretty good job, and long tenure provides the mayor with time to achieve his or her goals. The tenures of two of Chicago's mayors were cut short by assassination: the World's Fair mayor, Carter Harrison I, was assassinated in 1893 by a disgruntled office seeker, and Mayor Anton Cermak was killed in 1933 in Florida by a foreign anarchist who aimed at Democratic president-elect Franklin Roosevelt but missed, fatally shooting Chicago's mayor. The Democratic party claimed ten of the top twelve. The two others were Republicans: Chicago *Tribune* owner Joseph Medill and John Wentworth, who left the Democrats for the Republican party over the slavery and pro-Union issues. Finally, six were Roman Catholics and six were not, including Cermak, who was a nonbeliever and a freethinker. Chronologically, four governed during the nineteenth century (Ogden, Wentworth, Medill, and Harrison I); one shared both centuries (Carter Harrison II), and the other seven (Dunne, Dever, Cermak, Kelly, the two Daleys, and Washington) belong to the twentieth century.

Summary

Richard J. Daley emerged as the overall winner in all sections of the poll. The six-term Daley ranked first in both the since-1933 test of eight mayors and the leadership dimensions measured in table 16.2. Finally, in the historical best-ever race, Daley the elder came in first, nearly one mean rank above the second-place winner. No candidate came near Daley in the times-ranked-first column: only his son, Richard M., and Harold Washington garnered even half the number of first-place votes that Chicago's highest-ranked urban leader earned.

Although Richard J. Daley was controversial in life and still somewhat so in death, his appeal has to be viewed as more than that of a contemporary phenomenon who runs well against his own class of ethnic and machine politicians. He clearly holds his own and emerges as a winner, even when matched against a sizable body of blue-ribbon founding fathers and nineteenth-century political worthies.

Like the reputations of presidents, those of mayors benefit from what happens after they leave office. In the light of four post-Daley administrations (Bilandic, Byrne, Washington, and Sawyer: 1977–89), political turmoil, falling bond ratings, council wars, ugly racial battling, and less-than-citywide leadership make it seem likely that the relative stability of the six-term Daley would have some appeal to the experts. And it did. Of these post-Daley mayors, only Washington salvaged high ranking among the experts, probably because he was the city's first African American mayor, was an outstanding campaigner and speaker, and helped to move blacks from the periphery into the center of politics for at least two elections.[6]

Elected in 1989, the younger Daley won the high ranking of third on the historic list. He was completing his forth term when this poll was conducted. Richard II's ranking probably came about because of the electorate's exhaustion with racial political battling, and because Daley has been widely perceived as having calmed the troubled waters of political turmoil and returned politics to a cooler, saner political equilibrium.[7]

Comparing the 2002, 1994, and 1985 Polls

Overall, the results of the 2002 poll are similar to those of the 1994 and 1985 polls and reflect growing consensus among the experts. Two mayors, Harold Washington and Richard M. Daley, can account for the difference between the three surveys almost wholly. The movement upward and repositioning of one mayor, Washington, and the entry of a new mayor, Richard M. Daley, into the mix in the 1994 survey explains more than 90 percent of the tiny change in rankings. Washington moved most dramatically in the "since 1933" measure, rising from fourth place in 1985 to second in the 1994 survey and dropping back to fourth in the 2002 rankings.[8] When the 1985 evaluation was conducted, Washington was still in his first administration and thus we predicted that Washington would move up or down in subsequent surveys for key reasons: in 1985 he was locked into a political and legislative stalemate called "council wars" and had not completed his first term. After the 1985 survey had been completed and by spring 1986, Washington, with the help of the courts and aldermanic redistricting, had taken control of the city council and handily won reelection in 1987. Success in the last eighteen months of his public life and Washington's effort to remake himself as the mayor of all of the city and not just his core constituency probably helped pull Washington into high ranking in subsequent surveys.[9]

The second change was entry into the top ranks by the incumbent mayor, Richard M. Daley. Young Daley had not been mayor in 1985 and thus was not ranked in the first expert poll. In the 1994 poll that ranked mayors since 1933, Daley was in fourth place and rose dramatically to second best in the 2002 survey. His rank in the since-1933 section was not surprising, given that there were only eight viable contenders for the top five slots and that the administrations of three (Bilandic, Byrne, and Sawyer) are generally viewed as failures. The upward movement of young Daley was even more dramatic in the since-1837 surveys. In the 1994 poll, Daley junior ranked ninth. But in the 2002 survey, in which the experts evaluated all of Chicago's mayors elected since 1837, the experts ranked young Daley as third best in the city's history.

Securing high rank in the "historic" best ten is a much tougher challenge, for here each mayor must compete against a much larger field and a much larger historic hunting ground. Here the movement of young Daley into third place and Washington into fourth had positive consequences for them but a negative result for some high rank holders of the 1985 poll, except postfire mayor and *Tribune* publisher Joseph Medill, who rose from eleventh to seventh place. Some of the rank holders in the 1994 poll slipped downward slightly, by a notch or so, but remained in the top twelve categories in 2002. Also, their rank order remained similar to that of earlier surveys.

We can see that nearly all the variance from 1994 to 2002 can be accounted for by the rapid political climbers Richard M. Daley and Harold Washington. Subtracting those two names would have left the 2002 survey almost a mirror image of the 1994 poll, which lends credence to its reliability. Clearly a strong consensus is emerging among the experts on who are Chicago's ten best mayors. Finally, Richard J. Daley's commanding position in both surveys and the relatively low standard deviation that characterizes his vote suggests that expert opinion has crystallized on who is number one.[10]

Chicago Mayor Ranking Poll Respondents, September 2002

1. Biles, Roger
   East Carolina University
2. Binder, John
   University of Illinois, Chicago
3. Branham, Charles
   Du Sable Museum
4. Buenker, John
   University of Wisconsin–Parkside
5. Bukowski, Douglas
   Berwyn, IL
6. Crotty, William
   Formerly Northwestern University
7. Cutler, Irving
   Chicago State University
8. Gove, Sam
   University of Illinois, Urbana
9. Graber, Doris
   University of Illinois, Chicago
10. Greeley, Andrew
    Chicago
11. Green, Paul M.
    Roosevelt University, Chicago
12. Joravsky, Benjamin
    Chicago *Reader*
13. Kantowicz, Edward
    Chicago
14. Karamanski, Theodore
    Loyola University
15. Keating, Ann Durkin
    North Central College
16. Kennedy, Eugene
    Loyola University
17. Mazur, Edward
    Chicago City College
18. McCaffrey, Lawrence
    Loyola University

19. McClory, Robert
    Evanston, IL
20. Merriner, James
    Chicago City Club
21. Miller, Donald
    Lafayette College
22. Mooney-Melvin, Patricia
    Loyola University
23. Pacyga, Dominic
    Columbia College
24. Parot, Joseph
    Northern Illinois University
25. Pelissero, John
    Loyola University
26. Pfeffer, Paula
    Loyola University
27. Riess, Steven
    Northeastern Illinois University
28. Simpson, Dick
    University of Illinois, Chicago
29. Starks, Robert
    Northeastern Illinois University
30. Teaford, Jon
    Purdue University
31. Tischauser, Leslie
    Prairie State University
32. Washington, Laura
    Chicago Sun-Times

17.

MAYORING IN CHICAGO, 1837–2004: A STEPPING STONE TO HIGHER OFFICE OR A DEAD-END JOB?

Melvin G. Holli

Whether the mayoralty is a stepping stone to higher public office or a ticket to political oblivion remains a matter of some dispute. Operation PUSH's Jesse Jackson boldly proclaimed, during the primary victory celebration for mayoral candidate Harold Washington in 1983, that "this is a stepping stone to higher ground."[1] We presume that Jackson's statement implied more than simply winning the mayoral race and that he was enunciating a cardinal principle in the American dream of upward mobility—that the mayoralty was a stepping stone to higher public office at the statewide and national level.

Jackson's remark that the Chicago mayorship could be a stepping stone to higher office and bigger and better things seems to be at variance with the facts of mayoring in Chicago. Chicago, in a century and a half of mayor-council government, has never produced a U.S. president, as did Buffalo in the case of former mayor Grover Cleveland and tiny Northampton, Massachusetts, with Calvin Coolidge; or a vice president, as did Minneapolis with ex-mayor Hubert Humphrey; or even a U.S. senator, as did San Francisco with Dianne Feinstein; or a cabinet member, as did Denver with Federico Pena.

Unlike the study of the upward movement of blue-collar workers to higher white-collar status, which Stephan Thernstrom pioneered in 1964 and which has spawned a library of monographic studies, no such large corpus of literature exists for the study of upward political mobility. Yet a few landmark studies are evident in this smaller subfield. The principal pioneer in the study of political mobility is Joseph Schlesinger, who persuasively argued that politicians were just as ambitious as other Americans and saw the political system as a hierarchal ladder to ascend. Other scholars have studied this process of political climbing in single cities or limited spans of time. The main outlines of this historiography can be seen in the works of Marilyn Gittell, Theodore J. Lowi, and Wallace Sayre. Gittell, in a survey of big-city mayors for the period 1940–60, found relatively little upward progress to higher office and pronounced the mayoralty a dead-end job. Whether Gittell's study was a fair test of upward mobility is open to question, because 1940–60 was a period of almost nonstop crises, scandal, fiscal stress, and racial conflict in big-city politics. These issues and events may have crippled the efforts of mayors to move up to bigger and better offices. Theodore Lowi and Wallace Sayre examined the upward movement of mayors in a single city, New York, and their conclusion became "Sayre's law": "New York mayors come from anywhere and go nowhere." The door to the mayor's office led to a dead-end job.[2]

Does Sayre's law or the dead-end job thesis then apply to Chicago, or did city hall occupants escape the career-killing aspects of the mayoralty and move upward in the political world? Upward mobility in the political system is defined as attaining higher elective office, which in turn is related to the size of the electorate. Thus an upward progression would lead from city mayor to state governor or U.S. senator and then, finally, the presidency. The electoral base is illustrated today by the fact that the Chicago mayor is elected from a district holding about 3 million people; governors and senators are elected from a population base of more than 11 million in Illinois; and presidents from an electoral base of more than 250 million. The political opportunity ladder ascends upward from mayor to governor and senator and then to president. The only exception to this electoral-base measure of upward mobility is a House of Representatives seat, which is considered neither an upward nor downward movement but a lateral one, because Congress historically has been a good launching platform for higher office. Appointments to offices such as presidential cabinet posts, Supreme Court justiceships, and important ambassadorships are also regarded as upward mobility. Downward progression on the scale goes from mayor to state senator to state representative and to alderman or to any office that has a smaller electoral base than mayor or to any citywide office other than mayor. Thus having established our political pecking order, let us return to examine the evidence at hand.

Is the mayoralty a dead-end job? Has the Chicago mayorship been a dead-end job? Yes. It was literally a dead-end job for two mayors who were assassinated in office, Carter Harrison in 1893 and Anton Cermak in 1933, and for two others who died of natural causes while still clutching the reins of power, Richard J. Daley, 1976, and Harold Washington, 1987. For that foursome it was a terminal office and ended any hopes they might have had for higher office.

What about the other forty-one who have served from the time of Chicago's first mayor in 1837 to 2004?[3] Was it for them a springboard to higher public office, or was it, as in the case of our unfortunate four, a dead-end street?

Twentieth-Century Mayors

A short review of Chicago's twentieth-century occupants at city hall may illustrate some of the problems that blight upward career mobility via the Chicago mayor's office. Retreating to the turn of the century, we pick up our story with Carter Harrison II, descended from two presidents, as his name suggests, and a five-term mayor like his father who preceded him. First elected in 1897, Mayor Harrison was one of the shrewdest and most adept politicians who ever practiced politics in the Windy City, and although he nursed serious White House ambitions, he ran out of steam and public support on the eve of World War I. Not able to make a comeback as mayor and not able to reach higher office, Harrison coasted through the 1920s and skidded downward to a low-level patronage job, as collector of internal revenue in Chicago in 1933. He hit his job ceiling as mayor and then bounced downward.

His successor, Mayor Edward Dunne, a reformist judge, was the only mayor to climb upward from the mayor's seat to higher office, the governorship. Yet Dunne's break through the job ceiling brought no permanent change, for Dunne's successor was another regular organization type, Mayor Fred Busse, who gained minor notability on three accounts: (1) Busse was the first German American and the first non-Anglo-Irish mayor to come to office; (2) he was the first mayor to serve a four-year term; and (3) "Fat Fred" (as he was known to his North Side cronies) died in 1914 a pauper, leaving his wife with a mere pittance of fifteen cents as his total estate and reduced to the life of a charwoman, scrubbing floors to exist. Poverty is something that usually does not happen to Chicago mayors; their estates for the most part have been known to enlarge, not diminish, while in office. Not only was Mayor Busse's career blighted but his family was blighted by impoverishment. It was hard not to escape the conclusion that this gruff, blunt-spoken, portly burgher lacked the intellectual equipment and political polish to rise to higher office.

Next in the line of succession came Prohibition-era mayor William Hale Thompson, better known as "Big Bill," who in the parlance of the day "took the lid off" and practiced the politics of the "wide open town" to the delight of bootleggers, wets, and the voters of the Roaring Twenties. Yet gang wars, the St. Valentine's Day Massacre, and the widespread belief that Al Capone had influence in city hall incurred the wrath of the electorate and defeat for Big Bill in 1931. An outrageous mayor who mistakenly thought he was advancing his presidential ambitions by saying he would like to punch "King George in the snout," Thompson never got serious consideration for a presidential nomination. Ex-mayor Thompson made a bid in the 1930s for higher political office, the governorship, but was rebuffed by the voters. Stunned by how the crowds had turned on him, Big Bill died a disappointed man. However, unlike Fred Busse, ex-mayor Big Bill left his widow a tidy sum—$1.5 million in cash found in safety deposit boxes after his death. Needless to say, the widow Thompson never had to scrub floors or do windows.[4]

Sandwiched between two of Big Bill's three-term, three-ring circuses was an oddly puritanical Irish Catholic named William E. Dever, a one-term mayor from 1923–27 and a judicial careerist. Once in office, Mayor Dever ruthlessly sought to enforce the Prohibition laws, declared war on booze, and closed down some five thousand speakeasies, blind pigs, and soda fountains on the South Side. By putting "the lid back on," he dug his own political grave. Chicago voters rewarded Mayor Dever by defeating his reelection bid in 1927 and sending him packing to political oblivion. They called back into office as their chief executive that rascal of rascals, Big Bill Thompson. Chicago voters seemed unable to make up their minds whether they wanted the lid on or off. But they were certain that Mayor Dever was not the kind of man to send to the White House or the governor's mansion.

Then in 1931 came Chicago's second non-Anglo-Irish and only foreign-born mayor, Anton J. Cermak, of Czech, or Bohemian, birth. Cermak's political career was cut short by an errant assassin's bullet in 1933. Riding in an open car and sitting next to President-elect Franklin D. Roosevelt, Mayor Cermak was hit either by mistake or because of bad aim. (Someone quipped wryly that that may have been as close as any Chicago mayor ever got to the presidency.) Cermak lingered for a few weeks with his wound and then died, becoming known in pious ethnic circles as "Anton the Martyr." Sainthood, maybe, but no presidency.[5]

Chicago's next elected mayor was neither a saint nor a martyr but Edward Kelly, one the founders of the famous or infamous Kelly-Nash machine that would pull the sons of Erin and the Bridgeport neighborhood down victory road for the next half century. Mayor Kelly wielded awesome, raw, naked power after 1933 but was scandalized out of office and asked by his party to step aside for a blue-ribbon reformer in 1947. No one ever considered Mayor Kelly a candidate for higher office (and indeed, his enemies considered him a candidate for Cook County jail, one critic calling Kelly's years in the Chicago Sanitary District an "orgy of corruption"). With that kind of reputation, Mayor Kelly was not likely to rise beyond city hall.

Kelly's reformist replacement was Martin J. Kennelly, a trucking, storage, and moving firm magnate, whom the machine barely tolerated for eight years and then threw out unceremoniously in 1955. Although Kennelly was handsome in an executive kind of way—the silver-maned look of a presidential candidate (or TV anchorman)—he was a disaster as a party leader, and his career was over in 1955, when Richard J. Daley beat him in the Democratic primary. After Kennelly came the late, great Richard J. Daley, who set a record by being elected six times to the mayoralty. Whatever Daley's reputation may have been as a political powerhouse in national and regional Democratic circles, it is doubtful whether he could have been elected to anything outside Chicago's Cook County. Mayor Daley was never a serious prospect for higher office; if anything, others who sought higher office made their reputations attacking him and his city. He was the lightning rod for irate reformists who wished to put him down, not up. His hapless successor was Michael Bilandic, who was defeated by a snowstorm and a blitz by Jane Byrne and is unlikely to be slated again for the mayorship or higher elective office. He has, however, slid into a comfortable, low-tension, high-paying job as a justice on Illinois's highest court. Yet the indignities heaped on ex–Chicago mayors follow them out of office: the Chicago Council of Lawyers, which ranks judicial candidates, once labeled Bilandic "unqualified."[6] Finally we come to the last of the twentieth century and the first of the twenty-first century: Jane Byrne, the first female mayor, in 1979; Harold Washington, the first black mayor, 1983; his successor, Eugene Sawyer, 1987; and the 1990s mayor, Richard M. Daley, reelected in 2003, none of whom has progressed to higher office.

Upward career mobility does not seem to be part of the political future for Chicago mayors. In the twentieth century, the Chicago mayoralty has been an end-of-the-line job, with little prospect for political promotion up the electoral job ladder.

One might wonder whether that were the case in the nineteenth century. It could be argued that the twentieth century has been an aberrant period with an aberrant group in office. After all, the twentieth-century Chicago mayoralty has been populated by plebeians and ex-plebeians such as "Fat Fred" Busse, a small-time coal dealer; Anton Cermak, a firewood seller and ex–coal miner; Richard J. Daley, a stockyards cowboy whose father was a sheet metal worker; and Edward Kelly, a sanitary district axman, born of an Irish Catholic immigrant family with blue-collar antecedents. Maybe their collectively low position on the socioeconomic ladder and their Catholic, ethnic, blue-collar character plays poorly with the outstate, downstate, and suburban voters who would have to support them if they were to rise politically.

It may be possible that nineteenth-century Chicago mayors came from a higher social class and could weather the local political storms and sail on to higher office.

Part of that assumption is correct. Chicago mayors from incorporation of the city in 1837 through the Great Fire of 1871 were drawn from the upper reaches of the socioeconomic ladder. To be sure, they were not patricians, because Chicago was not old enough to have a patrician class nor a North Shore version of the Back Bay Brahmans. Yet they were upscale and a representative sample of the commercial and social elite. Chicago's first mayor, William B. Ogden, was later the president of the Chicago and North Western Railroad, an investor in the transcontinental railroad system, and an economic titan without peer in 1840s Chicago. Ogden was doubtless the wealthiest and socially most prominent person ever to serve as the mayor of Chicago. He was also a founding father, since he helped to write the city's first charter. Also prominent in business life was Chicago's third mayor, Benjamin Raymond, who founded the Elgin Watch Company. The city's fifth mayor, Francis Sherman, was a brick manufacturer and real estate investor whose wealth permitted him to retire at an early age and build the Sherman House Hotel, a Chicago landmark. Augustus Garrett, the city's sixth mayor, ran an auction house and invested in real estate; his fortune was used to establish the Garrett Bible Institute. The seventh mayor, Alson Sherman, established the first saw-mill in Chicago, developed the Lemont marble quarry, and was known to be a public-spirited citizen as well as one of the original trustees of Northwestern University. One of the city's earliest meatpackers, John Chapin, a New England Yankee and one of the founders of the Board of Trade, was the eighth mayor. The tenth, James Woodworth, is described as having "acquired a comfortable fortune in the milling of flour, land speculation, and banking" and fits the upper-income profile. Eleventh in our list of city hall worthies is Walter S. Gurnee, who came from a well-to-do family and amassed a sizable fortune for himself in the saddle and tanning business, claimed to be one of the largest in the West. Gurnee also founded the village of Winnetka on land he had purchased and was at one time the president of the Chicago and Milwaukee Railroad. Chicago's eighteenth mayor, Julian Rumsey, the owner of a grain commission firm, was once the president of the Board of Trade and one of the prime movers behind a stringent grain inspection system that would establish for Chicago grains a solid reputation in national markets. He was also the president of the Corn Exchange Bank. Even those mayors not from the commercial elite ranked high in income and public recognition. Dr. Levi D. Boone, the fourteenth person to occupy the mayor's chair, was the first president of the Chicago Medical Society and a prosperous physician whose wealth came from canal lands and downtown real estate. The city's twenty-first mayor, Joseph Medill, served from 1871 through 1873, and was the owner, publisher, and editor of the Chicago *Tribune* and a public-spirited leader and civic watchdog.

Thus from incorporation as a city in 1837 to the decade of the Great Fire in 1871, Chicago mayors were generally drawn from a higher socioeconomic level than their twentieth-century counterparts. A few were founding fathers, many others were wealthy and socially prominent, with quite a number being movers and shakers in shaping the city's economy and establishing its corporate government.[7] Even so, their upper-class status seemed to make no difference. These notables produced no presidents, no governors, no U.S.

senators or presidential cabinet appointees or Supreme Court justices or important ambassadors, despite their generally high social and economic standing and importance in the political system. The rich did no better than the poor; white collars conferred no mobility advantage over mayors with blue collars; the would-be patricians and founding fathers did no better than the plebeians or ex-plebeians. Thus it seems reasonable to conclude that it was not socioeconomic status nor class position that blocked upward political mobility.

Neither does it appear to have been place of birth, ethnicity, or religion. Mayors from high-status churches such as the Episcopal and Presbyterian along with the middle-status Methodist or Baptist drawn from Yankee, English, Scottish, or old-stock American heritages did no better in climbing upward from mayor than did new-stock immigrants drawn from Catholic Irish or Central European heritages. (The nephew of Daniel Boone and the two nephews of President Benjamin Harrison did no better in upward mobility than the sons and grandsons of the famine Irish or of the peasant migrations from Central Europe.)

How do we begin to explain this stunted and sluggish career mobility in the office of mayor? Some of the standard explanations that mobility scholars have employed, such as slow upward movement of social groups, seem not to apply to our office. We have probed the influence of class origins, ethnicity, and religion, and they appear to have little explanatory value. Being Catholic did not cripple the upward movement of our one overachiever, mayor-governor Edward F. Dunne, and being a WASP did not confer any unusual advantage on our three most visible aspirants for the presidency, the two Carter Harrisons and Mayor Big Bill Thompson. Five other possibilities remain to be explored, which I have called (1) the inferior man (or woman) thesis, (2) the low job horizons and modest career expectations factor, (3) the weak mayor system, (4) grassroots perils and easy access, and (5) antiurbanism. The elusive variable, that white whale of destruction that emerges from time to time to destroy mayoral careers in midpassage, may be lurking in those waters.

Inferior Man (or Woman) Thesis

This thesis argues that inferior politicians with flawed characters are drawn to the office of mayor and that their inferiority shows when they try to run for higher office. The argument, tautologically reasoned back from their collective mayoral failures, is that we know they are inferior men because of their failure to reach higher office. The literature on the subject can be traced back to John Stuart Mill, who believed that men at the lower levels in government were drawn from inferior stock. Another Englishman, James Bryce, published an enormously influential book at the end of the nineteenth century called *The American Commonwealth*, in which he asserted that American city government was the "conspicuous failure" in the American experiment and that "droves of squalid men . . . not fit for suffrage" put into office not the "best men" but the unqualified and unfit to lead. More recently, an American scholar, Marilyn Gittell, in an article published in 1963 gave us the second part of the inferior man corollary, which reads, "The office of mayor offers so little opportunity for advancement" that "men of inferior calibre are, and must be, attracted to it."[8] The problem with this argument is that it would be difficult to demonstrate that mayors are intrinsically inferior or somehow have flawed characters—unless one were to find some external objective measure of flawed character, such as criminal misdeeds or arrest records broadly shared by the group of people we call mayors. Yet this is not the case, since only three of the forty-five mayors have served time in jail: ex-mayors Levi Boone and Buckner Morris were suspected of rebel sympathies during the Civil War and went to jail after having been in office. More recently, Harold Washington went into office after having been in jail. But three of forty-five does not stamp mayors as a criminally prone inferior class unfit for higher office. (Imprisonment may put a blight on individual careers but certainly not on the whole class of people we call mayors.)

Secondly, even if we wish to examine mayors as John Stuart Mill might have and as James Bryce did, we know that their descriptions of urban populations as unfit, "squalid men" off immigrant ships who put their own kind of misfits into office does not fit. Our nineteenth-century mayors were not squalid men off immigrant ships but men drawn overwhelmingly from the top of the social and economic order, many of them founding fathers, economic titans, or the natural leaders of their time. On the basis then of our biographical evidence, it is possible to reject the inferior man thesis.

Low Job Horizons and Modest Career Expectations Factor

Do Chicago mayors have low job horizons and modest career expectations? Are they non–risk takers with civil servant mentalities? Do they forsake mobility for security and not pursue progressive, upward career paths as most politicians do? One way to investigate these questions is to examine the postmayoral careers and what our careerists did after mayoring. Because four died in office and three are still living, I will reduce the number of mayors to thirty-eight for examination. The collective behavior of the thirty-eight does not show low job horizons or the civil servant mentalities of non–risk takers. After having been mayor, the members of the group sought reelection to the office thirty-seven times, winning seventeen elections and losing twenty. The ex-mayors also ran for Congress nine times, winning three and losing six elections. They also put themselves forth nine times for the governor's office, losing eight and winding up only once in the governor's mansion. One also tried for the U.S. Senate and lost. Although they lost more than they won, they clearly behaved as a group of upwardly mobile strivers. Their dismal record in seeking higher office is not a commentary on ambition. They were progressively ambitious.[9] Thus on the face of the evidence, we can reject the low job horizons and modest career expectations thesis.

Weak Mayor System

The office of mayor, unlike the two other executive offices in the American political system, the president and the governor, is not a constitutional office but a statutory one provided for by state statute and legislative ordinance. Mayorship was not codified in any of the charter documents, such as a state or federal constitution, and thus lacks the protection and power of the other two political executives. The office, in modern form, evolved only after 1820 and has been subject to the whims, caprices, and winds of change coming out of state legislatures.

Although the mayor lacks the constitutional authority and power of the other two chief executives, the public seems to be unaware of this difference and expects from the mayor leadership on a par with that of a governor or president. The root of the problem lies in the fragmentation of authority of the urban chief executive and the mayor's diminishing power in the twentieth century.

In big cities, governmental authority is dispersed among federal, state, county, and special tax districts such as public parks, mosquito abatement districts, public schools, a county hospital, and federally supported public housing. An agency exception is the authority over the public schools given to Chicago's mayor in 1995. Although the mayor has little or no formal control over these tax districts and agencies, the voting public thinks he or she does and blames him or her when things go wrong. The only mechanism the mayor ever had for informally controlling these fragmented, uncoordinated agencies in his or her city—the urban machine—was done away with by the reformers. The rising urban middle classes rebelled against the machines, wiped them out in most cities, moved to the suburbs, and left behind no formal or informal set of arrangements to give the mayor the clout of the other two executive offices. Even in Chicago, reform has consistently and steadily taken its toll for the past quarter of a century, and the Shakman decrees of 1972 and 1979, which wiped out all political hiring and firing, are simply the last nails in a coffin long in the making. A power failure has occurred in city hall.

The other pillars of power are party discipline and voter loyalty. Party discipline, the glue that has held together the squabbling urban Democratic coalitions, has weakened, and so has voter loyalty, as evidenced in the Chicago 1983 mayoral elections in which blacks overwhelmingly ignored the party's advice in the primary and whites overwhelmingly ignored the party's advice in the general election. Thus the two informal sources of power, the machine and party loyalty, no longer enhance and enlarge the authority of the mayor. The Chicago mayoralty, after a brief fifty-year bout of machine power, has now returned as an office to its historically weak statutory character.[10] Nonetheless, voters still harbor illusions of executive omnipotence in city hall.

Grassroots Perils and Easy Access

The other factor is the availability of the mayor: everyone seems to have easy public access, if not in person, through letters to the editor in the newspapers, through aldermen, civic groups, and now the omnipresent and ubiquitous square-eye, television. The mayor, unlike the president and the governor, lives among his or her immediate constituents. Every conceivable thing that goes wrong is brought to the mayor's door: dog feces in the parks, crime in the streets, bad schools, lewd entertainment, unplowed streets, corruption in the city council, and inoperable elevators in the public housing projects. And the time lag is nonexistent. Faster than a speeding bullet do the aggrieved and aggravated converge on city hall to assault the mayor. The mayor hears about problems instantly and cannot escape.

By contrast, governors and presidents are far removed from the centers of their constituencies and insulated from complaints by legions of yes-men. Governors generally sit in small and medium-sized cities and towns near the middle of a given state, away from the big city news media and hungry junior reporters out to make a reputation by carving up and exposing some politician. The president is even more distantly removed from the center of his constituency and is seldom confronted by angry potato growers from Maine, cotton farmers from Mississippi, or auto workers from Detroit. These special interest groups send well-mannered lobbyists dressed in three-piece business suits with mellow voices and silver tongues to talk in hushed tones in the cloakrooms of Congress or the anterooms of the statehouses.

No such polite discourse occurs in the city. There, angry gay activists, indignant taxpayers, black power advocates, and Gray Panthers pounce on the mayor at every opportunity and denounce him or her sometimes in the vilest and most outrageous language imaginable—to increase the likelihood of making the evening television news or the front page of the next day's paper. The mayor is then subjected to a constant guerrilla warfare with parts of his or her constituency, and there is no mountain retreat such as a Camp David to which to repair to lick his or her wounds before the next encounter.

The mayor is exposed twenty-four hours a day, seven days a week, and fifty-two weeks of the year to citizens who are unhappy about snowplowing, want their garbage picked up more expeditiously, or want the city to ban or subsidize abortions, feed the hungry, heal the abrasions of urban life, educate the illiterate, enlarge the tax base, and provide more services and levy fewer taxes at the same time, as well as bring harmony, peace, tranquility, and love to the city. The citizens are not unreasonable. They want a St. Augustine, a St. Francis, a Machiavelli, and a King Midas all wrapped up in one. What they usually get is a Jane Byrne or a Harold Washington. These grass-roots demands make the mayorship the most perilous political job in America.

Antiurbanism

Because of the grassroots nature of the executive office, mayors seem to be more responsive to the true character of their electorates (or the noisiest parts of them) than are the holders of the other two executive offices. Mayors seem to be uniquely in tune with their local urban constituencies, who are not replicas of their states, regions, or nation. Chicago is not a microcosm of Illinois, the Midwest, or the United States. In its ethnic and racial composition, its educational attainments, the skills of its workforce, its crime rates, and its urban pathologies, it does not resemble the rest of Illinois. Neither does it in its sense of priorities of cultural values. Chicago's social system is heavily skewed toward the side of concern with pathologies, and her dominant political values openly profess big government, an even bigger welfare state, and more federal intervention into the lives of citizens and the economy. The demographic makeup of the city and the political ethos that derives from it are not representative of the larger electoral districts that control upward political mobility. The diverging political and social values that result are a form of urban-rural conflict.

One convenient illustration of that value conflict can be seen in the next logical step on the political ladder above mayor: the governorship. If Chicago mayors do not take that next logical step to the governor's mansion, then who does? And what does it tell us about the office of mayor?

In all of Illinois' history from statehood in 1818 on to 2000, thirty-four men have sat in the statehouse as governor. Of that thirty-four, eighteen were recruited from what I have called the law-and-justice nexus and thirteen from state and national legislative bodies. The governors of Illinois appear to have avoided city hall the way medieval travelers avoided plague-ridden cities. Governor James Thompson, 1977–91, illustrates, perhaps in extreme form, how the law-and-justice nexus operates to give a progressively ambitious politician good credentials for the upward climb to Springfield. James Thompson not only avoided city hall in his movement upward but spent a good deal of his career as U.S. attorney for the northern district of Illinois from 1971 to 1975 putting down city hall. He declared open season on Chicago Democrats, and before he was through, he had bagged Tom Keane (Mayor Daley's barn boss who ran the city council); Daley's long-term protégé Edward Barrett, then county clerk; and the Mr. Clean of Chicago Democratic politics, Otto Kerner, for granting favorable racetrack dates to a friend at Arlington Park in exchange for money. And fearless Jim actually lobbed one of his prosecutorial salvos right into the mayor's office when he picked up Daley speechwriter, confidant, and office aide Earl Bush for mail fraud, extortion, and general hanky panky. Other Daley lieutenants, such as Paul Wigoda, were put behind bars for income tax evasion and zoning payoffs as Big Jim cleansed Chicago's Augean stables and cleaned house in city hall. Thompson built a formidable reputation and public image putting city hall politicians and the mayor's cronies into jail.

When Thompson first ran for governor in 1976, he devoted a good deal of his campaign to putting down Daley and Chicago. He told downstaters, outstaters, and suburbanites that the people of Illinois "don't want a governor who is under the influence of the mayor of Chicago." Actually in doing that, Thompson had craftily borrowed the anti-Chicago and anti-Daley rhetoric of the previous governor, Daniel Walker. Walker had made his reputation blaming the 1968 convention riots on Daley and the Chicago police, and had defeated Paul Simon in the 1972 gubernatorial primary by calling Simon a puppet and minion of the Chicago machine. Walker's predecessor was a World War II tank commander named Richard Ogilvie, who began his law enforcement career as an assistant U.S. attorney in 1954, graduated to special assistant U.S. attorney in 1958, and led the legal battle against the Chicago mob. In 1962 Ogilvie was elected Cook County sheriff to keep an eye on that Sodom on the lakeshore, Daley's Chicago. Thus three relatively recent governors have gained office partly by running not from but against city hall.[11]

These three Illinois governors illustrate what I have called the law-and-justice nexus, the most fertile recruiting ground for the Illinois governorship. It includes U.S. attorneys, state's attorneys, district attorneys, prosecutors, sheriffs, and judges. Of the thirty-two men who served as governor from statehood to 1991, eighteen came from the law-and-justice nexus and thirteen from the state and federal legislatures. What does this finding mean? The statewide election process and the voters of Illinois seem to be saying that the only people from Chicago to be trusted in the governor's mansion in Springfield are those who make a career of fighting the evil ways of the big city and the corruption of city hall and the mayor's office. (Beyond the city limits, the most common element in the pregubernatorial careers of future governors also appears to be the jobs of prosecutor and judge.) Chicagoans who are ambitious and want to move up the political career ladder instinctively learn to avoid city hall.

Summary

We began our investigation with the question, Is the Chicago mayoralty a dead-end job? And the answer is that by all common measures of political mobility, it is. Next we asked why, and proceeded to examine our mayors against all of the standard explanations for upward mobility, such as socioeconomic status, class background, religion, and nativity. We found that our mayors, whether rich or poor, of foreign stock or native-born, from the top of the social register or from the wrong side of the tracks, and regardless of religion, were not able to escape the deadly political downdraft that sucks postmayoral careers into political oblivion. The wealthy founding fathers and descendants of American presidents, such as the Harrisons, did no better than the blue-collar plebeians drawn from the Central European peasant migrations or the famine Irish. Ironically, our one overachiever, mayor-governor Edward Dunne, was an Irish Catholic. Thus the standard explanations for upward mobility do not help to explain the blighted political careers of our mayors.

Next we turned to investigating several reasons given in the scholarly literature for the stunned and sluggish career mobility of the nation's mayors. We weighed our mayors on the inferior man (or woman) scales and found that explanation tautological and wanting. We then tested their careers for low job horizons and modest career expectations and found them not to be a satisfactory answer, for our mayors were clearly upward strivers, albeit unsuccessful ones.

Then we turned to three other factors and found plausible answers for which the evidence offers support. The first of these was a systemic problem, the weak mayor system, which undercut the mayor's ability to deliver services, often disappointing citizens. Next we found a problem in political ecology common to a city's chief executive—the grassroots peril and easy access—which made the job of mayor a lightning rod for political discontent and city hall a hot seat that lacked the insulation governors and presidents enjoyed.

Finally we turned to the last and most powerful explanation, which, combined with the two above, becomes the real white whale of destruction: antiurbanism. Antiurbanism in all of its grand varieties has crippled the political upward movement of Chicago mayors. We illustrated this city-outstate value conflict in looking at the next important leadership step on the political ladder, the governorship, and showed how the Chicago mayoralty was not a step up but a stumbling block. Chicago does not put up candidates for the governor's job because candidates for the governor's job spend their campaign time putting down Chicago. We concluded that the Illinois voters seem to be saying at the ballot box that the only people they will send to the governor's mansion from Chicago are those who make their careers fighting the evil ways of the big city and corruption in city hall. And accordingly, the evidence shows that political strivers avoid city hall the way medieval travelers did plague-ridden cities.

The best that can be said from the historical record is that the Chicago mayorship is an excellent springboard for the Chicago mayorship or for downward skidding to lower office. Chicago mayors do not make much of a splash in national politics, for they have not appeared to be attractive possibilities for appointments by national policymakers; no presidential cabinet posts, no ambassadorships, no Supreme Court justiceships have been entrusted to ex–Chicago mayors. When Jesse Jackson proclaimed in his euphoric moment that the Chicago mayoralty was a "stepping stone to higher ground," he must not have known what a quicksand bog it has been and is, and that it is more like a one-way ticket to political oblivion.

18.

RICHARD M. DALEY AND THE POLITICS OF ADDITION

Paul M. Green

Richard M. Daley is lucky to be the mayor of Chicago. Never in Chicago history has a defeated mayoral candidate been resurrected to the epitome of political power as quickly or as totally as the son of Chicago's legendary six-term mayor, Richard J. Daley (1955–76).

In 1983 Rich Daley, the Cook County state's attorney, suffered a bone-crushing loss in Chicago's Democratic mayoral primary. This epic battle (called by some the "Super Bowl of Chicago politics"), which pitted the incumbent mayor, Jane Byrne (the city's first and only female mayor) against Congressman Harold Washington (the city's first and only elected African American mayor) and Daley, electrified the city and the nation because of its ferocity, cost, and racial divisiveness.

Washington's primary win and subsequent equally heated general election victory over Republican Bernard Epton catapulted the new mayor into national prominence. After a few years of battling his city council (the so-called Council Wars), Mayor Washington gained control over the aldermen, won another mayoral primary and general election in 1987, and seemed destined to reach his stated goal of a twenty-year mayoral run.

Richard M. Daley fell back into Chicago's political shadows, carefully watching his words and actions while continuing to serve as the county's state's attorney.

Then the unexpected happened. Harold Washington, at the height of his political power, suddenly died in late November 1987. Political chaos returned to the city. In a famous all-night council meeting, an African American alderman, Eugene Sawyer, was selected acting mayor. Richard M. Daley kept quiet.

A lawsuit was filed by several Washington supporters and black activists, who demanded a special mayoral election as soon as possible. This anti-Sawyer coalition rallied around Alderman Tim Evans, an African American, as the true heir to the Washington legacy. Richard M. Daley kept quiet.

On November 8, 1988, State's Attorney Daley won a landslide reelection victory over his Republican opponent. A few weeks later, the Illinois Supreme Court ordered a special mayoral election for February 1989. Richard M. Daley *no longer* kept quiet. Instead, he unleashed a massive display of political power as he began his march to the fifth floor of city hall (the mayor's office). With almost military precision, Daley and his allies rolled over old foes, won over new allies, and demonstrated a surprising amount of tactical and strategic political shrewdness.

In six short years, Richard M. Daley had blossomed into a one-man political organization. Unlike his sometimes fumbling and inward 1983 effort, the Daley political operation in 1989 was smooth and expanding. Though Daley remained a poor public speaker and somewhat shy campaigner, his persona was transformed from "The Mayor's" political son to a public manager. One has to go back to the era of former mayor Anton J. Cermak (1931–33) to find a comparable makeover. Then, the long-time political infighter Tony Cermak repositioned himself as the "master executive" who could help Chicago survive the Depression.

Daley's jump was not as great but was equally effective. Since becoming Chicago's mayor, Richard M. Daley has remained true to his 1989 mantra as an urban problem solver, workaholic city booster, and no-nonsense administrator.

The Climb to City Hall

Richard M. Daley (RMD) was born on 24 April 1942. He was the fourth of seven children (and the eldest son) born to the union of Richard and Eleanor Daley. By the time RMD was a teenager, his dad had become Cook County Democratic chairman (1953) and Chicago mayor (1955).

Though he has often denied the notion that he was destined to be a politician or public official, the fact remains that RMD's childhood and young adult years centered on government and politics.

RMD was not an exceptional student but managed to graduate from Providence College (1965) and DePaul School of Law (1968). He eventually passed the bar, became a lawyer, and quickly moved into the political arena. He was elected to the state's 1970 constitutional convention from his family's Bridgeport neighborhood base. And two years later, the same citizens elected RMD to the Illinois state senate.

In Springfield, Senator Daley was seen as the eyes and ears of his powerful father. Unlike his dad, who also had served in the state legislature decades before and who had carefully and painfully climbed up the very crowded Chicago Democratic power ladder, "young Daley" was an untested and unseasoned political player. State capital insiders, especially downstate legislators and media, derided his abilities, using words like "spoiled" and "nasty" to describe his political personality and governmental skills.

His father's death on 20 December 1976 shoved RMD into the Democratic Eleventh Ward committeeman's post. The new acting mayor was Eleventh Ward alderman Michael J. Bilandic, a man who was even more reluctant than RMD to be thrust into political prominence. Admittedly, following a legend like RJD would have been tough for anyone, but neither RMD nor Mayor Bilandic had the "old man's" zest and love for Chicago's brutal ward and precinct politics.

In February 1979, after winning a special mayoral election in 1977, Mayor Bilandic lost to political newcomer Jane Byrne in the snow-filled Democratic mayoral primary (see previous chapters on Bilandic and Byrne). Byrne's subsequent landslide win over a no-name Republican in April 1979 gave her city hall and unleashed on Chicago's citizens the most thrilling, dangerous, and emotional decade of local politics in city history. This combination of political melodrama and shoot-out would not end until RMD's 1989 mayoral victory.

Byrne's 1979 triumph left RMD vulnerable for the first time in his political life. Even now, political scientists and psychologists cannot fully explain Mayor Byrne's desire to "get RMD" and drive him out of Chicago politics. But in no uncertain terms, Byrne declared war on state senator Richard M. Daley.

Finding himself growing more isolated in Chicago Democratic politics, RMD surprised nearly everyone by declaring his candidacy for Cook County state's attorney in November 1979. (This was the only county office held by a Republican). Byrne knew well the spotlight an antagonistic state's attorney could shine on the mayor's office, and she immediately searched for a heavy-hitting Democrat to take on Daley in the 1980 primary. In a bold move, she selected Fourteenth Ward alderman Ed Burke, also from a longtime Chicago political family, to defeat Daley and thus rid her of her real or imaginary nemesis.

What is seldom discussed in analyses of RMD's long political career is that when the chips were down in 1980 (both in the primary and in the general election), young Daley, the son of the Chicago Democratic machine's greatest boss, ran as a political *outsider*. Thus began a significant change in RMD's faith in party politics and the notion that the party's central committee endorsement (a huge tool of his dad) or even the committee itself truly mattered anymore.

Burke, with Byrne's help, was endorsed by the Democratic central committee and most ward leaders over Daley. The race was not between Burke and Daley but between Byrne and Daley. In the end, Daley crushed Burke by more than a two-to-one margin, aided in large part by RMD's surprising suburban strength.[1]

In November 1980, when most Americans watched Ronald Reagan easily defeat Jimmy Carter for president, Cook County residents were mesmerized by the tight race for Cook County state's attorney. As in the primary, Byrne went all out for RMD's opponent, even though incumbent state's attorney Bernard Carey was a Republican. As in the primary, Byrne's vendetta against RMD pushed the latter's actual foe into a sideshow posture at best. It got so bad for Carey that just prior to election day, he made an incredible admission concerning his predicament, stating, "Daley has portrayed himself as martyr or victim, when in fact, I have been the victim because it [Byrne's vendetta] has caused the voters to overlook the relative qualifications of both candidates. Its like standing too close to Mount St. Helens. Every time it [Byrne] erupts, I get covered with ashes."[2]

RMD beat Carey by sixteen thousand votes in one of the closest state's attorney races in county history. Byrne did her best to knife RMD in the city's African American wards, but the winner's strength in the city's heavily ethnic Southwest Side and its adjoining suburbs gave young Daley enough votes to squeak out a narrow win.

Much has been written about the 1983 Chicago Democratic mayoral primary. For the purpose of this chapter, it is important to point out that as a politician and government official, State's Attorney Daley was simply not ready to take on both Byrne and Congressman Harold Washington at the same time. RMD was obviously not comfortable running in 1983. Why? First, his political operation was not smooth (an uneven mixing of several of his father's old loyalists and a few of RMD's younger allies); second, his governmental track record was minimal, especially to take on an incumbent mayor and a longtime (though relatively unknown) political sharpshooter like Harold Washington; third and most important, RMD's campaign, both its policies and tactics, aimed inward, not outward. His campaign did not reflect the city's changing demographics or the types of issues that affected its citizens. As one old pro told me, "1983 was the ultimate 'pissing match' and Rich Daley's Bridgeport-based campaign could not overcome Byrne's citywide money and incumbency or Washington's racial appeal and rhetoric."[3] Nevertheless, RMD ran a close third to Washington and Byrne, he did receive the mayoral endorsements of both major newspapers, and he took his defeat with dignity and honor. Most important, he learned.

Mayor Richard M. Daley, the Politician

In his second run for mayor, young Daley made few mistakes. Granted, one of his former great adversaries, Harold Washington, had died and Jane Byrne had lost two election bids in trying to make a comeback. Also, former Democratic party chairman, Ed Vrdolyak, a bitter Daley foe, had switched parties twice (Republican and Solidarity) and was no longer a major political force. Still, in the 1988–89 campaign period, it was a new Rich Daley who was willing and able to take advantage of the mayoral opportunity unexpectedly dropped on his doorstep.

Strategically, Daley understood city residents were "simply tired of the tensions, tirades and turmoil of local politics."[4] Independent-minded lakefronters remained socially liberal but were seeking fiscal stability and were growing economically conservative, especially concerning the two magic words *property values*. Hispanics were frustrated at being used as bargaining chips between two racially based political camps. African Americans were split politically and philosophically as some searched futilely for another Harold Washington. And the city's remaining white ethnics were looking for someone with whom they could identify but, equally important, a leader who could restore peace to an exhausted, war-torn city.

Tactically, Daley in 1989 made a series of lightning political moves. First, he broke out of his political "Bridgeport blockade" by hiring two young, progressive consultants, David Wilhelm and David Axelrod, to run his campaign. Both men were veterans of Paul Simon's 1984 upset victory over incumbent U.S. senator Charles Percy of Illinois. Second, RMD's fund-raising was placed in the capable hands of prominent lakefronters Paul Stepan and John Schmidt. Third, unlike his actions in 1983, RMD aggressively sought out female political leadership and hit a home run by naming rising political star Julie Hamos deputy campaign manager. Fourth, he persuaded progressive Twenty-sixth Ward alderman Luis Gutierrez, a Harold Washington loyalist, to endorse his candidacy, thereby solidifying his appeal to the city's growing Hispanic community. Lastly, he selected noted black city hall reporter Avis LaVelle, of WGN radio, to be his press spokesperson. This move not only gave RMD a top-notch press secretary but also told lakefronters and Hispanic Chicagoans that this was indeed a new Daley running for mayor.

While expanding his coalition, RMD locked in ethnic Chicago support by convincing any would-be white opponent that challenging him would amount to political suicide.

Daley's twin 1989 victories—defeating Eugene Sawyer in the primary (56 percent to 44 percent) and Tim Evans in the general election (55 percent to 41 percent; Ed Vrdolyak received 4 percent)—set the mayoral vote pattern for the rest of the century and beyond. RMD's political and governing coalition consisted of white ethnics, lakefronters, and Hispanics. These groups have held firm for RMD throughout his mayoral career as a string of African American candidates failed to dent the mayor's *personal* machine.

Though some people write and talk of RMD resurrecting his dad's old political apparatus, they are wrong. The old ward and precinct machine is dead. The new machine is not loyal or beholden to an organization but to a person—Richard M. Daley. The mayor, unlike RJD, does not expend politi-cal capital or energy in countless political battles but picks and chooses his fights and candidates. Thus, the new machine is truly operational only when RMD runs for reelection or when there is a contest that the mayor goes all out to win.

This new machine has produced staggering results for RMD. Just look at the numbers. Starting in 1989, RMD has run eight times for mayor (1989, 1991, and 1995 Democratic primary and general elections, and 1999 and 2003 nonpartisan mayoral elections). In those eight campaigns,

1. except for Sawyer and Evans in 1989, no opponent has hit the 40 per-cent mark;
2. no foe has been able to win more than nineteen of fifty wards;
3. no opponent has come within one hundred thousand votes of RMD's winning total; and most important,
4. RMD's vote percentage has jumped from the midfifties in 1989 to nearly 80 percent in 2003. Moreover, in 2003, RMD unbelievably lost just *six* of the city's 2,712 precincts.

The last point is truly breathtaking, given the racial divisiveness of the mid-1980s. In 2003, by carrying every African American ward in the city (most of them with over 60 percent of the vote), RMD eliminated the last large pocket of organized anti-Daley voters in the city. Obviously, this could change by 2007, but it will not make an electoral difference unless a potential RMD rival can also break up or at least make large holes in the mayor's original 1989 coalition of ethnics, lakefronters, and Hispanics. In the 2003 election, twenty-four wards, containing a large chunk of RMD's 1989 base, gave the mayor at least 85 percent of their vote.

RMD's political transformation from Southwest Side ethnic leader to citywide coalition builder involved far more than a personal attitudinal shift. The mayor and his advisers recognized clearly that the citizen makeup of Chicago had undergone a remarkable change. And to update the favorite dictum of his late father, the current mayor obviously believes "good politics makes good demographics, and good demographics make good politics."

Look at the city of Chicago. The 2000 census reveals that no racial group dominates the city,[5] and moreover, both whites and blacks lost population between 1990 and 2000. Asians and Pacific Islanders saw their Chicago num-bers increase by over forty thousand residents, but the real demographic story involves the booming Hispanic population.

In the last decade of the twentieth century, Chicago's Hispanic population grew by over two hundred thousand. This fact alone is the reason the city's total population increased for the first time since the 1950 census.

Not only have there been recent population leaps in Chicago's racial minorities that have increased total numbers, but there also have been important shifts in residential location—another fact that has huge political implications.

Overall, the population growth in the city has occurred on Chicago's North and Northwest Sides and Near South and Southwest Sides. Broken down by racial group, these movements give vivid insight into RMD's political strategy and tactics.

Chicago's white residents continue to live in large numbers along most of the city's periphery. Wards in the Far North and Northwest Sides and Far Southwest and Southeast Sides (so-called ethnic wards) remained middle-class, home-owning vote bastions for Rich Daley. However, the combination of gentrification, returning baby boomers, and yuppification has transformed former manufacturing or low-rent neighborhoods northwest, west, and south of the Loop into "destination locations" for middle- and upper-middle-class whites of all ages. These Starbucks-drinking, cute-restaurant-dining, condo- and town-home-buying urban newcomers or returnees demand efficient government, first-rate city services, and stability. As will be seen in a later section of this chapter, most of these new inner-city white residents do not have school-age children but nevertheless support RMD's all-out attack on improving Chicago public schools, in part because they support Rich Daley.

Most Chicago blacks still reside heavily in the longstanding geographical upside-down "L" that stretches north from the city's Far South Side to a connecting line of wards pushing west from downtown fringe areas to the suburbs (the eastern end of this West Side black area having been pushed farther west by the upscale residential renaissance taking place west of the Loop). Many middle-class blacks have also moved into Southwest Side wards and wards in the northeastern part of the city. Though racial integration is far from massive, three points are important: (1) rising economic status for African Americans has spurred more integrative residential racial movement in the city during the 1990–2000 period than at any time in the city's history; (2) the historic South Side "black belt," home to the poorest African Americans, is undergoing a depopulation process as high-rise public housing is torn down; and (3) market-price housing has become the battle cry in middle-class South Side black wards, as residents there argue against more public, or low-income, housing in their neighborhoods, no matter the color of the potential resident.

Population expansion and intracity movement for Hispanics can be summed up in one word: *remarkable*. The historic Near North Side Latino neighborhoods (largely Puerto Rican in ancestry) have grown, as have those on the Near Southwest Side (predominantly Mexican). But the main growth of Chicago Latinos has taken place on the Northwest and Southwest Sides, where huge numbers of Hispanics have moved into formerly white city neighborhoods.

A community-by-community breakdown reveals the incredible surge of Hispanic outward movement within the city since the 1990 census. For example, the Belmont-Cragin neighborhood on the city's Far Northwest Side had a Latino population of 17,066 in 1990, but the 2000 census showed more than fifty thousand Hispanics living in that community. Other examples exist on the Northwest and Southwest Sides in communities heretofore not considered Hispanic, and the ramifications of this phenomenon go beyond basic socioeconomic change; it is political change as well. More and more Hispanics are becoming traditional homeowners, whose goals and demands play perfectly into Chicago-style neighborhood politics, a fact Mayor Daley understands better than anyone else in the city.

Rich Daley's multiethnic, multiracial personal political operation, stressing family, work, pride, racial sensitivity in hiring, and a middle-class ethos for the city, has simply overwhelmed any potential foe, either individual or group. It recognizes the city's changing demographics and the striving for middle-class status by African Americans and Latinos, and it simply trumps or empowers any individual or group that attempts a challenge. Even the usual hot-button schools issue, an area historically open to mayoral challengers, is now Daley-dominated.

It is important to remember that Chicago is a political town and RMD is a hard-nosed politician. He and his allies have cornered the market on fundraising and, equally important, have made it nearly impossible for any challenger to raise big dollars against him. And though the mayor often preaches against negative campaigning or personal attacks against opponents, he can unleash his well-known temper against anyone who comes at him personally or challenges his views on major issues. One of RMD's greatest political strengths is the potential for massive political retaliation, and given the lack of organized resistance against him, few individuals of substance want to risk facing a RMD onslaught.

On the political front, RMD has benefited from a change in how Chicago elects its mayors. In May 1995, Republican governor Jim Edgar (no Daley pal) and the GOP-controlled Illinois state legislature (the same body that *gave* RMD control of the Chicago Public Schools) passed legislation creating nonpartisan mayoral elections in Chicago. According to Chicago *Tribune* political writer Rick Pearson, "Republicans . . . thought eliminating party labels in city elections would remove for the GOP the stigma of running for mayor in a Democratic city."[6]

Unfortunately for Chicago Republicans, this new law was useless, since the city council had already been electing its members on a nonpartisan basis for decades with no positive results: currently Chicago has one Republican alderman, while forty-nine are Democrats. But for RMD, this 1995 election law was the equivalent of a political insurance policy. Why? A nonpartisan election prevents the possible repeat of the 1983 Democratic mayoral primary, when Harold Washington won the coveted party nomination in a multicandidate, biracial campaign with less than 50 percent of the vote. This new law almost guarantees RMD that if such an unlikely political scenario would rise again, there would have to be a one-on-one runoff between the top two vote getters. In sum, a racially driven divide-and-conquer campaign strategy against an incumbent white mayor is no longer feasible—its merely history.

Mayor Richard M. Daley, the Manager

There is little disagreement about RMD's rise to power or his political coalition skills; the continuous election victories speak for themselves. However, there is little agreement about how RMD runs the city. To his loyalists, he is a dedicated, no-nonsense leader who challenges himself and those around him to pursue an efficient and modern management model for Chicago. To his opponents (seldom expressing themselves publicly), he is a hot-tempered demagogue who rewards his friends, punishes his enemies, and dismisses public debate on important issues as a waste of time. And given his unwillingness to emulate his father and become the city's dominant Democratic party leader, almost all criticism aimed at RMD is due to *policy* and not *political* matters.

Any discussion of RMD as mayor-manager must come to grips with a crucial historical fact: Chicago has a weak mayor–strong council form of government. Historically, successful Chicago mayors (as shown in this book) have been individuals who dominated their city council through their own personal or political popularity and power. Sometimes persuasion was easy; at other times, old-fashioned Chicago muscle was used to persuade city alderman to follow the lead of the mayor. Though some academics lament this de facto power reversal and long for an active and open city council with teeth, the chances of such a change under RMD are slim to none.[7] Why?

Like his father, the current Mayor Daley distrusts the council that helps him govern the city. Instinctively, he understands that for most of the city's history, Chicago aldermen were ward- and not city-oriented. And though race has replaced ethnic background as the great ward boundary decider, RMD, like many of his mayoral predecessors, remains suspect of many local council members' knowledge, integrity, and work ethic. Another legal change beneficial to Daley, one that allows Chicago mayors to select new aldermen for council vacancies between elections, has only somewhat eased RMD's reluctance to share power with his legislative body. However, when it comes to policy crunch time, RMD has little patience for council committee meetings or debate; he would much rather depend on his handpicked administrative team to resolve crucial issues.

In the summer of 1991, I interviewed RMD about his first two years in office.[8] It was the first time he described his mayoral-managerial style in detail, and his answers were a blueprint of how he would run Chicago government. On the type of management he was looking for in his staff and department heads, Daley said, "I want in government . . . people who are hardworking but, most of all, people who are creative and willing to go to the edge of something."[9] About his own administrative style, especially as it relates to staff and city employees, RMD was blunt in his response, "I'm one who demands a lot from people. I'm not afraid to look at alternative ways in city government. That's what I've done in my two years and will continue to do in the next four."[10]

Perhaps his most insightful answer, which among other things outlined his goal to centralize power in his office, dealt with the issue of public service accountability. At a time when many big-city mayors were trying to deflect or duck responsibility for urban ills and problems, RMD clearly stated a governing philosophy that would soon see him take over the day-to-day operations of the city's public schools and public housing. According to Daley, "you get . . . accountability through service. You're a manager. *I'm* the one who is going to be accountable. . . . *I'm* the one who gets called about a problem. . . . *I* get blamed for it, not one of my employees. So let's begin. The accountability is right here, right in this office."[11]

From this interview early in his mayoral reign, one sees RMD playing the role like a confident baseball pitcher. He wants the ball and believes he and his team have the ability to win any game (issue) as long as he is on the mound (in office) getting people out (his opponents) with blazing fastballs (hard work and political power). In a large city like Chicago, this kind of managerial confidence can occur only if the mayor has competent people around him. And in this respect, RMD has been both very lucky and shrewd in selecting department heads and mayoral staff.

What is seldom mentioned about RMD's mayoral run is the seemingly endless supply of mainly young public administration professionals who have worked for him. Though their stint of service may not be long, their ability to perform municipal tasks has seldom been equaled in Chicago history or, for that matter, anyplace else. Many of his top-line administrators have had little political experience, but they learned quickly how to play the game. Obviously, it helped that RMD towered over every obstacle as the great protector.

Two points about Daley and his governmental team are crucial. First, when they or the mayor concludes that their time in city government is over, many move on to other public bodies or the local private sector. Incredibly, they often keep connections with the mayor and his people and many times act as unofficial liaisons to these other units of government or business. Second, and corollary to point one, *no* former RMD confidant or high-level city employee (for that matter, no low-level city employee either) has ever turned on the mayor. RMD commands total loyalty from his past and current city personnel, who remain forever faithful to the mayor. Why? Theories range from RMD charisma to political retaliation and all ideas in between, but the fact remains that the media and potential RMD foes have *never* found a source to dump dirt on the mayor or his closest associates.

Perhaps no single issue reflects RMD's leadership style better than public education in Chicago. Like most other big-city school systems, Chicago's elementary and secondary educational programs hit the skids as the twentieth century was winding down. Historically, most Chicago mayors avoided public school issues; instead they deflected criticisms to the appointed school board or superintendent, who, they claimed, controlled their own budget, personnel, and policies. However, in 1988 (a year before RMD was elected), Chicago public schools hit rock bottom when then Secretary of Education William Bennett called the city's schools the worst in the nation.

Chicago area businessmen and -women, along with educational advocacy groups, began a reform movement to give parents and community residents greater governing control over their schools through the creation of local school councils. Still, huge problems festered—bad administrative leadership, mismanagement, poor union relations, and inadequate student performance. In 1995 the Illinois general assembly and the state's governor (all GOP-controlled) gave RMD near total control of public education in the city. Republican motivation for this move (only a handful of Democrats supported this radical legislation) ranged from a desire to stick it to Democratic legislative foes and their potent ally, the Chicago Teachers Union, to a heartfelt belief that only RMD could change the city's educational system.

The mayor jumped at the opportunity with a combination of joy and fury. The legislation "gave the Mayor of Chicago" the power to appoint a five-member corporate-style board of school trustees to oversee the system and, more important, a "chief executive officer" to run the system.[12] This CEO was given the power to appoint the top management officials with board approval, but all in the know knew the boss was RMD.

The mayor's choices of Paul Vallas to be CEO and Gerry Chico to be board president were met with near unanimous approval. Part of the excitement of this unprecedented power shift in school administration was the simple recognition that both of these talented men were top RMD loyalists (Vallas, the city budget director; Chico, the mayor's chief of staff). In effect, the public, the media, and school personnel generally concluded that if the mayor was going to run things, he might as well have his people in charge.

The Vallas-Chico combine ran the schools for a little more than six years. During that period, they improved classroom performance, contained costs, and cut bureaucracy. At the same time, they created innovative programs like *ending* social promotions and mandatory summer school for failing students, and in the process diminished greatly the racial tensions both in the schools and in the surrounding communities. That both men had a falling out with the mayor in the spring of 2001 simply meant that new Daley partisans would take their places.

Involvement in Chicago's public schools showcased RMD's managerial can-do, get-it-done style. He took on a longstanding problem that many viewed as political quicksand. He lobbied for and received the power to make him accountable for the city's schools. He shrewdly selected individuals who had both administrative competency and political loyalty (to him) to run the entire bureaucracy. And in the process, he turned this most critical urban issue from a liability to an asset by becoming its chief spokesman and cheerleader. In the end, Chicago public schools are better than they were in 1995 but nowhere near where they need to be. However, no Daley political foe has used the once combustible education issue against him.

Most Chicagoans have accepted the notion that good government is good politics, especially RMD-style. In an October 2000 interview with *Business Week* magazine, Daley clearly stated his proudest accomplishment as mayor was education. According to RMD, "education . . . it's the only priority we've had in this city."[13] Though he may not have turned the city's educational lemon into lemonade, RMD has made the issue politically drinkable to the vast majority of his constituents.

Conclusion: The Future

Political

RMD's political future looks bright. Assuming that no problems with health or family occur, RMD looms as an overwhelming favorite for reelection in 2007. Why? Two basic reasons. First, not only does his expanding electoral coalition seem unstoppable, but chances of potential real political opposition appear to be nonexistent. Second, if RMD wins in 2007, he would tie his dad's Chicago mayoral victory total (six) and, at the end of that term, he would break his father's twenty-one-year mayoral longevity record.

A Daley victory in 2007 would also provide one of the most astounding political statistics in American urban history. RMD and his dad will have won together twelve of Chicago's last sixteen mayoral elections and, if RMD completes the 2007 term, will have occupied the mayor's office for forty-three of the last fifty-six years!

Can anyone or anything thwart RMD's political juggernaut? No candidate or campaign is unbeatable, given the right circumstances or powerful opponents. Since 1989 RMD has avoided the following big three political land mines, any one of which (if outlandish enough) could endanger his carefully constructed political apparatus: first, financial ethics—RMD or members of his immediate family reaping huge monetary awards for clout-based illegal activities; second, personal ethics—RMD discovered to be involved in illicit personal behavior; third, racial ethics—RMD committing a significant race-based mistake that rekindles 1980s-style "skin color" politics.

The chances of RMD involving himself in any of these ethical lapses range from remote (financial and racial) to you-must-be-kidding (personal). Though stories about Daley pals enriching themselves through political clout have appeared in various media outlets, nothing of substance has come close to tying RMD to any of the activities. Like his dad, the current Mayor Daley has traded dollars for power. His personal lifestyle is beyond reproach, and though he no longer lives in his family's ancestral Bridgeport "bungalow belt" neighborhood, his philosophy, politics, and financial needs remain blue-collar. In short, for RMD, the glory is in being and remaining Chicago's chief executive and no other potential monetary or personal reward can compete with the title "Mayor."

Governmental

The search for revenue remains job one. As in other major American big cities, Chicago's manufacturing base has diminished, and though tourism, conventions, and trade shows have picked up some of the slack, the city and RMD continually search for a steady stream of new dollars.

Externally, this quest means RMD must look to Washington, DC, and Springfield for support and assistance. This fact alone (besides his own personal proclivities) will prevent RMD from becoming a Democratic party insider, kingmaker, or party boss at the national or state level. He and his city cannot risk alienating government leaders on the basis of differing party identities. Therefore RMD will continue to play down party labels and will continue to "schmooze" Republicans with zeal and respect.

Internally, RMD must find new ways to govern efficiently and effectively. Chicago is not Madison, Wisconsin (a city with a long history of progressive politics), and moreover, Professor Woodrow Wilson's nineteenth-century managerial maxim of the need to separate "politics from administration" is not an accepted Windy City tradition. Moving to a more Wilsonian model will remain a huge RMD challenge but one he must accept. Why? He and his city simply will not have the revenue to fund no-show, no-work, underperforming employees.

In sum, the mayoral Chicago political tradition is about to face its toughest test. RMD's massive political muscle must be used to encourage and enforce more city worker governmental productivity. Revenue pressures combined with an expanding gentrified center city populace will demand fiscal sanity and excellent public service. At the same time, RMD must satisfy the hopes and ambitions of the city's growing Hispanic population while continuing to address the other critical urban needs of better education, health care, crime reduction, and affordable housing. Governing Chicago has never been easy, and despite his impressive arsenal of political and governmental weapons, Mayor Richard M. Daley faces several ongoing battles that will test his managerial skill and political will.

19.

RICHARD M. DALEY'S RECORD

Surpassing the Boss

Steve Neal

His success is no accident.

As the eldest son of Chicago's most durable chief executive, Richard Michael Daley had a better political education than anyone who has ever held the mayor's office. He was a teenager when his father was elected mayor in 1955 and began their family's half-century dominance of the prairie metropolis. The younger Daley learned from his father the importance of forging coalitions, adapting to change, and having a vision for the future of the city.

"I may not be the best speaker in town," he said in declaring his candidacy for the 1989 special mayoral election, "but I know how to run a government, and how to bring people together."

Richard M. Daley prevailed in that race and would go on to become the city's first nonpartisan mayor and, in the 1990s, the first mayor to win three four-year terms in a single decade. After winning his fifth term in 2003 to become the city's second-longest-serving mayor, he showed that he has the staying power to break his father's longevity record and may also surpass the elder Daley's legacy of accomplishment.

In an era of term limits, the second Mayor Daley has become the dean of big-city mayors. Since he was first elected in 1989, the cities of New York and Los Angeles imposed term limits and seven men have presided over the nation's two largest cities. His seniority makes him unique among the nation's urban leaders and is among the reasons that presidents of both parties and congressional leaders have sought his advice on the problems of the cities. "He is a poster child against term limits," said former Los Angeles mayor Richard Riordan. "I think Rich Daley is a fantastic mayor."

Daley has brought calm and stability to a city that had been sharply divided along racial lines, developed innovative programs that have gained national acclaim, and done much to improve the city's quality of life. R. W. Apple of the New York *Times* has written that Chicago under Daley's leadership "is a prosperous, well-governed model for the rest of the country."

According to the 2000 census, for the first time in five decades, the city's population increased. New and former residents are moving into the central district and into the neighborhoods. The conversion of lofts and construction of new townhouses are attracting people from the suburbs and newcomers to the Chicago area. With his own family's move from Bridgeport to Central Station on the Near South Side, Mayor Daley played an important role in this housing renaissance.

From the renovation of Navy Pier through the consolidation of the Museum Campus and the relocation of the Outer Drive, he has sparked a revival of downtown Chicago. He dedicated a new central library in the South Loop, promoted a revival of the Loop's theater district, and oversaw the construction of the massive new Millennium Park along Michigan Avenue from Randolph to Adams streets. "The city has never looked better," said former Republican governor James R. Thompson, who credits Daley's leadership.

At the same time, Daley is attentive to the neighborhoods and is out and about more than predecessors, including the first Mayor Daley. Through his Neighborhoods Alive program, Daley has invested billions of public dollars in new or repaved streets, alleys, sidewalks, and sewers. He has spent more than $500 million for the acquisition of new parks and improvement of the city's vast park system. The city has planted more than five hundred thousand trees during the Daley years. Daley also launched a citywide recycling program and has removed spray paint from hundreds of thousands of buildings and sidewalks through his Graffiti Busters program. "He's just the kind of guy who goes on tours of the neighborhoods and sees a streetlight out and demands to know why the damn streetlight is out," said Fran Spielman, city hall correspondent for the Chicago *Sun-Times.* "He is a nuts and bolts guy."

The improvement of Chicago's public schools is Daley's most notable achievement. During President Ronald Reagan's administration, Education Secretary William Bennett had referred to Chicago's public schools as "the worst in the nation." Daley embraced legislation in 1995 that gave him control of the schools and allowed him to install a new management team that eliminated a deficit of $1.5 billion, set higher standards, made homework mandatory, ended social promotions, and demanded accountability. The mayor obtained more than $2 billion to build seventy new school buildings and renovate another six hundred. "I knew I had to have some responsibility for education," Daley said, "because if the middle class won't put its kids in the city schools, then we lose the middle class."

In the wake of Daley's school reforms, math and reading scores improved to their highest level in decades. The success of Daley's education initiatives could also be measured in increased enrollment, attendance, and graduation rates. "We have shown that if you set high academic standards, give students the support they need, and create the proper environment for learning," he said, "children will respond."

Daley, who served from 1980 through 1989 as Cook County state's attorney, has made the reduction of crime a priority. In 1993 he convened an emergency meeting of the U.S. Conference of Mayors in Chicago and took the lead in shaping an anticrime package that included a federal ban on assault weapons and a mandatory waiting period for the purchase of all firearms. Former White House press secretary James S. Brady, a leading advocate of gun control, said in 1998 that Daley was more committed to this cause than any mayor in America.

As part of this effort, Daley in 1998 became the first big-city mayor to wage a legal battle against the gun manufacturers and dealers who provide weapons to urban criminals. During his administration, local law-enforcement officials have confiscated and destroyed more than 160,000 illegal weapons. Since his program of community policing began in 1995, crime has declined by 27 percent. For eleven consecutive years, the city's overall crime rate has dropped.

Not all of Daley's initiatives have succeeded. In the early 1990s, he failed to win the Illinois senate's approval for the construction of a new regional airport at Lake Calumet and Republican governor Jim Edgar thwarted his proposal to open up Chicago for casino gambling.

But Daley has done much to bolster the local economy. By expanding McCormick Place, he consolidated Chicago's position as the nation's most popular site for conventions and trade shows. His expansion of O'Hare airport is expected to produce 195,000 new jobs and have an economic impact in the tens of billions of dollars. The renovation of O'Hare and Midway airports mean that Chicago will remain the hub of the nation's aviation system. He has reduced taxes on local businesses and offered tax incentives to attract new industry. In his fourth term as mayor, Daley won a national competition to lure the Boeing Company to Chicago. Over the last decade, the Chicago area has gained more than 476,000 jobs, according to the U.S. Bureau of Labor Statistics.

Daley has had to run the city with fewer public resources than his father had available. The federal government provides funding for only 13 percent of his budget, compared with a third in the elder Daley's era. He has responded to this challenge by reducing the city's workforce, merging departments, and hiring private firms to run city parking garages, provide janitorial services at public buildings, and take over more than thirty other city functions. "From day one," said Daley, "I've operated under the assumption that we have to do more with less."

As the mayor of a city that is racially diverse, he has sought to reach out to all communities. He appointed a panel early in his administration that developed an ordinance requiring that 25 percent of all city contracts be awarded to minority-owned firms and 5 percent to women-owned businesses. Congressman Jesse Jackson Jr. has praised the mayor's commitment to affirmative action. Daley has promoted the recruitment and hiring of minorities for his administration, and there is a general perception that he has been fair in providing city services to the African American and Hispanic communities. He has launched a ten-year, $1.5 billion program to replace old and crumbling public-housing high-rise buildings with new, more accessible homes. Over the last decade, the Daley administration has helped build or renovate thirty-seven thousand units of affordable rental housing and provided loans that enabled eight thousand moderate-income families to buy homes and another twenty-five thousand to improve their homes.

Daley, who received only 7 percent of the black vote in 1989, has slowly but steadily increased his support among African Americans to 28 percent in 1995 and 44.5 percent in 1999. In the 2003 election, Daley swept all twenty African American wards and received nearly 60 percent of the black vote. "I take pride in the fact that Chicago's united today," Daley said, "and that our victory was built in every community."

He has been more enduringly popular than any Chicago politician of his era. As the state's attorney of Cook County, Daley became the first person in that office in forty-eight years to win three terms. His only loss was in the three-way 1983 Democratic mayoral primary won by Harold Washington and in which Daley finished third behind former mayor Jane M. Byrne. Since then he has won a dozen consecutive elections, including primaries, general elections, and two nonpartisan mayoral elections. Although Daley has made most of these victories seem effortless, his winning streak is impressive when measured against others who have held these offices. His two predecessors as state's attorney were defeated for reelection, as were two successors. Three of his four predecessors in the mayor's office were defeated in their bids for second terms. "I don't have the power," Daley said after winning a fifth term. "The people have the power."

Daley, heir to the most famous name in Chicago Democratic politics, is less political than his father, who served in a dual role as the chairman of the Cook County Democratic Central Committee. In contrast to his father, Daley does not serve in a party leadership role, nor is he even acquainted with most suburban members of the Democratic county committee. When the General Assembly voted in 1995 to eliminate party labels in Chicago's mayoral elections, the mayor did not object. "The elephants or donkeys are not what younger people look to," Daley once told Chicago political historian Paul M. Green. "They look at individual candidates' philosophy, and I think it's a different time and a different generation."

Bungles and Botches

Steve Rhodes

Much of the good that has been said about the mayoralty of Richard M. Daley is true. He has shined up a tourist-friendly, international city. The downtown sparkles. And he's tended to the city services so important to residents, from garbage pickup to well-kept alleys to improved roads and bridges. He has overcome a shaky start to create a sense of a city on the move. It's no surprise voters have elected him mayor five times. They like what they see.

They also have had very little choice, as Daley has effectively co-opted his rivals and stamped down dissent. He doesn't debate his campaign opponents and rarely gives a serious answer to media inquiries. Beyond the hype of the flowers he's planted and the image building of a sophisticated PR machine, Daley's mayoralty has been uneven at best and downright dismal at worst.

Perhaps no incident epitomizes the dark side of this mayor better than the midnight raid on Meigs Field. Under cover of darkness on 30 March 2003, he sent city crews in bulldozers to carve up the runway of Meigs Field and render the tiny lakefront airport inoperable. Daley claimed he was acting to protect the city from a potential terrorist attack, invoking the specter of 9/11.

A little more than a week later, U.S. homeland security chief Tom Ridge said his department was not consulted about Meigs and had not determined the airport's existence to be a threat. In fact, Ridge said he was disappointed the mayor had closed the airport. Daley eventually admitted that he simply wanted to turn the airport into a park—long a well-known dream of his, and perhaps a creditable idea, but not a plan anyone, least of all former governor George Ryan, who had a deal with Daley to keep Meigs Field open until at least 2006, expected to be executed in secret.

In other words, Richard M. Daley exploited the tragedy of 9/11 to avoid public input about a lakefront proposal that most citizens probably agreed with, while reneging on a deal made with a governor. The rights of the vocal Meigs lobby to have their say—for the mayor to be forced to achieve a political solution, the way democracies are supposed to work—went by the wayside.

This is a great mayor? The Meigs Field embarrassment displayed one of Daley's worst characteristics—namely, that he often acts like an arrogant bully with no regard for actual democracy. A closer look at his record, adapted from a *Chicago* magazine article I authored, reveals a few consistent strains that have consistently gotten him in trouble.

An Arrogant, Antidemocratic Autocrat

Using his statutory power to fill aldermanic vacancies, Daley has appointed more than a third of the city council. Daley did not make the law allowing him to fill vacancies, but he has leveraged it to the fullest extent, while ignoring calls for reform. Chicago *Sun-Times* political columnist Steve Neal once wrote, "There isn't another major political executive in the country with comparable power."

By populating the city council with his own appointments and using brute political strength to subdue any pockets of resistance, Daley has rendered the city council virtually powerless, reduced to a tool for political theater when he needs procedural validation or a show of support from the city's legislative body. Even as he insists he is not a political boss, he demands the council's loyalty and punishes members who dare to step out of line.

Daley's control extends well beyond the council and sister city agencies such as the Chicago Transit Authority (CTA) and the Chicago Housing Authority. Daley also controls the Cook County board through its president, John Stroger. Daley's brother John is the board's finance chairman. Perhaps the most egregious example of Daley's control of the county board occurred when the mayor asked it to overturn its 17-0 vote decision to relocate the county's domestic violence court to the upscale River North neighborhood. The mayor got his way even though the alternative site will cost taxpayers an additional $22 million.

Challenging Daley is difficult not only because vengeance is swift but because getting on the ballot has become much more difficult in Chicago than in other major cities—and even more difficult than ballot requirements for many statewide and federal offices. When the General Assembly passed legislation in 1995 making Chicago's mayoral race nonpartisan (relieving Daley of potential primary challenges prior to general elections), it curiously left out a petition signature requirement for ballot access. Lawyers for the Chicago Board of Election Commissioners set the level at twenty-five thousand. By contrast, when Daley was first elected, he needed only forty-four hundred petition signatures to get on the ballot. It takes one thousand signatures to get on the mayoral ballot in Los Angeles and seventy-five hundred to get on the ballot in New York City. Steve Neal has described the signature requirement as "a lifetime lease on the mayor's office."

Contract Cronyism

Perhaps the most consistently troubling aspect of the Daley administration is the never-ending stream of contract scandals enriching the mayor's political friends. What's more, the mayor has failed not only to put a stop to the shenanigans but also to act like he cares. His lack of outrage is outrageous.

The short list of the Daley scandals is depressingly familiar to regular Chicago newspaper readers: Michael Marchese, a mayoral pal, gets a cut-rate deal on a CTA parcel in Lincoln Park and a West Side property for a buck. Jeremiah Joyce, a mayoral confidant, earns a reported $1.8 million in a single year brokering concessions contracts at O'Hare airport for McDonald's. Patrick Huels, a mayoral protégé, is forced to resign as Daley's city council floor leader after he accepts a $1.25 million business loan from city contractor Michael Tadin, a friend of the mayor's who once had $100 million in city contracts. Another mayoral pal, Oscar D'Angelo, a disbarred lawyer, brokers lucrative newsstand contracts at O'Hare that cuts in two friends of the mayor's wife, and gave an interest-free loan to top mayoral aide Terry Teele. And those are just the highlights.

The most disturbing deal of all is the Duff family affair. In a thirty-count indictment, federal investigators have charged two members of the Duff family with conning the city into awarding $100 million in janitorial contracts meant for woman- and minority-owned businesses. The Duffs, led by patriarch John Duff Jr., a generous Daley campaign supporter, are white, and John Duff Jr. is most assuredly a man.

What makes this scandal particularly hot for Daley is that the well-known broadcaster Bruce DuMont has said that his late wife, Kathy Osterman, once confided in him when she was the city's special events director that Daley told her to make sure the Duffs got the contracts to clean up after summer festivals. (Daley has denied the charge.)

Asked by the *Sun-Times* about the Duffs' reputed Mob ties, Daley said, "I don't know anything about it." For the price of a newspaper, the mayor could have enlightened himself.

Even if Daley is innocent in the long string of contract scandals—if, say, a lot of people whom he doesn't really know very well are exploiting his name and their perceived connections to him—he has failed to demand that the madness simply stop. Instead, he seems to take each new scandal in stride as the unfortunate result of human nature, never taking responsibility for overseeing the public till.

Bungling of Big Projects

An oft-repeated theme of the Daley regime is that in the early going of his mayoralty, he tried to do some Big Things and failed. The prime examples are the Lake Calumet third airport, a downtown casino and hotel complex, and the downtown trolleylike "circulator." He began to succeed as mayor only when he focused on the smaller but important details of running a city: the beautification and infrastructure programs that have won him wide notice. A return to big projects—namely, a remodeled Soldier Field and the lakefront Millennium Park—in recent years seems to bolster the notion that he isn't very good at managing them.

Next to Meigs Field, there is no better example of this mayor's modus operandi than Soldier Field. Daley strong-armed a controversial $632 million plan through the state legislature in just two weeks. The Chicago Plan Commission approved the deal at the end of an eight-hour meeting, wearing down protesters waiting for the vote, which was a fait accompli anyway. The city council approved the required zoning change on bended knee, as usual. A park district committee held what the Chicago *Tribune* called a "kangaroo-court" hearing in which not a single commissioner asked a single question of officials from the stadium's prime beneficiary, the private corporation known as the Chicago Bears, or of city staff, before approving the plan.

The result is an edifice almost universally derided as the "Mistake by the Lake," for both its architectural miscues and its controversial location on the lakefront. The absence of democratic debate—of governing bodies actually doing their institutional duties and of the public actually participating in a momentous decision involving public money and public land—was appalling.

Another example is Millennium Park. The grandiose park may very well turn out to be the postcard for Chicago that its supporters insist, but it's hard to get around the fact that it was supposed to open in the summer of 2000 at a cost of $150 million. It finally opened in the summer of 2004 at a cost of $475 million.

Finally, there is O'Hare airport. In 1986 a state study showed that the area needed a third airport. In 1990 Daley proposed one, at Lake Calumet on the city's Southeast Side. When that deal faltered and a site in suburban Will County emerged instead, Daley changed his tune. An airport in the suburbs would put its patronage out of the mayor's control. The Daley administration began to insist that a third airport wasn't needed after all. City hall and its consultants reportedly fudged the numbers on air traffic estimates to bolster their case. And then, when he thought the time was politically ripe, Daley switched gears again and proposed an O'Hare expansion he said was absolutely necessary for the city's air travelers and the region's economy. Unfortunately for the mayor, his change of heart occurred just in time for a recession and the aftereffects of 9/11, which landed the hometown United Airlines in bankruptcy court and cast doubt on O'Hare expansion while a third airport remained in limbo.

Mismanagement of Crises

Rudy Giuliani's reign as New York City's mayor was a controversial one until 9/11. But even Giuliani's most ardent opponents had to admit that his leadership in the wake of the attacks was more than anyone could have reasonably asked for. In the worst of times, Giuliani showed true leadership. Daley seems to crumble into a defensive mess at times of great tragedy.

Arguably the worst disaster to strike the city happened on Daley's watch. More than seven hundred people died in the heat wave of 1995. While no one can blame the mayor for the weather, sociologist Eric Klinenberg persuasively argued in his 2002 book *Heat Wave* that the mayor failed to recognize the unfolding disaster and that once he did, he was more interested in managing the public relations of the tragedy than the public health issues before him. To my knowledge, Daley has never challenged Klinenberg's inside account.

Likewise, Daley's initial response to the 2003 fire inside the county administration building that killed six people was to criticize the media for asking questions. One question the media had was why the mayor had promised three times to require sprinklers in old high-rises like the county building, only to back down each time after building management associations lobbied against the requirement.

As with disasters such as the South Side E2 nightclub horror and the North Side Lincoln Park porch collapse, Daley and his administration moved quickly to absolve the city of blame and point fingers elsewhere.

And in one of the city's great crises unfolding over time, Chicago has held for a number of years the nation's highest murder rate for big cities. While the murder rate is the result of a complex set of factors, Daley has resisted, for example, redeploying beat officers according to where crime is actually occurring. Daley prefers to cater to the many white, upper-class homeowners and their aldermen who don't want to see a potentially corresponding reduction in police patrols in their neighborhoods.

There is no doubt that Daley has had a strong run as mayor and that his accomplishments are many. His electoral opponents have run weak campaigns. It's hard to argue that he hasn't been the best candidate in many of these races.

But the widespread acclaim that Daley has garnered is beyond the man's record, and historians may take a more measured view. No mayor can be perfect, and anyone who serves a long time will have a long list of failings. But this mayor's failures are large and consistent, and usually boil down to the simple fact that he too often rules like a childish bully instead of a mature leader.

Perhaps what the record really shows is that Daley is a far more complicated figure than he is usually portrayed. The record suggests he is not simply a neighborhood guy with good instincts but a perplexing and often inscrutable mayor who runs roughshod over anyone in his way.

20.

PUTTING HAROLD TO REST

Laura S. Washington

When Harold Washington was elected the first black mayor of Chicago in April 1983, he declared, "The city will never be the same." He was right then. But now he must be turning over in his grave in Chicago's old Oakwood Cemetery. Since his death in November 1987, progressive politics has not been the same. In fact, the coalition that elected him—blacks, Latinos, and lakefront liberals—no longer exists. Defunct. History. Gone. As Washington himself long ago pronounced of the legendary Democratic machine, his own coalition is "dead, dead, dead."

Washington was catapulted to victory by a record turnout of 79 percent of Chicago's registered voters. African Americans saw the chance to make history and seized it with a vengeance. Virtually every black that could, 99 percent of African Americans, punched "10." My father, a mail carrier and lifelong South Sider, had not voted in twenty years. But he turned out for Harold. Yet it was the support of more than 70 percent of Latino voters and as many as one third of the progressive whites that edged him over the top.

Cut to twenty years later. It's a new millennium, in more ways than one. In 2003, Richard M. Daley, son of the machine, was reelected for a fifth term with 79 percent of the vote. His victory came with 60 percent of the African American vote, even with three black opponents. That's up from an estimated 7 percent black support Daley won in the 1989 primary, which paved the way for his takeover of city hall. So what happened to the Washington movement and the coalition it spawned?

Remnants did linger, for a while. In 1992, blacks, women, and progressives teamed up to propel Carol Moseley Braun, a longtime state legislator and Washington protégé, to become the first black woman in the U.S. Senate. Today there are African American officeholders at nearly every level of city, county, and state government, and black voters were a major force in putting them there. There are more Latinos in the Chicago City Council and Illinois General Assembly than ever. Illinois' first and only Hispanic congressman, Luis Gutierrez, started his career in the Washington coalition.

Still, for activists of color and other reformers, the Daley years offer many reasons to pick up the pieces. Chicago has held the title of murder capital of the nation. The city is being strangled by a historic shortage of affordable housing. More than a fourth of African American males are dropping out of Chicago public high schools. Public housing is being dismantled, leaving the city's poorest citizens with few options, all of them bad. As in cities around the nation, Chicago officials are staggering under a shaky economy and, desperate for new revenues, are taxing everything in sight. Property taxes are already out of sight.

Many of the city's biggest catastrophes have beset communities of color, especially African Americans: In 1998 a shortsighted and stunning rush to judgment led the Chicago Police Department to charge two black boys, aged seven and eight, with the murder and rape of eleven-year-old Ryan Harris. The charges were later dropped, but five years later, the city was still fighting a multimillion-dollar wrongful prosecution lawsuit. In 1999 two unarmed motorists were shot to death in separate altercations with police, leading to tens of millions of dollars in settlements. In early 2003, twenty-one young people were trampled to death at E2, a dance club frequented by African Americans. The investigation is pending, while the city wades through a stack of personal injury lawsuits alleging that officials failed to regulate safety conditions at the club.

There's plenty to beef about, so where are the beefers? Why, in a city that is 60 percent minority, have black and Latino activists been unable to rebuild a progressive political movement and elect one of their own?

The New Machine

Some pundits would pose that like Washington's movement, the legendary Richard J. Daley machine is a memory. The current mayoral administration, however, is just a new kind of machine. Since "Boss" Daley's son, Richard M. Daley, snatched city hall from the hapless Eugene Sawyer in 1989, he has built a tightly held, nonideological administration that has effectively avoided the kind of incendiary racial moves and insults that doomed his predecessor, Jane Byrne.

Instead, Daley has run a co-option game, placing talented but devoutly apolitical professionals of color in top jobs and dictating to every significant policymaking board and commission in Chicago. And foreseeing the explosion in Latino population long before the U.S. census made it official, Daley crafted a Latino network around the Hispanic Democratic Organization.

To his credit, Daley has cultivated the Washington legacy in ways that have curried favor with the black middle class. He has appropriated some of Washington's pet causes and done them one better. He beefed up the participation of minority- and women-owned enterprise in city programs, which Washington launched and championed, to record levels. He approved city council initiatives that appeal to blacks but carry little political risk, like slave reparations. Daley took over the public schools and, in a nod to Washington's passion and pastime, proclaimed reading a top priority.

Buoyed by an unprecedented economic boom of the 1990s, development soared, unemployment rates were at all-time lows, and there was plenty of federal and state pork to go around. Daley plumbed a rich vein of pork in President Bill Clinton's Empowerment Zone initiative. It was new-fangled political patronage masquerading as economic development. Daley, who had a close relationship with the Clinton administration, could also count on an assist from brother Bill Daley, once Clinton's campaign finance chair and later his U.S. commerce secretary. Clinton sent Chicago a $100 million goodie basket for Daley to share with community groups and aldermen who behaved. He found a lot of eager takers.

Paying Homage

Richard M. Daley pulled a page from his father's political prayer book and learned the art of cultivating the black church. A September 2000 investigation by the Chicago *Reporter* revealed that since Daley's 1989 election, fourteen of the city's largest black congregations and their nonprofit affiliates had received close to $10 million in city payments.

The funds went to legitimate do-gooding: to help run day care programs, build affordable housing, administer social service programs. But those monies no doubt were more likely to end up in the coffers of churches and groups who kept their heads down than they were to be given to the rabble-rousers.

Church leaders don't apologize for accepting the support, saying they are not being bought off but are just taking advantage of city programs that aid their members, who are taxpayers, don't you know. Daley's critics point to the endorsement press conferences at which dozens of black ministers flank the mayor. They argue that it's just one more way the mayor has co-opted the black community.

Changin' Times

Chicago is a changed city. The joke in Washington's city hall was that most of the high-ranking blacks came from one zip code area: 60615, used in Washington's home base, which included middle-class Hyde Park.

With gentrification and the growth of the black middle class, many families have since opted out of the city for the suburbs, eroding the political base. And the transformation of the city's notorious public housing high-rises into mixed-income developments is scattering poor blacks throughout the city and suburbs, decentralizing the opposition.

The nationalists who dominated black politics in the 1960s and 1970s have not adjusted to the new demographics and times. While many of those nationalists helped bring Washington to power, they never bought the concept of multiracial organizing. Their mantra: "It's our turn."

They never heard the saw that power comes with addition, not subtraction. They can't hear that race-based exclusionary politics is "antediluvian," as Washington loved to say.

Even today the nationalists reject the truism that Washington had to reach out beyond blacks to stay in power. Some black activists still chafe at sharing power with Latinos, gays and lesbians, and others who feel cut out of the system.

The Black Hack

Washington won the mayorship because he pledged to dump "the ancient, decrepit and creaking machine," as he put it. The machine hack's motto, "Where's mine?" was jettisoned for a promise of fairness to all Chicagoans. Washington's agenda was based on need and equity, not on clout.

But many of the aldermen in Washington's coalition of twenty-one were products of the machine and thus reluctant partners in the coalition. From day one, they muttered, all they wanted was their city contracts and jobs, and they weren't getting enough.

Washington knew fairness was the right thing and that he had to abide by it. His fragile coalition would fracture, he knew, if all the good stuff went to the black base.

Today, some of the aldermen who writhed under Washington's massive political thumb are still in the Chicago City Council. A good many others have been appointed by Daley to fill the seats of officials who have died or, in time-tested Chicago tradition, gone to jail. Just about all of them have been co-opted by Richard M. Daley.

Chapter Three

Washington is the first chapter of a postmachine Chicago, and Richard M. Daley is the second. The third chapter dawns on a twenty-first-century city.

People of color who want to revive a progressive agenda must reach beyond race to class. It's not just a challenge for activists in Chicago. President George W. Bush has made capturing the Latino vote a key priority in his reelection campaign, and Democratic presidential contender and former Vermont governor Howard Dean has conjured up images of—and a lot of heat for—voters who drive Confederate flag–bearing pickup trucks to drive home the case that the national Democratic party cannot rebuild without an economic message.

In April 2003, at the Harold Washington Library, the late mayor's disciples gathered to commemorate his movement and ponder its future. Jacky Grimshaw, Washington's top political operative, noted the pathetic turnouts in recent elections. "We need to have the participation of the electorate if we are to elect a progressive leadership," she said. "Or we continue to get what we got, which ain't very much."

That's pretty basic. In the 1983 race, the citywide turnout was 79 percent. In the 2003 mayoral election, just 34 percent of registered voters showed up at the polls, the most tepid showing since 1947. And voter registration efforts have been sporadic and lackluster. That's got to change.

If progressive politics, or anyone's politics other than Daley's, will ever prevail, activists must stop waiting for the next charismatic figure to come along and spark a movement. And they need to know it's not just about race anymore. African American leaders must reach out beyond the base, particularly to Latinos, and pay more than lip service to the political and economic issues that resonate across racial, ethnic, and class lines.

The future of a progressive movement in Chicago and Illinois may rest with a new generation of elected officials and activists who are bypassing city hall by building grassroots support and new coalitions. A key one to watch is Barack Obama, an Illinois state senator who won a crowded primary race to become the Democratic nominee for an open U.S. Senate seat in 2004. The legislator and civil rights activist has a law degree from Harvard and was the first African American to serve as editor of the *Harvard Law Review.*

In 1992 Obama directed Illinois Project VOTE!, a statewide voter registration and education campaign that helped bring in Illinois for Bill Clinton and secure Braun's senate win. Obama, who, like Washington, made his home in Hyde Park, is one of a new breed of black professionals who are getting it. He is building a multiracial, multieconomic cadre of wealthy residents from Chicago's north lakefront and North Shore, labor unions, senior citizens, antiwar activists, and of course, his African American base. If a few ventures like this one succeed, then perhaps, just perhaps, Harold Washington can finally rest and get a little peace out at old Oakwood.

21.

THE CHICAGO POLITICAL TRADITION: A MAYORAL RETROSPECTIVE

Paul M. Green

A review of Chicago's modern mayors reveals a simple fact: there is no one way to win city hall. Some past Chicago mayors have been clever political strategists who outfought and outsmarted their mayoral rivals; some have been loyal party stalwarts who eased their -way to the top; others have been non-traditional candidates whose leading attribute was their lack of political acumen. Through it all, city hall has been the ultimate political prize for Chicago politicians. Only one mayor, Edward Dunne, has ever gone on to higher political office after his or her stint as the city's chief executive.

Of the themes that mark the landscape of Chicago politics, the pursuit and exercise of power towers above them all. In no other American city are the possession and dispensation of political power—or as Chicagoans call it, "clout"—as central to the operation of its government or to the daily lives of its citizens. Chicago's mayors have reflected this overriding theme despite their governing the city under a weak mayor–strong council system. Successful mayors have used this political power to take command of the city and dominate the council while balancing the various interests of Chicago's diverse residents. Unsuccessful mayors were those unwilling to use their power and unable to deal with the council while taking positions that did not match their constituents' needs.

Prior to Anton Cermak, Chicago's mayors were personality-oriented leaders who represented political factions within a major party. Following Cermak and the emergence of the Chicago Democratic machine, the city's mayors were organization-oriented, either selected by the machine or allowed to administer with its acquiescence. In 1983 Harold Washington became the first mayor in the machine era to win and govern city hall without organization party support. In the long run, this fact may be far more important than the color of Washington's skin.

Given the total party involvement in Chicago's mayoral history, it is not surprising that no mayor has been able to bring true reform to the city. At the same time, no word in Chicago history has had more meanings, more champions, and more causes than *reform*. From Medill to Richard M. Daley, no mayor has run for office without espousing major reforms to improve city life. However, once in office, Chicago's chief executives have found that most of their constituents were not "ready" to replace power politics with reform politics. From the civil service reforms in the 1890s to the Shakman decrees in the 1970s, Chicago's mayors have been able to sidestep laws and procedures aimed at reforming the governance process. Ironically, the most impressive governmental and administrative reforms in Chicago history occurred during the terms of those mayors most associated with "boss politics." Cermak, Kelly, and Richard J. Daley were professional politicians who sought total political control and yet were open to innovative improvements in governmental efficiency as long as it did not hinder their political activities.

Given the above logic, one sees how easily Chicagoans could accept machine domination in return for "a city that works." Early-twentieth-century party factionalism that gave the people a city council filled with gray wolves and inconsistent mayoral leadership succumbed to united Democratic party dominance that eventually curtailed council flamboyance and mayoral high jinks. The rhythm of Chicago politics became a relatively simple ins-versus-outs or professional-versus-amateur melody. The fight for power was the key element, and post-Cermakian mayors have stressed their executive competence based on balanced budgets, deliverance of outstanding city services, and a professional governmental demeanor. Until recently, even the periodic shouting matches, scandals, and sensational stories of waste and criminal wrongdoing have made little difference to Chicago voters. A culture of comfort based on narrow neighborhood or ward interests and not the general welfare of all city residents has guided the decisions of Chicago's voters.

A corollary theme to the overriding issue of power is the historic diversity of Chicago's electorate. Ethnicity, religion, and race have been and still are key determinants of mayoral style and political behavior. Patrician mayors like Medill battled newly arrived immigrants for control of the city, while a shrewd compromiser like Carter Harrison II was able to rally most of the different nationalities around his banner. Under Cermak, the various ethnic groups united to run the city themselves by forming a multinational political organization. This ethnically based machine ruled Chicago for over fifty years until another group of voters, blacks, unified and took over city hall.

As for religion, the old joke that "Republicans divide the city into wards, while Democrats divide it into parishes" rang true for many years in Chicago. This strong Catholic influence has played havoc with mayoral policies on the issue of personal liberty—drinking, vice, gambling, and having a good time. From the segregated vice policies of Harrison, through the Capone era of Big Bill Thompson, down to the machine era of Richard J. Daley, religion and revelry have battled it out for the city's soul. Stuffed-shirt mayors like Medill, Dunne, and Dever were too strict for the electorate, while Kelly and Thompson were eventually ousted for letting the city become too wide open.

Chicago has had a growing black population throughout the twentieth century. Neither its government nor its citizens have been able to change the "black belt mentality" that makes Chicago the most racially segregated city in America. However, persistent racial separation coupled with Chicago's ward-based politics has produced a tradition of black elected officials and party leaders in the city. These individuals have cut political deals whereby their black constituents have been the deciding factor in electing to the mayoralty Thompson in 1919, Daley in 1955 and 1963, and of course, Washington in 1983. Black voters were also crucial to Byrne's 1979 mayoral primary victory. Yet no mayor has ever come to grips with the underlying issue of how to incorporate racial integration into the ward and neighborhood lifestyle of the city.

Now Chicago is undergoing a surge in Hispanic migration, thereby adding a massive new voting bloc to the political mix. Coming from many nations (though Mexico is the dominant country of origin), these newcomers have not yet jelled as a big-time player in city politics. For the most part, Hispanics have gravitated to Richard M. Daley, recognizing the need to associate themselves with the authority center of Chicago life. Eventually Hispanic Chicagoans will have to decide where their political future rests as they become more intermeshed into the city's political structure. Can they establish themselves as a new power core or will they remain adjuncts and allies of an existing political base?

Perhaps the notion of neighborhood identification is the most persistent theme in the administrations of past Chicago mayors. Clearly, individual loyalty to an ethnic community, a parish, a ward, or a street corner has meant Chicago has not been one huge city but rather a collection of little villages tied together politically but not culturally. Most of Chicago's mayors in this study have reflected this diversity in their governmental and political actions. Men like Richard J. Daley and Kelly could overcome the label of boss and be revered and feared for their ability to centralize political authority while they decentralized city services. On the other hand, weak mayors were those who could not organize politically and were unable to deliver the goods to the neighborhoods. Chicagoans for generations have accepted city hall as its "fountain of clout," but it has been the clever mayor that has sprinkled the goodies to the various communities as well as downtown. Unlike the mayors of most other American cities, Chicago mayors have faced a tradition of neighborhood solidarity even while a powerful political machine dominated its governmental process. Short-term mayors were those who refused to accept that almost any type of skullduggery could be justified and allowed as long as the sanctity of the neighborhood was not violated. Long-term mayors, even a buffoon like Thompson, were able to identify with neighborhood problems, to voice their concerns, and to echo their fears. This geographic parochialism may explain why good government independents with their citywide concerns have historically been restricted to a narrow band along the city's lakeshore while the rest of the city residents lived their lives inland in family-oriented communities.

Lastly, the twenty-first century finds the Chicago political tradition still thriving, even though the city has lost (or is losing) its unique neighborhoods, manufacturing base, and nationality makeup. What is perhaps most remarkable about the current Mayor Daley is that despite all the above changes and others described earlier in this book, he has modified, not revolutionized, mayoral governing in the city. To be sure, he has become a lifestyle and administrative lakefront reformer, but he has buttressed this new image with a personal (not party) political machine to enforce his will. Like his famous father, he brokers goods and service needs between neighborhoods even though they are becoming more similar in a gentrifying city. He balances the interests and rewards of his black and Hispanic coalition allies while, like a high wire juggler, maintaining near total loyalty from the city's remaining white residents. And he reflects five of his dad's six wellsprings of power (not the supremacy of the Democratic party) even though the city has undergone a dramatic demographic shift in the last half century.

Like all politicians, however, RMD is potentially vulnerable to events and new personalities. The Chicago *Sun-Times* 2003–4 "Hire a Truck" scandal series shook the mayor's persona as the newspaper exposed old-fashion patronage, cronyism, and waste of public dollars. The newspaper not only questioned the use of taxpayer funds to rent private vehicles for city projects but also resurrected the old war cry against organized crime in city business.

In early 2004 a new African American leader emerged. State senator Barack Obama from Chicago won the Democratic U.S. Senate nomination, garnering Harold Washington–like support from Chicago's black voters, many of whom had lost interest in local politics. Questions immediately rose about Obama's mayoral potential and whether his candidacy would energize other ambitious and talented minority politicians who could eventually challenge Daley.

Time is also a looming threat to the incumbent mayor. He has been in office for a decade and a half. Many of his original team of outstanding administrators and shrewd political operatives are no longer with him. Whispers circulate around city hall that the mayor is less willing to take advice and listen to alternative arguments from this new circle of confidants.

Still it would take quite a high-risk gambler to wager against Mayor Richard M. Daley. Problems aside, his larger-than-life presence in "his" city makes it doubtful that any opponent could ever unseat him. However, one prediction about Chicago's future is almost a sure bet. When RMD lays down his gavel for the final time, a political firestorm of pent-up ambitions and emotions will sweep the city. Mayoral succession in Chicago has seldom been neat or tidy; the post-RMD selection process will be no different in its ferocity and tension. Yet whoever emerges as Chicago's next mayor, he or she will be successful only through recognizing and mastering the city's established political tradition.

APPENDIX

NOTES

CONTRIBUTORS

INDEX

APPENDIX: CHICAGO MAYORS

Chicago Mayors

William Ogden (1837–38)
Buckner Morris (1838–39)
Benjamin Raymond (1839–40, 1842–43)
Alexander Loyd (1840–41)
Francis Sherman (1841–42, 1862–65)
Augustus Garrett (1843–44, 1845–46)
Alson Sherman (1844)
John Chapin (1846–47)
James Curtiss (1847, 1850)
James Woodworth (1848–49)
Walter Gurnee (1851–52)
Charles Gray (1853)
Isaac Milliken (1854–55)
Levi Boone (1855)
Thomas Dyer (1856–57)
John Wentworth (1857–58, 1860–61)
John Haines (1858–60)
Julian Rumsey (1861–62)
John Rice (1865–69)
Roswell Mason (1869–71)
Joseph Medill (1871–73)
Lester Legrant Bond (1873)

Harvey Colvin (1873–76)
Monroe Heath (1876–79)
Carter Harrison I (1879–87, 1893)
John Roche (1887–89)
DeWitt Cregier (1889–91)
Hempstead Washburne (1891–93)
George Swift (1893, 1895–97)
John Hopkins (1893–95)
Carter Harrison II (1897–1905, 1911–15)
Edward Dunne (1905–1907)
Fred Busse (1907–11)
William H. Thompson (1915–23, 1927–31)
William Dever (1923–27)
Anton Cermak (1931–33)
Frank Corr (1933)
Edward Kelly (1933–47)
Martin Kennelly (1947–55)
Richard J. Daley (1955–76)
Michael Bilandic (1976–79)
Jane Byrne (1979–83)
Harold Washington (1983–87)
Eugene Sawyer (1987–89)
Richard M. Daley (1989–   )

Mayors Who Served in the Council

	Mayor	Alderman
Ogden, William Butler	1873–1838	1840–1841
		1847–1848
Morris, Buckner Stith	1838–1839	1839–1840
		1844

Raymond, Benjamin W.	1839–1840	1847–1848
	1842–1843	
Loyd, Alexander	1840–1841	1850–1851
Sherman, Francis C.	1841–1842	1837–1838
	1862–1865	
Garrett, Augustus	1843–1844	1840–1841
	1845–1846	
Sherman, Alson S.	1844–1845	1842–1843
		1849–1851
Chapin, John P.	1846–1847	1844–1845
Curtiss, James	1847–1848	1838–1839
	1850–1851	1846–1847
Woodworth, James H.	1848–1850	1845–1846
		1847–1848
Milliken, Isaac	1854–1855	1850–1854
Boone, Dr. Levi D.	1855–1856	1846–1847
		1847–1848
Dyer, Thomas	1856–1857	1853
Haines, John C.	1858–1860	1848–1854
Heath, Monroe	1876–1879	1871–1875
Swift, George B.	1895–1897	1879–1882
		1892–1894
Thompson, William Hale	1915–1923	1900–1902
	1927–1931	
Dever, William E.	1923–1927	1902–1910
Cermak, Anton J.	1931–1933	1909–1912
Bilandic, Michael A.	1976–1979	1969–1976
Sawyer, Eugene	1987–1989	1973–1987

Source: Holli, Jones, *Biographical Dictionary of American Mayors, 1820–1980.*

NOTES

1. Joseph Medill: Chicago's First Modern Mayor

1. Medill may be described as a "class reformer," part of a group of patrician Republicans concerned with promoting governmental efficiency. This distinguishes him from "party reformers," whose concern is with increasing political representation, and "status reformers," who promote socioeconomic equality. See William J. Grimshaw, "Is Chicago Ready for Reform?—or, A New Agenda for Harold Washington," in Melvin G. Holli and Paul M. Green, eds., *The Making of the Mayor, Chicago 1983* (Grand Rapids, Michigan: Eerdmans Pub. Co., 1984), 141–65.

2. In their seminal article on the mayors of Chicago, Bradley and Zald labelled Medill as a "transition" mayor between the "commercial elite" and the first machine mayors. See Donald S. Bradley and Mayer N. Zald, "From Commercial Elite to Political Administrator: The Recruitment of the Mayors of Chicago," *American Journal of Sociology* (Fall 1965), 153–67.

3. Letter from Joseph Medill to R. W. Patterson (Medill's son-in-law), 4 November 1871 Chicago *Tribune* Archives collection.

4. Ibid.

5. In the 1870s, Chicago had twenty wards with two aldermen serving from each ward. For an analysis of the demographic composition of the wards, see Wayne Andrews, *The Battle for Chicago* (New York: Harcourt and Brace, 1946).

6. State of Illinois, "An Act concerning the appointment and removal of city officers . . . , conferring additional powers upon Mayors . . . , and concerning appropriation bills and ordinances passed. . . ." Passed 9 March 1872; implemented 1 July 1872.

7. *Journal of the Proceedings of the Common Council of the City of Chicago*, 4 December 1871. (hereafter, *Journal*).

8. Ferdinand Rex, *The Mayors of Chicago* (Chicago: Municipal Reference Library mimeograph, 1933), 55–56.

9. Letter form Joseph Medill to U.S. Vice-President Schuyler Colfax, 5 February 1872, Chicago Historical Society Archives Collection.

10. Rex, 56.

11. *Journal*, 2 December 1872.

12. One historian described Medill as "sick at the thought of compromise with immigrant voters." (See Andrews, 67.) This is perhaps unfair, given his repeated efforts to reach such compromises during the first year of his administration. Still, there is little question that the official explanation of fatigue and

"ill-health" (see John Moses and Joseph Kirkland, eds., *History of Chicago,* vol. 1, Chicago: Munsell & Co., 1895, 216) is incomplete. The absence of primary historical documents on this subject will cause it to remain somewhat of a mystery.

13. *Journal,* 18 August 1873.

14. Ibid., 26 January 1874.

15. Ibid., 4 December 1871.

16. Moses and Kirkland, 216.

17. *Journal,* 26 February 1872.

18. On 11 March 1872, Alderman Charles C. Holden (10th), who Medill had defeated for mayor the previous year, introduced a resolution to the city council demanding that the Chicago Relief and Aid Society give to the city treasury more than one million dollars it had collected to provide assistance to victims of the fire. The council passed the resolution and Medill signed it reluctantly on 3 May 1872. State of Illinois, Secretary of State Archives Division. (Springfield, Illinois: Records of official city business prior to 1875, n.d.)

19. Rex, 55.

20. *Journal,* 29 July 1872. On 25 September 1872 Alderman Holden responded to Medill's demand that "the practice of appointing police on the recommendation of aldermen must stop." He claimed that Medill's allegation was largely unfounded and provided a list of "sponsors" of policemen for six months to support his contention. State of Illinois, Secretary of State Archives Division.

21. *Journal,* 4 December 1871.

22. Chicago *Tribune,* 15 January 1881.

23. On 15 July 1872 the complaint of a private citizen that "Irish [have been] excluded from nominees to the Board of Education" was introduced to the city council as a Remonstrance measure. No action was taken on the complaint, and all of Medill's nominees were approved. State of Illinois, Secretary of State Archives Division.

24. J. Robert Nash, *People to See* (New Century Publishers, 1981), 5.

25. Alfred Theodore Andreas, *History of Chicago,* vol. 3 (New York: Arno Press, 1975), 855.

26. Quoted from a resolution adopted by a mass meeting of German citizens, 24 October 1872, which was submitted to the city council as a "Communication Relative to the Enforcement of the Sunday law" on 28 October 1872. Secretary of State, Archives Division.

27. Andreas, 855.

28. On 7 February 1874, the Chicago *Tribune* republished the allegation made by the *Staats-Zeitung* and provided evidence that it was incorrect.

29. Andrews, 49.

30. Nash, 19.

31. Lincoln responded by calling Medill a "coward. You and your Tribune

have had more influence than any paper in the Northwest in making this war. . . . Go home and send us these men." Medill admitted afterwards that "it was the first time I was ever whipped, and I didn't have an answer." Quoted in Ida M. Tarbell, *The Life of Abraham Lincoln*, vol. 2 (New York: Lincoln History Society, 1903), 218–19.

32. Quoted in Nash, 9.

33. Medill was not the first newspaperman to serve as a mayor of Chicago. "Long John" Wentworth, publisher of the Chicago *Democrat*, was elected mayor in 1857. However, Wentworth was completely unconcerned with the press's coverage of his administration. According to Nash, Wentworth "grew tired of his newspapering" and sold the *Democrat* to the Chicago *Tribune*. Nash, 3.

34. "Colonel" Robert R. McCormick ultimately became the dominant influence in the management of the *Tribune* from 1911 to 1955. See Gwen Morgan and Arthur Veysey, *Poor Little Rich Boy* (Carpentersville, Illinois: Crossroads Communications, 1985).

35. *Journal*, 20 March 1899.

2. Carter H. Harrison II: The Politics of Balance

1. Jon Teaford, *The Unheralded Triumph: City Government in America, 1870–1900* (Baltimore: Johns Hopkins University Press, 1984) overturns James Lord Bryce's oft-quoted dictum that city government in America was a "conspicuous failure." I would like to consider my essay on Carter Harrison a part of this large reevaluation of city politics at the turn of the century. Teaford discusses Harrison briefly on pages 49–50, 52–53, 59–60.

2. G. K. Chesterton, *Orthodoxy* (Garden City, NY: Doubleday, 1959), 99.

3. The basic sources on the Harrisons are: Claudius O. Johnson, *Carter Henry Harrison I: Political Leader* (Chicago: University of Chicago Press, 1928); Carter H. Harrison, Jr., *Stormy Years* (Indianapolis: Bobbs-Merrill Co., 1935); Carter H. Harrison, Jr., *Growing Up with Chicago* (Chicago: Ralph Fletcher Seymour, 1944). A highly sanitized collection of Harrison papers resides at Newberry Library.

4. A city census of 1878 recorded 436,739 residents; in 1880, the city census counted 491,516 and the U.S. Census 503,298 (*Chicago City Manual* [1913] 188). For the growth of Chicago's geographic boundaries, see Harold M. Mayer, Richard C. Wade, *Chicago: Growth of a Metropolis* (Chicago: University of Chicago Press, 1969), 177.

5. Harrison, *Stormy Years*, 18, 26; "Message of Carter H. Harrison, Mayor, 1887," Chicago Historical Society.

6. *Chicago City Manual* (1913) 205; (1912) 208.

7. Edward R. Kantowicz, "The Ghetto Experience: Chicago as a Case Study," (paper delivered at the National Archives Conference on State and Local History, May 1975); Kantowicz, "Church and Neighborhood," *Ethnicity*

7 (December 1980), 349–66; John M. Allswang, *A House for All Peoples* (Lexington: University Press of Kentucky, 1971).

8. For a perceptive study of Chicago's "moral geography," see Perry R. Duis, *The Saloon* (Urbana: University of Illinois Press, 1983).

9. *Chicago City Manual* (1912) 209.

10. All biographical information on Harrison, Sr., is from Johnson, *Carter Henry Harrison I*, and from Frederick Rex, *The Mayors of the City of Chicago, 1837–1933* (Chicago: Municipal Reference Library, 1947).

11. "Last Speech of Carter H. Harrison, 28 October 1893," Chicago Historical Society.

12. *Skandinaven*, quoted in Johnson, *Carter Henry Harrison I*, 119.

13. See Harrison's two autobiographies: *Stormy Years* and *Growing Up with Chicago*.

14. "Scrapbook of Articles under Pen Name Cecil Harcourt," Chicago Historical Society.

15. Theodore Roosevelt, *Autobiography* (New York: Macmillan, 1913), 63.

16. Paul M. Green, "The Chicago Democratic Party, 1840–1920," (Ph.D. diss., University of Chicago, 1975), 85ff.

17. The historical literature on progressivism is immense. My thinking on progressivism has been shaped by Richard Hofstadter, *The Age of Reform* (New York: Vintage, 1955); Robert Wiebe, *The Search for Order* (New York: Hill and Wang, 1967); and Richard Abrams, *The Burdens of Progress 1900–1929* (New York: Scott Foresman, 1978); Melvin Holli, *Reform in Detroit* (New York: Oxford University Press, 1969) is an admirable study of Hazen Pingree, a "reform boss" similar in many ways to Harrison.

18. Chapter 3, "Anatomy of a Reform Movement," in Steven J. Diner, *A City and Its Universities* (Chapel Hill: University of North Carolina Press, 1980) provides a good overview of reform in Chicago.

19. Joseph Bush Kingsbury, "Municipal Personnel Policy in Chicago, 1895–1915," (Ph.D. diss., University of Chicago, 1925), 4–7.

20. William T. Stead, *If Christ Came to Chicago* (Chicago: Laird and Lee, 1894); Lloyd Wendt and Herman Kogan, *Lords of the Levee* (Garden City, NY: Garden City Publishing Co., 1944), 91–96.

21. Ibid., 117–20; Green, "Chicago Democratic Party," 55–57; "Ogden Gas Company—Legal Research, Dated August 4, 1939," in Harrison Papers, Newberry Library.

22. Harrison, *Stormy Years*, 304–14; Harrison to Major Clifton P. Williamson (undated), in Harrison Papers; Wendt and Kogan, *Lords of the Levee*, 159–60.

23. Lincoln Steffens, *The Shame of the Cities*, (New York: Hill and Wang, 1957), 162–94; Kingsbury, "Municipal Personnel Policy," 57–68; Ralph Russell Tingley, "From Carter Harrison II to Fred Busse," (Ph.D. diss., Univer-

sity of Chicago, 1950), 32–33; "Mayor's Annual Message, April 10, 1905," Chicago Historical Society.

24. "Mayor's Annual Message, April 10, 1905"; "The Truth About Harrison," March 1901 campaign pamphlet; Green, "Chicago Democratic Party," 57.

25. "The Truth about Harrison," March 1901; "Mayor's Annual Message, April 10, 1905"; Rex, *Mayors of Chicago*, 88.

26. "The Truth about Harrison," March 1901; "Mayor's Message, 1900."

27. For background on Chicago traction, see John A. Fairlie, "The Street Railway Question in Chicago," *The Quarterly Journal of Economics* 21 (May 1907), 371–404; and Paul Barrett, *The Automobile and Mass Transit* (Philadelphia: Temple University Press, 1983).

28. Sidney I. Roberts, "Portrait of a Robber Baron: Charles T. Yerkes," *Business History Review* 35 (Autumn 1961), 344–71; and, for a more favorable view of Yerkes, Robert D. Weber, "Rationalizers and Reformers: Chicago Local Transportation in the Nineteenth Century," (Ph.D. diss., University of Wisconsin, 1971).

29. Roberts, "Portrait of a Robber Baron," 356–70; Harrison, *Stormy Years*, 136–75; Fairlie, "Street Railway Question," 380.

30. Roberts, "Portrait of a Robber Baron," 368, 371.

31. "Mayor's Message to the City Council, Outlining the Provisions of a Street Railway Franchise Renewal Ordinance, January 6, 1902"; and "Carter H. Harrison to the Citizens of Chicago, April 4, 1903," both in Harrison Papers. I believe that Paul Barrett, in *The Automobile and Mass Transit*, misinterpreted Harrison's policy, when he stated: "Harrison had no clear position on the transportation issue" (22).

32. Fairlie, "Street Railway Question," 388–400.

33. "Report of the Committee on Local Transportation to the City Council of the City of Chicago, January 15, 1907," Chicago Historical Society; Barrett, *The Automobile and Mass Transit*, 37–44.

34. *Chicago Times-Herald*, 14 July 1897, quoted in "The Truth About Harrison," March 1901, Chicago Historical Society.

35. Edward R. Kantowicz, *Polish-American Politics in Chicago* (Chicago: University of Chicago Press, 1972), 75–76.

36. Ibid., 77–83; Michael McCarthy, "Prelude to Armageddon: Charles E. Merriam and the Chicago Mayoral Election of 1911," *Journal of the Illinois State Historical Society* 67 (November 1974), 505–18; Harrison, *Stormy Years*, 291–95; Charles E. Merriam, *Chicago: A More Intimate View of Urban Politics* (New York: Macmillan, 1929), 283–86.

37. Wendt and Kogan, *Lords of the Levee*, 294–304; Harrison, *Stormy Years*, 304–14; John Landesco, *Organized Crime in Chicago* (Chicago: University of Chicago Press, 1929), 26–31; Chicago Vice Commission, *The Social Evil in Chicago* (Chicago, 1911).

38. Green, "Chicago Democratic Party," 172–241; William Jennings Bryan to Carter Harrison, 17 September 1914, and 9 November 1914, in Harrison Papers.

39. Carter Harrison to Graham Taylor, 7 January 1936, in Graham Taylor Papers, Newberry Library.

40. Wendt and Kogan, *Lords of the Levee*, 229.

41. Carter Harrison to Major Clifton P. Williamson (undated), in Harrison Papers.

42. "Mayor's Message to the City Council, Outlining the Provisions of a Street Railway Franchise Renewal Ordinance, January 6, 1902," in Harrison Papers.

43. For Tom Johnson, Frederic Howe, and the idea of a civic renaissance, see chapter 10, "The City Republic," in Frederic C. Howe, *The City: Hope of Democracy* (New York: Charles Scribners Sons, 1905).

44. See, for example, Green, "Chicago Democratic Party," 75, and Nick A. Komos, "Chicago, 1893–1907: The Politics of Reform," (Ph.D. diss., George Washington University, 1961), 243.

45. "Mayor's Annual Message," 3 April 1915, Chicago Historical Society.

46. *Chicago City Manual*, 1913, 99.

47. Harrison, *Stormy Years*, 339.

3. Edward F. Dunne: The Limits of Municipal Reform

1. The charges of radicalism were typical of those found in most Republican newspapers of the day, especially the *Tribune* the *Daily News*, and the *Record-Herald*. Dunne's version of his mayoral career can be found primarily in Edward F. Dunne, *Illinois: The Hearst of the Nation*, (Chicago: The Lewis Publishing Company, 1933) v. 2, 188–207 and in William Sullivan, comp., *Dunne: Judge, Mayor, Governor*, Chicago: The Lewis Publishing Company, 1916). The Illinois History Survey at the University of Illinois-Urbana/Champaign also has a collection of Dunne scrapbooks that contain mostly newspaper clippings. I am grateful to John Hoffman, director of the survey, for his cooperation.

2. The best sources for Dunne's intellectual development are his own works cited in note 1 and Richard E. Becker, "Edward Dunne, Reform Mayor Chicago; 1905, 1907," (Ph.D. dissertation, University of Chicago, 1971) 1–24. On "Catholic social liberalism" see Aaron I. Abell, American Catholic Thought on Social Questions, (Indianapolis: Bobbs-Merrill, 1968), 143–264. On social reformers see Melvin G. Holli, *Reform in Detroit: Hazen S. Pingree and Urban Politics,* (New York: Oxford University Press, 1969), 157–84. On "urban liberalism," see John D. Buenker, *Urban Liberalism and Progressive Reform,* (New York: Charles Scribners' Sons, 1973). On the significance of being "co-ethnic" see Edgar Litt, *Beyond Pluralism: Ethnic Politics in America,* (Glenview, Illinois: Scott, Foresman and Company; 1970), 1–74, 127–41. No less an authority than Carter H. Harrison II observed that it was taking one's life in one's

hands to campaign against Dunne in such Irish Catholic strongholds as Bridgeport or Back-of-the-Yards. See note 6.

3. John A. Fairlie, "The Street Railway Question in Chicago," *Quarterly Journal of Economics* 21 (1907): 371–404.

4. Dunne, *Illinois*, 227–35; Sullivan, *Dunne*, 177–85, 188–218.

5. Dunne, *Illinois*, v. 2, 228–39; Sullivan, *Dunne*, 197–218.

6. Dunne, *Illinois*, v. 2, 242–48; Chicago *Record-Herald*, 26 February 1905.

7. Sullivan, *Dunne*, 205–18.

8. Dunne, *Illinois*, v. 2, 244–45.

9. Becker, "Edward Dunne," 1–24; Nick A. Komons "Chicago, 1893–1907; The Politics of Reform," (Ph.D. diss. George Washington University, 1961), 310–25; Ralph Tingley, "From Carter Harrison to Fred Busse . . ." (Ph.D. diss. University of Chicago, 1950), 170–78; Paul M. Green, "The Chicago Democratic Party, 1840–1920," (Ph.D. diss., University of Chicago, 1975), 89–90.

10. Chicago *Tribune*, 27 June and 14 December 1904; Sullivan, *Dunne*, 170–75; Chicago *Evening Post*, 19 December 1904.

11. Chicago *Tribune*, 23 January 1905; Dunne, *Illinois*, v. 2, 255; Becker, "Edward Dunne," 31–35: Chicago *Chronicle*, 26 February 1905; Sullivan, *Dunne*, 177–85.

12. Linda J. Lear, *Harold L. Ickes: The Aggressive Progressive, 1874–1933* (New York: Garland Publishing Company, 1981), 56–64. In Ickes's view, "the formerly fierce traction opponent and IMO advocate had become bland and timid—safe and sound—dull and conservative," with ideas that were "more or less of a hodge podge."

13. Green, "Chicago Democratic Party," 103–10; Becker, "Edward Dunne," 35–38; Sullivan, *Dunne*, 186–87. Green styles Dunne's campaign a "brilliant combination of politics and reform zeal."

14. Becker, "Edward Dunne," 49–57; Komons, "Chicago, 1893–1907," 325–37; Green, "Chicago Democratic Party," 114–18; Lear, *Harold Ickes*, 58–62. Green concludes that Dunne handled the Traeger incident "with the ease and polish of a party professional."

15. Becker, "Edward Dunne," 37–49. Typical of Dunne's volunteer organizations were the Women's, Austin, Southside Women's, Scandinavian, and German-American Municipal Ownership Clubs, and the E. F. Dunne Workingman's Club, the Chicago Teacher's Federation Dunne Club, the Northwestern Law School Club, and the Ben Franklin Club.

16. *Tribune*, 5–6 April 1905. The voting analysis is based upon the comparison of the returns found in the *Tribune* with the ward map of the city and data found in U.S. Bureau of the Census, *Thirteenth Census of the United States*, 1910, v. 2, *Population*, 512–14. Especially useful in understanding the city's geographical makeup were Harold M. Mayer, Richard C. Wade, and Glen E. Holt, *Chicago: Growth of a Metropolis*, (Chicago: University of Chicago Press,

1969); Harvey Warren Zorbaugh, *The Gold Coast and the Slum: A Sociological Study of Chicago's Near North Side*, (Chicago: University of Chicago Press, 1929); and Glen E. Holt and Dominic A. Pacygca, *Chicago: A Historical guide to the Neighborhoods; The Loop and the South Side*, (Chicago: Chicago Historical Society, 1979).

17. *Tribune*, 6 April 1905. The Socialist candidate John Collins received 23,034, most of which presumably might have gone to Dunne if he had not been in the race.

18. Fairlie, "Chicago Railway question," 390–92; *Barrett, Automobile and Urban Transit*, 33–35; *Tribune*, 6 April 1905.

19. Becker, "Edward Dunne," 61–84; Komons, "Chicago, 1893–1907," 342–44; Jane Addams, *Twenty Years at Hull House*, (New York: Macmillan Co., 1910), 330–38; Dunne, *Illinois*, v. 2, 297–98.

20. On his European tour, Dunne had been impressed with the Glasgow system managed by A. C. Young. The man that he unwittingly invited to Chicago was James Dalrymple, Young's successor. Dalrymple accepted Dunne's hospitality and repaid him by writing a report that emphasized the political and financial difficulties of achieving MO. Dunne's attempt to suppress the report and its subsequent release by his opponents caused the mayor considerable embarrassment. See Fairlie, "Street Railway Question," 392; Komons, "Chicago, 1893–1907," 355–56.

21. Fairlie, "Street Railway Question," 390–98; Barrett, *Automobile and Urban Transit*, 33–36; Dunne, *Illinois*, v. 2, 270–89.

22. Charles E. Merriam, *Chicago: A More Intimate View of Urban Politics*, (New York: Macmillan Co., 1929), 90–133; Harrison, *Stormy Years*, 240–57; Green "Chicago Democratic Party," 117–9; Chicago *Record-Herald*, 3 April 1905.

23. Komons, "Chicago, 1893–1907," 346–54; Becker, "Edward Dunne," 69–73; Dunne, *Illinois*, v. 2, 268.

24. Dominic Candeloro, "The Chicago School Board Crisis of 1907," *Journal of the Illinois State Historical Society* 68 (1975): 396–406; *Tribune*, 10 October 1906; *Chronicle*, 4 April 1907.

25. Becker, "Edward Dunne," 165–97; Komons, "Chicago, 1893–1907," 366–68; *Record-Herald*, 30 May, 30 September, and 4 May 1905; 6, 7, and 24 March and 4 April 1906.

26. Alex Gottfried, *Boss Cermack of Chicago: A Study of Urban Political Leadership*, Seattle: University of Washington Press, 1962) 48–61; John M. Allswag, *A House for All Peoples: Ethnic Politics in Chicago, 1890–1936*, (Lexington: University Press of Kentucky, 1971), 3–36; *Tribune*, 19 March 1906; Dunne, *Illinois*, v. 2, 295.

27. Chicago *Inter-Ocean*, 22 February 1907.

28. Arthur F. Bentley, "Municipal Ownership Interest Groups in Chicago: A Study of Referendum Votes, 1902–1907," (Typescript in Regenstein Library, University of Chicago, n.d.); *Tribune*, 9 January 1907. A *Colliers* edi-

torial concluded that the voters had chosen "immediate seats in the cars rather than immediate municipal ownership."

29. Green, "Chicago Democratic Party," 117–21; Becker, "Edward Dunne," 184–97; Komons, "Chicago, 1893–1907," 378–98; *Tribune*, 22 February 1907.

30. Becker, "Edward Dunne," 197–211; *Tribune*, 12, 21, and 25 March 1907. The MO cause was carried by such Chicagoans as William Dever, Louis F. Post, and George Hooker and by such nationally recognized advocates as Tom Johnson and Brand Whitlock, with the latter calling Dunne a "co-partner in municipalization." For a discussion of William Randolph Hearst's role see Herbert S. Rosenthal, "William Randolph Hearst and Municipal Ownership," *Tamkang Journal of American Studies* 1 (1984): 6–36.

31. Becker, "Edward Dunne," 197–204. Dunne, *Illinois*, v. 2, 294–307. Busse was a member of the Lorimer faction of the GOP which had close ties to the traction companies and which the moderates regularly condemned for its alleged corruption, machine tactics, and preference for a wide-open city. Presumably, the combination of their antipathy toward the Dunne administration and the support of settlement was powerful enough to overcome their normal aversion. See Joel A. Tarr, *A Study in Boss Politics: William Lorimer of Chicago,* (Urbana: University of Illinois Press, 1971).

32. Lear, *Harold Ickes,* 69–70; Barrett, *Automobile and Urban Transit,* 38–45; Fairlie, "Street Railway Questions," 399–401. Dunne later claimed that he was indirectly offered a $50,000 campaign contribution if he would keep open the brothels on Custom House Place and that "in the river wards where money counts most, my candidacy was literally slaughtered at the polls." See Dunne, *Illinois*, v. 2, 294–97; and Becker, "Edward Dunne," 190–201.

33. *Tribune*, 3 April 1907. The electoral analysis was accomplished by the same sources cited in note 20 above. The Socialist candidate, George Koop, received 13,429 votes, slightly more than Busse's margin over Dunne. See also Edward R. Kantowicz, *Polish-American Politics in Chicago, 1880–1940,* (Chicago: University of Chicago Press, 1975).

34. *Tribune*, 3 April 1907; Becker, "Edward Dunne," 205–11; Bentley, "Municipal Ownership Interest Groups in Chicago," n.p.

35. See Dunne, *Illinois*, v. 2, 268–88. For a view that Dunne bungled MO and produced a "mottled victory," see Ginger, *Altgeld's America,* 295–303. Just two weeks after the election, the Supreme Court ruled that the street car certificates counted against the city's total bonded indebtedness, thus rendering the Mueller Law virtually useless.

36. Dunne, *Illinois*, v. 2, 290–92; Becker, "Edward Dunne," 74–75; Sullivan, *Dunne,* 315–23; *Daily News*, 22 April 1905.

37. Dunne, *Illinois*, v. 2, 290–91; Becker, "Edward Dunne," 165–78; *Tribune*, 10 February, 14 March, 12 April 1906.

38. Becker, "Edward Dunne," 170–77; Sullivan, *Dunne,* 315–23, 336–49;

Tribune, 18 April 1906; *Daily News,* 11 December 1965, 30 June 1906.

39. Becker, "Edward Dunne," 170–71; Sullivan, *Dunne,* 336–49; *Tribune,* 14 and 22 December 1906.

40. Dunne, *Illinois,* v. 2, 300–304; Becker, "Edward Dunne," 80–82; *Daily News,* 22 April 1905.

41. Candeloro, "School Board Crisis," 397–405; Dunne, *Illinois,* v. 2, 293, 304–5; *Tribune,* 10 October 1906, 13 November 1908; *Chronicle,* 28 May 1907.

42. Becker, "Edward Dunne," 212–17. Dunne narrowly lost the Democratic mayoral nomination to Harrison in 1911 and was elected governor of Illinois in 1912. His administration, although handicapped by lack of a legislative majority, made an impressive progressive record in labor, welfare, regulatory, and penal legislation and enacted limited woman suffrage. Defeated for reelection in 1916, Dunne devoted the rest of his life to his family, Democratic politics, and Irish-American causes. In 1919, he led an Irish-American delegation to the Versailles Conference pleading Irish independence, and in 1933 at the age of 80, he published his five volume *Illinois: Heart of the Nation.* He died in Chicago on 24 May 1937 at the age of 83.

4. Fred A. Busse: A Silent Mayor in Turbulent Times

1. George C. Sikes, "Chicago's New Mayor," *The American Monthly Review of Reviews* (May 1907), 585.

2. See Maureen A. Flanagan, "Charter Reform in Chicago: Political Culture and Urban Progressive Reform," *Journal of Urban History* (February 1986).

3. Nick A. Komons, "Chicago, 1893–1907: The Politics of Reform" (Ph.D. Dissertation, George Washington University, 1961) provides a detailed description of the role of the traction issue in municipal politics. See especially 295–96 and 311–26.

4. Chicago *Tribune,* 22 March 1907, 2; 23 March 1907, 3; and 29 March 1907, 4.

5. Ibid., 26 March 1907, 2.

6. At all the Chicago Federation of Labor meetings in January 1907 and 3 and 17 February 1907 this issue was of particular concern. See Chicago Federation of Labor, *Minutes* (Chicago Historical Society).

7. *Tribune,* 29 March 1907, 4.

8. See Carter Harrison, *Stormy Years: The Autobiography of Carter H. Harrison, Five Times Mayor of Chicago* (Indianapolis: Bobbs-Merrill, 1935), 110–12; Lloyd Wendt and Herman Kogan, *Bosses in Lusty Chicago* (Bloomington: University of Indiana, 1943), 38 for accounts of Yerkes; see Sikes, 588 and the *Tribune,* 20 March 1907, 2 for Busse and traction.

9. *Tribune,* 23 March 1907, 4; 26 March, 1; 28 March, 3; 27 March, 1; 26 March, 3; and 24 March, 1.

10. Ibid., 23 March 1907, 2; 26 March 1907, 3; and 23 March 1907, 1.

11. Ibid., 23 March 1907, 3; 26 March, 2; and 30 March, 2.

12. In the same way, Busse's Republican support from elsewhere in the

country was *ipso facto* good, Edward Dunne's outside Democratic support was bad. Because of his stand on municipal ownership, Republicans linked Dunne with the political aspirations of the notorious "outside agitator" William Randolph Hearst, accusing the Mayor of taking orders directly from "carpet-bagger" Hearst and his "mud-slinging" cronies who would descend upon Chicago, determined to put it under the thumb of New York City. That the Republicans were quite willing to place Chicago under the control of Theodore Roosevelt and the Republican party in Washington, was beside the point. Or rather, once again, it seems to have been a case of the other guy's partisanship being wrong, while the Republicans' was of course right. For examples, see the *Tribune*, 27 March 1907, 1; 28 March, 2; 29 March, 1; 23 March, 1; and 28 March, 1.

13. In the municipal elections of 1900, for example, when the Republicans won control of the city council, the Municipal Voters League discarded its hitherto sacred call for nonpartisan constitution of council committees. They backed the Republican plan to form committees along strict party lines saying "it is understood, however, that most, even of the more prominent reform members, do not regard the [nonpartisan] pledge as binding in the event it can be shown that better results can be accomplished by the majority party having control of the committees and working machinery of the Council." The notorious democratic alderman Johnny Powers, looking through the jaundiced eye of a seasoned politician, pronounced the situation for what it was: "to the victor belong the spoils." See the *Tribune*, 4 April 1900, 1–2 and 8 April 1900, 1.

14. *Tribune*, editorial 22 March 1907, 2 and 31 March 1907, 5.

15. For further accounts of the history of the conflict and the arguments of each position, see especially the *Public*, 17 November 1906; Chicago Federation of Labor, *Minutes*, 2 December 1906; Chicago *Record-Herald*, 3 December 1906; Adade Wheeler and Marlene Wortman, *The Roads They Made: Women in Illinois History*, (Chicago: Charles Kerr, 1977), 87–89; Mary E. Dreier, *Margaret Dreier Robins: Her Life, Letters, and Work* (New York, 1950); and Chicago *Daily News Almanac* (1905) 358.

16. *Tribune*, 18 May 1907, 1.

17. *Tribune*, 28 May 1907, 1–2; CFL, *Minutes*, 16 June, 21 July, and 4 August 1907; *Record-Herald*, 5 August 1907.

18. See Maureen A. Flanagan, "Charter Reform in Chicago, 1890–1915: Community and Government in the Progressive Era" (Ph.D. Dissertation, Loyola University of Chicago, 1980).

19. Flanagan, "The Ethnic Entry into Chicago Politics: The United Society for Local Self-Government and the Reform Charter of 1907," *Journal of the Illinois State Historical Society* (Spring 1982).

20. *Abendpost*, 3 April 1907.

21. *Abendpost*, 6 and 7 September 1907; Illinois *Staats-Zeitung*, 7 and 8 September 1907; *Record-Herald*, 6 September 1907.

22. *Record-Herald*, 14 September 1907.

23. *Record-Herald,* 29 April 1909 and 12 May 1909.

24. See *Tribune,* 21 May 1907, 2.

25. *Union Labor Advocate,* February 1911, 6–11.

26. Michael P. McCarthy, "Prelude to Armageddon: Charles E. Merriam and the Chicago Mayoral Election of 1911," *Journal of the Illinois State Historical Society,* (November 1975), 505–18.

5. Big Bill Thompson: The "Model" Politician

1. Article reprinted in *Congressional Record,* Senate, 70th Cong., 1st sess., 1928. vol. 69, pt. 4, 3697–3700; Washington, D.C.: U.S. Government Printing Office, 1928 (copy of pamphlet on file at Chicago Historical Society). Senator Thomas Heflin of Alabama followed Watson and inserted "The Law of Eligibility" from the *Protestant* magazine. The article contended canon law made it virtually impossible for a Catholic to hold the presidency.

2. Federal Bureau of Investigation, Subject: William Hale Thompson, File: 87–3286.

3. For the standard treatment of Thompson, see Reinhard H. Luthin, *American Demagogues* (Boston: 1954). Journalists have been the most fascinated by Thompson. William Stuart, *Twenty Incredible Years* (Chicago: 1935), treats his subject as a prophet scorned, which is not surprising since Stuart was a Hearst newspaperman and Thompson confidant. More balanced is Herman Kogan and Lloyd Wendt's *Big Bill of Chicago* (Indianapolis: 1953). As working reporters, the two had access to newspaper clipping files now destroyed or denied public use. Daniel J. Boorstin, *The Americans: The Democratic Experience* (New York: 1973), 83; FBI, Subject: William Hale Thompson, File: references, page stamped "60305"; Joel Tarr, *A Study in Boss Politics: William Lorimer of Chicago* (Urbana: 1971), chs. 4 and 7.

4. Chicago *Tribune,* 23 January 1915; Kogan and Wendt, *Big Bill,* 92; *Tribune,* 5, 14, 24, and 25 February 1915.

5. Chicago *Tribune,* 3, 12, 18, and 31 March 1915.

6. Chicago *Tribune,* 28 January and 17 February 1915; Arthur W. Thurner, "The Impact of Ethnic Groups on the Democratic Party, 1920–1928" (Ph.D. diss., University of Chicago, 1966), 13; *Tribune,* 26 January 1915; Kogan and Wendt, *Big Bill,* 108. A copy of the handbill is in the graphics collection of the Chicago Historical Society.

7. Edward H. Mazur, "Minyans for a Prairie City: The Politics of Chicago Jewry, 1850–1940" (Ph.D. diss., University of Chicago, 1974), 235. In all, Sweitzer lost the Bohemian, German, Jewish, and Swedish as well as the black vote. See John Allswang, *A House for All People: Ethnic Politics in Chicago* (Lexington: 1971), Table A-2.

8. *Daily News Almanac and Yearbook* (1916) at Chicago Historical Society; *Chicago Tribune,* 7 and 16 April 1915; Thomas E. Vadney, *The Wayward Liberal: A Political Biography of Donald Richberg* (Lexington: 1970), 32–34; *Tri-*

bune, 25 April 1915; on economy drive and Eastland, *Tribune,* 5 and 30 June and 29 July to 1 August 1915.

9. Chicago *Tribune,* 15–17 June 1915; *Chicago Commerce,* vol. 11, no. 7, 18 June 1915, at Chicago Historical Society (CHS); *Tribune,* 2 October 1915; Howard Barton Myers, "The Policing of Labor Disputes in Chicago: A Case Study" (Ph.D. diss., University of Chicago, 1929), 813 and 837; *Tribune,* 30 November 1915.

10. James W. Errant, "Trade Unionism in the Civil Service of Chicago, 1895 to 1930" (Ph.D. diss. University of Chicago, 1939), 113–14 and Chicago *Tribune,* 11, 17, and 19 July 1916; for Loeb Rule, *Tribune,* 26 August 1915, and Mary J. Herrick, *The Chicago Schools* (Beverly Hills: 1971), 122.

11. Open letter of the Illinois Manufacturers' Association, 9 September 1915, Box 162, Illinois Manufacturers Association Collection, CHS; Herrick, *Schools,* 128 and 135.

12. Perry Duis, *The Saloon: Public Drinking in Chicago and Boston, 1880–1920* (Urbana: 1983), 286–87; Chicago *Tribune,* 5 and 6 October 1915.

13. Chicago *Tribune,* 29 May to 8 June 1916; William T. Hutchinson, *Lowden of Illinois: The Life of Frank O. Lowden* (Chicago, 1957), vol. 1, 104, 263–66; Charles Gates Dawes to Lawrence Y. Sherman, 1 July 1915, Lawrence Y. Sherman Papers, Illinois State Historical Library, Springfield.

14. Kogan and Wendt, *Big Bill,* 133–34 and 137–43; Chicago *Tribune,* 22 February, 21 March, and 3 April 1916; "The Truth About Civil Service," CHS; *Tribune,* 19 March 1916.

15. Chicago *Tribune,* 14 and 17 September 1915; for rally and leaflet, *Tribune,* 16 and 30 September 1915.

16. Chicago *Tribune,* 11 and 24 October 1916, and 19 January 1917. The trials are covered in Kogan and Wendt, *Big Bill,* 147–48, and Harold F. Gosnell, *Negro Politicians* (Chicago: 1935), 172–74. On wiretaps, *Tribune,* 15 and 28 November 1917.

17. Chicago *Tribune,* 12 September 1915; on preparedness, *Tribune,* 4 June 1916.

18. Kogan and Wendt, *Big Bill,* 153; *Congressional Record,* House, 65th Cong., 1st sess., 1917. vol. 55, pt. 1, 413. The "no" votes were cast by Fred A. Britten, Charles E. Fuller, Edward J. King, William E. Mason, William A. Rodenberg, and Loren E. Wheeler. Britten represented a Chicago district; Mason resided in Chicago as a congressman-at-large. The others represented downstate districts. According to William Stuart, Thompson worked for Lowden in 1916 in exchange for support of his Senate ambitions. William Hutchinson argues there was no clear understanding between the two. See Stuart, *Twenty Incredible Years,* 27 and Hutchinson, *Lowden,* vol. 1, 265 and vol. 2, 383–84.

19. For Thompson's problems with the press, see Kogan and Wendt, *Big Bill,* 149–60. "Food Shortage Warning," 26 April 1917, Chicago Municipal

Reference Library (CMR); *The Republican*, 2 and 23 June and 28 July 1917, CHS.

20. Chicago *Tribune*, 2 and 9 March 1917.

21. Chicago *Tribune*, 3 August 1917; *Chicago Plan Commission Proceedings*, 953, CHS.

22. Address of William Hale Thompson, *Proceedings of the Chicago City Council*, 1918–1919, 13 May 1918, 90–98; for Thompson's versions of the incidents, "The Truth About William Hale Thompson," CMR; on People's Council, Chicago *Tribune*, 1 to 5 September 1917, and Hutchinson, *Lowden*, vol. 1, 378–80; *Tribune*, 26 August 1917, and 25 March, 8 April, and 7 May 1918.

23. Copy of letter marked "personal," Samuel Graham to Charles F. Clyne, U.S. district attorney for northern Illinois, 17 May 1917, and explanation by Joseph B. Fleming to Clyne, 29 May 1917, correspondence numbered 9-5-390-1 and 2, Record Group 60, National Archives; Department of Justice Central Files, Record Group 60, no. 9-19-1206, National Archives; Melvin G. Holli, "The Great War Sinks Chicago's German Kultur," in Melvin G. Holli and Peter d'A. Jones eds., *Ethnic Chicago*, (Grand Rapids: 1984), revised and expanded edition, 501–2; Chicago *Tribune*, 8 August 1917.

24. Chicago *Tribune*, 29 August 1917; Emerson Hough, *The Web* (Chicago: 1919), 182–85, 491, CHS.

25. Chicago *Tribune*, 4 September 1917; Holli, "Great War," 501–2; "A Year of Americanization Work, July 1918–July 1919," CHS. The individual lessons were collected and turned into a text, *A First Book in English for Non-English Speaking Adults* (Chicago: 1920), by Frances K. Wetmore. Lessons included Goggles—"Wear goggles at work and save your eyes."—and Time (on the dangers of buying a defective watch)—"The timekeeper docked me for lost time."

26. "The Truth About William Hale Thompson," CMR.

27. Chicago *Tribune*, 7, 8, and 12 September 1918; *Daily News Almanac and Yearbook* (1919) CHS.

28. *The Republican*, 15 February 1919; Charles E. Merriam, Spencer D. Parrott, Albert Lepawsky, *The Government of the Metropolitan Region of Chicago* (Chicago: 1933), 10. Ickes lived in the Hubbard Woods section of Winnetka; his law partner Richberg lived in south suburban Palos Park.

29. Chicago *Tribune*, 17 February 1919; for Olson's views on eugenics, *Tribune*, 4 September 1915; pamphlets "Win With Merriam" and "Chicago's Hope is Its Free Men and Women" in Charles E. Merriam Papers, University of Chicago.

30. Chicago *Tribune*, 12 and 14 February 1919; on vigilantes, *Tribune*, 18, 19, 20 and 25 February 1919; *Tribune*, 19 and 26 February 1919. Barry D. Karl in his *Charles E. Merriam and the Study of Politics* (Chicago: 1974) makes no mention of Merriam's campaign tactics. See pp. 97–98.

31. Kogan and Wendt, *Big Bill,* p. 167; Chicago *Tribune,* 10 and 11 March 1919; "How Sweitzer and Thompson Appealed to Race Prejudice for Votes," CMR; *Daily News Almanac and Yearbook,* 1920. The campaign included a fourth candidate, John Fitzpatrick, president of the Chicago Federation of Labor, who polled 56,000 votes.

32. Chicago *Tribune,* 29 March 1915. A Thompson speaker made the Sweitzer-Johnson charge. Charles Branham, "The Transformation of Black Political Leadership in Chicago, 1864–1942" (Ph.D. diss., University of Chicago, 1981), 154–57. Movie ads for "Birth" are in *Tribune,* 14 July 1915; 16 November 1916; and 8 June 1917. Here, too, the Democrats failed to capitalize. When the film again played in Chicago in 1924, the administration of William Dever cited state law to ban it but then quickly reversed itself in fear of a possible lawsuit by exhibitors. See Chicago *Defender,* 2, 9, and 16 February 1924. Michael Wallace Homel, "Negroes in the Chicago Public Schools, 1910–1941" (Ph.D. diss., University of Chicago, 1972), 38–40.

33. The reports were not confined to the press. See undated statement by Merriam on the "support of patriotic colored people" for his 1919 candidacy, Merriam Papers, and a letter form Raymond Robins to "Dear Captain-General," 12 March 1927, in the Raymond Robins Papers, Wisconsin State Historical Society, Madison. A social reformer, Robins hoped that the opposition of Edward H. Wright to Thompson could be used to sway black voters to Dever in the 1927 mayoral election. Six years earlier, when Wright was allied with Thompson, he was the object of press criticism for a $30,000 legal bill he sent city hall. See Chicago *Tribune,* 14 and 16 April 1921. Chicago *Defender,* 16 June and 30 October 1926.

34. Gosnell, *Negro Politicians,* pp. 200 and 250; Leonard D. White to Charles E. Merriam, 11 July 1931, in Merriam Papers.

35. William M. Tuttle Jr.'s *Race Riot: Chicago in the Red Summer of 1919* (New York: 1975) and Allan H. Spear's *Black Chicago: The Making of a Negro Ghetto, 1890–1920* (Chicago: 1967) both view the riot largely as a clash over public facilities, housing, and jobs. Thomas Lee Philpott's *The Slum and The Ghetto: Neighborhood Deterioration and Middle-Class Reform, Chicago, 1880–1930* (New York: 1978) ignores environmental and ethnic factors and emphasizes the role of racism. *Dziennik Zwiazkowy,* 27 May 1918, in I-C Polish of Chicago Foreign Press Survey, Works Progress Administration (Foreign Press Survey); *Lietuva,* 31 May 1918, in III-H Lithuanian, Foreign Press Survey, Chicago *Tribune,* 10 June 1919.

36. *Narod Polski,* 28 May 1919, in I-C Polish, Foreign Press Survey; *Jewish Courier,* 19 May and 14 July 1919, in II-D-10 Jewish, Foreign Press Survey; Chicago *Tribune,* 22 May and 8 and 9 June 1919; *Courier,* 25 July 1919, in I-C Jewish, Foreign Press Survey.

37. For Dunne, Chicago *Tribune,* 12 and 18 April, 30 May, 2 and 8 June,

and 9 July 1919; on rallies, *Tribune,* 8 and 25 June and 14 and 15 July 1919.

38. Tuttle, *Race Riot,* 141; Chicago *Tribune,* 28 June and 12 July 1919; on Star Order incident, *Tribune,* 21 June 1920.

39. Chicago *Tribune,* 24–28 July 1919; Hutchinson, *Lowden,* vol. 2, 456–57, and *Tribune,* 6–13 June 1920; Kogan and Wendt, *Big Bill,* 184.

40. Chicago *Tribune,* 1 November 1920. M. A. Michaelson to Warren G. Harding, 27 June 1921; Harry Daughtery to Harding, 29 June 1921; and Andrew Mellon to Harding, 6 July 1921, are all on microfilm roll 195, presidential case file Illinois, Warren G. Harding Papers, Ohio Historical Society. Copy of letter William M. Offey to Mac Gregor Bond, 28 January 1922, and handwritten note by Daughtery on bottom of summary of his phone conversation with Bond are in Department of Justice Central Files, Record Group 60, no. 220285, National Archives. The state supreme court in 1930 reversed a lower court ruling that Thompson was personally liable for the funds in the experts' fee suits. See Kogan and Wendt, *Big Bill,* 194, 310–11, and 320. *Tribune,* 21 June 1922; copy of letter William Hale Thompson to Herbert Hoover, 21 October 1921, in John Fitzpatrick Papers, CHS.

41. Kogan and Wendt, *Big Bill,* 210–13.

42. Sprague's name appears on a list of those accepting appointment to the committee, in John Fitzpatrick Papers, CHS. Chicago *Tribune,* 8 September 1921; Royal E. Montgomery, *Industrial Relations in the Chicago Building Trades* (Chicago: 1927), 275–81; undated leaflet in pamphlets for Citizens' Committee to Enforce the Landis Award, CHS.

43. "The Landis Award: Its Purpose and Accomplishments," CHS. Dever's union membership is cited in "Dever Did Deliver," in Box 3 of Agnes Nestor Papers, CHS. *Landis Award Journeyman,* vol. 1, no. 7, 1 May 1924, CHS. Both Samuel Insull and Col. William Pelouze, Thompson's political supporter and brother-in-law, respectively, were committee members, a connection the Democrats did not exploit in the 1927 election.

44. Stephen D. London, "Business and the Chicago Public School System, 1890–1966" (Ed.D., University of Chicago, 1968), 99; Herrick, *Chicago Schools,* 144–54. The "platoon" system increased the number of children an individual school could handle.

45. William Hale Thompson to William W. Borah, 1 February 1926, Illinois Invitations, William Borah Papers, Library of Congress; Carroll Hill Wooddy, *The Chicago Primary of 1926: A Study in Election Methods* (1974 Arno reprint of 1926 edition), 64–67, particularly Thompson speech contained in footnote.

46. Chicago *Tribune,* 9 January 1927; Kogan and Wendt, *Big Bill,* 253–54, and *Tribune,* 9 March 1927; Thurner, "Impact of Ethnic Groups," 248; on music, *Tribune,* 3 April 1927; for Hoyne and Robins, *Tribune,* 24 March 1927.

47. Chicago *Tribune,* 23 and 30 March and 1 April 1927.

48. Chicago *Tribune,* 17 and 19 March 1927; Thompson speech dated 31 March 1927 in Merriam Papers; *Tribune,* 26 February and 10 April 1927.

49. Chicago *Tribune*, 6 April 1927; Orville James Taylor to Julius Rosenwald, 11, 18, and 19 March 1927, Julius Rosenwald Papers, University of Chicago; for ad by Independent Republicans, *Tribune*, 31 March 1927; Alice Reichel to Julius Rosenwald, 18 May 1927, Rosenwald Papers.

50. Errant, "Trade Unionism," 118–19; Herrick, *Chicago Schools*, 168–70; Kogan and Wendt, *Big Bill*, 340, and Chicago *Tribune*, 8 August 1927; on the new labor-political relationship, Errant, 170–72.

51. Estimates in Kogan and Wendt, *Big Bill*, 268–69; M. R. Werner, *Julius Rosenwald: The Life of a Practical Humanitarian* (New York: 1939), 295–315.

52. Serritella's trial coincided with the 1931 general election. His conviction was overturned on appeal. See Harold F. Gosnell, *Machine Politics: Chicago Model* (1968 Greenwood reprint of 1937 edition), footnote, p. 12. The link between the syndicate and politics is detailed in Len O'Connor, *Clout: Mayor Daley and His City* (New York: 1975), and Mike Royko, *Boss: Richard J. Daley of Chicago* (New York: 1971).

53. Chicago *Tribune*, 22–27 April and 3 June 1927; "America First-Farm Relief-Inland Waterways-National Flood Control to Prevent Disaster," CMR; San Francisco *Examiner*, 16 September 1927, Thompson Clipping file.

54. Chicago *Tribune*, editorial, 8 June 1920: Chicago *Herald-Examiner*, 27 January 1923. San Francisco *Examiner*, 21 July 1926 and 8 April 1927 and undated New York *American* editorial are all contained in Thompson clipping file, courtesy of the San Francisco *Examiner*. Hearst editorial in the Baltimore *American*, 5 November 1927, courtesy of the Baltimore *New-American*.

55. Chicago *Defender*, 24 April and 8 May 1926; copy of letter marked "personal," Victor Olander to Oscar F. Nelson, 16 April 1927, in Box 10, Victor Olander Papers, CHS.

56. Herrick, Chicago Schools, 168–70. McAndrew was charged with insubordination and tainting the school histories with pro-British propaganda. His contract expired before a "guilty" verdict was reached. See Chicago *Tribune*, 22 March 1928. Thompson sent a letter to the school board, 22 November 1927, on ethnic heroes of the Revolution. See George S. Courts, *School and Society in Chicago* (1971 Arno reprint of 1928 edition), 280–83. Chicago *Tribune*, 1 December 1927, and Rupert Costo, ed., *Textbooks and the American Indian* (San Francisco: 1970), 2–3.

57. On Pineapple Primary and Thompson breakdown, Kogan and Wendt, *Big Bill*, 304–8 and 312–14; Chicago *Tribune*, 10 October 1930.

58. Clarence Darrow to Donald Richberg, 15 June 1930, in Box 9, Donald Richberg Papers, CHS; Karl, Merriam, 235; Harold Ickes, *Autobiography of a Curmudgeon* (New York: 1943), 267–70 and 281; Vadney, *Wayward Liberal*, 120.

59. Chicago *Defender*, 4 April 1931; on St. Patrick's Day Meeting, *Defender*, 20 March 1926.

60. Chicago *Tribune*, 6 April 1931; Alex Gottfried, *Boss Cermak of Chicago: A Study of Political Leadership* (Seattle: 1962), 180–200; on Cermak and Jar-

ecki, Douglas Bukowski, "Judge Edmund K. Jarecki: A Rather Regular Independent," *Chicago History*, vol. 8, no. 4, Winter 1979–1980; Allswang, *House for All Peoples*, Table 8: 2, p. 161.

61. The most comprehensive treatment of the public works of Thompson's successor is Carl W. Condit's *Chicago, 1930–1970: Building, Planning, and Urban Technology* (Chicago: 1974).

62. Chicago *Tribune*, 7 April 1931; on Citizens' Committee, *Tribune*, 14 March 1929; O'Connor, *Clout*, 17.

63. Ickes, *Autobiography*, 173.

6. William E. Dever: A Chicago Political Fable

1. Dever's background and early career are detailed by the writer in "Dever of Chicago: A Political Biography" (Ph.D. dissertation, University of Chicago, 1983). See also the William E. Dever Papers and the William E. Dever Scrapbooks, both at the Chicago Historical Society.

2. The best contemporary study of Chicago politics in the early twentieth century is Charles E. Merriam, *Chicago: A More Intimate View of Urban Politics* (New York: The Macmillan Co., 1929). For the evolution of the Democratic organization, consult Paul M. Green, "The Chicago Democratic Party, 1840–1920: From Factionalism to Political Organization" (Ph.D. diss., University of Chicago, 1975).

3. Chicago *Daily News*, 19 December 1922, 4 January 1923; Chicago *Tribune*, 7, 11 January 1923.

4. Brennan's selection of Dever is described in Parke Brown, "Brennan of Illinois," *Century Magazine* 112 (September 1926): 596–97. See also Harold L. Ickes, *The Autobiography of a Curmudgeon* (New York: Reynal and Hitchcock, 1943), 247–48; George Sikes to Martin J. O'Brien, 11 November 1922, Dever Papers.

5. Chicago *Journal*, 2 March 1923.

6. Chicago *Herald and Examiner*, Chicago *Tribune*, both 17 April 1923.

7. At least one contemporary magazine essay on Dever's beer war was published in booklet form: Neil McCullough Clark, *Mayor Dever and Prohibition: The Story of a Dramatic Fight to Enforce the Law* (Westerville, OH: American Issue Publishing Co., 1925).

8. Chicago *Tribune*, 8, 15 January 1925.

9. Dever wrote his own account of the cleanup for the New York *Herald*, 25 November 1923; the article was syndicated and appeared in other papers. See also Chicago *Tribune*, 8 October 1923.

10. Chicago *Herald and Examiner*, 10 April 1925.

11. Chicago *Tribune*, 10 January 1925.

12. The McAndrew controversy is described in George S. Counts, *School and Society in Chicago* (New York: Harcourt, Brace, 1928).

13. U.S., Congress, Senate Subcommittee of the Committee on the Judi-

ciary, *The National Prohibition Law*. Hearings on bills to amend the National Prohibition Act, 5–24 April 1926, 69th Cong., 1st sess., 1926, 1377–78, 1384–85.

14. Chicago *Herald and Examiner*, 3 October 1926; William E. Dever, "Get at the Facts." *Atlantic Monthly* 138 (October 1926): 518–24.

15. Chicago *Herald and Examiner*, 5 January 1927.

16. Chicago *Daily News*, 23 February 1927; John Bright, *Hizzoner Big Bill Thompson: An Idyll of Chicago* (New York: Jonathon Cape and Harrison Smith, 1930), 250–51.

17. Quoted in Elmer Davis, "Portrait of an Elected Person," *Harper's Magazine* 155 (July 1927): 183.

18. Besides the Davis article cited above, other national magazine commentaries on the 1927 election include: Nels Andersen, "Democracy in Chicago," *Century Magazine* 115 (November 1927): 71–78; Kate Sargent, "Chicago: Hands Down!" *The Forum* 78 (November 1927): 708–24; William Allen White, "They Can't Beat My Big Boy!" *Collier's* 79 (18 June 1927): 8–9, 46–47; "What 'Big Bill's' Victory Means," *Literary Digest* 93 (6 April 1927): 5–7; "Why Chicago Did It," *New Republic* 50 (20 April 1927): 234–36.

19. Chicago *Herald and Examiner*, 18 March 1924; Arthur W. Thurner, "The Impact of Ethnic Groups on the Democratic Party in Chicago, 1920–1928," (Ph.D. diss., University of Chicago, 1966), 263–64.

7. Anton J. Cermak: The Man and His Machine

1. Alex Gottfried, *Boss Cermak of Chicago: A Study of Political Leadership* (Seattle: University of Washington Press, 1962), viii.

2. H. K. Barnard, *Anton the Martyr* (Chicago: Marion Publishing, 1933), 20.

3. Gottfried, 369.

4. Personal Interview. Chicago, 1985.

5. Personal Interview. Chicago, 1970.

6. Chicago *Tribune*, 7 May 1915.

7. See Paul M. Green's "Irish Chicago: The Multi-Ethnic Road to Machine Success," in Melvin G. Holli and Peter d'A. Jones, eds., *Ethnic Chicago* (Grand Rapids: Eerdman's Publishing Company, 1984), 434–39.

8. Personal Interview. Chicago, 1970.

9. Chicago *Herald and Examiner*, 13 February 1927.

10. See Gottfried, 169–99. Mike Royko, *Boss: Richard J. Daley of Chicago* (New York: E. P. Dutton, 1971), 36. Andrew Greeley, *That Most Distressed Nation* (Chicago: Quadrangle Books, 1972), 206. Eugene Kennedy, *Himself! The Life and Times of Mayor Richard J. Daley* (New York: The Viking Press, 1978), 51.

11. Chicago *Herald and Examiner*, 30 October 1929.

12. Ibid. 7 October 1929.

13. Ibid. 25 April 1929.
14. Chicago *Tribune,* 24 March 1931.
15. Ibid. 14 May 1931.
16. Personal Interview. Chicago, 1971.
17. See Kip Sullivan, "Politics and Educational Policy: The Control of Chicago Public Schools During the Administration of Anton J. Cermak" (Unpublished Ph.D. diss., Loyola University of Chicago, 1985).
18. Chicago *Tribune,* 13 July 1931.
19. Chicago *Tribune,* 21 May 1931.
20. *Public Service Leader,* 5 December 1932.
21. See Green, *Ethnic Chicago,* 451–52.

8. Edward J. Kelly: New Deal Machine Builder

1. Roger Biles, *Big City in Depression and War: Mayor Edward J. Kelly of Chicago* (DeKalb: Northern Illinois University Press, 1984), 13–19. On Cermak, see Alex Gottfried, *Boss Cermak of Chicago: A Study in Political Leadership* (Seattle: University of Washington Press, 1962). Prior to selecting Kelly, Nash chose Alderman Francis J. Corr as "acting" mayor. He served from March 10 to April 14.
2. "Mayor Kelly's Own Story," Chicago *Herald-American,* 5 May 1947; Donald S. Bradley and Mayer N. Zald, "From Commercial Elite to Political Administrator: The Recruitment of the Mayors of Chicago," *American Journal of Sociology* 71 (September 1965): 153–67.
3. Broadus Mitchell, *Depression Decade* (New York: Rinehart and Co., 1947), 105; Irving Bernstein, *The Lean Years: A History of the American Worker, 1920–1933* (Boston: Houghton Mifflin, 1966), 297–98.
4. Paul Douglas, "Chicago's Financial Muddle," *New Republic* 61 (12 February 1930): 324–26; Lyman B. Burbank, "Chicago Public Schools and the Depression Years of 1928–1937," *Journal of the Illinois State Historical Society* 64 (Winter 1971): 365–81; *New York Times,* 27 November 1932.
5. *Newsweek* 5 (13 April 1935): 7; Charles T. Holman, "Chicago Elects a New Mayor," *Christian Century* 50 (26 April 1933): 567–68; New York *Times,* 16 April 1933; Chicago *Tribune,* 26 April 1933; John T. Flynn, "These Our Rulers," *Collier's* 106 (20 July 1940): 18, 19.
6. *Lightnin'* (July 1933): 10; Burbank, 375; Chicago *Tribune,* 28 April 1933.
7. "Elected to Fill Former Mayor Cermak's Unexpired Term," *Newsweek* 1 (22 April 1933): 19; New York *Times,* 16 April 1933; Harold M. Mayer and Richard C. Wade, *Chicago: Growth of a Metropolis* (Chicago: University of Chicago Press, 1969), 362–64; Arthur G. Lindell, *City Hall Chronology,* 1966, Municipal Reference Library of Chicago, vol. 2.
8. Chicago *Tribune,* 24 February 1935 (quote); *Newsweek* 5 (13 April 1935): 7; *Chicago American,* 3 April 1935 (Wetten quote).
9. New York *Times,* 4 March 1935 (first quote), 20 October 1936 (Krock

quote); "Chicago's Record of Accomplishment Under Mayor Edward J. Kelly," 1940, Chicago Historical Society (Sutherland quote).

10. Gottfried, 207; John M. Allswang, *A House For All Peoples: Ethnic Politics in Chicago, 1890–1936* (Lexington: University Press of Kentucky, 1971), 42–43; Edward R. Kantowicz, "American Politics in Polonia's Capital: 1888–1940," Ph.D. diss., University of Chicago, 1972, 429–30.

11. Henry F. Gosnell, *Machine Politics: Chicago Model* (Chicago: University of Chicago Press, 1937); Sonya Forthal, *Cogwheels of Democracy: A Study of the Precinct Captain* (New York: William-Frederick Press, 1946).

12. "Mayor Kelly's Chicago," *Life* 17 (17 July 1944), 75; "The Kelly-Nash Political Machine," *Fortune* 14 (August 1936), 126–39.

13. Donald G. Sofchalk, "The Chicago Memorial Day Incident: An Episode of Mass Action," *Labor History* 6 (Winter 1965): 17; U.S. Congress, Senate Committee on Education and Labor, "The Chicago Memorial Day Incident: Hearings before a Subcommittee of the Senate Committee on Education and Labor," 75th Cong., 1st sess., 1937, 37–40; Barbara Newell, *Chicago and the Labor Movement: Metropolitan Unionism in the 1930s* (Urbana: University of Illinois Press, 1961), 178–79, 224–25, 250.

14. Roger Biles, "'Big Red in Bronzeville': Mayor Ed Kelly Reels in the Black Vote," *Chicago History* 10 (Summer 1981), 99–111.

15. Ibid.

16. Perry R. Duis, "Arthur W. Mitchell, New Deal Negro in Congress," M.A. thesis, University of Chicago, 1966, 26–38; John M. Allswang, "The Chicago Negro Voter and the Democratic Consensus: A Case Study, 1918–1936," *Journal of the Illinois State Historical Society* 60 (Summer 1967), 172.

17. James Q. Wilson, "Negro Leaders in Chicago," Ph.D. diss., University of Chicago, 1959, 102 (quote); James Q. Wilson, *Negro Politics: The Search for Leadership* (Glencoe, IL: Free Press of Glencoe, 1960), 50.

18. Mike Royko, *Boss: Richard J. Daley of Chicago* (New York: E. P. Dutton, 1971), 132; Len O'Connor, *Clout: Mayor Daley and His City* (New York: Avon Books, 1975), 178–79.

19. William H. Stuart, *The Twenty Incredible Years* (Chicago: M. A. Donahue, 1935), 536; Virgil W. Peterson, *Barbarians in Our Midst: A History of Chicago Crime and Politics* (Boston: Little, Brown, and Co., 1952), 165; Warren H. Pierce, "Chicago: Unfinished Anomaly" in Robert S. Allen, ed., *Our Fair City* (New York: Vanguard Press, 1947), 177; Chicago *Daily News*, 30 October 1934; John Bartlow Martin, "Al Capone's Successors," *American Mercury* 68 (June 1949): 733; Biles, *Big City Boss*, 107.

20. Chicago *Daily News*, 30 October 1934; Paul Douglas, *In the Fullness of Time* (New York: Harcourt Brace Jovanovich, 1971), 90; Pierce, 177; John T. Flynn, "Too Much Fun," *Collier's* 104 (7 October 1939): 35–36; Martin, 733; Peterson, 165.

21. Chicago *Daily News*, 30 October 1934.

22. Biles, *Big City Boss*, 8–11, 107–8; Pierce, 177; Douglas, *In the Fullness of Time*, 91; Eugene Kennedy, *Himself!: The Life and Times of Mayor Richard J. Daley* (New York: Viking Press, 1978), 62 (quote).

23. Harold L. Ickes, *The Secret Diary of Harold L. Ickes: The First Thousand Days, 1933–1936* (New York: Simon and Schuster, 1954), 246, 494, 557; Arthur M. Schlesinger, Jr., *The Age of Roosevelt: The Politics of Upheaval* (Boston: Houghton Mifflin, 1960), 442–43; Edward J. Kelly to Harry Hopkins, memo of telephone conversation, 10 September 1935, Harry Hopkins Papers, Box 93, Franklin D. Roosevelt Library, Hyde Park, New York.

24. James A. Farley, *Jim Farley's Story: The Roosevelt Years* (New York: McGraw-Hill, 1948), 92; Ickes, 463; Jim Farley to Edward J. Kelly, 17 September 1936, Democratic National Committee Papers, Illinois File, FDR Library.

25. Edward J. Kelly to Franklin D. Roosevelt, received 30 August 1932, Franklin D. Roosevelt Papers, Personal File 3166, FDR Library; Franklin D. Roosevelt to Edward J. Kelly, 12 September 1932, ibid.; Samuel I. Rosenman, *Working With Roosevelt* (New York: Harper and Row, 1952), 123; Biles, *Big City Boss*, 80–83.

26. Lyle W. Dorsett, *Franklin D. Roosevelt and the City Bosses* (Port Washington, New York: Kennikat Press, 1977), 93; Ralph Madison, "Letter from Chicago," *New Republic* 112 (23 April 1945): 549–51.

27. Dorsett, 93; Biles, *Big City Boss*, 83–85.

28. On Roosevelt's role in the 1936 Illinois gubernatorial race, see: Thomas B. Littlewood, *Horner of Illinois* (Evanston: Northwestern University Press, 1969).

29. Gene Delon Jones, "The Local Political Significance of New Deal Relief Legislation in Chicago: 1933–1940," (Ph.D. diss., Northwestern University, 1970), 244; City of Chicago, *Chicago's Report to the People, 1933–1946*, (March 1947), 7, 9; Carl W. Condit, *Chicago, 1930–1970: Building, Planning, and Urban Technology* (Chicago: University of Chicago Press, 1974), 24, 30, 34, 48n.

30. Jones, 206 (quote); Biles, *Big City Boss*, 71–80.

31. Walter Davenport, "From Whom All Blessings Flow," *Collier's* 96 (20 July 1935), 7, 8, 34–36; Lorena Hickok to Harry Hopkins, 18 July 1936, Lorena Hickok Papers, FERA Reports, Box 11, FDR Library (quote); Gosnell, 78; Chicago *Tribune*, 26 April 1937; Speech of Wayne McMillen, 25 January 1938, Records of the National Association of Social Workers, Chicago Chapter, Box 5, Chicago Historical Society; Leo M. Lyons, "Illinois Investigates the Relief Situation," *National Municipal Review* 27 (January 1938): 26 (quote).

32. Edwin O'Connor, *The Last Hurrah* (Boston: Little, Brown, and Co., 1956), especially 101, 329–31. In agreement with this critique of the Last Hurrah thesis are: Bruce M. Stave, *The New Deal and the Last Hurrah: Pittsburgh Machine Politics* (Pittsburgh: University of Pittsburgh Press, 1970); Lyle

W. Dorsett, *The Pendergast Machine* (New York: Oxford University Press, 1968); and Jones, "Local Political Significance of New Deal Relief Legislation."

33. Littlewood, 208–11; Flynn, "Too Much Fun," 36; Chicago *Tribune*, 1 March 1939; Chicago *Herald and Examiner*, 2 March 1939; New York *Times*, 5 April 1939. The only biography of Dwight Green is Robert J. Casey and W. A. S. Douglas, *The Midwesterner: The Story of Dwight H. Green* (Chicago: Wilcox and Follett, 1948).

34. Chicago *Tribune*, 23 February 1943 (McKibbin quote), 7 April 1943; Chicago *Sun*, 8 April 1943.

35. Paul F. Barrett, "Mass Transit, the Automobile, and Public Policy in Chicago, 1900–1930," Ph.D. diss., University of Illinois at Chicago Circle, 1976, 72, 95, 108, 230; Lindell, 248.

36. "Millenium for Straphangers," *Time* 50 (8 September 1947): 24–25; City of Chicago, *Chicago's Report to the People*, 192, 196; Paul F. Barrett, "Public Policy and Private Choice: Mass Transit and the Automobile in Chicago Between the Wars," *Business History Review* 49 (Winter 1975): 473–97.

37. Biles, *Big City Boss*, 47 (quote); O'Connor, 56–58; Kennedy, 79–80; Chicago *Sun*, 17 April 1947.

38. Ralph Whitehead, Jr., "The Ward Boss Who Saved the New Deal," *Chicago* 26 (May 1977): 179 (quote); Milburn P. Akers, "Twilight of Boss Kelly," *Nation* 162 (April 13, 1946): 425–26; "Protected Gambling in Chicago," *Criminal Justice* 74 (May 1947): 20–23.

39. Biles, *Big City Boss*, 147; Melvin G. Holli interview with J. Greenough, 14 April 1985, River Forest, Illinois.

40. Ibid., 147–48; O'Connor, 58–59; Milburn P. Akers, "Chicago Dumps Kelly," *Nation* 164 (4 January 1947): 8; Chicago *Tribune*, 16 April 1947, 21, 24 October 1950; "Funeral of a Boss," *Life* (6 November 1950): 40–41.

41. Ibid.

42. Walter Johnson and Carol Evans, eds., *The Papers of Adlai E. Stevenson* (Boston: Little, Brown, and Company, 1973), vol. 3, 311 (Stevenson quote); Alfred Steinberg, *The Bosses* (New York: Macmillan, 1972), 8 (first Kelly quote); Victor Rubin, "You've Gotta Be a Boss," *Collier's* 116 (25 September 1945): 36 (second Kelly quote).

9. Martin H. Kennelly: The Mugwump and the Machine

1. Perry R. Duis and Glen E. Holt, "The Real Legacy of 'Poor Martin' Kennelly," *Chicago* 27 (July 1978): 162–65; Charles B. Cleveland, "Look What He's Doing to Chicago," *Saturday Evening Post* 221 (July 3, 1948): 15ff.

2. Cleveland, "Look What He's Doing to Chicago," 16 and passim.; "Biographical Sketch of Mayor Martin H. Kennelly," (n.p., n.d.) in the Martin H. Kennelly Papers, Department of History, University of Illinois at Chicago; Interview with Leon Despres, Chicago, Illinois, 19 August 1985.

3. New York *Times*, 22 December 1946.

4. Despres interview, 19 August 1985; Len O'Connor, *Clout: Mayor Daley and His City* (New York: Avon Books, 1975), 85.

5. "Biographical Sketch of Martin H. Kennelly"; "Martin H. Kennelly, Chicago's Thirty-ninth Mayor: Biography—History," (n.p., n.d.); The Greater Chicago Committee for the Re-Election of Mayor Kennelly, "Meet Martin Kennelly," (n.p., n.d.), all in the Kennelly Papers. Peter J. O'Malley, "Mayor Martin H. Kennelly of Chicago: A Political Biography," (Ph.D. diss., University of Illinois at Chicago, 1980), ch. 1.

6. Duis and Holt, "The Real Legacy," 164; O'Malley, "Mayor Martin H. Kennelly," ch. 1.

7. O'Malley, "Mayor Martin H. Kennelly," ch. 1.

8. Roger Biles, *Big City Boss in Depression and War: Mayor Edward J. Kelly of Chicago* (DeKalb, IL: Northern Illinois University Press, 1984), 148–50; O'Malley, "Mayor Martin H. Kennelly," 36.

9. Biles, Kelly's biographer, doubts this version of events. In addition to the sources cited in note 8, above, see also Milton L. Rakove, *We Don't Want Nobody Nobody Sent* (Bloomington: Indiana University Press, 1979), 12.

10. New York *Times*, 22 December 1946. While there is no firsthand account of the bargain struck between Arvey and Kennelly, John Bartlow Martin provides some insight with his account of Arvey's dealings with gubernatorial candidate Adlai Stevenson. According to Martin's reconstruction, Arvey said: "I will tell you the same thing I told Kennelly in 1947. The only thing I ask of you is that you help the Democratic Party as much as you can in a decent way. We want the patronage when a Democrat can fill the job. I am not talking about cabinet appointments or your own personal appointments. Get the best men you can for those. We want you to get the best. That's the way you can help the party the most. You're our showcase. If you do well, then we'll look good. All I ask is that you be loyal to the party—don't make an alliance with the Republicans." See John Bartlow Martin, *Adlai Stevenson of Illinois* (Garden City, NY: Doubleday and Company, Inc., 1976), 279. If, in fact, Arvey made such a deal with Kennelly, it was a shrewd one that protected the Cook County Democratic organization's interests at a time when the Republicans controlled a significant minority in the city council.

11. Statement of Martin H. Kennelly to the members of the Democratic Central Committee, 20 December 1946, in the Kennelly Papers.

12. Speech by Russell W. Root over radio station WLS, 18 February 1947; Address by George B. McKibben over radio station WENR, 10 March 1947, both in the Kennelly Papers; Independent Voters of Illinois, Minutes of the State Central Committee Meeting, 9 December 1946, in the Independent Voters of Illinois Papers, Chicago Historical Society (CHS).

13. Martin H. Kennelly for Mayor, press releases, 7 and 24 March 1947; Martin H. Kennelly, radio address no. 1, "Chicago Is My Home Town," all in the Kennelly Papers.

14. O'Malley, "Mayor Martin H. Kennelly," ch. 2.

15. Inaugural Address of Mayor Martin H. Kennelly, Council Chambers, City Hall, 15 April 1947, in the Kennelly Papers.

16. O'Malley, "Mayor Martin H. Kennelly," ch. 3; Leon Despres interview, 19 August 1985.

17. Martin H. Kennelly, "State of the City" address, 2 February 1954, in the Kennelly Papers; O'Malley, "Mayor Martin H. Kennelly," ch. 5.

18. Mary J. Herrick, *The Chicago Schools: A Social and Political History* (Beverly Hills: Sage Publications, 1971), 259–77.

19. Herrick, *The Chicago Schools*, 277–78; Margaret Hancock to Mitchell McKeown, 13 March 1951, in the Kennelly Papers.

20. Herrick, *The Chicago Schools*, 279–300.

21. Chicago *Tribune*, 7 March 1954.

22. O'Malley, "Mayor Martin H. Kennelly," 81–83; A Democratic precinct captain to Mr. Mayor, 12 March 1951, in the Kennelly Papers; Chicago *Tribune*, 7, 8 March 1954; Chicago *Sun-Times*, 8 March 1954; Chicago *Daily News*, 5 March 1954; O'Connor, *Clout*, 84.

23. Duis and Holt, "The Real Legacy," 162–65; O'Malley, "Mayor Martin H. Kennelly," ch. 4.

24. Kennelly, "State of the City" address, 2 February 1954.

25. O'Connor, *Clout*, 91; O'Malley, "Mayor Martin H. Kennelly," ch. 5.

26. In addition to the sources cited in note 25 above, see also Chicago *Tribune*, 24 January 1951.

27. O'Malley, "Mayor Martin H. Kennelly," ch. 5; Statement of Mayor Martin H. Kennelly left with Senate Crime Investigation Committee, 5 October 1950; Memorandum Re Organized Syndicated Vice and Gambling (n.d.), both in the Kennelly Papers; "News on the Spot," 14 November 1950, in the Len O'Connor Papers, CHS.

28. The Greater Chicago Committee, Martin H. Kennelly for Mayor, press release, 14 February 1947 and n.d., both in the Kennelly Papers.

29. Interview with Robert E. Merriam, Chicago, Illinois, 23 September 1985.

30. O'Connor, *Clout*, 89; Stephen E. Hurley to J. H. Dillard, 31 August 1954 and "Requested Increase in Civil Service Budget Rejected Up To Now," 6 December 1954, both in the Kennelly Papers; O'Malley, "Mayor Martin H. Kennelly," ch. 3; Merriam interview, 23 September 1985.

31. Merriam interview, 23 September 1985.

32. Chicago *Sun-Times*, 27 March 1950; Rakove, *We Don't Want Nobody Nobody Sent*, 276.

33. Biles, *Big City Boss*, 152; Chicago *Sun Times*, 8 March 1954; Francis W. McPeek to Mayor Kennelly, 20 October 1954, in the Kennelly Papers; O'Connor, *Clout*, 13, 86; Rakove, *We Don't Want Nobody Nobody Sent*, 299; Merriam interview, 23 September 1985.

34. O'Malley, "Mayor Martin H. Kennelly," ch. 3.

35. Milton C. Mumford to Hughston McBain, 16 May 1947, in the Holman D. Pettibone Papers, CHS; Metropolitan Housing and Planning Council, Minutes of the Executive Committee, 29 October 1953; Sydney Stein, Jr. to Edward Eagle Brown, 27 April 1953; Metropolitan Housing and Planning Council, Minutes of the Board of Governors Meeting, 3 April 1953, all in the Metropolitan Housing and Planning Council Papers, Special Collections, University of Illinois at Chicago; Interview with Julian Levi, Chicago, Illinois, 29 July 1980; Interview with Ferd Kramer, Chicago, Illinois, 4 August 1980. For a detailed examination of the legislative background to slum clearance and renewal in Chicago, see Arnold R. Hirsch, *Making the Second Ghetto: Race and Housing Chicago, 1940–1960* (New York: Cambridge University Press, 1983), 100–170.

36. Interview with Ira J. Bach, Chicago, Illinois, 24 July 1980.

37. Martin Meyerson and Edward C. Banfield, *Politics, Planning, and the Public Interest* (New York: The Free Press, 1955), 171–72.

38. Martin, *Adlai Stevenson of Illinois*, 450–51, 460; O'Malley, "Mayor Martin H. Kennelly," ch. 7.

39. Rakove, *We Don't Want Nobody Nobody Sent*, 13; Herrick, *The Chicago Schools*, 277; Chicago *Sun-Times*, 15, 17 April 1953; 22 July 1953; and unidentified clippings in the Daniel M. Cantwell Papers, CHS.

40. For Kelly's record on racial issues, see Biles, *Big City Boss*, 89–102; Interview with Vernon Jarrett, Chicago, Illinois, 28 August 1985.

41. Chicago *Defender*, 22, 29 March 1947; Chicago *Bee*, 5 January 1947.

42. Rakove, *We Don't Want Nobody Nobody Sent*, 12; Eugene Kennedy, *Himself! The Life and Times of Richard J. Daley* (New York: Viking Press, 1978), 80–81; Biles, *Big City Boss*, 146–48.

43. Chicago Commission on Human Relations, "Memorandum on the Fernwood Park Homes" (mimeo., n.d.), Chicago Urban League Papers (CUL Papers), Special Collections, University of Illinois at Chicago; "The Peoria Street Incident" (mimeo., n.d.), Municipal Reference Library (MRL), City Hall, Chicago, Illinois.

44. Sidney Williams to Homer Jack, December 1949, in the Archibald J. Carey, Jr. Papers, CHS; Sidney Williams to Mayor Martin H. Kennelly, 29 November 1949, in the Catholic Interracial Council Papers (CIC Papers), CHS; Arvarh E. Strickland, *History of the Chicago Urban League* (Urbana, IL: University of Illinois Press, 1966), 172–74; Hirsch, *Making the Second Ghetto*, 61–62, 246–47.

45. Chicago Council Against Racial and Religious Discrimination to Martin H. Kennelly, 24 February 1949 and Archibald J. Carey to Val J. Washington, 27 April 1949, both in the Carey Papers; Chicago *Defender*, 5 March 1949.

46. Elizabeth Wood to the Commissioners, 28 July 1947, Business and Pro-

fessional People in the Public Interest Papers (BPI Papers), CHS; Meyerson and Banfield, *Politics, Planning, and the Public Interest,* passim.; Address by Elizabeth Wood, Executive Secretary of the Chicago Housing Authority at "A Tribute to Good Government" dinner given in her honor by Chicago citizens at the Red Lacquer Room of the Palmer House on Thursday, 9 October 1952, CUL Papers; *Southeast Economist,* 26 May 1949, clipping in the Cantwell Papers.

47. Address by Elizabeth Wood; Institute for Community Design Analysis, "Review and Analysis of the Chicago Housing Authority and Implementation of Recommendations; Final Report of Phase I: Recommended Changes and Resulting Savings," 31 March 1982, MRL: Wood's firing is discussed in greater detail in Hirsch, *Making the Second Ghetto,* 234–38.

48. O'Malley, "Mayor Martin H. Kennelly," 147, 222–23; Willard Townsend to J. S. Knowlson, 9 April 1951; Willard Townsend to Mayor Kennelly, 16 April 1951; J. S. Knowlson to Martin H. Kennelly, 7 June 1951; [Olive M.] Diggs, Memo, 13 March 1951, all in the Kennelly Papers.

49. O'Malley, "Mayor Martin H. Kennelly," 192; Timothy J. O'Connor to Martin H. Kennelly, 13 January 1955, n.p.; Patrolman C. Ryan to Aide to the Commissioner, n.d.; Summary of Gambling Arrests Made for the Year 1951, n.d., all in the Kennelly Papers, Mike Royko, *Boss: Richard J. Daley of Chicago* (New York: Signet Books, 1971), 62; Bach interview, 24 July 1980.

50. Jarrett interview, 28 August 1985; Chicago *Tribune,* 13 January 1952, 6 February 1955; Chicago *Sun-Times,* 31 December 1953; unidentified clipping in the C. C. Wimbish Papers, CHS.

51. O'Malley, "Mayor Martin H. Kennelly," 222; Chicago *Defender,* 7 April 1951.

52. Merriam interview, 23 September 1985.

53. Report on the Community Forum's Meeting on Trumbull Park, 23 May 1954, in the Irene McCoy Gaines Papers, CHS; Chicago *Defender,* 15 May 1954, 26 March 1955; Elizabeth Wood to Members of the CHA Advisory Committee on Race Relations, 27 April 1954, in the BPI Papers; Duckett-Lawrence Associates, et al., "A Specialized Public Relations and Promotional Program Proposed for Robert E. Merriam, Candidate for Mayor of Chicago (Aimed at the Negro Community)," n.d., in the Carey Papers.

54. Kennelly campaign press release, 30 January 1955, in the Kennelly Papers, Chicago *Sun-Times,* 28 January 1955; Chicago *Defender,* 5, 19 February 1955, 26 March 1955; Claude A. Barnett to Frederick D. Jordan, 21 February 1955 in the Claude A. Barnett Papers, CHS.

55. The South Deering Improvement Association employed a sound truck to drum up votes for Daley in the Trumbull Park area. See Illinois Division, American Civil Liberties Union, Executive Committee Minutes, 7 April 1955, 16 June 1955, in the Illinois Division-American Civil Liberties Union Papers,

Special Collections, Regenstein Library, University of Chicago; see also *Daily Calumet*, 21 February 1955; Chicago *Defender*, 19 February 1955; O'Malley, "Mayor Martin H. Kennelly," ch. 8; O'Connor, *Clout*, 106–25.

56. Chicago *Sun-Times*, 24 February 1955.

10. Mayor Richard J. Daley and the Politics of Good Government

1. Robert Lineberry, George Edwards, and Martin Wattenberg, *Government in America: People, Politics and Policy*, 5th ed. (New York: Harper Collins, 1991), 263; Eugene Kennedy, *Himself: The Life and Times of Mayor Richard J. Daley* (New York: Viking Press, 1978); *Time*, 15 March 1963; Len O'Connor, *Clout: Mayor Daley and His City* (New York: Avon Books, 1975), xi; Personal interview with Tom Jacobs, 21 January 1992.

2. A. J. Liebling, "Profile of Chicago," *New Yorker*, (26 January 1952), 33.

3. Ira Katznelson, *City Trenches: Urban Politics and the Patterning of Class in the United States* (Chicago: University of Chicago Press, 1981), 6.

4. O'Connor, *Clout*, 8.

5. Ralph Whitehead, "The Organization Man," *American Scholar* (Summer 1977), 352.

6. Harvey Karlen, *The Governments of Chicago* (Chicago: Courier Publishing Company, 1958), 229.

7. Milton Rakove, *Don't Make No Waves—Don't Back No Losers* (Bloomington: Indiana University Press, 1975), 44.

8. Harry Barnard, "Reflections By A Traditional Liberal On The Future Of Chicago As Related to The Coming Mayoralty," Personal Memorandum (23 November 1948), 1.

9. *Nation*, 22 December 1951.

10. *New Republic*, 31 August 1953.

11. James V. Cunningham "Political Battle in Chicago," *Commonweal* (11 February 1955), 497.

12. Chicago *Tribune*, 21 April 1955.

13. Edward C. Banfield, *Political Influence* (New York: Free Press, 1961), 235–36.

14. Ibid., 237.

15. Ibid., 257.

16. Paul E. Peterson, *School Politics Chicago Style* (Chicago: University of Chicago Press, 1967), 15.

17. Ibid., 17.

18. *New York Times*, 15 April 1956.

19. Mike Royko, *Boss: Richard J. Daley of Chicago* (New York: E. P. Dutton and Company, 1971), 92.

20. Personal interview, 5 February 1985.

21. Ibid.

22. James Dugan, "Mayor Daley's Chicago," *Holiday* (December 1963), 86.

23. Ibid.
24. Carl Chatters papers, Box 1, Chicago Historical Society.
25. Personal interview with Tom Jacobs, 21 January 1992.
26. Personal interview, July 1983.
27. Personal interview with Jane Byrne, 24 February 1992.
28. John Kay Adams, "Reforming Chicago," *Harper's* (June 1958), 76.
29. Chicago *Tribune*, 3 April 1959.
30. Ibid.
31. Chicago *Tribune*, 2 April 1963.

11. Michael A. Bilandic: The Last of the Machine Regulars

1. Chicago *Tribune*, 23 December 1976.
2. Ibid., 26 December 1976.
3. Ibid., 29 December 1976.
4. Personal interview, May 1986.
5. From 1933 to the early 1940s Chicago Mayor Edward J. Kelly shared power with Cook County Democratic party chairman Pat Nash.
6. Chicago *Tribune*, 18 April 1977.
7. Ibid., 19 April 1977.
8. After losing to Bilandic, Block joined most of his former Chicago Republicans by moving to the suburbs. In short, he got out of town.
9. Personal interview, June 1986.
10. Personal interview, June 1986.
11. Milton Rakove, "Jane Byrne and the New Chicago Politics," in Samuel Gove and Louis Masotti, eds., *After Daley: Chicago Politics in Transition* (Urbana: University of Illinois Press, 1982), p. 227.
12. Michael Bilandic speaking at the Milton Rakove Memorial Seminar, University of Illinois, Chicago, November 1985.
13. Peter W. Colby and Paul M. Green, "The Consolidation of Clout: The Vote Power of Chicago Democrats from Cermak to Bilandic," *Illinois Issues* (February 1979). Reprinted in Paul M. Green, David Everson, Peter Colby, and Joan Parker, eds., *Illinois Elections*, 3d ed. (Springfield: Sangamon State University, 1986).
14. Chicago *Tribune*, 25 February 1979.
15. Chicago *Sun-Times*, 18 February 1979.

12. Jane M. Byrne: To Think the Unthinkable and Do the Undoable

1. Bill and Lori Granger, *Fighting Jane: Mayor Jane Byrne and the Chicago Machine* (New York, 1980), 19.
2. Ibid., 221–22.
3. Robert Davis, "Evil Cabal to a Crew of Haters," Chicago *Tribune*, 2 September 1980; David Axelrod, "City Transition Team Transits," Chicago *Tribune*, 29 April 1979.

4. Eugene Kennedy, "An Opinionated Psychobiography of Mayor Jane Byrne," Chicago *Sun Times,* 9 February 1983; Paul McGrath at the Chicago Political Tradition Conference, Chicago Historical Society, 2 December 1985; Milton Rokave, "Jane Byrne and the New Chicago Politics," in Samuel Gove and Louis Masotti, eds., *After Daley* (Urbana: University of Illinois Press, 1982), 234–35; Haider cited in Alfredo Lanier, "Jane Byrne's High Hopes and Hard Times," *Chicago* (December 1981): 198; Byrne cited in Chicago *Tribune,* 6 April 1980.

5. Interview with Jane Byrne, 4 March 1986.

6. Chicago *Tribune,* 28 December 1979; Bob Wiedrich, "Byrne's Strident Strike Rhetoric," Chicago *Tribune,* 21 December 1979; Sidney Lens, "What CTA Workers are Asking For," Ibid.

7. A. F. Ehrbar, "Financial Probity: Chicago Style," *Fortune* 101 (2 June 1980): 100–105; "Byrne Tells New Plan for Schools," Chicago *Tribune,* 25 January 1980; N. Shepperd, Jr., "It's Mayor Byrne vs. the Rest," New York *Times,* 7 January 1980.

8. "Byrne Halts Strike Talks," Chicago *Tribune,* 19 February 1980; see also editorial, ibid.; "Byrne Vows to End Strike," ibid., 15 February 1980; Granger, *Fighting Jane,* 227–29.

9. "Reflective Byrne," Palm Beach *Post,* 17 April 1983.

10. Ehrbar, "Financial Probity: Chicago Style," 100–105.

11. Ibid.; "Byrne Hits Past Mayors for City's Financial Woes," Chicago *Tribune,* 31 December 1980; "City Bond Rating . . . ," Chicago *Tribune,* 9 February 1980; Haider cited in Lanier, "Jane Byrne's High Hopes . . . ," 198.

12. Interview with Jane Byrne, 4 March 1986; Donald Haider, "A Multi-Year Financial Projection of and Options for the Corporate Budget, City of Chicago, 1985–1989" (Prepared for the Committee on Finance, City Council, November 1985), 14, 16.

13. "Mayor's Record of Achievement," Chicago *Tribune,* 22 June 1980.

14. Robert Davis, "Byrne's Crusade," Chicago *Tribune,* 5 April 1981.

15. David Axelrod, "The Battles," Chicago *Tribune,* 5 April 1981.

16. McMullen quoted in "Byrne, McMullen Hit Abusive Press," Chicago *Tribune,* 19 January 1980, and in Christopher Willcox "Chicago: How the City Works," Detroit *News magazine* (20 July 1980): 18.

17. Harry Golden, "Byrne's Mercurial Record of Feats, Fests," Chicago *Sun Times,* 15 February 1983; Ira Bach, "Byrne has Been Good for the City," Chicago *Tribune,* 19 February 1983.

18. Granger, *Fighting Jane,* 27–31; "Jane Byrne." *Current Biography 1980,* 33. For early life see also Kathleen Whalen Fitzgerald, *Brass: Jane Byrne and the Pursuit of Power* (Chicago 1980).

19. On her move to Cabrini-Green see Anne Keegan, "I Can't Wait Till She Moves In," Chicago *Tribune,* 23 March 1981. McMullen on Mayor Byrne's legs cited in Granger, *Fighting Jane,* 102.

13. Harold Washington: The Enigma of the Black Political Tradition

1. Robert McClory, "Up from Obscurity: Harold Washington," in Melvin G. Holli and Paul M. green, eds., *The Making of the Mayor: Chicago, 1983* (Grand Rapids: Eerdmans Press, 1984), 3.

2. Ibid., 3.

3. Ibid., 4.

4. Edward C. Banfield and James O. Wilson, *City Politics* (Cambridge, MA: Harvard University Press and M.I.T. Press).

5. Ibid.

6. Election returns are from the Chicago Board of Election Commissioners.

7. An earlier version of this argument is in my article, "Is Chicago Ready for Reform?" in Holli and Green, *The Making of the Mayor.*

8. Population data are from the *Local Community Fact Book* series published by the University of Chicago Press.

9. The material for this and the other sections on Harold Washington comes from interviews with him and other politicians who were involved in the incidents discussed.

10. Interview with Edison Love, one of Dawson's top precinct captains. On Love, see Milton L. Rakove, *We Don't Want Nobody Nobody Sent,* (Bloomington: Indiana University Press, 1979), 37–45.

11. Dawson vehemently opposed Metcalfe's nomination behind the scenes, but he was no match for Daley. Interview with Corneal Davis, President of the Second Ward organization.

12. An excellent and densely detailed discussion of this period can be found in Arnold R. Hirsch, *Making the Second Ghetto* (Cambridge: Cambridge University Press, 1983).

13. Ibid. Realtors regularly charged blacks exorbitant prices for housing beyond the black belt.

14. Chicago *Sun-Times,* 1 February 1955.

15. Chicago *Defender,* 5 February 1955.

16. An interesting discussion of this period is contained in Joe Mathewson, *Up Against Daley* (LaSalle, IL: Open Court Press, 1974), 121–34.

17. Chicago *Sun-Times,* 19 January 1986.

18. Ibid.

19. Ibid.

20. Edward T. Clayton, *The Negro Politician,* (Chicago: Johnson Publishing Co., 1964), 73.

21. Interview with Mayor Washington.

22. *Chicago* magazine selected Washington as one of the top ten legislators, and the Chicago *Sun-Times* ranked him "the most capable black in the legislature." Both citations came in 1977.

23. Basil Talbott, Chicago *Sun-Times,* n.d.

24. Polling in the 1983 mayoral campaign is discussed by a pollster, Richard Day, "Polling in the 1983 Mayoral Election," in Holli and Green, *The Making of the Mayor.*

15. The Daley Era: Richard J. to Richard M.

1. Melvin G. Holli and Paul M. Green, *Bashing Chicago Traditions: Harold Washington's Last Campaign, Chicago, 1987* (Grand Rapids: Eerdmans, 1989), 139–40.

2. See mayoral biographies in Melvin G. Holli and Peter d'A. Jones, eds., *Biographical Dictionary of American Mayors, 1820–1980* (Westport, CT: Greenwood Press, 1981).

3. "Chicago's Daley," *Newsweek,* 5 April 1971, 80.

4. Walter Jacobson, "Daley," Chicago *Tribune Magazine,* 28 March 1971, 27; Sheehan quoted in Mike Royko, *Boss: Richard J. Daley of Chicago* (New York: Dutton, 1971), 190; Adamowski quoted in Milton Rakove, *We Don't Want Nobody Nobody Sent: An Oral History of the Daley Years* (Bloomington: Indiana University Press, 1979), 278; Hoellen quoted in Rakove, *We Don't,* 278.

5. Singer cited in Rakove, *We Don't,* 373; Grimshaw quoted in Williams Braden, "Daley Remembered," Chicago *Sun-Times* (spec. repr.), 9 December 1986.

6. Chicago *Tribune,* 18 April 1977.

7. Milton Rakove, "Jane Byrne and the New Chicago Politics," in Samuel Gove and Louis Masotti, eds., *After Daley: Chicago Politics in Transition* (Urbana: University of Illinois Press, 1982), 227.

8. Chicago *Tribune,* 25 February 1979.

9. Byrne quoted in Bill Granger and Lori Granger, *Fighting Jane: Mayor Jane Byrne and the Chicago Machine* (New York: Dial Press, 1980), 19.

10. Jane Byrne, interview with authors, 4 March 1986; Alfredo Lanier, "Jane Byrne's High Hopes and Hard Times," *Chicago* (December 1981), 198.

11. Byrne, interview; Bob Wiedrich, "Byrne's Strident Strike Rhetoric," Chicago *Tribune,* 2 December 1979; "Byrne Halts Strike," Chicago *Tribune,* 19 February 1980.

12. McMullen quoted in "Byrne, McMullen Hit Abusive Press," Chicago *Tribune,* 19 January 1980; Robert Davis, "Byrne Crusade," Chicago *Tribune,* 5 April 1981.

13. For campaign coverage, see Melvin G. Holli and Paul M. Green, eds., *The Making of the Mayor, Chicago, 1983* (Grand Rapids: Eerdmans, 1984). Bernard Epton, interviews with author, 10 June and 9 August 1984.

14. "The Media and the Mayor," WBBM-TV, November 26, 1987; Washington quoted in Holli and Green, *Bashing,* 143–44.

15. John McDermott, interview with author, 19 November 1987; Nancy

Isserman, "Conduct Press Releases and Numerical Summary of Complaints" (CONDUCT staff report, Chicago, 1987).

16. WBBM-TV news, Chicago, 18 November 1987; T. Hardy, "Mayor Keeps Byrne off Democratic Slate," Chicago *Tribune,* 19 November 1987.

17. William Raspberry, "Jesse Jackson's Selective Application of His Fairness Principle," Chicago *Tribune,* 28 March 1989; WMAQ-TV news, Chicago, 2 December 1987; L. Gorov, "Long Night Was Hard to Stomach," and R. Feder, "480,000 Homes Maintained a TV Vigilance," Chicago *Sun-Times,* 5 April 1989.

18. Clarence Page, "A Racial Campaign That Didn't Work," Chicago *Tribune,* 9 April 1989; Jim Merriner and Fran Spielman, "Evans Never Had a Chance," Chicago *Sun-Times,* 5 April 1989.

19. David Axelrod, interview with author, 7 February 1990.

20. Axelrod, interview; "Daley Turns Down Chicago's Fire," *Insight,* 11 September 1989, 23; John McDermott, "Our New, Positive Racial Politics," Chicago *Tribune,* 14 March 1989.

21. *Chicago Enterprise,* February 1991; Holli and Green, *Bashing,* 156.

22. J. Kass, "Daley at Mid-term," Chicago *Tribune,* 7 February 1993; Mayor's press secretary handouts, April, May, 1993.

23. G. Washburn, "Clinton Kills Airport Cash for Peotone," Chicago *Tribune,* 2 October 1993.

24. "Chicago's Casino Dream Is Still That," New York *Times,* 3 October 1993; "Daley Cool for Now to Casino Plan," Chicago *Tribune,* 10 February 2003.

25. T. Hardy, "Daley Enjoys Widespread Approval," Chicago *Tribune,* 6 June 1993; Daley poll, Market Shares Incorporated, Chicago, 13–18 May 1993; "Daley Romps to 5th Term," Chicago *Tribune,* 26 February 2003; Fran Spielman, "Mayor Wins Nearly 60% of Black Vote," Chicago *Sun-Times,* 26 February 2003.

26. Jacky Grimshaw, "Divided We Fall," *Chicago,* August 1993, 35–37.

27. Richard M. Daley, February 1991 speech, transcripts, mayor's file, city hall.

28. One dimension of the scholarly study of equilibrium theory can be seen in Drew Fudenberg and Jean Tirole, *Game Theory* (Cambridge, MA; MIT Press, 1991); "Reinventing Da Mayor," *U.S. News and World Report,* 23 March 1992, 40–41.

29. Richard M. Daley, "We're Not a Dynasty," Chicago *Sun-Times,* 18 December 2002.

30. "Daley Picks a Gay Alderman," Chicago *Sun-Times,* 20 December 2002; Mark Brown, "Daley Greases the Council's Last Squeaky Wheel," Chicago *Sun-Times,* 20 January 2003; John Kass, "FBI Pays Call on Towing Firm with Daley Ties," Chicago *Tribune,* 23 March 2003.

31. David Axelrod, "10 Votes for Daley," Chicago *Tribune,* 23 February 2003.

32. Ibid; "Graffiti Crew Hits 10 Year Mark," Chicago *Tribune,* 11 March 2003.

33. "Daley Wins Big," Chicago *Sun-Times,* 26 February 2003; Mike Dorning and Jeff Zeleny, "The Daley/Bush connection," Chicago *Tribune,* 10 March 2003; Steve Neal, "Daley Joins Pantheon of Marathon Mayors," Chicago *Sun-Times,* 26 February 2003.

16. Ranking Chicago's Mayors: Mirror, Mirror on the Wall, Who Is the Greatest of Them All?—An Updated Poll

1. Arthur M. Schlesinger, Sr., *Life,* 1 November 1948, 65–66, 73–74; *New York Times Magazine,* 29 July 1962, 12–13, 40–43; Robert K. Murray and Tim H. Blessing, *Greatness in the White House: Rating the Presidents, Washington Through Carter* (University Park: Penn State Press, 1989), 10–24; Steve Neal, "Our Best and Worst Presidents," Chicago *Tribune Magazine,* 10 January 1982, 9–18.

2. Melvin Holli, "The Experts Choose Chicago's Greatest Mayors," *Public Perspective* 6.5 (1995): 54–56; Melvin G. Holli, "Ranking Chicago's Mayors: Mirror, Mirror, on the Wall, Who Is the Greatest of Them All?" in *The Mayors: The Chicago Political Tradition,* rev. ed., ed. Paul M. Green and Melvin G. Holli, 233–42 (Carbondale: Southern Illinois University Press, 1995).

3. For example, see Robert K. Murray and Tim H. Blessing, "The Presidential Performance Study: A Program Report," *Journal of American History* 70 (December 1983): 538.

4. For biographical information, see Peter O'Malley, "Edward J. Kelly," in *The Biographical Dictionary of American Mayors, 1820–1980,* ed. Melvin Holli and Peter d'A. Jones (Westport, CT: Greenwood Press, 1981), 190–91, hereafter cited as Holli and Jones, *BDAM.* See also Roger Biles, *Big City Boss in Depression and War: Mayor Edward J. Kelly of Chicago* (DeKalb: Northern Illinois University Press, 1984); Edward H. Mazur, "Carter H. Harrison I," and Andrew K. Prinz, "Carter Harrison II" in Holli and Jones, *BDAM,* 151–52; Peter O'Malley, "Anton J. Cermak," in Holli and Jones, *BDAM,* 60–61; Alex Gottfried, *Boss Cermak of Chicago: A Study of Political Leadership* (Seattle: University of Washington Press, 1962); Roger Biles, "John Wentworth," in Holli and Jones, *BDAM,* 387. See also Don E. Fehrenbacher, *Chicago Giant: A Biography of "Long John" Wentworth* (Madison, WI: American History Research Center, 1957); Andrew K. Prinz, "Edward Dunne," in Holli and Jones, *BDAM,* 106–7; John D. Buenker, "Edward F. Dunne: The Urban New Stock Democrat as Progressive," *Mid-America* 50 (January 1968): 3–7; Paul M. Green, *Paul Green's Chicago* (Springfield, IL: Illinois Issues, Sangamon State University, 1988); Richard E. Becker, "Edward Dunne, Reform Mayor of

Chicago, 1905–1907" (Ph.D. diss., University of Chicago, 1971); John R. Schmidt, *The Mayor Who Cleaned Up Chicago: A Political Biography of William Dever* (DeKalb: Northern Illinois University Press, 1989); Douglas Bukowski, "William Dever and Prohibition," *Chicago History* (Summer 1984); Paul Barrett, "Joseph Medill," in Holli and Jones, *BDAM*, 251–52; Thomas Bullard, "William Ogden," in Holli and Jones, *BDAM*, 273; Eugene Kennedy, *Himself: Life and Times of Mayor Richard J. Daley* (New York: Viking, 1978); William Grimshaw, *Bitter Fruit: Black Politics and the Chicago Machine* (Chicago: University of Chicago Press, 1992).

5. For more about mayor-governor Dunne, see chapter 17.

6. For example, ex-president Dwight Eisenhower was placed on the "ten worst" list in 1962 by his contemporaries, but after his successors stumbled through the Bay of Pigs, the Vietnam War, burning cities, Watergate, and the Middle Eastern oil embargo, Eisenhower's prosperous and peaceful 1950s appeared much better and elevated Ike onto the list of the ten best presidents in Neal's 1982 *Tribune* poll.

7. See Melvin G. Holli, "Daley to Daley," in *Restoration: Chicago Elects Another Daley*, ed. Paul M. Green and Melvin G. Holli, 193–207 (Chicago: Lyceum Books, 1991).

8. Melvin G. Holli, "Ranking Chicago Mayors" in the 1987 edition of Green and Holli, *Mayors*, 203.

9. See "Requiem for a Heavyweight," in Melvin G. Holli and Paul M. Green: *Bashing Chicago Traditions: Harold Washington's Last Campaign* (Grand Rapids: Eerdmans, 1989), 181–95.

10. For stability that tends to emerge in leadership polls, see Murray and Blessing, *Greatness*, 23–24.

17. Mayoring in Chicago, 1837–2004: A Stepping Stone to Higher Office or a Dead-End Job?

1. Quoted in Anne Keegan, "Will Wise Words Outlast the Hot Ones?" *Chicago Tribune*, 25 February 1983.

2. Stephan Thernstrom, *Poverty and Progress: Social Mobility in a Nineteenth Century City* (Cambridge, MA: Harvard University Press, 1964); also, Thernstrom's *The Other Bostonians: Poverty and Progress in the American Metropolis, 1880–1870* (Cambridge, MA: Harvard University Press, 1973); Thomas Kessner, *The Golden Door: Italian and Jewish Immigrant Mobility in New York City, 1880–1915* (New York: Oxford University Press, 1977); Joseph A. Schlesinger, *Ambition and Politics: Political Careers in the United States* (Chicago: Rand McNally, 1966), 2–5, 195–97; Marilyn Gittell, "Metropolitan Mayor: Dead End," *Public Administration Review* 23 (March 1963): 20–24; Theodore J. Lowi, "Why Mayors Go Nowhere," *Washington Monthly* 3 (January 1972): 55–60; Wallace S. Sayre and Herbert Kaufman, *Governing New York*

City: Politics in the Metropolis (NewYork: Russell Sage Foundation, 1960), 697; Russell Murphy, "Whither the Mayors? A Note on Mayoral Careers," *Journal of Politics* 42 (February 1980): 277–90. See also Raymond E. Wolfinger, *The Politics of Progress* (Englewood Cliffs, NJ: Prentice-Hall, 1974), 397–401.

3. Biographical information about Chicago mayors is derived from Melvin G. Holli and Peter d'A. Jones, eds., *Biographical Dictionary of American Mayors, 1820–1980* (Westport, CT: Greenwood Press, 1981), hereafter cited as Holli and Jones, *BDAM*.

4. Richard E. Becker, "Edward Dunne, Reform Mayor of Chicago, 1905–1907" (Ph.D. diss., University of Chicago, 1971), 217; John D. Buenker, "Edward F. Dunne: The Urban New Stock Democrat as Progressive," *Mid-America* 50 (January 1968): 3–7; Andrew K. Prinz, "Fred A. Busse, 1866–1914," "William Hale Thompson," and "Carter H. Harrison II," in Holli and Jones, *BDAM;* John Bright, *Hizzoner Big Bill Thompson: An Idyll of Chicago* (NewYork: Cape and Smith, 1930), 242.

5. Douglas Bukowski, "William Dever and Prohibition," *Chicago History* 7 (Summer 1984), 109–18; John R. Schmidt, "Dever of Chicago: A Political Biography" (Ph.D. diss., University of Chicago, 1983), 156–64; H. K. Barnard, *Anton the Martyr* (Chicago: Marion, 1933), 80 ff.

6. Roger Biles, *Big City Boss in Depression and War: Mayor Edward J. Kelly of Chicago* (DeKalb: Northern Illinois University Press, 1984); see also biographies by Peter J. O'Malley of Martin H. Kennelly and Richard J. Daley, and by Roger Biles of Jane Byrne, in Holli and Jones, *BDAM;* William H. Stuart, *The Twenty Incredible Years, as "Heard and Seen."* (NewYork: Donohue, 1935), 545–46; Chicago *Tribune,* 17 February 1984.

7. For nineteenth-century mayors, see biographies in Holli and Jones, *BDAM;* Don E. Fehrenbacher, *Chicago Giant: A Biography of "Long John" Wentworth* (Madison, WI: American History Research Center, 1957); Patrick McLear, "William B. Ogden: A Chicago Promoter," *Journal of the Illinois State Historical Society* 70 (November 1977): 283–391; Bessie L. Pierce, *A History of Chicago. Vol. 2, From Town to City, 1848–1871* (NewYork: Knopf, 1940), 304–5; C. Buettinger, "Economic Inequality in Early Chicago," *Journal of Social History* 11 (Spring 1978): 416, 418. D. S. Bradley and M. Zald, "From Commercial Elite to Political Administrator: The Recruitment of Mayors of Chicago," *American Journal of Sociology* 71 (September 1965): 154–55.

8. John S. Mill cited in Murphy, "Whither the Mayors?" 286n; James Bryce, *The American Commonwealth* (NewYork, 1927), 1:642; Bryce, *American Commonwealth* (London, 1888 ed.), 2:67, 335; Gittell, "Metropolitan Mayor," 23; Melvin G. Holli and Paul M. Green, eds., *The Making of the Mayor: Chicago, 1983* (Grand Rapids: Eerdmans, 1984), chap. 1. See also Edward H. Mazur, "Carter H. Harrison I," in Holli and Jones, *BDAM.*

9. For political ambition theory, see Joseph A. Schlesinger, *Ambition and Politics.* Milton Rakove has argued that upward progression is sometimes reversed by Chicago politicians, who find the local scene a far more fertile field in which to make a buck and get in the limelight, in *Don't Make No Waves— Don't Back No Losers: An Insider's Analysis of the Daley Machine* (Bloomington: Indiana University Press, 1975), 7. More recently Rakove has suggested that upward climbing on the political ladder is the norm even for Chicago politics in "Observations and Reflections on the Current and Future Direction of the Machine," in Holli and Green, *Making of the Mayor.*

10. Edward A. Greenlaw, "Office of Mayor in the United States," *Municipal Affairs* 3 (March 1899): 55–56; Samuel Edwin Sparling, *Municipal History and Present Organization of the City of Chicago* (Madison, WI, 1898), 159–67; see also Rakove, "Observations," in Holli and Green, *Making of the Mayor.*

11. John Clayton, *The Illinois Fact Book and Historical Almanac, 1673–1968* (Carbondale: Southern Illinois University Press, 1970), 9–158; Robert E. Hartley, *Big Jim Thompson of Illinois* (Chicago: Rand McNally, 1979), 38–62, 88, 99.

18. Richard M. Daley and the Politics of Addition

1. Peter W. Colby and Paul Michael Green, "The Irish Game: Watch Byrne—Watch Daley—Watching Byrne," *Illinois Issues* (September 1980).

2. Bernard Carey quoted in Paul Michael Green, "Daley's Victory: A Prelude to the Big Brawl," *Illinois Issues* (January 1981), rptd in *Illinois Elections*, ed. Paul M. Green et al. (Springfield, IL: Sangamon State University, 1996), 71.

3. Interview with author.

4. Paul M. Green, "Chicago Politics: A Tradition of Toughness," in *Political Conduct: A Look at Campaign Bigotry in Chicago Election Behavior*, ed. Louise Kerr (Chicago: Conduct, 1989), 21.

5. Marie V. Bousfield, "The Population of Chicago in the year 2000" (Chicago Department of Planning and Development, September 2001).

Chicago's Racial Breakdown by Percentage and Population

African American	37%	1,065,009
Caucasian	31%	907,166
Latino	26%	753,644
Asian and Pacific Islander	4%	127,762
Native American	0%	10,290
Mixed	3%	84,437
Total population		2,896,016★

★The above numbers do not add up to this total because groups overlap.

6. Chicago *Tribune*, 11 March 1999.

7. Dick Simpson, *Rogues, Rebels, and Rubber Stamps* (Boulder, CO: Westview Press, 2001).

8. Paul M. Green, "Mayor Richard M. Daley: His Views of the City and State," *Illinois Issues* (August-September 1991).

9. *Ibid.*, 18.

10. *Ibid.*

11. *Ibid.*, 20.

12. The 1995 Illinois law gave RMD power to appoint a temporary, five-member "superboard," labeled the Chicago School Reform Board of Trustees. In 1999 the board (by order of the same law) was expanded to seven members and was renamed the Chicago Board of Education.

13. *Business Week*, 16 October 2000.

CONTRIBUTORS

Monroe Anderson served as press secretary for and political confidant to acting mayor Eugene Sawyer.

Roger Biles is a professor of history at Northern Illinois University and the author of *From Tenements to the Taylor Homes: In Search of an Urban Housing Policy in Twentieth-Century America.*

John D. Buenker is a professor of history at the University of Wisconsin–Parkside and the author of many books, including *Historical Dictionary of the Progressive Era, Progressivism,* and *Urban Liberalism and Progressive Reform.*

Douglas Bukowski, a Chicago writer and historian, is the author of *Big Bill Thompson, Chicago, and the Politics of Image.*

Maureen A. Flanagan, a former editor of the *Journal of the Gilded Age and Progressive Era,* teaches at Michigan State University.

Paul M. Green is the Arthur Rubloff Professor and the director of policy studies at Roosevelt University in Chicago.

William J. Grimshaw is a professor of political science at the Illinois Institute of Technology.

Arnold R. Hirsch is the Ethel and Herman L. Midlo Professor for New Orleans Studies and a university research professor of history at the University of New Orleans.

Melvin G. Holli is a professor emeritus of history at the University of Illinois at Chicago and the author of a number of books, including, most recently, *The Wizard of Washington: Emil Hurja, Franklin Roosevelt, and the Birth of Public Opinion Polling.*

Edward R. Kantowicz is an independent scholar living in Chicago.

Steve Neal was the political columnist for the Chicago *Sun-Times.*

David L. Protess of Northwestern Journalism School is the author of numerous articles about Chicago politics and urban reform.

Steve Rhodes is a reporter for *Chicago Magazine.* His journalistic interests center on politics and policy issues in the Chicago region.

John R. Schmidt is a Chicago public school teacher and the author of *The Mayor Who Cleaned Up Chicago: A Political Biography of William E. Dever.*

Laura S. Washington, a former aide to Mayor Harold Washington, is the Ida B. Wells Barnett University Professor at DePaul University in Chicago and a columnist for the Chicago *Sun-Times.*

INDEX

The letter *t* following a page number denotes a table.

Index

Mitchell, Arthur W., 118
Mitchell, Grayson: quoted, 200
mobility, career. *See* career mobility
Morris, Buckner, 253
Moseley Braun, Carol, 226, 283–84, 287
Municipal Voters League, 23
Murray-Blessing president-ranking poll, 235

Nash, Patrick, 107, 111, 123, 150
nativity: and career mobility, of mayors, 250–52, 258
Neal, Steve, 235, 279
Newhouse, Richard, 194
Newsweek, 218
New York Times, 274

Obama, Barack, 287, 291
Oberman, Martin, 161, 169
O'Connor, Len: quoted, 147
Ogden, William B., 251; ranking of, 240t, 241, 242
Ogden Gas franchise, 22, 24, 29
Ogilvie, Richard, 257
Olson, Judge Harry, 62, 70
Operation PUSH, 225, 246
Orr, David, 226
Osterman, Kathy, 280

Paterson, Robert W., 15
Patterson, Joseph Medill, 47–48
Pearson, Rick, 267
Pena, Federico, 246
Percy, Charles, 264
Peterson, Paul: quoted, 154
Pincham, R. Eugene, 225, 232
Polish Americans, 18, 28
Polish-Jewish conflict, 72
Polish-Lithuanian conflict, 71–72
Post, Louis, 57
presidents, ranking of, 235
Public Perspective journal, 236
Pucinski, Aurelia, 226
Pucinski, Roman C., 161, 162, 220–21, 226

Rakove, Milton, 168, 221, 333n. 9
Raymond, Benjamin, 251
Rayner, J. J., 190
Reagan, Ronald, 275
religion: and career mobility of mayors, 250–52, 258
Ridge, Tom, 278
Riordan, Richard, 274
Robins, Raymond, 57
Rochon, Reynard, 213, 215
Roddewig, Clair, 157
Roosevelt, Franklin D., 241, 249
Rose, Don, 169, 170, 176
Rosenwald, Julius, 77
Rumsey, Julian, 251
Rush, Bobby, 200, 216, 232
Ryan, George, 278

Sanchez, Al, 234
Savage, Gus, 227, 228
Sawyer, Eugene, 232, 236, 284; as acting mayor, 226–27, 260–61; administration of, 208, 211; and campaign for mayor, 206; career mobility of, 250; and deal with Alderman Timothy Evans, 213; elected mayor, 199; and Erwin France, 210, 211; and Harold Washington, 200; and mayoral primary (1989), 214, 264; and media manager Reynard Rochon, 213, 215; political image of, 207; ranking of, 238, 242, 243; and Steve Cokely affair, 208–10; sworn in as mayor, 207
Sayre, Wallace, 247
Schiller, Helen, 233
Schlesinger, Arthur M., Sr., 235
Schlesinger, Joseph, 246–46
Schmidt, John, 264
Serritella, Daniel, 77
Sheehan, Timothy, 157, 218–19
Sherman, Alson, 251
Sherman, Francis, 251
Simon, Paul, 257, 264
Simpson, Dick, 161, 169
Singer, William, 191; and mayoral primary (1975), 219

342